The Jews in Modern

Publications on t
University of V
Numbe

Gudrun Krämer

The Jews in Modern Egypt, 1914–1952

UNIVERSITY OF WASHINGTON PRESS
SEATTLE

Sponsored by
the Department of
Near Eastern Languages and Civilization
and the
Middle East Center
of the Henry M. Jackson
School of International Studies
University of Washington

Printed in the United States of America.

The Library of Congress Cataloging-in-Publication Data will be found at the back of this book.

UNIVERSITY OF WASHINGTON PRESS
Seattle

To the memory of my grandmother

Contents

Acknowledgments

This study grew out of a doctoral dissertation, which was first published in German in 1982 and was then revised and translated into English in 1985–87. The intellectual debt accumulated over the years is large, and I hope that those to whom I owe it will forgive me if I do not name them all. Professor Albrecht Noth supervised the original thesis, and with his intellectual rigor and moral encouragement, helped me over many hurdles in my research. Professors Ami Ayalon, Jere Bacharach, Werner Ende, Peter Freimark, Jacques Hassoun, Albert Hourani, and Reinhard Schulze are foremost among those who gave me their generous support and advice. I am, of course, greatly indebted to my interview partners and the staffs of the archives and libraries I consulted for their patient assistance. Special patience was required of Felicia J. Hecker, director of the Near Eastern Publications program at the University of Washington, who with her commitment and competence made long Germanic sentences shorter and the distance between Seattle and Hamburg bridgeable.

That the debts I incurred in the course of my research are intellectual rather than financial I owe first and foremost to the Scholarship Foundation of the German People (Studienstiftung des deutschen Volkes), which supported me throughout my studies, making it easier for me to chose a research topic that demanded time and considerable travel. Its support was supplemented, in 1979–80, by a travel grant from the Volkswagen Foundation. In 1985, a fellowship from the Stroum Fellowships for Advanced Research in Jewish Studies and a leave of absence from the Stiftung Wissenschaft und Politik finally allowed me to spend some time in Seattle to begin translating the German original into English. Without the generous support from these institutions, the present study could indeed have been neither written nor published.

The chapter on Zionism is based on an earlier version published in *Egypt and Palestine: A Millennium of Association*, edited by Amnon Cohen and Gabriel Baer (Jerusalem, 1984). I am obliged to the editors for permission to use it here.

The Jews in Modern Egypt, 1914–1952

Abbreviations

AA	Auswärtiges Amt (Bonn)
Abt.	Abteilung
AJEPO	*Annuaire des juifs d'Egypte et du Proche Orient*
AIU	Alliance Israélite Universelle (Paris)
AMJY	*American Jewish Yearbook*
AS	*Annuaire statistique*
CAHJP	Central Archives for the History of the Jewish People (Jerusalem)
CZA	Central Zionist Archives (Jerusalem)
DW	Dār al-Wathā'iq (Cairo)
DW/MW	Dār al-Wathā'iq, Majlis al-Wuzarā' (Cairo)
FO	Foreign Office (Public Record Office, London)
HADITU	al-Ḥaraka al-Dīmuqrāṭīya lil-Taḥarrur al-Waṭanī
£E	Livre Egyptienne, Egyptian Pound
LICA	Ligue Internationale Contre l'Antisémitisme
LISCA	Ligue Internationale Scolaire Contre l'Antisémitisme
MAE	Ministère des Affaires Etrangères (Paris)
MDLN	Mouvement Démocratique pour la Libération Nationale
MELN	Mouvement Egyptien pour la Libération Nationale
OH	Oral History Department (Institute of Contemporary Jewry, Hebrew University, Jerusalem)

Introduction

The minority question has played, and continues to play, so prominent a rôle in the history and politics of widely differing societies that it has always been certain of widespread attention. The striking position of specific minorities in the local economy—Protestants in Catholic areas of Western Europe, Jews in Eastern Europe, Greeks and Armenians in the Middle East, Chinese in South East Asia or Indians in East Africa—has attracted a considerable amount of scholarly research. The Middle East is, therefore, just one area where the minority question poses itself, affecting all aspects of social, cultural, and political life, but it has always been an area where it does so with particular virulence. The existence of a large number of ethnic and religious groups has seriously hampered the process of nation building in which the young states of the Arab Islamic world engaged after becoming independent of the Ottoman Empire and European colonial rule. The Ottoman Empire, a plural society par excellence, had never pursued the ideology of the melting pot. Rather, it had cemented the lines of ethnoreligious division with its administrative *millet* system based on semiautonomous religious groups headed by their respective religious hierarchies. Iraq, Syria and, of course, Lebanon offer ample material to study the tensions between these groups thrown together in artifical boundaries—Sunnī and Shī'ī Muslims, Christians of various denominations, 'Alawīs, Druze, Bahā'īs, Kurds, Armenians, and others. Compared to these societies, Egypt appears relatively homogeneous. But even Egypt with its minority of indigenous Christian Copts is not, and never has been, free of sectarian tension.

The Jews, and this fact deserves to be emphasized, have always been only one of the many minorities living in the Middle East. Until the middle of this century, Jews were to be found in almost all countries of the area, although their numbers varied considerably. In the late 1940s, the great exodus of Middle Eastern Jewry to Europe, the Americas, Australia and, first and foremost, to Palestine/Israel began. While in 1947 there were about 800,000 Jews in the Islamic countries of the Middle East (including North Africa), of whom 650,000 lived in the Arab countries, only a few thousand remained in the 1980s. Of the 75,000 Jews who resided in Egypt in the 1930s and 1940s, some 20,000 left the country after the first Arab-Israeli War of 1948, to be followed by another 40,000 to 50,000 after the Suez War of 1956. The nationalization of private business in 1961–62 and the June War of 1967 caused thousands more to emigrate. By the 1980s, some 300 to 400 Jews, mainly elderly, were left in Cairo and Alexandria.[1] This massive exodus calls for an explanation.

It does, of course, suggest that there was serious tension between the Muslim majority and the Jewish minority, and that the Muslim Arab societies were either unable or unwilling to integrate their Jewish minorities—provided that the Jews themselves were willing to accept, or attempt, integration. This leads to the questions of whether the Jews were in any way a special minority, distinct from the Copts, the Kurds or the ʿAlawīs, and whether there was in the modern Middle East a Jewish question similar to the one known in contemporary Christian Europe.

The subject of the position of non-Muslim minorities in general, and of Jews in particular, under Islam has always been highly controversial. Two major lines of interpretation have evolved, one stressing traditional Muslim-Jewish coexistence and harmony, the other emphasizing oppression based on Islamic intolerance and fanaticism.[2] The contradiction between these two interpretations of Muslim-Jewish relations can, to a certain extent, be explained by the position their proponents take on the Palestine conflict, and by the historical period to which they mainly refer. While the advocates of the "theory of harmony" emphasize the golden ages of Islamic and Jewish culture in Muslim Spain and Fāṭimid Egypt their opponents point to periods of great upheaval such as the rule of the Almohads and the Almoravids in medieval North Africa, the reign of the eccentric caliph al-Ḥākim bi-amri'llāh in tenth-century Egypt, and the modern experience under the impact of the Palestine conflict. But even this difference in emphasis cannot resolve the contradiction altogether. Given these conflicting schools of thought, substantial evidence on the state of Islamic tolerance was only to be expected from the detailed analysis of a specific area over a limited period of time.

For the modern period, three larger areas offer themselves for examination: (*a*) the Maghreb, (*b*) the Arabian Peninsula, and (*c*) the states bordering on, or closest to, Palestine/Israel, namely, Syria, Lebanon, Egypt, Jordan (which can be excluded because it did not have any significant Jewish population), and Iraq. This last group of states is of special interest because of its advanced degree of socioeconomic, political, and cultural development and the relative freedom of action its political leadership enjoyed after the end of direct colonial rule. Iraq excepted, their Jewish communities are, moreover, less well known and researched than those of North Africa and the Yemen.

As a case study for the position of the Jews in modern Middle Eastern society, Egypt is particularly interesting but also problematic. While its urban population had been exposed to Western influence for several decades, it had always preserved a strong sense of Egyptian identity. This sense of Egyptian identity not only shaped its approach to Western culture and civilization; it also restricted the appeal of pan-Arab sentiment and solidarity. Thus it was only in the 1930s that (pan)Arabism was gaining ground among (urban) Egyptian intellectuals and political activists. In this respect, Egyptians differed considerably from the Syrians or the Lebanese. They were, therefore, not directly representative of Muslim Arabs in general. Nor was

Egyptian Jewry with its high degree of internal differentiation and Westernization fully representative of Middle Eastern Jewry as a whole.

At the same time, it is precisely the complexity of Egyptian society, and of Egyptian Jewish society, that may help us identify and analyze a number of factors determining the position not only of the Jews but of other non-Muslim minorities as well. Included among these factors were the modernization of the economy and society under European influence or direct control, that is, integration in a world market dominated by the industrialized Western nations; nationalism in its various forms; Islamic revival, and, last but certainly not least, anti-Zionism linked to the Palestine conflict. In spite of strong British influence, Egyptian political leaders were, moreover, able to take independent action, especially with regard to domestic politics, making it easier to specify internal factors of political change and behavior.

Two sets of questions offer themselves for closer analysis. First, what was the position of the Jews in Egyptian society in the years between 1914 and 1952, particularly in the interwar period? Did it differ in any significant manner from the position of other non-Muslim minorities, who, while they may have been of Egyptian nationality, were not of Egyptian origin and culture, such as the Greeks, the Italians or the Armenians? Did there exist a Jewish question in the period under review? The analysis here is, to a certain extent, based on a comparison with other minorities living in the country in order to avoid an isolationist interpretation, which is liable to view as specifically anti-Jewish events and measures that may have affected other minorities as well. Throughout this study, the focus will be on the social and economic position of the Jews in Egyptian society as well as on their political activities. Aspects of culture and religion, daily life, the position of women, and related questions, interesting and important as they are, must be left to a separate study.

Closely related to this first set of questions is the second one: What were the factors leading to the mass departure, or expulsion, of the Jews from Egypt after the Arab-Israeli wars of 1948, 1956, and 1967? Here the analysis is based on the assumption that it was not so much changes within the local Jewish population, which caused the deterioration in Muslim-Jewish relations, but rather changes in Egyptian society and politics at large, which, therefore, have to be studied in some detail. While there can be no doubt that the position of the Jews in twentieth-century Egypt was strongly linked to the Arab-Jewish, or to be more precise the Arab-Zionist, conflict over Palestine, the specific weight of the Palestine factor still remains to be defined. In this context, the way Egyptian Jews tried to adapt to, or respond to, changed conditions in Egypt and the region at large is of special interest.

As for the time limits of the present study, the starting point of 1914 requires little explanation: World War I constituted a watershed in the social, economic, and political life of both Egyptian and Egyptian Jewish society. The year 1952 is admittedly more arbitrary. The revolution of July 1952 was of critical relevance to general Egyptian history. The position of the Jews, by contrast, was more directly affected by the wars of 1948, 1956, and 1967. Originally, 1952 was chosen because archival material of the kind used for the earlier period was not yet available when I did the archival research for this study in 1979–81. The loss is, however, limited because the basic problems involved in Muslim-Jewish, or Arab-Jewish, relations inside Egypt had become apparent by the 1940s. The change in government policy in 1956, mass departure and mass expulsion were the practical outcome of these underlying problems. The stereotyped image of the Jews as Zionists and enemies of all human society was only spread in the 1960s, after the overwhelming majority had already left the country.

1

Communal Structure and Composition

IMMIGRATION

From the middle of the nineteenth century into the first quarter of the twentieth, Egypt was a country of immigration: a country rich in possibilities, well-placed strategically, highly fertile, and inhabited by a hardworking population, which was said to be easily roused but peaceful at heart.[1] The government with its policy of almost unlimited laissez faire opened its doors to foreigners, and the system of the Capitulations, originally meant to protect non-Muslim foreign merchants, granted them a status of virtual exterritoriality. Highly favorable conditions, then, were further guaranteed by the political, economic and, if necessary, military pressure of the European powers headed by Great Britain.

With the expansion of the economy and administration under Muḥammad ʿAlī (1805–48) and his successors, the influx of foreigners coming from other areas of the Mediterranean basin and the Ottoman Empire, which were either less developed economically or politically unstable, increased dramatically. Foreign colonies formed and gained influence, among them the Greeks, the Italians, the Syrians, and the North Africans, the Armenians, and finally the Jews.[2] This wave of massive immigration, which began in the mid-nineteenth century, continued well into the 1920s, bringing the number of foreigners living in Egypt up from about 15,000 in the 1850s to 100,000 in the 1880s and over 200,000 in the years after World War I. The late 1920s marked the end of this trend. Under changing economic and political conditions, the number of foreigners declined to about 150,000 in 1947, mostly as a result of emigration.

Official data on the number of foreigners living in Egypt are, however, somewhat misleading. A large percentage of those listed as French, British or Italian subjects or protégés had not actually come from Great Britain, France or Italy, but from areas controlled or occupied by these powers, such as India, North Africa, Malta or, after the dismemberment of the Ottoman Empire in 1918, from Iraq, Syria, and Lebanon. Quite a few of these foreigners belonged to the local non-Muslim minorities, who, by obtaining in some way or another, foreign passports, came to enjoy the privileges attached to the Capitulations. The Egyptian census of 1917 serves to show this very well: out of the 24,354 British subjects registered there, only about 45 percent came from Great Britain itself, another 25 percent from Malta, roughly 10 percent from Greece, 954 from India, 824 from Egypt and 3,908 from other parts of the British Empire. Out of the 21,270 French subjects registered in 1917, only about 40 percent hailed from France proper, whereas 33 percent came from Morocco, Tunisia, and Algeria, 17 percent from Egypt, 871 from Syria, and 213 from other countries.[3]

Among the immigrants to Egypt from various parts of the Ottoman Empire, North Africa, and Europe were also a large number of Jews. They joined a small Jewish community of perhaps 6,000 to 7,000, which had been established in the country for many centuries. As a result of immigration, the Jewish community grew rapidly to 25,000 in 1897 and over 60,000 in 1920. Reliable estimates for the interwar period gave the real number of Jews, as opposed to those officially registered, as 75,000 to 80,000. If the Jewish immigrants were attracted to Egypt by the same pull factors as the others, they had frequently been exposed to particularly strong push factors in their countries of origin. To the economic crisis in parts of the Ottoman Empire and Eastern Europe and political instability or actual war in the Mediterranean area, which affected all groups of the local population, were added incidents of persecution on religious or racial grounds in parts of Eastern Europe or outright expulsion, as in the case of Palestine during World War I.

TABLE 1

Growth of Selected Minorities, 1840–1947

Year	Greeks	Italians	British/ Maltese	Jews
1840	5,000	6,000	1,100	5,000–7,000
1871	34,000	13,905	6,000	–
1882	37,301	13,906	6,118	–
1897	38,208	24,454	29,262	25,200
1907	62,975	34,926	20,356	38,635
1917	56,735	40,198	24,354	59,581
1927	76,264	52,462	34,169	63,550
1937	68,559	47,706	31,523	62,953
1947	57,427	27,958	28,246	65,639

SOURCES: Figures for 1840–71 from Maḥmūd, *al-Jālīyāt*, pp. 33, 45, 48; and Jacob M. Landau, *Jews in Nineteenth-Century Egypt* (New York, 1969), pp. 4–5; for 1882–97, Henein b. Henein, "La population de l'Egypte et l'exode estival," in *L'Egypte: Aperçu historique et géographique, gouvernement et institutions, vie économique et sociale*, edited by Joseph Cattaoui (Cairo, 1926), pp. 371–82; for 1907–47, see the respective volumes of the *AS* (Egyptian census, French edition); and Cohen, *The Jews*, p. 70.

TABLE 2

The Jewish Population of Egypt, 1840–1947

Year	Total	Cairo	Alexandria	Other Areas
1840	5,000–7,000	–	–	–
1897	25,200	11,608	9,831	3,761
1907	38,635	20,281	14,475	3,879
1917	59,815	29,207	24,858	5,516
1927	63,550	34,103	24,829	4,618
1937	62,953	35,014	24,690	3,249
1947	65,639	41,960	21,128	2,651

SOURCES: Landau, *Jews*, pp. 4–5; Egyptian census, 1897–1947 as quoted in Cohen, *The Jews*, p. 70.

The immigration of Jews from the Ottoman Empire, Greece, the Balkans, Corfu, and Italy, who were mainly of Sephardi (i.e., Spanish) origin, began in the early nineteenth century and continued until the 1920s. Sephardi and Oriental Jews from North Africa went to Egypt chiefly between 1897 and 1907, when the country experienced a stock market crash brought on by speculation. They settled mostly in Cairo and in certain trading centers in the Delta, notably Ṭanṭā. Jews from Yemen and Aden on their way to Palestine often got no further than Egypt when their funds ran out. Most of them arrived between 1900 and 1914 and settled in the Suez Canal Zone or in Cairo. Ashkenazi Jews from Russia, Rumania, and Poland arrived in the late nineteenth and early twentieth centuries, and, for the most part, went to Cairo. In 1914–15, over 11,000 Ashkenazi Jews expelled from the district of Jaffa by the local Ottoman commander fled to Alexandria, Cairo, and Suez but returned to Palestine or Eastern Europe after the end of the war.

Apart from the basic fact that they were all Jewish, these immigrants of widely differing regional origin and social background had a few other features in common: most were young (under thirty), poor, and eager to make a living in Egypt. The community leaders in Cairo, Alexandria, Ṭanṭā, and Suez were aware of the financial burdens and potential social problems linked to this massive influx, and their attitude toward the newcomers was accordingly rather ambivalent. They showed themselves very generous to the victims of political or racial persecution, providing them with food, shelter, clothing, and various other forms of support. But at the same time they made repeated attempts to redirect the tide of immigrants toward some other destination, preferably Palestine. In several instances, they went so far as to approach the authorities for help in stopping Jewish immigration into the country altogether.[4]

Jewish leaders were, however, unable to prevent the constant influx of immigrants from fundamentally changing the ethnic and social composition of the local Jewish community. These changes had a profound impact on their position in the Egyptian economy and society as well. In the four decades from the British occupation of Egypt in 1882 to the end of World War I, Egyptian Jewry underwent a process of sociocultural differentiation that continued well into the 1930s and even the 1940s. While this process of differentiation and social rise within Egyptian society was closely linked to general economic and cultural development in the country, it was greatly enhanced by the continuous flow of immigrants bringing special skills, experience, new ideas, and in some cases, even capital.

If large-scale immigration improved the social status of the Jews in Egypt, it certainly did not create unified, socially and culturally homogeneous communities, much less a single Egyptian Jewish community. Even before the mid-nineteenth century, the Jews of Egypt had not formed a homogeneous group. In Fāṭimid, Ayyūbid, and Mamlūk times, that is, from the middle of the tenth to the early sixteenth centuries, the local Jewish community was composed of immigrants from Mesopotamia, Palestine, North Africa, and their descendants who, according to the rites they followed, were divided into Rabbanites, Karaites, and Samaritans. At certain times, the government recognized a single head for all Jews in the country, such as the *nagid* or *ra'īs al-yahūd* in the late Fāṭimid and Ayyūbid eras, that is, from the mid-eleventh century onward, and the chief rabbi in late Ottoman times. In actual fact, however, the various groups and local communities maintained a high degree of autonomy.[5] In the early sixteenth century, growing numbers of Sephardi refugees arrived from Spain and Portugal, soon to be followed by the first immigrants from Eastern Europe. At that time, the Jewish minority was split into the separate communities of Egyptian, Sephardi, North African, and Karaite Jews; the small Ashkenazi minority does not seem to have been separately organized.

Few and impoverished, all Jewish groups except the Karaites, had again merged into one community by the end of the eighteenth century. In the 1850s, new attempts were made to form independent communities on the basis of rite, regional origin or affiliation to prominent personalities.[6] In their social position and cultural orientation, however, the Jews were highly homogeneous. They were mostly poor—poorer than the other non-Coptic minorities, though better off than the Muslim and Coptic lower class. They concentrated almost exclusively in certain living areas as well as in specific occupations and skills, such as money changing and lending, gold and silver smithery, and petty trade. They had little formal education and were closely attached to Jewish tradition, but had assimilated into their Egyptian environment in life-style, language, and popular beliefs.[7] All this was to change in the second half of the nineteenth century.

RITE AND REGIONAL ORIGIN

Among the various local minorities—the indigenous Christian Copts on one hand and the Muslim and Christian Syrians, North Africans, Greeks, Italians, Armenians, and Maltese on the other—the Jews did, perhaps, constitute the most diverse community. Their inner cleavages into subgroups of different regional origin, rite, language, cultural orientation, and social status make it very difficult to speak of Egyptian Jewry as a unified whole. In the following, the factors of rite and regional origin, language, nationality, occupation and social status, residence and regional distribution will be examined separately and interdependently.

Rite and regional origin form the most obvious criteria for distinguishing among various subgroups of Egyptian Jewry. The ethnic factor, which here refers to regional origin and language, was reflected on all levels, ranging from an individual sense of identity based on language and culture over status within the community to the structure of communal organization. The basic distinctions to be made are among the so-called Sephardi Jews (including, among others, the indigenous Egyptian, Oriental, and Italian Jews), the Ashkenazi Jews, and the Karaites.

The Sephardim

In order to fully understand the structure and organization of the community as well as the status of its individual members, it is necessary to distinguish further among those commonly referred to as Sephardim. The most important subgroups were constituted on the basis of regional origin, and included indigenous Egyptian as well as Italian, Greek, North African, Iraqi, and Yemeni Jews, who frequently preserved their own languages and customs and grouped around their own synagogues.

Only a small minority of the Jews living in Egypt in the twentieth century were strictly speaking Egyptian Jews in the sense that their families had been living in Egypt for several generations. Although Egyptian Jewry could boast a venerable tradition of scholars and community leaders including Saʿadia Ga'on and Moses Maimonides, it is next to impossible to establish any direct links between the Jewish communities of Hellenistic and medieval times and those of the modern era. What can be said is that because of continuous immigration, even this group, which in modern times was considered truly autochthonous, in actual fact included many descendants of immigrants from earlier centuries. Socially and culturally, however, they were largely homogeneous. In the mid-twentieth century, the number of indigenous Jews was estimated at about 10,000, that is, some 15 percent of the entire community.[8] They lived mostly in the Cairo Jewish quarter, the *ḥārat al-yahūd*, and in certain smaller towns of the Delta and Upper Egypt. There is little information available on the indigenous Jews, and the little we have is often biased and decidedly unsympathetic.

The most detailed information available concerns the Jewish quarter of Cairo, which, in the twentieth century, had about 7,000 inhabitants, most of them indigenous Jews or immigrants from other Arab countries.[9] The evidence indicates that the indigenous Jews engaged mostly in traditional occupations in small trade and various crafts and that they were generally poor. A significant number seems to have been without any regular occupation and income, or were openly unemployed. They, therefore, depended on the charity of the community or of their wealthy coreligionists, if they did not live by begging altogether.[10] In life-style, customs, dress, and eating habits, the indigenous Jews had assimilated into their Egyptian environment. They also spoke Egyptian Arabic, not any specific Judeo-Arabic dialect.

Despite this high degree of cultural assimilation, which was also reflected in their religious life combining Jewish traditions with practices common to local Muslims, Christians, and Jews, there seems to have been little social interaction with Muslims or Copts outside the sphere of business. The Jews lived in their separate quarter (*ḥāra*) which, though it was neither a ghetto nor a *mellāḥ* as known in North Africa, set them apart, and they sent their children to Jewish schools, which were maintained by the community or by wealthy individuals. Naturally, dependence on communal welfare tended to reinforce vertical loyalties, binding the Jewish poor to their richer coreligionists rather than to their Muslim and Coptic neighbors.[11] As beneficiaries of communal welfare the Jews from the *ḥāra* were not represented on the communal boards, and even among the various social and political groups, they were rarely to be found. In the smaller towns of the Delta and Upper Egypt, the proportion of indigenous Jews in communal organizations seems to have been larger, and their status relatively higher. Al-Manṣūra is a case in point.[12] In certain villages of the Delta—some of them actually called *tall al-yahūd* or *tall al-yahūdīya* (hill of the Jews)—there were still some Jews living as peasants (*fallāḥīn*).[13] But in the absence of documentation on indigenous Jewish families, it is very difficult to establish their history and precise social status at any given time.

Closest to the indigenous Egyptian Jews culturally and socially were the Oriental or Arab Jews from North Africa and other areas of the Ottoman Empire, Yemen, and Aden, most of whom had come to Egypt for essentially economic reasons. Many of them settled in their ports of arrival: Alexandria, Suez or Port Said. But there were also small colonies of North African and Yemenite immigrants in Cairo, who preserved their specific customs and dialects over several generations. Having arrived poor and frequently without any training in the skills and languages required locally, they shared the low status of the indigenous Egyptian Jews.[14]

Yet Oriental immigrants were not all poor. They also included a large number of merchant families from Tunisia, Syria, Iraq, and Aden, who, with their experience, language skills, international connections, and independent capital were quickly able to establish themselves in Egypt. Although in the large communities of Cairo and Alexandria they were usually unable to gain quick access to the leading circles, they formed the dominant stratum in the smaller and newer communities in the Suez Canal Zone. The second and third generations of Oriental immigrants frequently adopted the language and cultural outlook of the cosmopolitan Jewish middle and upper classes, leaving Arabic culture and language to their poorer coreligionists in the provincial towns and the Cairo *ḥāra*.[15]

The first genuine Sephardi, that is, Spanish Jews had come to Egypt in the course of the Christian *reconquista* of Muslim Spain, particularly after the expulsion of the Jews from Spain and Portugal in 1492 and 1497 respectively. They were followed by many more Sephardi immigrants from other parts of Europe and the Ottoman Empire. Superior to their Egyptian coreligionists in scholarship and general education, international connections and, in some cases, even wealth, they soon came to dominate the local community, which had been greatly reduced in the last decades of Mamlūk rule.[16] The majority of Sephardim arrived in the late nineteenth and early twentieth centuries with the main wave of immigration from North Africa, Greece (notably Salonika), Italy, present-day Turkey (Izmir), Syria, and Iraq. They joined the commercial and entrepreneurial middle class, and in many instances succeeded in making a fortune and in gaining influence in the community within a relatively short period of time. The large number of Sephardi (and Oriental) lawyers, doctors, and engineers testifies to their success in the professions.[17] Even in the twentieth century, many outside observers commented on the dynamism of the Sephardi immigrants, who seemed to them more active, bright, and intelligent—or, as is to be suspected, simply more Western and European—than their Egyptian coreligionists.[18] Their language skills put them at a clear advantage, since in addition to Ladino most Sephardi immigrants also knew French, Italian, Greek or some Arabic dialect.[19] The élite of the Cairo and Alexandria communities regarded themselves as Sephardim, being able to trace their presence in Egypt back to at least the early nineteenth century.

Italian Jews formed a distinctive group within the so-called Sephardi community. Numbering between 8,000 and 10,000 in the interwar period, they lived mainly in Alexandria, where they played a prominent rôle in both the Jewish and the Italian colonies. Italians were particularly influential in the commercial and financial circles of this cosmopolitan Mediterranean port, and in the early twentieth century, Italian was still used there as the lingua franca. In 1854, the Italian Jews of Alexandria had even felt strong enough to set themselves up as a separate community. Having failed to win the necessary support, they rejoined the Communauté Israélite d'Alexandrie a year later.[20] While many so-called Italian Jews had in fact come from Italy, notably from Livorno/Leghorn, many others had arrived from other parts of the Mediterranean area and only later adopted Italian nationality. Regardless of their real origin, however, most "Italian Jews" identified with Italy, its language, culture, and politics—even under fascist rule.[21] Among the Italian Jews there were many craftsmen, clerical workers, salespeople, and some laborers (who made up a significant portion of the non-Jewish Italian colony in Egypt). But there were also numerous professionals, merchants, and bankers. Some of the richest and most respected Jewish families in the country, such as the Mosseris, Pintos or Rossis, had Italian nationality.[22]

The distinction between indigenous Egyptian, Oriental, Italian, and Sephardi Jews proper that is made here for analytical purposes was in actual practice frequently disregarded. In Cairo, all Jews from the Mediterranean area, the Ottoman Empire, and the other Muslim lands, who, with some local variations, followed the Sephardi rite, formed La Communauté Israélite du Caire, headed by the (Sephardi) chief rabbi of Egypt. Only the small Ashkenazi and Karaite minorities were actually organized into independent communities. Nevertheless, a sense of separate identity based on regional origin was preserved even among the Sephardim. This was reflected in associations such as the Società Israelitico-Corcirese di Mutuo Soccorso, founded in Alexandria in 1913, the Association des Juifs Orientaux established in 1916 and renamed the Union des Juifs Orientaux in 1930, the Cercle de la Jeunesse Judéo-Espagnole formed in Cairo in 1920 and in Alexandria in 1929, and the Union des Juifs Héllènes founded in 1934.

The Ashkenazim

As early as the sixteenth century, a certain number of Ashkenazim were living in Egypt. Their numbers were reinforced in the seventeenth century by refugees who had escaped from the persecutions of the Chmielnicki cossacks in the Ukraine in 1648. The size of the Ashkenazi element increased markedly when, between 1880 and 1914, and after the Kishinev pogrom of 1903 in particular, hundreds of Ashkenazi refugees from Russia, Poland, and Rumania arrived in Egypt, almost all of them young and without means of support. The pressure seemed so great that in several instances the local communities tried to stop the immigration of this essentially alien element. The Alexandria community was faced with its greatest challenge when, in December 1914, the commander of the Fourth Ottoman Army Corps stationed in Palestine, Ahmed Cemal Paşa, expelled all Russian and Polish Jews from the Jaffa district. Between December 1914 and the summer of 1915, over 11,000 of these exiles found refuge in neighboring Egypt, notably in Alexandria. As soon as the war was over, however, a large majority returned either to Palestine or Eastern Europe.[23]

In spite of this wave of immigration, the Ashkenazim remained a minority of between 5,000 and 6,000 individuals, 8 percent at most of all Jews living in Egypt in the interwar period.[24] It was a minority that was, moreover, further divided along the lines of origin, language, and customs. By far the largest part of the Ashkenazi immigrants had come from present-day Russia and Rumania, 90 percent of whom spoke Yiddish as their native language and the remaining 10 percent Russian. Only a very small minority came from German-speaking areas. In the Ashkenazi quarter of Cairo, the Darb al-Barābira, Yiddish was preserved well into the 1950s. At the beginning of the century, two short-lived Yiddish papers were published (*Die Yiddishe Zeitung* in 1907 and *Die Zeit* in 1909). A theater group founded in 1912, the Groupement Artistique Juif du Caire, performed Yiddish plays and as late as the 1940s was even heard on Egyptian radio.[25]

Most Ashkenazi immigrants worked as cigarette rollers, at least until the decline of this industry during World War I; as artisans (tailors, shoemakers, opticians, gold and silver smiths); or as clerks and salespeople. Many remained in these fields, while others engaged in small-scale trade or opened their own shops, especially in the textile and fashion industries.[26] In the second generation, a considerable number of Ashkenazim made their way into the professions, particularly in the medical field.[27] While a number of self-made men and their families did acquire wealth and education, especially during and after World War I, the large majority of Ashkenazim remained poor, and their plight was noted and commented upon by almost all outside observers.

Poverty certainly did not help to improve the Ashkenazi standing in an environment that was as conscious of status and money as was Egyptian society. The Sephardi and Oriental majority, moreover, had some misgivings about the moral standards of the Ashkenazim. Certain immigrants from Rumania (Wallachia) engaged in disreputable if not illegal business in the demimonde and underworld of Cairo, Alexandria, and the Suez Canal Zone, which as a result of the Capitulations was effectively beyond the reach of the Egyptian authorities. Some Jews kept bars or brothels, others were involved in the international trade in "white slaves," which brought Greek, Syrian, and Jewish women to Egypt. There is nothing to indicate that the Ashkenazim had a significant share in the business, or that they had a bad reputation in Egyptian society at large.[28] Among the Sephardim, the Ashkenazim were, nonetheless, called *schlechtes* (bad or evil ones). It was widely believed that it was not so much the bad (*schlecht*) circumstances in which they were living that earned them this epithet, but rather their alleged moral deficiencies. The harshest criticism of local Ashkenazim came from foreign observers, many of them sympathetic to the Jewish national movement, such as the journalist Rudolf Nassau, who in 1904 published several extremely critical articles in the Viennese journal *Die Welt*.[29]

For obvious reasons, the Ashkenazim had greater difficulty integrating into the local Jewish community and into Egyptian society at large than did Oriental immigrants. They tended to settle in separate living areas, which in Cairo, where most Ashkenazim lived, was the Darb al-Barābira, and they soon tried to establish a separate community organization. The Ashkenazi Community, founded in 1865, was, however, denied official recognition—partly because the Sephardi community resisted all attempts at institutionalized separatism. But for all practical purposes the Ashkenazim formed an independent community in Cairo, with their own rabbi, president, and council. It was only in the areas of education and health, and in questions that concerned all Jews living in Egypt regardless of rite and origin that they cooperated with the larger Sephardi community.[30] All attempts subsequently made on either side to overcome this division failed because of Ashkenazi resistance.

During World War I, a well-to-do Ashkenazi middle class evolved, which assumed the leadership of the community. They, therefore, feared that in merging with the dominant Sephardi and Oriental majority they would lose their separate identity. They were also reluctant to assume the burden of providing for the poor in the *ḥāra* at a time when their own welfare service was widely regarded as exemplary. Yet the institutional division between Sephardim and Ashkenazim, which many regarded as harmful and unnatural, was only valid in Cairo. In Alexandria and the provincial towns, where the Ashkenazim formed a small minority, they remained within the larger community. Only in Alexandria did they form a charitable organization of their own.[31]

On the whole, relations between Ashkenazim and Sephardim seem to have been reasonably good, though in certain circles they were strained by prejudice and mutual feelings of superiority. Ambivalence and animosity resulting from the differences in origin, culture, political experience, and social status seem in many cases to have emerged only after their departure from Egypt, being reinforced by later experiences of Ashkenazi-Sephardi tension in countries like Israel. Yet it cannot be denied that some tension had already existed in Egypt. The generation living before World War I was still very much aware of the difference, and *schlechtes* clearly had a pejorative connotation. Cultural factors were reinforced by social ones. Members of the rich Sephardi families, who were educated in French, Italian or British schools and who belonged to the cosmopolitan élite of Egyptian society, looked down with contempt, or at best with condescension, on the Ashkenazi craftsmen, tradespeople, medical doctors, and dentists who did not even know proper French. In certain instances women of good Sephardi society even refused to sit with Ashkenazi women on charitable boards. On the other hand, many Ashkenazim, however poor they might have arrived in Egypt, still felt superior to their Oriental and Sephardi coreligionists, who appeared to them fatalistic and uneducated, or quite simply "typically Oriental" like Egyptian society in general. The following report written by the sharp-tongued Rudolf Nassau in 1904 reflects this view:

The bearers of culture in this country so rich of development potential are Europeans.... The mental and moral habitus of the Egyptian has not been changed in its essence: [they are] full-blooded Orientals with a thin layer of European culture [*Talmikultur*]. And Arab Egypt has the Arab Jews it deserves. In their thinking and feeling they are Arabs rather than Jews, in their morals and customs [they are] Orientals.... Their social and national awareness is nil. In rich circles, indolence and the lack of education are hidden behind a thin veneer of pseudo-French culture, which is displayed in so demonstrative a way; the poor Arab Jews vegetate in the limitation of their ghetto, good natured, oppressed, neglected people without intelligence, education [and] ambition. They are said to be very religious, and so they are to the extremes of superstition. The "Sohar," [*sic*] the main work of the Kabbala, is their favorite book and the gospel of their scholars [*Schriftgelehrten*].[32]

But these were signs of mutual ambivalence, based on cultural and political differences as much as on social distance, which appear to have by and large disappeared in the second and third generations of immigrants. Their children went to school together, be it the communal schools for the poor or the French lycées for the middle and upper classes, and they met in clubs and associations of all kinds. In the forties, foreign observers noted with regret that even the Ashkenazim had become Levantinized, after the Sephardim had succumbed to these regrettable influences even earlier.[33] It was mainly on the issue of marriage that parental resistance did occasionally resurface. In certain circles mixed marriages between Sephardim and Ashkenazim were still regarded as a *mésalliance*.[34] But even in Cairo, where this kind of social snobbery seems always to have been more marked than in other communities including Alexandria, resistance had subsided almost completely by the late 1940s.

The Karaites

Little is known about the history of the Karaites in Egypt.[35] And yet the Karaites, as a minority within a minority, combining basic features of Judaism with certain influences of Islam, could be of special interest to anyone interested in either or both religions. The Karaite movement, which was probably founded in eighth-century Baghdad by ʿAnan ben David, is distinguished from mainstream Judaism by its acceptance of only the Pentateuch (Torah) as the scriptural basis of faith, rejecting the post-biblical rabbinical tradition codified in the Talmud. From this, as it were "fundamentalist," approach the name *ḳara'im* or *bene miḳra* (readers of the scriptures) is derived. The exegesis of the Torah was originally achieved by studying the scriptures (cf., the Islamic concept of *ijtihād*), and conclusions were drawn on the strength of the literal meaning of the text (*ketav*, cf., *naṣṣ*), the consensus of the interpreters (*ʿeda*, cf., *ijmāʿ*), analogy (*heḳḳesh*, cf., *qiyās*), or common sense (*ḥokhmat ha-daʿat*, cf., *ra'y*). In order to avoid chaos in interpretation, a certain set of binding rules regarding the creed and rite were agreed upon between the twelfth and fifteenth centuries, and even a limited number of rabbinical traditions accepted insofar as they helped to clarify difficult passages in the Torah.

The major distinctions between Karaites and Rabbanites were not so much related to faith or dogma, but rather to matters of rite and practice. Karaism was originally characterized by its greater emphasis on ritual purity, implying, among other things, stricter limitations on contacts with non-Jews and on marriage. The concept of incest, for instance, was more comprehensively defined than in Rabbinical Judaism. There were also certain differences in the calendar and hence the celebration of the holidays, in religious service and the decoration of the synagogues, which betrayed clear influences of Islam. These differences varied considerably among the various centers of Karaite life, depending on economic and political conditions in their countries of residence. In Russia, which for most of the time was the center of Karaism, the tension between Karaites and Rabbanites grew sharper under the impact of rising anti-Jewish feeling until in the seventeenth century the Karaites dissociated themselves completely from mainstream Judaism. By contrast, their coreligionists in the Islamic world went in the opposite direction, drawing again closer to the Rabbanite Jews.

Soon after the establishment of the Karaite movement, a small community was founded in Egypt, which in Ṭūlūnid and Fāṭimid times, that is, from the ninth to the twelfth centuries, was fairly wealthy and influential. In spite of sharp conflicts about matters of religious practice, Rabbanite-Karaite relations were, for the most part, harmonious, as reflected in a certain number of mixed marriages. The rift widened again in the twelfth century as a result of the anti-Karaite position taken by Moses Maimonides.[36] In the following centuries, the Karaites must have suffered from political instability and economic decline just as much as the other Jews, or, as a matter of fact, all other groups in Egyptian society except the changing rulers.

By the nineteenth century, their former wealth and prestige had long since disappeared.

In the mid-twentieth century, the Egyptian Karaites numbered several thousand—4,507 in 1927 according to the Egyptian census, 5,264 in 1937, and 3,486 in 1947; Maurice Fargeon gave their number as 7,000, and unofficial Karaite sources as 8,000 to 10,000.[37] With few exceptions, they lived in Cairo, where they had their own quarter, the *'aṭfat al-yahūd al-qarā'īn*, bordering on the Jewish *ḥāra*. The large majority of Karaites were poor. According to the census of 1927, almost 50 percent were illiterate. By 1937, the illiteracy rate had declined to about one-third (1,676 of 5,264); some 60 percent (2,822) were able to read and write.[38] Most Karaites were craftsmen, working especially with gold, silver, precious stones, and perfumes, and a certain number worked as opticians, pawnbrokers, money changers, traders, and peddlers. Of the 1,767 inhabitants of the Karaite quarter fifteen years and older that were registered in the Egyptian census of 1937, 516 were employed in public and social services and 210 in trade.[39] These data have to be treated with caution, however, since apart from the lack of precision in the criteria employed, they apply to the inhabitants of the *'aṭfat al-yahūd al-qarā'īn* only. Yet by the end of World War I, many Karaites, particularly the better-off middle and upper classes, had already left the quarter for middle class areas such as 'Abbāsīya and Khurunfish.[40]

By the end of World War I, a commercial middle class had evolved among the Karaite community as well. Unlike the Rabbanite Jews, their children were primarily educated in Egyptian or British, rather than Jewish or French, schools and then either entered the professions or trade and banking. The wealthy families of Mas'ūda, Līsha', Levi, Cohen, Marzūq, Ṣāliḥ, Shammā', Ṭawīl or Manjūbī, who also dominated communal affairs, did not match the Sephardi élite in wealth and prestige.[41] But in their life-style they, too, came increasingly to imitate the tastes of the cosmopolitan élite. Individual members of these rich families excepted, the Karaites in general had assimilated much from their Egyptian Arab environment. Family life was very similar with the exception that Karaite women, rather than veiling themselves, seem to have displayed their beauty quite openly, at least within their quarter.[42] In 1904, Rudolf Nassau reported twenty-five cases of polygamy among Karaite Jews.[43] Their first and family names were generally of biblical or Arabic origin (Yūsuf, Ibrāhīm, Zakī, Murād, Ṭawīl, Ṣāliḥ, 'Abd al-Waḥīd, etc.). Assimilation was also reflected in the high number of Karaites who were registered as Egyptians. In 1927, 1,848 out of 4,507 Karaites were registered as foreigners and 2,659 (over 50%) as Egyptian subjects. In 1937, 1,737 out of 5,264 Karaites were listed as foreigners, and the remaining 3,527 as Egyptians. By 1947, the number of foreign nationals had dwindled to a mere 322 as opposed to 3,164 Egyptians. Stateless persons were not listed separately.[44]

Given their high degree of assimilation into Egyptian society, the distance the Karaites maintained from the Rabbanite Jews, both Sephardim and Ashkenazim, was all the more striking. Although in the twentieth century, both groups recognized each other as Jews, mixed marriages were accepted only with great difficulty.[45] With the exception of a few individuals, notably the writer and lawyer Murād bey Faraj Līsha' (1866–1956) and the Karaite chief rabbi Ibrāhīm Cohen (1922–33), Egyptian Karaites avoided close contacts with the Rabbanites. If there was no longer any mention of mutual hatred and aversion, as was occasionally reported in the nineteenth century, the distance between the two groups nevertheless persisted.[46]

This distance was expressed in the separate communal organization maintained by the Karaites, which, however, like that of the Ashkenazim, was not officially recognized by the Egyptian government. In the late 1930s, the Karaite community maintained three synagogues and two schools; in 1945, it also established a social center for its poor.[47] Cooperation with the Rabbanite Jews was restricted to polite visits on the Jewish holidays and individual contributions to charitable institutions such as La Goutte de Lait. It was only in the 1940s that a Karaite representative joined the school board of the Sephardi community. In Alexandria, the small Karaite minority formed part of the local Jewish community but was placed under the jurisdiction of the Karaite chief rabbi of Cairo in matters of personal status.[48] In Cairo, the first community council (*majlis millī*) was elected in 1901, and composed of the great families, who, under the leadership of the Karaite chief rabbi and their president, continued to run communal affairs until the 1940s. Up until that time, elections were held at long and irregular intervals. Signs of opposition to the dominance of the ruling families first appeared in the 1920s. A Karaite youth club called Jamʿīyat (or Ittiḥād) al-Shubbān al-Isrā'īlīyīn al-Qarā'īn bi-Miṣr (Association of Karaite Jewish Youth in Egypt) was active on behalf of social and cultural reform and worked for a cultural-religious revival on the lines of spiritual Zionism. It found a forum in several Karaite papers, such as *al-Ittiḥād al-Isrā'īlī* (1924–29), *al-Shubbān* (1937), and *al-Kalīm* (1945–57), which called for a religious revival and a democratization of communal affairs in the tradition of earlier Karaite papers like *al-Tahdhīb* (1901) or *al-Irshād* (1908).[49]

If, therefore, the Karaites tried to keep relations with the Rabbanites friendly, but decidedly distant, they were nevertheless regarded as Jews by all outside observers, even though it was generally known that there were indeed differences separating Karaite and Rabbanite Jews. When in May 1948, the Wafdist paper *Ṣawt al-Umma* published blacklists of Jewish merchants and entrepreneurs allegedly linked to Zionism, the names of several Karaites were also included. And in June 1948, when a bomb exploded in the Karaite quarter of Cairo, a note attached to it claimed that it had been set by the Rabbanite Jews—a claim that few were inclined to believe.[50] But since the Karaites never played an influential rôle in the Egyptian Jewish community, they will once again find themselves largely ignored in the following pages.

LANGUAGE

Repeated reference has been made to the different languages Jewish immigrants brought with them from their countries of origin, and which, in many cases, they preserved in Egypt. Language and regional origin were originally more closely correlated than were language and social status. The indigenous Jews and the Karaites spoke the Egyptian Arabic dialect, and some of them were even able to read and write Modern Standard Arabic as used in the press and modern literature. The immigrants from Arab countries preserved their specific Arabic dialect, and as a result, often had some difficulty understanding each other unless they were able to resort to Modern Standard Arabic. The Sephardi immigrants spoke Ladino (Judeo-Spanish derived from Latin), but frequently also knew French, Italian, Turkish or Arabic. Greek Jews spoke Greek, Italian Jews Italian, Turkish Jews Ladino and the Ashkenazim Yiddish, Polish or Russian—altogether a babel of tongues, which went some way to imitate the biblical precedent.

However, this linguistic chaos was mainly characteristic of the time of massive immigration, that is, the last third of the nineteenth century and the first two decades of the twentieth. At that time, several papers were published in Arabic, Ladino, and Yiddish, but soon disappeared for lack of readers. After World War I, some ethnic groups retained their native tongue in the family circle. In dealings both with Jews from other areas and with non-Jews, however, the middle and upper classes adopted one of the leading European languages. In the late nineteenth century this was mainly Italian, which until 1876 served as the language of administration and until 1905 as the chief language of instruction in the community schools of Alexandria. By that time, French had become the lingua franca of the local foreign minorities and the Turko-Egyptian élite alike. Interestingly, it was the women who in most middle- and upper-class families adopted Italian and French rather than Arabic and Hebrew, which, in the majority of cases, they either did not know well or not at all. While most middle- and upper-class Jews knew English quite well, they used it mainly in business and official contacts, but very rarely in private life. The Jewish communities held their meetings in French, and until the 1930s, French was also the main language of instruction in the community schools, as well as, of course, in the schools of the Alliance Israélite Universelle. Even the Zionist movement was forced to rely on French rather than Hebrew or Arabic.[51]

Arabic, by contrast, was increasingly losing ground, and in the interwar period was relegated to a low rank as the language spoken by the poor inhabitants of the Cairo *ḥāra*, the provincial towns, and the Karaites. The Arabic edition of the Zionist paper *Israël*, which was first published in 1920, had to be abandoned in 1933, and *al-Shams*, though frequently cited here, had only a limited number of readers. Most local Jews knew just enough colloquial Egyptian Arabic to be able to deal with shopkeepers, waiters, domestic servants, and the man in the street; a minority had a sufficient command of Modern Standard Arabic to be able to read and write it. It was only at the time of heightened national consciousness in the late 1930s and the 1940s that certain Jewish groups began to devote more attention to Arabic. The Jewish youth club Association de la Jeunesse Juive Egyptienne and its platform, *al-Shams*, called for the adoption of Arabic, not only to prove their willingness to integrate into Egyptian society, but also to overcome the inner cleavages of language and origin dividing the community itself. At the same time, the communal schools replaced the French curriculum with the Egyptian one; in 1943 the annual reports of the Cairo community council were translated into Arabic. Yet Arabic was never able to replace French and Italian as the languages of Jewish and non-Jewish members of the local foreign minorities.[52]

Knowledge of Hebrew remained even more restricted. Whereas in the mid-nineteenth century, many Jews still spoke both Arabic and Hebrew, only a tiny minority were able to do so a century later. In the Jewish community schools, Hebrew was taught as a secondary language only, and in the French schools, it was accorded the same rank as the classical languages of Latin and Greek. The religious talmud torah schools as well as the Zionist groups did offer courses in Hebrew, but in the 1940s only one small Zionist group, the ḳevutsa Bar Kokhba, was actually able to use Hebrew in their daily life.[53]

Except for the poorest sections of the community, most Jews in Egypt were true polyglots, and many members of the educated middle and upper classes had a command of four or five languages. Linguistic skills contributed greatly to the success of Jewish immigrants in the economic field. At the same time, their adoption of French and Italian in family and social life could not fail to affect their cultural and even their political orientation in general. If the multiplicity of languages made contacts with non-Jews sharing a similar education and socioeconomic status easier and more intense, it also added considerably to the factors weakening the internal cohesion of Egyptian Jewry.

NATIONALITY

After the British occupation of Egypt, nationality gradually began to assume a relevance it had never had before. Formal citizenship, as opposed to religious affiliation, gained further importance when, in the late 1930s, the Egyptian government started to Egyptianize the economy and administration by reserving a growing number of positions for Egyptian citizens.

Previously it had been particularly advantageous for local foreign minorities either to keep or acquire foreign passports in order to enjoy the legal and economic privileges attached to the Capitulations. The name of this institution is both telling and misleading. It is not derived from the usual sense of the word, but rather from its original meaning of treaties composed of many individual chapters (Lat., *capitula*). The Capitulations originally were treaties of commerce and protection between Muslim rulers and European (Christian) princes or republics, as they were first granted to Genoa in A.D. 1149, to Pisa in 1154, and to Venice in 1220, later to be followed by the king of France in 1535, the queen of England in 1580, and the Netherlands in 1612.[54] These treaties guaranteed the lives and property of foreign subjects during their stay in the territory of the respective Muslim ruler, placing them under their own jurisdiction which, as early as the thirteenth century, was in some cases exerted by local foreign consuls. This safeguard of life and property, which excluded the foreigners from Islamic jurisdiction and taxation, notably the poll tax (*jizya*) imposed on local *dhimmīs*, in fact continued pre-Islamic Byzantine and even pharaonic practices. It was originally interpreted as an extension of the limited state of protection or *amān*, which any Muslim was able to grant a non-Muslim (*musta'min*) for a limited period of time, but was successively extended to cover the entire reign of the ruler who had first entered into the treaty and finally of his successors, too, until canceled. And while the Islamic laws concerning non-Muslims (*dhimmīs*) were abolished by the Ottoman reform decrees of 1839 (Hatt-ı Şerif of Gülhane) and 1856 (Hatt-ı Humayun), which were reflected in similar Egyptian legislation in 1882, the Capitulations, as a result of the British presence in Egypt, were constantly gaining in weight. Not only could they now be enforced at any given time; they were also expanded far beyond their original intent.

What made them so attractive was no longer the safeguard of life and property, the exemption from the *jizya* (abolished by the reform decrees of 1856 and 1882 respectively) or the right freely to practice one's religion. It was the legal and economic privileges granted to foreigners, which exempted them from local taxation (unless all European capitulary powers agreed to its imposition), and from Egyptian jurisdiction, placing them under the jurisdiction of their consuls. As a result of established custom, these consuls gradually came to deal with all types of civil, commercial, and criminal cases involving one or several of their subjects.[55] The principle *actor sequitur forum rei*, forcing the plaintiff to follow the defendant to the latter's consular court caused juridical chaos, which the establishment, in 1875, of the Mixed Courts was meant to remedy. The Mixed Courts unified the legal codes and procedures by creating special codes based on the French Code Napoléon, and they were soon able to monopolize all court action involving, however remotely, the interests of foreigners and their companies. Yet even after 1875, most cases of criminal and of personal status law remained within the jurisdiction of either the different consular or the religious courts. The multiplication of codes, courts, and procedures was only reduced after the Capitulations and the Mixed Courts were abolished in 1949 to be followed by the religious courts in 1955.

Until the late 1930s, the prospects of legal and fiscal exemption and of foreign protection in general made it much more attractive for local minorities to apply for foreign rather than Egyptian nationality, which would have placed them under the jurisdiction of the so-called Native (after 1937: National) Courts. Like all other minorities, local Jews, both indigenous and newly immigrated, attempted to obtain some sort of foreign protection or nationality.

The British consuls, representing the dominant European power in the country, could afford to impose strict limits in granting any kind of British protection. During World War I, when a number of wealthy Jewish families lost their Austro-Hungarian protection and considered applying for British nationality, a member of the local embassy staff suggested a more liberal and farsighted policy vis-à-vis these applicants:

> These Jews are decent people and would I am convinced be a useful nucleus for a Colony after our direct withdrawal from the control of Egyptian Affairs and I should be sorry to lose this unique opportunity of shepherding them into our fold. Many of them can even now acquire other nationalities ... and if we want to catch them no time should be lost.[56]

If this was not done, he feared, they might see themselves obliged to adopt Egyptian nationality, "the idea of which does not smile upon them as Semi-Europeans."[57] However, the reply from the Foreign Office was brief and cool. There was not much interest on the part of the Office in names like de Kraemer, Menasce, and Green ("which at one time used to be Gherein").[58]

The French, having to use more indirect ways of winning influence, were much more generous. The Jews were an important factor in the economic and social life of the country and deserved to be treated with careful attention. Granting French decorations was one way of showing this attention, French protection and citizenship another. The French minister in Cairo, Gaillard, did not hesitate to articulate the need for local support, when he wrote in 1921 that lacking a sufficient number of French citizens living in Egypt, France had to ask for this support among "true friends."[59] And the French prime minister succinctly summarized the official line vis-à-vis the Jewish community in Egypt when he stated in 1930: "The Jewish community [*milieu*] is one of the most important and most French groups in Egypt; a possible reduction in our influence on them could not leave the government indifferent."[60]

In 1939, when the French consular records were revised it turned out that at least 90 percent of those registered as French protégés of Algerian descent, a total 4,000 to 5,000 individuals, most of them Jews, had no legal claim to French protection whatsoever, as neither they nor their ancestors had ever set foot on Algerian soil.[61] The representatives of the lesser European powers finally, intent on expanding their influence vis-à-vis the British presence in the country, were only too happy to increase both the number of their protégés and their personal income, as passports and documents of foreign protection had, of course, to be bought.[62]

Under these circumstances, a large number of Jews of various backgrounds came to acquire some kind of foreign protection or nationality. This, coupled with large-scale immigration, meant that the majority of Jews living in Egypt in the twentieth century did not have Egyptian citizenship. In the interwar period, 25 to 30 percent at most were Egyptian nationals, with another 25 percent being either foreign nationals or foreign protected and the remaining 45 to 50 percent being stateless (and hence not eligible for the privileges attached to the Capitulations). In 1917, the English edition of the Egyptian census registered 24,980 "Jews by religion" (of whom only 14,417 were defined as "Jews by race") out of 59,815 Jews as local subjects, about 40 percent.[63] The French edition of the same census ignores this strange and unexplained distinction. It lists only those "Jews by race" as Egyptian subjects (22%) and registers 70 percent as stateless (*apatride*). Again according to the French edition, this category was reduced to 45 percent in 1927. The Arabic and English editions of the Egyptian censuses of 1927, 1937, and 1947 unfortunately do not list stateless persons at all. In

1927, the number of Egyptians and foreigners was roughly equal (32,320 and 31,230 respectively out of a total of 63,550). In 1937, 40,300 out of 62,953 Jews were registered as Egyptians (65%) as against 22,653 foreign nationals (35%). In 1947, it was 50,831 Egyptians (almost 80%) as against 14,808 foreign nationals (20%) out of a total 65,639 Jews. While these figures leave many questions open (were those listed as Egyptians actually Egyptian nationals or at least eligible for Egyptian nationality, or were they simply not foreign nationals?) they clearly indicate the rapid reduction of the number of foreigners from 31,230 in 1927 to 14,200 in 1947. The census data conflict sharply with the figures given in the *Tribune Juive* (no. 523) of September 1947, which mentions 30,000 to 40,000 stateless Jews on one hand, and *al-Shams* of 7 November 1947 on the other, which mentions 15 percent Egyptian and 15 percent foreign nationals as opposed to 70 percent stateless Jews. One way to explain the apparent contradiction is to assume that the Egyptian census included stateless persons under Egyptian subjects. All evidence suggests that the majority of those who lost, or gave up, their foreign nationality as well as of the indigenous Egyptian and the Oriental Jews (mostly former Ottoman subjects) in fact did not obtain Egyptian passports.[64]

The decree law number 19 of February 1929, which, for the first time, attempted to clarify the questions related to Egyptian nationality, was essentially very liberal, recognizing as Egyptian nationals: (1) all those whose families had resided in the country without interruption since 1 January 1848 (the proof of which, however, was very difficult to provide given the absence of proper registration); and (2) those former subjects of the Ottoman Empire who made their "habitual residence" in Egypt on 5 November 1914 (when Great Britain declared war on the Ottoman Empire) and had stayed there since. The children of foreigners born in Egypt and habitually resident there were eligible for Egyptian nationality within one year of attaining their majority, provided they gave up their foreign citizenship. In all other cases, the requirements of naturalization included a ten-year residence in the country, an adequate command of

Arabic, sufficient means of support and, finally, the proof of good conduct.[65] In spite of these generous regulations, which were meant to facilitate the integration of former Ottoman subjects, the Egyptian government did in fact make it very difficult for non-Muslim foreigners to become naturalized, especially so in the 1940s. If until the 1930s most Jews had seen little advantage in applying for Egyptian citizenship, they found it exceedingly difficult to do so after the Convention of Montreux in 1937, when Egyptianization intensified, rendering Egyptian papers valuable. As a result, it was precisely the poorer and less educated sections of local Jewry—among them the large majority of highly assimilated indigenous and Oriental Jews—who, in spite of their legal eligibility for Egyptian nationality, were in fact left stateless.

TABLE 3

Nationality of the Jews in Egypt, 1917 and 1927

Year	Nationality	Absolute Figures	Percentages
1917			
	Local subjects	14,417	22
	Ottoman	1,081	
	French	776	10
	Italian	668	
	British	343	
	Others (stateless?)	42,296	70
	Total	59,581	100
1927			
	Egyptian	21,994	33
	Turkish	1,243	
	French	5,764	22
	Italian	4,949	
	British	2,130	
	Others (stateless?)	29,632	45
	Total	63,550	100

SOURCES: *AS* 1917 (Cairo, 1918), table 12, p. 22; and *AS* 1933–34 (Cairo, 1936), table 5, p. 20.

TABLE 4

Nationality of Jewish Notables in Egypt, ca. 1922

Nationality	Alexandria	Cairo/ Sephardim	Cairo/ Ashkenazim
		(In percentages)	
Egyptian	33	8	30
Italian	25	30	–
French	15	18	2
British	15	15	6
Austro-Hungarian	*	7	6
Ottoman	–	10	6
Russian/ Soviet Union	–	–	20
Others	5.5	12	10
Unknown	–	–	25
Absolute Figures	184	140	56

SOURCES: "Liste des notables israélites d'Alexandrie" (1922?); "Liste des notables israélites Sépharades du Caire" (1922); "Liste des notables Achkénases du Caire" (n.d.), all in DW/MW, al-Ṭawā'if al-qibṭīya (4).

* In Alexandria, Austro-Hungarian subjects were listed separately (25 families).

Naturally, it was mostly the affluent and educated middle and upper classes, which were able to obtain either foreign or Egyptian passports. In the years after World War I and the dissolution of the Ottoman and the Habsburg empires, the number of British, French, and Italian nationals was swelled by many former subjects of these empires. In the 1930s, about 9 percent of the Jews living in Egypt were French nationals or protégés; nearly 8 percent were Italians, about 3 percent had British and another 1.5 percent Turkish protection or nationality. For the upper-middle and upper classes, a slightly different distribution emerges from a "List of Notables," which was probably drawn up during or immediately after World War I. While it will come as no surprise that among this class the proportion of foreign nationals was higher than among the general Jewish public (25–30% Italian and 15–18% French citizens, 6% British subjects, 15% British protégés), it seems remarkable that at least in Alexandria, Egyptian nationals made up one-third of the notables included on the list (see table 4).

Again it should be remembered that foreign nationality or protection was not necessarily related to foreign origin. A large proportion of Italian Jews had thus not come from Italy, and neither had their ancestors. In spite of this, they developed a strong sense of their Italian identity, particularly during World War I and the fascist rule. This diminished only when, in 1938, Mussolini introduced anti-Semitic legislation. The Greek, French, and German Jews tended to be just as patriotic as the Italians. The issue of (double) loyalty, therefore, posed itself from the outset, to be further sharpened by the rise of Zionism and of anti-Zionism in the late 1930s and the 1940s.

OCCUPATIONAL AND SOCIAL STRUCTURE

Economic development under the viceroy (khedive) Ismāʿīl (1863–79) and, from 1882 on, under British rule, which protected the local minorities and gave privileges to the foreigners, brought about a considerable improvement in the economic and social position of the Jews in Egypt. Until the mid-nineteenth century, Jews worked primarily in certain urban occupations traditionally filled by non-Muslims, notably in the field of credit and finance as money changers, moneylenders or pawnbrokers, as traders and craftsmen dealing with gold, silver, precious stones, and perfumes, as tailors, silkweavers, workers (cigarette rollers), and, last but not least, as traders dealing in fruit, tobacco, silk, cotton, and cloth.[66] These were areas and occupations in which Jews were strongly represented in other parts of the Ottoman Empire, too, where the ethnic division of labor typical of the medieval Islamic world had, to a certain extent, been preserved intact.[67] It will also be noted that these are precisely the fields that the Karaites still engaged in in the mid-twentieth century. After the Jews lost the profitable customs and tax farms to the Copts and Syrian Christians under ʿAlī bey al-Kabīr in the second half of the eighteenth century, the number of wealthy and influential families declined significantly.[68] In the reign of Muḥammad ʿAlī, only a few families such as the Tilche, Aghion, and Adda, merchants involved in the European trade, or money changers and moneylenders were still considered prosperous. In social stratification, the Jewish minority was thus largely homogeneous and clearly poorer than the other non-Coptic *dhimmī* groups living in the country.

The introduction, in 1820, of long-staple (i.e., long fiber) cotton, which soon accounted for over 80 percent of Egyptian exports, and later of sugar cane brought Egypt into the international market economy.[69] Agriculture was transformed, infrastructure widely expanded, and demand for credit and capital soared. In the course of this process the outlines of the traditional mosaic of ethnic division of labor came to be increasingly blurred, without, however, being completely erased. Muslim Egyptians rose to leading positions in the government, administration, and the army, obtained large landholdings, and engaged in wholesale trade. At the same time, local non-Muslims, who because of their religious and educational backgrounds were much more receptive to European influence, took advantage of the newly evolved economic opportunities. The policy of economic liberalism and legal privilege that was guaranteed by British rule allowed these local foreign minorities to acquire a position within the Egyptian economy totally out of proportion to their actual numbers.

Like other immigrants, Jews profited from the favorable conditions offered to them in Egypt. For the most part, not only were they highly achievement-oriented and hence hard-working, having come to Egypt either because they had suffered from economic hardship, political insecurity or religious persecution in their countries of origin, or because they were attracted precisely by the prospects of quick success Egypt seemed to offer at the time. In many cases, they could also rely on an international network of family and kinship ties, which were particularly useful in the fields of commerce and finance. Among their highest qualifications were, of course, their relatively high standard of education and their language skills.

In Egypt from the 1860s on, Jewish education had been gradually transformed from the traditional system of religious schools (*ḥeder*) into a modern system adapted to European, notably French, standards. From the 1890s to the 1920s, and in certain provincial towns such as Ṭanṭā up to the late 1930s, the Alliance Israélite Universelle played an important rôle in the spread of French culture and education. After World War I, it was only the poorer segments of the community that continued to send their children to the inexpensive communal schools. The middle and upper classes preferred foreign private schools, many of them run by Catholic missionaries. For the period up to 1947, literacy and education have been studied by Hayyim Cohen. His analysis shows that in spite of an illiteracy rate of 20 percent in 1947, Jewish educational standards roughly equaled those of the other non-Coptic minorities, while they were far superior to those of the Muslim and Coptic majority of the population (see tables 5 and 6).[70]

TABLE 5

Jewish Pupils in Egypt, 1907–46

Year	Boys	Girls	In Jewish Schools		Percentage of Jews in Foreign Schools
			Boys	Girls	
1907–8	4,000	3,194	906	504	80.3
1912–13	4,523	3,815	1,154	744	77.2
1924–25	7,461	6,230	4,097	3,119	47.3
1930–31	7,928	6,621	4,542	3,969	41.5
1936–37	7,635	6,657	4,474	3,960	41.0
1945–46	6,733	5,374	2,883	2,056	59.2

SOURCE: Cohen, *The Jews*, p. 110. Pupils at Egyptian state schools not included.

In the early phase of economic expansion and socioeconomic transformation, covering the period from the 1860s to the 1880s, the banking and credit sector played a crucial part—the very field in which Jews had traditionally been strongly involved. The rise of the Jewish families most influential in communal affairs—

the Cattaoui (Qaṭṭāwī), Mosseri, de Menasce, Suarès, Rolo, and Aghion—can be traced back to their rather humble origins as money changers and moneylenders (*ṣarrāf*) in the Jewish quarter of Cairo. Money changing and moneylending were gradually transformed into modern banking, and frequently combined with trade with Europe and the Levant. In the process of expansion, family business became increasingly diversified. Investment in land and real estate, infrastructure, and construction as well as, to a lesser extent, in industry were added to banking and trade. A few examples from the Suarès and Mosseri families may serve to illustrate this development.

TABLE 6

Literacy among Jews in Egypt, Five Years and Older, 1907–47

(In percentages)

Year	Male	Female	Total
1907	63.3	35.5	49.7
1927	81.7	63.9	72.2
1937	83.3	67.7	75.4
1947	89.7	75.9	82.2
1947[a]	90.2	80.4	85.0
1947[b]	56.1	30.6	43.8

SOURCE: Cohen, *The Jews*, p. 111.

[a] Non-Coptic Christians

[b] All communities

Raphael Suarès (1846–1902) was an eminent local banker and businessman who channeled foreign capital into Egyptian agriculture, banking, and industry.[71] Two members of the Suarès family, which had originally come from Spain (and hence was Sephardi) and later settled in Livorno, arrived in Egypt in the early nineteenth century. Menahem Suarès della Pegna settled in Alexandria and his brother Isaac in Cairo. In 1875, Isaac's three sons, Joseph (1837–1900), Félix (1844–1906) and, finally, Raphael, together with Simon Rolo, founded the Maison de Banque Suarès Frères et Compagnie, which, until its dissolution in 1906, closely cooperated with the bank of Cattaui Figli et Compagnie. Both the Rolos and the Cattaouis were prominent local Jewish families. Like the banking houses of the Cattaoui, Mosseri, de Menasce, and Zilkha families, the Banque Suarès served as mediator for European capital seeking local investment. Raphael Suarès directed French capital into the Crédit Foncier Egyptien, which was founded in 1880 and, as the main source of credit for large landowners, developed into one of the largest institutions of its kind.[72] Through his association with the British industrial magnate Sir Ernest Cassel, Suarès collaborated in channeling British capital into three major enterprises: the construction of the first Aswān dam, which was completed in 1902; the foundation, in 1898, of the National Bank of Egypt, of whose 100,000 shares issued in 1898 Cassel acquired 50,000 and Suarès 25,000 and, finally, the sale of the khedivial estates (*al-dā'ira al-sanīya*).[73]

The *dā'ira sanīya*, to take just one example, comprised vast estates in Upper and Lower Egypt—about half a million *faddān* at the date of their liquidation in 1880 (1 *faddān* = 1,038 acres), 10 percent of Egypt's cultivated land—which the khedive Ismā'īl had given as mortgage for loans granted by European banking houses in 1865, 1870, and 1877. In 1880, the *dā'ira* estates passed into the ownership of the Egyptian state and were placed under joint British, French, and Egyptian management. By 1897, about 40 percent of this land had been sold to private owners. In 1898, the council decided to sell the remaining 300,000 *faddān* to a private company. The Daira Saniyeh Company Limited, headquartered in London, with Cassel, Suarès, and E. Cattaoui as principal shareholders, was able to secure an option on the sale for some £6 million, although their value was even then estimated at £10 million. Cassel's share in the sale was 50 percent and Suarès' 25 percent. The *dā'ira* estates were then divided up and sold to individual landowners, both Egyptian and foreign, or to foreign-owned land companies.[74] Suarès' involvement did not end here. In the 1890s he had founded, with French capital, the Sugar Company of Egypt (Société Générale des Sucreries et de la Raffinerie d'Egypte), which in 1902 started to run a number of sugar factories on former *dā'ira* land it had acquired. Because of mismanagement, the enterprise found itself on the brink of bankruptcy in 1905. At this stage it was taken over by the Société du Wadi Kom Ombo, one of the largest joint ventures of the Cattaoui, Suarès, de Menasce, and Rolo families, which in 1904 already controlled about 70,000 *faddān*. Its directors, Henri Naus and later (Sir) Victor Harari, managed it so successfully that the Sucreries, after making enormous profits during World War I, gained a virtual monopoly in sugar production, employing over 20,000 workers in the 1920s. The S.A. du Wadi Kom Ombo developed into one of the largest companies in Egyptian agriculture. Economic power translated into political influence, and in the 1930s, members of the Cattaoui family entered Parliament as deputies of the district of Kom Ombo.[75]

The Suarès family was actively engaged not only in banking, credit, and land development, but also in transport and infrastructure. In Cairo, they established the first public transport company, the horse-drawn carriages of the Omnibus Company ('Arabīyāt Suwārīs), which, until 1940, serviced the busy Mūskī Street. Later they joined Moise de Cattaoui in building several railway lines (Cairo-Ḥulwān in 1880, Cairo-Asyūṭ in 1890, Qinā-Aswān in 1896, and later the Eastern and Delta Light Railways). In 1897–98, Raphael Suarès obtained the concession for the waterworks in Ṭanṭā, and a few years later for al-Manṣūra and Cairo as well.[76] Other members of the family owned large estates in Lower and Upper Egypt, with Raphael's brother Félix alone owning over 10,000 *faddān* in 1900, as well as extended real estate in the center of Cairo, where the Suarès Square (Maydān Suwārīs, renamed Maydan Muṣṭafā Kāmil in 1939) bore his name.[77] As shareholders, managers, and directors, the Suarèses were involved in a large number of companies in all sectors of the Egyptian economy, but played no significant part within the Jewish community. Only one family member, Edgar Suarès, served as president of the Alexandria community in 1914–17.

Even in the economic field, the Suarèses were soon outdone by another Jewish family, the Mosseris, who had had little share in the companies of the Cattaoui-Suarès-de Menasce-Rolo group. The Mosseris, too, had come to Egypt via Italy.[78] While they seem to have arrived in the second half of the eighteenth century, the first known family member is Mūsā al-Kabīr, who, like Ya'qūb Qaṭṭāwī and Ya'qūb Menasce, acquired wealth and real estate in the Cairo Jewish quarter in the second half of the nineteenth century. Though he continued to live in traditional Jewish Arab style, he was one of the first Jews to leave the *ḥāra*. It was, however, another branch of the large Mosseri family, descended from Yūsuf (Joseph) Nissim Sr., which was to gain the strongest influence in the Egyptian economy and the local Jewish community. Joseph Nissim Sr., unlike Mūsā al-Kabīr, Ya'qūb Qaṭṭāwī, and Ya'qūb Menasce, started in trade, where he made a moderate fortune first as a partner in the firm of Pinto, Mosseri, and Mandolfo and later on his own. After their father's death in 1876, his four sons founded the first family bank, J. N. Mosseri Fils et Compagnie. The eldest son, Nissim J. bey Mosseri (1848–97), rather than marrying a cousin as was customary among the Mosseris, chose Hélène Qaṭṭāwī, daughter of Ya'qūb Qaṭṭāwī, a wealthy merchant-banker and president of the Cairo Jewish community. The links connecting the various Jewish families, and hence their trading and banking houses as well, were thus cemented by a tight network of intermarriage. As the son-in-law of the president, Nissim bey was also the first Mosseri to assume the office of vice-president of the Cairo community, which for the next few decades was to remain hereditary within his family.

Yet the true rise of the house of Mosseri only occurred in the following generation, that is, after the turn of the century. The eldest of Nissim's eleven children, Joseph Nissim bey Mosseri Jr. (1869–1934), after his marriage to Jeanne Aghion in 1894, followed his father as head of the banking and trading firm of J. N. Mosseri Fils et Compagnie and vice-president of the Cairo community. The dominant figure of this generation, however, was Joseph Nissim's younger brother Elie N. Mosseri (1879–1940).[79] After studying economics at Cambridge, he, together with three of his brothers, founded a second banking house, the Banque Mosseri et Compagnie. His marriage to Laura Suarès, the daughter of Félix Suarès, was a brilliant match, and his personal ties to Ismā'īl Ṣidqī Pāshā, one of the best known politicians in the country, brought him into touch with Egypt's leading political and economic circles. In 1930, Ṣidqī made him a member of the prestigious Economic Council of Egypt (Conseil Economique d'Egypte). Elie Mosseri's links to a number of large Jewish banking houses such as Rothschild, Lazar, and Seligmann, his considerable interests in France and, above all, his numerous assignments as director and manager in many of the largest companies operating in the country (especially in the fields of land development, real estate, transport, and construction, including about thirty companies controlled either by himself or by other members of his family) made him one of the most influential figures in Egyptian business and a prototype of the local foreign minority member. In spite of his British education, he was regarded by the British as a representative of Italian interests, and did indeed carry an Italian passport, but also served as honorary consul of Portugal. He had a reputation of being strict in his religious practices, and in 1926 was elected vice-president of the Jewish community in Cairo.

None of his brothers reached Elie's position of influence in Egyptian business. Maurice N. Mosseri, after a distinguished business career, followed his brother as vice-president of the Cairo community (1941–43). Joseph Vita bey founded the Josy (Arab., Jawzī) film company in 1915, which developed into one of the largest companies in the Egyptian film industry. Their cousin and brother-in-law Victor M. Mosseri (1873–1928) became one of the most prominent agricultural engineers in the country, who on his large estates worked very successfully on the control of plant diseases.[80]

While certain Sephardi families that had established themselves in Egypt by the early nineteenth century won powerful positions in banking, international trade, land development, and infrastructure, it seems that the majority of Oriental immigrants, who started entering the country from the 1860s on, made their way to wealth and prestige primarily in the field of commerce. The Chemla, Cicurel, Dorra, Douec (Dwek), Haim, Mizrahi, Najar, Picciotto, Romano, Setton, Shalom, Smouha, and Toriel families, whose names appear frequently on the lists of company boards and communal institutions, were all initially engaged in the import and export trade with European industrial products, so-called Manchester goods, on one hand and Egyptian agricultural products, notably cotton, and textiles on the other.[81] Many of these new immigrants were affected by the economic crisis of 1907, which had been caused by excessive speculation in the real estate and stock markets, and forced a large number of Jews to re-emigrate.[82] But business flourished again during World War I, when Egypt was cut off from foreign imports, giving local industry its first chance to develop unthreatened by competition from the more advanced and better protected European economies.

The Chemla family, for instance, which had already owned a clothing store in native Tunis, moved to Cairo during the crisis of 1907, bringing with them most of their employees. Their store was so successful, particularly during World War I, that they were able to continuously expand it, and to acquire considerable wealth. By the second generation, they had also entered Jewish high society, but never occupied a prominent position in communal affairs.[83] Not so the Italian Cicurels, who within one generation rose from very humble origins to a position of great wealth and influence. In 1882, a member of the Jewish Hannaux family opened a haberdashery and toy shop on Cairo's Mūskī Street, which was later expanded into a general textile and fashion store called Au Petit Bazar. In 1887, Hannaux sold it to one of his former employees, an immigrant from Izmir named Moreno Cicurel. In 1909, Cicurel opened a new shop close to the Place de l'Opéra (Maydān al-'Ataba), which his three sons Salomon, Joseph, and Salvator made into Egypt's largest department stores, Les Grands Magasins Cicurel et Oreco, with branches in Alexandria and Ismā'īlīya.[84] Their generation also gained considerable influence in the Egyptian economy—Joseph bey Cicurel (1887–?) was a founding member of Bank Misr in 1920, Salvator bey (1894–?) sat on the board of several business associations—and in the Jewish community. Salvator bey Cicurel was even chosen to replace René Cattaoui as president of the Cairo community in 1946, ending almost a century of Cattaoui rule. Such rags-to-riches stories were, of course, not limited to Jews. The rise of the Sidnaoui (al-Ṣīdanāwī) brothers, Greek Catholic immigrants from Syria who, in the same period, opened a highly successful department store in Cairo, offers a striking parallel to the story of the Cicurels and Chemlas.[85]

With the expansion of the economy and administration in the second half of the nineteenth century, there developed a growing demand for administrative personnel trained in the appropriate managerial and technical skills as well as European languages. Their European education and language skills qualified many members of the local foreign communities, among them a large number of Jews, for leading positions in government administration and private business.

The career of (Sir) Victor Harari (Pasha) (1857–1945), whose father had come to Egypt from Beirut in the 1830s, is an excellent example.[86] Upon completing his studies in England and France, Victor Harari worked with the Egyptian Ministry of Finance, where he was promoted to comptroller general in 1884 and to budget director in 1886. In 1905, he went into private business as the local representative for Sir Ernest Cassel to reorganize, among others, the Société Générale des Sucreries et de la Raffinerie d'Egypte which, at the time, was virtually bankrupt. Later he became the director of several companies belonging to the Cattaoui-Suarès-de Menasce-Rolo group, among them the S. A. du Wadi Kom Ombo. He also sat on the boards of a large number of other banks and enterprises. His son Ralph A. Harari (1892–?) managed to follow his father in his distinguished career in administration and private business. Unlike the Sephardi and Oriental families referred to above, the Hararis moved into the highest circles of Jewish society not because of wealth accumulated in banking or commerce, but because of their managerial and technical skills obtained in Europe. In both the community and business circles, they represented British rather than French interests.

Virtually all the families listed in the relevant yearbooks as merchants, traders or bankers had members trained in (French) law, which they practiced as directors in private business and/or in the legal profession proper. The number of Jewish lawyers at the Mixed Courts, which applied their own codes based on the French Code Napoléon, was very high, 82 (14%) out of 545 lawyers registered in 1930. By contrast, there was only one Jewish lawyer, Simon bey Carasso, at the Native (since 1937: National) Courts in 1948. Emmanuel Misrahy Pasha as well as Moise bey Dichy and Isidore Feldman, who were among the delegation representing Egypt at the 1937 Montreux Conference, or Zaki bey Orebi, who as late as 1953 served as a member on the constitutional committee, were some of the most prominent lawyers in the country.[87] The majority of Jewish medical doctors were immigrants, with a striking dominance of Ashkenazim.[88] Within the community, the status of professionals was generally determined by the rank and prestige enjoyed by their families. Lawyers figured prominently among communal reformers and political activists in the various political organizations active among Egyptian Jewry. But it was only in the Ashkenazi community that professionals were able to rise to leading positions at an early stage of communal development.[89]

The large majority of the Jews, of course, did not belong to these upper-class families of bankers, merchants, landowners, entrepreneurs, managers, and professionals. Most self-employed shop-owners, commercial agents, and brokers belonged to the middle and lower-middle classes; the peddlers dealing in food or haberdashery and the lottery vendors were part of the lower class. A large number of Jews were employed as clerks or shop assistants in banks, firms, and stores or as government employees. Jewish craftsmen worked primarily with textiles, gold, and silver; Jewish workers were, especially in the period up to World War I, to be found mainly in the cigarette industry. The sources mention the aversion shown by Egyptian Jews to manual labor. They also note the high reputation enjoyed by Jewish merchants.[90] The description of Jewish economic life given by Rudolf Nassau at the turn of the century is valid for the entire interwar period:

In the field of business, the Jews of Cairo have to show undisputed success. Business and profit are the magical words dominating their entire life.... In Cairo the commission business is almost entirely in the hands of Jews. The clothing, shoe, draper's and jeweler's shops, too, are mostly Jewish. On the Mousky, the busiest street in Cairo, one Jewish shop is followed by another, representing all branches of business. There are very large department stores furnished in the most elegant fashion.... They find extremely favorable conditions for making profits. The rapid progress Egypt experienced since the early eighties [1880s] made the price of real estate go up considerably, and so there are big and small Jewish financiers [*Geldleute*] successfully engaged in real estate and building speculation, both on an occasional and a professional basis.... It is worth mentioning that the Jewish merchant or commission agent is very popular with the local population and that he is in most cases regarded as very honest. For the craftsmen and workers, who mostly come from the East [i.e., Eastern Europe], too, chances to make a living are more favorable than in other countries of Jewish immigration. Among the cigarette workers, Jewish proletarians from Russia and Rumania constitute the most intelligent, more class-conscious element.[91]

A considerable portion of the local Jewish population seems to have been without regular occupation, if not openly unemployed. The Egyptian census of 1937 listed almost one-third (1,115 of 3,601) of the inhabitants of the Cairo Jewish quarter (al-Yahūd al-Rabbānīyīn) as unemployed; the census of 1947 registered 368 unemployed and 957 "unproductive and ill-defined" out of 3,876 Jews living in the *ḥāra*.[92] The proportion of community members without sufficient means of support was high in the provincial towns of the Delta and in the Suez Canal Zone, whose commercial middle and upper classes migrated to Cairo and Alexandria. But even in the big cities, there were frequent complaints about the widening gap between the rich and the poor and about the indifference of the Westernized, de-Judaized rich to the plight of their poor coreligionists. The rising middle class of immigrant merchants and professionals who, by the end of World War I, had gained in wealth and self-assurance called, and actually worked for, communal reform. The local Jewish press did not hesitate to criticize the lack of adequate housing, high unemployment, the number of beggars, the persistence of illiteracy and what was perceived as a general state of spiritual and material neglect among the Jewish poor in Cairo, Alexandria, and the provincial towns.[93]

Many reports confirm that the Jews of Egypt were concentrated in certain fields of business and occupation: money changing, banking, the stock exchange, insurance, import-export and textile trade, certain crafts, the law, and medicine. But it is very difficult to provide precise data on their share in specific sectors of the Egyptian economy. While there is no lack of reports noting—usually in a critical vein—the influence individual Jews or Egyptian Jewry as a whole exerted on certain branches of the Egyptian economy, or on the Egyptian economy in general, they very rarely contain statistical evidence to substantiate their claim. The problem is further complicated in that generally the sources do not distinguish between the Jewish share of capital as opposed to management in specific companies or branches of business. The series of articles by Anas Muṣṭafā Kāmil on the rôle of Jewish capitalism in Egypt, published in the journal *al-Ahrām al-Iqtiṣādī* in spring 1981, is a case in point.[94]

Two major problems emerge from this approach. First, no detailed data are provided on the nature and volume of Jewish participation in individual firms or economic sectors. Yet obviously one Jewish board member does not make a company Jewish. Second, the argument is based on the (implicit) assumption that there was one general Jewish interest uniting all Jews irrespective of regional origin, language, nationality, and business ties, and that Jews are sufficiently defined by their being Jewish without need of further specification. Incidentally, the same approach can be observed with regard to political activity and orientation. In actual fact, specific individuals, families or firms frequently acted as representatives of specific national interests, be they French, British, German or Egyptian. Hence, there was no general Jewish interest uniting all these individuals, families, and firms. What can be defined is their rôle as mediaries or "bridgeheads" of European capital seeking investment in Egypt.

On the basis of the available data, it is indeed difficult to give the exact share of local Jews in the capital and management of specific companies and branches of the Egyptian economy in the inter- and postwar eras. In this context it should be noted that foreign companies owned or directed by Jews are not included here. One way of dealing with the problem is to analyze membership in the boards of joint stock companies registered under Egyptian law, which, from the late nineteenth century on, dominated most of the important branches of business. Like everybody else, Jews frequently established their firms as joint stock companies. On their boards, members of their own or other Jewish families as well as of other local foreign minorities were strongly represented. A limited number of (Muslim and Coptic) Egyptian landowners, merchants, and politicians were also included. The web of business contacts resulting from membership in these boards was further reinforced by intermarriage, creating strong links within the various ethnic and religious groups and, to a certain extent, even among them.[95]

The relevant yearbooks edited by, among others, Elie Politi and Edouard Papasian, indicate the proportion of Jews in the management of joint stock companies. According to Thomas Philipp, Jews held 15.4 percent (112) of a total 728 directorships and 16 percent (262) of a total 1,626 management positions in joint stock companies in 1943. Their share declined to 12.7 percent (140) of 1,103 directorships (12.6% of 2,411 management positions) in 1947–48 and to 8.9 percent (111) of 1,248 directorships (9.6% of 2,749 management positions) in 1951; by 1960, it had been reduced to a mere 0.5 percent (7 of 1,399 directorships) and to 0.4 percent (8 of 1,886 positions) respectively. His figures are considerably lower than those given by Charles Issawi, who maintains that Jewish managers held 18 percent of the positions on the boards of 1,406 joint stock companies registered in 1951. In comparison, Muslims occupied 31 percent and Copts 3 percent of all positions only, while Europeans (who may have included an additional number of Jews) amounted to another 31 percent, Syrians and Lebanese to 11 percent, Greeks and Armenians to 8 percent.[96]

Table 7 provides a picture of Jewish capital investment in specific sectors of the Egyptian economy in 1956, when for political reasons the Jewish share in the Egyptian economy and society had already declined significantly.[97] Unfortunately, it does not specify the Jewish share in relation to overall investment in these sectors. As table 8 serves to show, some of the areas in which Jewish entrepreneurs invested were also among the most profitable sectors of the Egyptian economy in the interwar period.

TABLE 7

Jewish Capital Investment in the Egyptian Economy, 1956

Economic Sector	Invested Capital in *£E*
Land development	5,231,627
Textiles	2,336,543
Banks and insurance	1,055,000
Machinery	337,625
Food processing	243,500
Transport	211,356
Building and construction	206,000
Import and export trade	138,000
Other sectors	827,520
Total investment	11,135,836

SOURCE: Maḥmūd Mutawallī, *al-Uṣūl al-tārīkhīya lil-ra'smālīya al-miṣrīya wa-taṭawwuruhā* (Cairo, 1974), p. 244.

TABLE 8

Annual Profit Rates of Selected Economic Sectors, 1928–39

Sector	Percentage of Profit Rate
Railways and electricity	15.23
Raw material processing and building material	11.07
Land and mortgage banks	10.33
Building and construction	5.83
Land development	4.70

SOURCE: Issawi, *Egypt at Mid-Century*, p. 92.

Statistical data and a number of narrative sources give us the following picture of the Jewish rôle in the Egyptian economy: Jews played a significant part in the crafts dealing with gold and silver as well as in money changing and moneylending. The capital they accumulated in money changing and moneylending, and later in modern banking and credit, combined with their connections to leading European bankers and industrialists (many of them Jewish as well), facilitated their rise in Egyptian society. Jewish family enterprises of the nineteenth century usually combined banking and international trade, importing so-called Manchester goods from Europe and exporting Egyptian agricultural products, notably cotton. In the twentieth century, almost all department stores ranging from Cicurel, Chemla, Cohenca, Gattegno, Adès, Lévi-Benzion, Orosdi-Back and Stein to the Simon-Arzt-Stores, Le Salon Vert and La Petite Reine were Jewish-owned. The notable exception was Sidnaoui's, a department store owned by Christian immigrants from Syria. The Jewish rôle in trade and commerce, therefore, was not only highly significant, it was also highly visible.

From the beginning, Jewish entrepreneurs took a leading part in land development, where they were still strongly represented in the 1950s. Speculation in agricultural land and urban real estate had assumed dangerous proportions at the height of agrarian development in the late nineteenth and early twentieth centuries. The crash of 1907 ruined many of the companies that had sprung up, frequently on very shaky financial footing, in the decade between 1885 and 1895. It also affected many Jewish businessmen, and quite a number were forced to leave the country again.[98] Certain land companies such as the S.A. du Wadi Kom Ombo also cultivated cotton, sugar cane, and other crops. Linked to the expansion of agriculture was the expansion of infrastructure, including canals, railways, and roads, electricity, water supply, and housing. Jewish entrepreneurs were strongly involved in railway construction and urban development, including, to give just a few examples, the Cité Smouha in Alexandria and the Ma'ādī quarter south of Cairo. Jews were also heavily engaged in the hotel industry and tourism.

Closely related to the banking and credit sector, Jews played a predominant rôle at the stock exchanges of Alexandria and Cairo. According to the stock exchange yearbooks edited by Clément Lévy, Jews made up 75 to 90 percent of all stockbrokers registered there in the 1930s and 1940s. In the 1920s, Greeks still comprised about 50 percent of the Alexandria brokers. Jews were also strongly represented in insurance companies.[99]

Corresponding to the structure of the Egyptian economy in the period under consideration, Jewish entrepreneurs thus concentrated on the tertiary or services sector, including banking, credit and insurance, the stock exchange, trade and commerce, infrastructure, and construction. The major exception was the highly profitable field of land development, and of cotton and sugar cane cultivation. Jewish entrepreneurs were less involved in industry, which started to expand during World War I, when Egypt was, for a limited time, shielded against foreign competition. Two prominent Jews—Joseph Aslan Cattaoui and Joseph Cicurel—sat on the board of Bank Misr, which in 1920 attempted to lay the groundwork for an independent Egyptian credit and industrial sector.

To return to the inner-Jewish perspective, statistical data on occupation and social stratification are, even for the twentieth century, rare and not very reliable. Moreover, statistics frequently use loosely defined categories that were created for their specific purposes and not applied in other statistics. One of the earliest attempts to combine data on the occupational and social composition of Egyptian Jewry was presented in 1901 by Albert Najar, an agricultural engineer, in a report to the president of the Alliance Israélite Universelle.[100] Among the 25,000 Jews included, he listed 10 percent in banking, money changing, and moneylending (3% large banks, 7% medium and small banks or exchange offices), 25 percent in commerce (5% wholesale and 20% retail trade), 36 percent employees (7% managers and senior civil servants earning over 6,000 F [French francs] per annum, 10% medium and 19% small employees), 4 percent professionals, 4 percent craftsmen, and 5 percent workers, especially cigarette rollers. He classified 8 percent as "very rich,"

38 percent as "well-off," 14 percent as "relatively well-off," 24 percent as poor, and 16 percent as very poor. Among the 60 percent whom he considered prosperous, 20 percent were so rich that the Jewish community as a whole found itself in a "preponderant social situation." Out of the remaining 40 percent, half, that is, 20 percent of the 25,000 Jews included, depended on the charity of the rich or on begging.

The Egyptian censuses of 1937 and 1947 limit themselves to occupation, without providing any data on income and social stratification (see table 9). The categories are defined according to fields of economic activity (agriculture, trade, service) rather than function and social status. "Trade" thus comprises wholesale traders and peddlers, "public, social, and personal services" include senior officials, managers, clerks, domestic servants, and possibly even housewives. The professions are not listed separately. The high number of those classified as "unproductive and ill-defined" in the census of 1937 is striking. This category remained virtually unchanged between 1937 and 1947, if those listed under "personal services" (including housewives?) in 1947 were registered as unproductive in 1937. The percentage of those active in commerce in the 1930s and 1940s (about 33%) had somewhat increased since 1901, when, according to Najar, commerce accounted for 25 percent of the sample. Considering the wide differences in the number of persons included and the categories used in these statistics, any conclusion drawn from a comparison between them must necessarily rest on rather shaky grounds.[101] The remaining statistics show similar disadvantages. The Cairo urban census of 1947 is restricted to the (male?) inhabitants fifteen years and over of the city quarters covered. However, both the Rabbanite and the Karaite quarters (presumably corresponding to *ḥārat al-yahūd* and *'aṭfat al-yahūd al-qarā'īn*) were inhabited by the poorest sections of the communities only and therefore were not representative of Egyptian Jewry as a whole (see table 9).

The Israeli census of 1961 is based on a sample of Jewish immigrants from Egypt and Sudan who arrived in the years before 1947, between 1948 and 1954, and after 1954 respectively.

TABLE 9

Occupation of the Jews in Egypt, Egyptian Census of 1937 and 1947

	1937				1947			
	Egypt	Cairo	Rabbanites	Karaites	Egypt	Cairo	Rabbanites	Karaites
Total number of Jews	57,833	35,014	3,601	1,767	58,891	41,860	3,874	1,725
Employed	32,060	21,202	2,486	1,739	55,749	37,301	3,506	1,565
Agriculture, fishing, and hunting	134	37	4	2	126	32	7	1
Industry, mining, and construction	4,289	2,341	240	258	4,301	2,705	369	314
Transport and communications	483	241	21	16	571	351	32	10
Trade	11,997	6,827	690	210	13,042	8,367	769	222
Public and social services	2,105	1,249	1,099	516	2,779	1,815	111	33
Personal services	1,280	686			22,009	13,779	1,361	653
Unproductive and ill-defined	11,762	6,871	–	–	12,921	8,390	957	332
Unemployed	25,773	13,808	1,115	28	3,142	1,862	368	160

SOURCES: Figures for 1937 from *Population Census of Egypt, 1937* (Cairo, 1942), table 35, p. 294; for Cairo, ibid., vol. 9, Muḥāfaẓat al-Qāhira (Cairo, 1940), table 13, pp. 80–81; for the Rabbanites and Karaites, ibid., table 4, pp. 20–21. Figures for 1947 from *Population Census of Egypt, 1947* (Cairo, 1954), table 44, pp. 444–45; for Cairo, ibid., vol. 15, Muḥāfaẓat al-Qāhira (Cairo, 1952), table 14, pp. 124–26; for the Rabbanites and Karaites, ibid., table 4, p. 51.

Here the distortion works in the same direction as in the Cairo urban census as the more prosperous strata, especially those previously engaged in commerce, banking, and industry, who mostly went to Europe, Australia, and the Americas rather than to Israel, are underrepresented (see table 10). Nonetheless, the share of traders, commercial agents, and salespeople (30%) roughly equals what is given in the Egyptian statistics for the Jewish community as a whole. Moreover, there is a possibility that a certain number of those listed as managerial and clerical workers in the Israeli census (36.2% before 1947) were counted in the commerce category in the Egyptian census. Workers and craftsmen are grouped together in one bracket. Their percentage was highest among the pre-1947 immigrants (36.2%), who came to Palestine on certificates favoring craftsmen and laborers, and declined to 22.4 percent for those immigrants who arrived after 1954.

For the late 1940s, the *American Jewish Yearbook* of 1947–48 (p. 469) provides interesting, though unsubstantiated data. It considered 10 percent of the Jews in Egypt "well-to-do" and 15–20 percent "middle class," while the remaining 70–75 percent lived in "abject poverty" (as compared to 95% in Yemen, 85–90% in Iraq, 60–70% in Lebanon, and 55% in Syria). If, therefore, statistical data on the social and occupational structure of Egyptian Jewry in the twentieth century remain, to a certain extent, unsatisfactory, they nevertheless provide the broad outlines. They are supplemented by a number of narrative, and often highly colorful sources.

To sum up, profound economic and political changes in the period between the British occupation in 1882 and the end of World War I, combined with large-scale immigration, completely transformed the social and ethnic composition of Egyptian Jewry. Above the old lower and middle classes of craftsmen, laborers, retail merchants, money changers, and peddlers there developed a new and rapidly growing middle class of employees, administrators, merchants, and professionals, composed largely

TABLE 10

Occupation of Jews from Egypt and the Sudan, Israeli Census, 1961

Occupation	Immigrated to Israel							
	Before 1947		1948–54		After 1954		Total Period	
Not in labor force	50	17.5%	340	12.3%	190	8.5%	580	11.0%
Workers in transport and communications, quarries and mines, crafts, services, sports, and recreation	85	36.2	685	28.3	460	22.4	1,230	26.2
Farmers, fishermen, and related workers	–	–	–	–	–	–	–	–
Traders, agents, and salesmen	65	27.7	680	28.2	655	31.9	1,400	29.8
Professionals, scientific, technical, administrative, executive, managerial, and clerical workers	85	36.2	1,050	43.5	940	45.7	2,075	44.1
Total	285	100.0	2,755	100.0	2,245	100.0	5,285	100.0

SOURCE: Israel, Central Bureau of Statistics, *Census of Population and Housing 1961, Labour Force, Part IV, Occupations Abroad*, publication no. 27 (Jerusalem, 1965), table 2, p. 14.

of immigrants and their children. In the interwar period, the lower and upper-middle class comprised an estimated 15 percent employees (clerical workers, junior officials, salespeople), 15 percent craftsmen, at least 30 percent merchants or commercial agents, and about 5 percent professionals. At the top there evolved a small, but exceedingly wealthy upper class of bankers, wholesale merchants, landowners, entrepreneurs, and managers, comprising at most 5 to 10 percent of the community, among whom a limited, and virtually closed, circle of Sephardi families acted as a kind of Jewish aristocracy. It was these affluent, educated, and influential middle and upper classes that outside observers usually had in mind when speaking about the Jews in modern Egypt. They tended to overlook, or pass over as insignificant, the fact that below them remained a Jewish lower class, which in Cairo and Alexandria may have constituted up to 25 percent of the community. Mostly indigenous or Oriental in origin, uneducated, and only irregularly employed if at all, the lower class often had to live off communal welfare, private charity, and begging. From the point of view of social stratification, then, the Jewish community with its thin upper, large upper-middle, and very broad lower-middle class merging into the lower class resembled an onion rather than the pyramid characteristic of Muslim and Coptic Egyptian society.

Within all social strata, wealth, which in the large majority of cases was accumulated locally, constituted the single most important factor of upward social mobility. Technical, managerial, and language skills in some cases offered an alternative to wealth. Both were, to a certain extent, correlated with regional (ethnic) origin and cultural orientation. The correlation between class and ethnic origin on one hand and language, culture, and nationality on the other, is illustrated in table 11.

Growing internal differentiation and the rise of Jewish bankers, traders, and entrepreneurs in the late nineteenth century rapidly widened the gap separating the various strata and subgroups among Egyptian Jewry. Growing differentiation on the social level was, in its turn, reflected in a growing diversity of life-style, residence, nationality, education, language, culture, and, as a result, of identity as well. Rite and ethnic affiliation, which in many cases tended to overlap, as the primary basis of solidarity and identity thus gradually began to be superseded by the element of class, without, however, ever being completely obliterated.

TABLE 11

Class Characterized by
Ethnic Origin, Language, and Nationality

Class and Ethnic Origin	Language	Nationality
Upper		
Sephardi	French, Italian, etc.	foreign, Egyptian
Upper-middle		
Sephardi, Oriental, Ashkenazi	French, Italian, Arabic, English Yiddish, etc.	foreign, Egyptian, stateless
Lower-middle		
Sephardi, Oriental, Ashkenazi	Italian, Greek, Arabic, French Yiddish, etc.	Egyptian, stateless, foreign
Lower		
Indigenous, Oriental, Ashkenazi	Arabic, Italian, French, Greek Yiddish, etc.	stateless, Egyptian, foreign

RESIDENCE AND REGIONAL DISTRIBUTION

The regional distribution of the Jews corresponded to the general pattern of economic and political development in the country. In the nineteenth century, the Jews lived in Cairo, Alexandria, and the centers of trade and administration in the Delta—Ṭanṭā, al-

Manṣūra, al-Maḥalla al-Kubrā, Zaqāzīq, Ziftā—where they were able to pursue their traditional urban occupations in commerce, the crafts, and finance. After the opening of the Suez Canal in 1869, Jewish communities established themselves in the new cities of the Suez Canal Zone, notably Port Said, Ismā'īlīya and the city of Suez itself. As a result of immigration, most of the medium-sized towns of Lower Egypt and the Canal Zone expanded rapidly in the period up to 1917, and in certain cases even up to 1927.[102] Many of the new immigrants stayed in their ports of arrival, Alexandria, Port Said or Suez. The chances offered in commerce and manufacturing attracted others to the larger cities in the Delta, Ṭanṭā in particular, but also Zaqāzīq. Nonetheless, most of these provincial communities, which were largely composed of indigenous and Oriental Jews from Morocco, Algeria, Yemen, and Aden, as well as a certain number of Ashkenazi Jews, were still poor at the beginning of the twentieth century.

Economic conditions improved significantly during World War I. In the Canal Zone, where Allied troops were stationed during the war, the communities experienced a noticeable, if short-lived upsurge. But when, after the war, the center of commerce, industry, and administration shifted back to Cairo and Alexandria, which offered better communal and educational services and much more entertainment, the better-off and better-educated Jewish middle and upper classes joined the general trend of migration to the big cities. In the small towns of the Delta, Damanhūr, Kafr al-Zayyāt, Mīt Ghamr, Simbillāwayn, Ziftā, and al-Dasūq, but also in al-Maḥalla al-Kubrā, the Jewish population had already started to decline in the 1880s. After World War I, every provincial town, including Ṭanṭā, lost a large portion of its Jewish inhabitants to Cairo and Alexandria, which on all levels of economic, cultural, and social life seemed so much more attractive. A certain number of Jews from Ṭanṭā, Port Said, and Suez migrated to Palestine, many of them no doubt former immigrants from Yemen and Aden, who had previously been forced to interrupt their journey (*'aliya*) in Egypt.[103] Only the poorer and less educated sections of the community were left behind in the provincial towns, employees, salespeople, unskilled workers, a small number of merchants and commercial agents, many unemployed people, and some beggars. From Ṭanṭā the head of the local Alliance school, Isaac Farhi, reported in 1924:

A period of great productiveness, which has led to a prosperous life-style, has been followed by a period of poverty and misery. This metamorphosis is one of the sinister results of the war which, in terms of finances, has made the fortune of some and the misfortune of others. The former, seeing their social position happily transformed, thought first and foremost about changing their place of residence. Tantah had become too narrow a field of action for them, too provincial and too monotonous for their social life. Cairo and Alexandria seemed highly attractive to them. This marked the beginning of the exodus of the rich families from our city. The example had been given; it was followed by several families, even of moderate means, and eventually included all those working in an independent position. As a result, the Jewish population of Tantah now is made up only of small merchants, employees, and salesmen in banks and stores. While there are still seven independent merchants and one medical doctor, they live in modest circumstances. These successive departures have caused the ruin of the Tantah community.[104]

Moreover, many of those registered as merchants, traders or commercial agents did not really reside in their place of work, but commuted on a daily or weekly basis to Cairo, Alexandria or, in some cases, Ṭanṭā. There their families lived, and there they celebrated the Jewish holidays. For obvious reasons, these commuters were not much interested in the communal life of their place of work. By the 1920s, this migration process had by and large come to an end. If Egyptian Jews had been a predominantly urban community even in the nineteenth century, they were now concentrated in the big cities. In the interwar period, 95 percent of the Jews lived in either Cairo or Alexandria (see table 12).

This migration wave was caused by economic rather than political factors. Still, in the late nineteenth and early twentieth centuries, the minorities felt undoubtedly better protected in the large cities under direct British control than in the small provincial towns. It is, at any rate, striking that the incidences of ritual murder (blood libel) accusations, which between the

TABLE 12

Regional Distribution of the Jews in Egypt, 1897–1947

Mudīrīya/Governorate City	1897	1907	1917	1927	1937	1947
Cairo	8,819	20,281	29,207	34,103	35,014	41,860
Alexandria	9,831	14,475	24,858	24,828	24,690	21,128
Canal Zone						
Port Said	400	378	602	1,012	777	748
Ismā'īlīya	39	11	95	110	87	116
Suez	120	74	157	126	78	84
Lower Egypt						
al-Gharbīya	1,414	1,403	1,512	1,123	687	320
Ṭanṭā	883	1,104	1,183	943	–	–
al-Maḥalla al-Kubrā	197	145	102	91	–	–
Ziftā	184	81	62	37	–	–
Kafr al-Zayyāt	61	32	68	15	–	–
Dasūq	50	4	12	16	–	–
al-Daqhalīya	828	734	887	725	427	302
al-Manṣūra	508	522	586	563	–	–
Mīt Ghamr	258	190	176	157	–	–
Simbillāwayn	51	20	8	16	–	–
al-Buḥayra	239	389	235	79	69	95
Damanhūr	228	?	53	53	–	–
al-Sharqīya	278	292	290	173	129	78
Zaqāzīq	238	240	245	147	–	–
al-Qalyūbīya	?	191	319	159	109	88
Banhā	?	?	178	77	97	–
Upper Egypt						
al-Gīza	17	36	482	646	450	587
Aswān	13	7	137	62	75	57
Asyūṭ	15	44	142	44	105	6
Girgā	19	?	143	34	36	?
Banī Suwayf	31	57	88	57	12	7
Qinā	42	?	114	88	57	28
al-Fayyūm	9	43	83	27	26	11

Summary

Year	1897	1907	1917	1927	1937	1947
Cairo and Alexandria	18,650	34,756	54,065	58,932	59,704	62,988
Canal Zone	439	463	854	1,248	942	958
Lower Egypt	?	3,057	3,287	2,302	1,447	897
Upper Egypt	?	353	1,362	1,046	823	790

SOURCES: Figures for 1897 from Fargeon, *Les juifs*, p. 306; and Landau, *Jews*, p. 9. Figures for 1907 from *AS* 1909 (Cairo, 1911); and for the smaller towns in Lower Egypt from Fargeon, *Les juifs*, pp. 306–11.

1870s and the 1920s were repeatedly raised against the Jews by local Christians, notably Greeks and Syrians, were almost all located in certain maritime ports and the smaller towns of the Delta. Port Said and Damanhūr witnessed a whole series of such accusations, but none were reported from Alexandria after the British occupation in 1882, and only two from Cairo. These incidents caused a number of Jews to move to the larger cities, which seemed more secure. However, their place was quickly taken by new immigrants.[105] That the political groups and the press, which in the 1930s and 1940s frequently adopted a strongly anti-Zionist, and in some cases took an openly anti-Jewish stance, were concentrated in Cairo and Alexandria did not lead to any significant Jewish migration out of these cities.

The Jewish communities of Cairo and Alexandria did not develop at an equal rate in the first half of the twentieth century. Although at the end of the nineteenth century, the Alexandria community was still slightly larger than that of Cairo, and although both experienced rapid growth between 1897 and 1917, Alexandria began to stagnate after World War I. The growth between 1907 and 1917, to a certain extent, must have been caused by the arrival of Ashkenazi refugees from Palestine, most of whom left again after the war. They must have been joined by other members of the local community, though it is impossible to give any precise figures based on the material available. The trend went in the opposite direction in Cairo, the center of government, the administration, and industry. Its Jewish population increased by 20 percent between 1917 and 1927, and then remained at the same level until 1937, so that there must have been some emigration. In the decade between 1937 and 1947, it grew again by 20 percent. The constant influx of immigrants certainly contributed to the comparative weakness of communal organization in the capital.

Within Cairo and Alexandria, another movement of migration was to be observed from the 1860s on—the dispersion of Jews and other non-Muslim minorities over the various city quarters reflecting social diversification within their communities.

The link between spatial and social mobility shows particularly well in the case of Cairo (see table 13).

From Ottoman times until the mid-nineteenth century, almost all Jews had lived in the Jewish quarter of Cairo, the *ḥārat al-yahūd*, situated in the Mūskī area in the Gamālīya quarter, one of the oldest and most traditional quarters of the city. The more prosperous families lived in larger houses (*hoch*, Arab., *ḥawsh*) combining a living and a work area, the poorer families in crowded rented apartments. Only a few families remained in Old Cairo (*miṣr al-qadīma* or *al-'atīqa*), where the Jewish cemetery was still located in the twentieth century (al-Basātīn in the Khalīfa quarter). The Jewish quarter was no ghetto, but offered its inhabitants protection, allowing them to lead a traditional communal life. In the late 1930s, Fernand Leprette was still able to describe the four gates of solid iron and beech wood of the *ḥāra*, which permitted the inhabitants to defend themselves against outside aggressors.[106] In the late 1860s, individual members of the wealthiest Sephardi families, the Mosseris, Cattaouis, and Suarès, began to leave the *ḥāra* to settle in the newly developed quarters to the west and north of the old city. For some time at least, their offices remained in the *ḥāra*, while they built spacious villas for themselves, often resembling palaces, in still uninhabited areas that were in the process of being converted into suburbs for the wealthy. Shubrā was then a rural area, 'Abbāsīya, Ismā'īlīya and Tawfīqīya were uncultivated plots, which the respective khedives sold to members of the upper class at a low price on condition that they build villas there. When, in the years preceding World War I, these suburbs, and 'Abbāsīya in particular, lost their character as exclusive residential enclaves for the rich and became middle-class neighborhoods, the members of the upper class moved into newly developed quarters along the Nile, namely, Zamālik, Garden City, Roda, and Gīza, where they were still to be found in the 1950s.[107]

From the late nineteenth century onward, the wealthy families were followed by the Jewish middle class of various ethnic origins, including the Karaites, who also moved to the 'Abbāsīya, Ismā'īlīya and Heliopolis quarters. Even before World War I,

TABLE 13

Residential Distribution of the Jews in Cairo, 1937 and 1947

Quarter	1937 Total Population	1937 Jews	1947 Total Population	1947 Jews	1947 Rabbanites	1947 Karaites
al-Azbakīya	54,549	1,356	75,422	2,037	1,995	42
Bāb al-Sha'rīya	87,113	2,868	132,824	3,658	3,635	23
Būlāq	156,638	241	232,423	386	368	18
al-Gamālīya	84,289	4,788	107,292	5,255	4,136	1,119
al-Khalīfa	81,045	12	122,194	8	7	1
Darb al-Aḥmar	81,120	505	122,080	537	532	5
Sayyida Zaynab	128,214	612	192,705	368	355	13
Shubrā Sharq	117,868	398				
Shubrā Gharb	115,757	178	227,003	377	360	17
'Abidīn	111,271	8,191	159,300	10,681	10,589	92
Heliopolis	87,771	3,586	164,919	4,069	3,983	86
Old Cairo	66,793	341	116,843	523	503	20
al-Mūskī	25,919	2,580	35,963	3,278	3,232	46
al-Wā'ilī	123,919	9,358	208,380	10,544	8,930	1,614
Rawḍ al-Faraj	?	?	193,906	139	130	9
All Cairo	1,312,096	35,014	2,090,654	41,860	38,755	3,105

SOURCES: Figures for 1937 from *Population Census of Egypt, 1937*, vol. 9, Muḥāfaẓat al-Qāhira (Cairo, 1940), table 5, p. 50. Figures for 1947 from *Population Census of Egypt, 1947*, vol. 15, Muḥāfaẓat al-Qāhira (Cairo, 1952), table 5, pp. 69–70.

'Abbāsīya had been largely Jewish. After the war, Jews were said to make up the majority of its inhabitants most of whom were Copts, Europeans or other members of the local foreign minorities, who also had their schools and hospitals there. The neighboring Ismā'īlīya quarter was also largely foreign. By 1922, Heliopolis (*miṣr al-jadīda*), which had been built by the Belgian industrialist Baron d'Empain at the turn of the century and which the first Jew reportedly moved to in 1908, had its own Association Israélite de Heliopolis. At the same time Būlāq, which in the nineteenth century had been a fashionable residential suburb, was completely transformed into a quarter inhabited mainly by craftsmen and workers, many of them immigrants from Upper Egypt as well as Greeks, Italians, Copts, and Jews. After World War I, the Jewish lower-middle class moved on to 'Abidīn, Bāb al-Lūq, and Daher (al-Ẓāhir), a subdistrict of the Sakākīnī quarter. As early as 1910, the head of the Alliance school in Cairo, S. Somekh, reported in a letter to Paris:

> The Jewish community in Cairo has its ghetto, too, where it was still confined yesterday. It has been a mere half-century since it has overcome its barriers to establish itself in all the new arteries of the capital. The high aristocracy lives in Ismailieh, the most fashionable quarter of Cairo, where some five years ago it opened a magnificent synagogue [on present 'Adlī Street], breaking the chains of tradition which attached it to its humble birthplace, the ghetto. Tewfikieh, of smaller size, is the meeting place of the grand bourgeoisie, and Abbassieh that of the small traders and employees who cannot afford high rents. It is only the poor—and they are legion—the workers of all categories and those still haunted by the cult of old memories who have remained in the ghetto, which, in spite of all desertions, is nonetheless too narrow to contain them. The flow of immigrants constantly fills the empty spaces created.[108]

Residence, then, was patterned according to two factors, rite and ethnic origin on one hand and social class on the other. After World War I, upward social mobility among the lower and the lower-middle classes was generally reflected in a move from the *ḥāra* to (lower-middle class) quarters inhabited by large numbers of Jews and other minorities such as Sakākīnī (including Daher) as well as Būlāq, Bāb al-Lūq, and 'Abidīn. Those who rose even further in status continued to move into middle-class areas such as 'Abbāsīya, Ismā'īlīya, and Heliopolis, which also had a large portion of other minority and foreign inhabitants. As mentioned previously, the rich lived mostly in the new residential areas along the Nile. In the Egyptian censuses of 1937 and 1947, the majority of Cairene Jews were registered in the 'Abidīn and Wā'ilī districts (including 'Abbāsīya, Ismā'īlīya, and Tawfīqīya) with 8,000 to 9,000 Jewish inhabitants each in 1937 and over 10,000 in 1947, followed by the traditional Gamālīya and Bāb al-Sha'rīya quarters with 3,000 to 4,000 Jewish inhabitants each, modern Heliopolis with over 3,500, and the Mūskī with some 3,000. Old Cairo numbered a mere 341 Jewish inhabitants in 1937 and 503 in 1947.

Their social rise removed large sections of the Jewish middle and upper classes physically and culturally from their poorer coreligionists, who continued to live in a traditional Jewish environment. In their new neighborhoods, the middle and upper classes integrated into a cosmopolitan subculture dominated by foreigners and non-Muslim minorities. Within the *ḥāra* and in its vicinity, the various subgroups of indigenous and immigrant Jews still lived close to their synagogues, of which the Egyptian, Turkish, Portuguese, and Ashkenazi were the most notable. The indigenous Egyptian Jews still constituted the largest of these subgroups, whose quarter was generally known as the "Sephardi quarter." Separated from them lived the Yemeni Jews and the Turkish Jews, who, in the 1940s, numbered about 40 families. As was mentioned before, the Karaite lower and lower-middle classes inhabited a living area of their own, the *'aṭfat al-yahūd al-qarā'īn*, where, in 1947, some 1,700 community members over the age of 15 were registered. Another 1,600 Karaites were listed in Khurunfish, in the Wā'ilī district. The Ashkenazi lower and lower-middle classes lived in the Darb al-Barābira area, bordering on the *ḥārat al-yahūd*, which as late as the 1940s resembled a traditional Eastern European Jewish *shtetl*.[109]

Alexandria did not present as clear a picture of ethnicity, social mobility, and residential distribution as Cairo. Even in the nineteenth century, Alexandria had had no Jewish quarter similar to the Cairo *ḥāra*, although Alexandrian Jews did concentrate in a certain residential area. By the twentieth century, they had dispersed over almost all districts of the city, following the criterion of social class rather than of rite and regional origin. Moreover, the residential areas most popular among Alexandrian Jews were also heavily dominated by other local foreign minorities. According to the Egyptian population census of 1937 and 1947 respectively, 9,735 (9,188) lived in Muḥarram Bey, 4,455 (2,451) in Gumruk, 4,440 (3,834) in al-Manshīya, 4,086 (3,558) in ʿAṭṭārīn and 1,112 (1,355) in Ramla out of the total 24,690 (20,885) Jews registered in Alexandria. The chief rabbinate, the community center, and the community school were all housed in a large complex in the center of town, where they were still to be found in the 1980s (present rue Nébi Daniel).[110] In al-Manṣūra, too, the Jews left the original Jewish quarter (*rubʿ al-yahūd*) in the twentieth century to settle throughout the town. In Port Said, the Jewish immigrants from Yemen and Aden lived in a separate neighborhood, while the other Jews settled in the European part of town. There is nothing to indicate that in other provincial towns Jews still inhabited special living areas after World War I.[111]

2

Communal Organization

Considering the diversity of Egyptian Jewry, caused to a large extent by massive immigration, it seems all the more remarkable that in the twentieth century, communal organization was relatively stable and efficient. In all towns except Cairo, the Sephardim, Ashkenazim, and Karaites were united in one community, ending the state of communal fragmentation characteristic of earlier centuries. Although the Rabbanite Jews were not, like the Orthodox Copts or the Armenian Catholics, officially recognized as a separate religious community (*millet*) by the Sublime Porte in 1839, they were treated as such by the imperial decree of 28 May 1891, which was confirmed by the Egyptian government in 1915. The Karaites, by contrast, who had not presented their statutes to the government, were never formally recognized as a separate community.[1] Like the other *millets*, the Rabbanite Jews enjoyed communal autonomy in the fields of religious cult, personal status, and education. They were thus entitled to deal with marriage, divorce, inheritance, and guardianship according to their religious law, to hold religious services and celebrate their holidays, and to maintain their places of worship and cemeteries as well as schools and charitable institutions.[2]

In the nineteenth century, the Jewish communities established a wide range of religious, social, and charitable institutions. This network was considerably expanded in the twentieth century, contributing to the diversification of the community, and of communal affairs. New organizations were created in the areas of education and services for the aged, both of which previously had been left largely to private philanthropy. In those areas where the community was unable to provide adequate services, philanthropic associations formed, which were mainly supported by the commercial middle and upper classes. The associations provided food and clothing for Jewish school children from poor families, dowries for Jewish girls and pregnant women, help for the sick and the aged. They continued a long tradition of Jewish welfare and self-help organizations, which had their counterparts in most of the Jewish communities of the Mediterranean area and the Ottoman Empire as well as among other, non-Jewish minorities of the Islamic world.

The basic pattern of communal organization was very similar among Cairo, Alexandria, and larger provincial cities such as Ṭanṭā. All Jews residing in town for a certain period of time, usually one year, were regarded as members of the community regardless of rite or personal observance. Membership, therefore, did not reflect individual choice or personal belief. While all Jews were thus members of their local community, only men over the age of eighteen, or twenty-one, in some cases, paying the fee (*'arikha*) were entitled to vote in the communal assembly. The *'arikha* was normally £E 11 per annum, but the wealthy families paid much higher sums. Communal organization was thus largely based on plutocratic principles. The general assembly of dues-paying members elected the council, which usually numbered twelve to eighteen members. The communal council in turn elected from among its ranks the president, one or two vice-presidents, the secretary general and the treasurer as well as their alternates. Unlike the *nagid* of Fāṭimid times, the president did not need to be confirmed in his office by the ruler, that is, the king of Egypt. By contrast, this official confirmation was required for the religious heads of the various communities, including the *shaykh al-Azhar*. The chief rabbi, who was nominated by the general assembly of the paid-up members, was thereby designated by the authorities as the official representative of the community.

In spite of this, the statutes of all major communities named the council and its president as their representatives vis-à-vis the government and all other non-Jewish groups or organizations. The communities were thus headed by the lay body of the community council, which represented the leading families and the affluent commercial and entrepreneurial middle class, who controlled communal affairs until the 1940s. In Cairo, the offices of president and vice-president were de facto hereditary within the Cattaoui and Mosseri families. In Alexandria the circle of eligible families was somewhat wider. The provincial communities were generally headed by a well-to-do merchant, who often served as president for several decades. The dominance of wealthy merchants and traders was not in itself new. In Fāṭimid and Ayyūbid times, the communities also had been headed by lay notables, and it was only in late Ottoman times that rabbis were officially regarded as chief representatives of their communities. Scholars no longer played a prominent rôle in communal affairs in modern times.[3]

By the twentieth century, the rabbis were clearly subordinate to the lay leadership. Early in the nineteenth century, the chief rabbis of Cairo and Alexandria were still directing communal affairs largely independently. Generally, however, their authority was supplanted by the rising class of merchants and bankers, and by the end of the century, it was restricted to religion and cult proper. The religious leadership's loss of power and authority has, of course, to be seen within the context of secularization among Egyptian Jewry in general, which on the cultural level was reflected in the growing orientation of the middle and upper classes toward Europe.[4] According to the statutes of 1927, the chief rabbi of Cairo was not even in charge of the administration of the synagogues, which was entrusted to a special council committee, and was hence utterly dependent on the council in all matters of finance and administration. In the case of conflict with the council, the rabbis were, therefore, left with few alternatives but to resign from office, which the council in more than one case was quite happy to accept. In the final analysis, the actual power of the chief rabbi was a matter of his personality rather than the letter of the communal statutes. This showed particularly well in Cairo, where, to judge by the law, his authority should have been weakest. Chief Rabbi Haim Nahum Efendi, who was appointed in 1925 and who, because of his experience and his good relations with the authorities, became the actual leader of the community in the 1940s, finally found his position recognized, when in 1948 a modification of the statutes made him, in conjunction with the council, the official representative of his community. This amendment, however, only served to demonstrate that in Egypt, much as in the Jewish communities of Western Europe, religious and lay authority were effectively separated and organized in two parallel hierarchies, headed by the chief rabbi on one hand and by the council and president on the other.

The Jews of Egypt had no countrywide organization until 1925, when King Fu'ād I made Haim Nahum Efendi chief rabbi of Egypt (grand rabbin du Caire et de l'Egypte). The chief rabbi of Egypt was, therefore, elected by the Cairo community only. When Haim Nahum died in 1960, his successor, Haim Dwek, was only designated *rabbin substitut* and hence did not inherit Nahum's extensive powers. The chief rabbinate of Cairo was also in charge of the communities of Port Said, al-Manṣūra, Banhā, and Mīt Ghamr, whereas Ṭanṭā, Damanhūr, and Kafr al-Zayyāt were under the jurisdiction of the chief rabbinate of Alexandria.[5] No similar unification existed on the lay level. Even in the late 1940s when political tension was rising in Egypt, the rivaling communities of Cairo and Alexandria were jealously guarding their independence. In 1943, a first coordinating committee was established, but did not achieve much. A similar attempt made in 1948 equally failed to bring about the much needed coordination between the two major communities in the country.[6]

The one communal association to have a countrywide organization were the lodges of the B'nai B'rith. Following the American example, they had been established first among Ashkenazi immigrants in Cairo, soon to be followed by Sephardi lodges in both Cairo and Alexandria and, in the 1920s, in all other major Jewish communities in the country. In the 1920s, a number of lodges were active among Egyptian Jews: the Ashkenazi Maimonides and the Sephardi Cairo lodges in the capital (established in 1887 and 1911 respectively), the Eliahu ha-Nabi lodge in Alexandria (1891), Ohel Moché in Ṭanṭā (1921), Maghen David in al-Manṣūra (1923), Israël in Port Said (1924). In 1934, the Grande Loge du District d'Egypte et du Soudan united them under one organization, which later also established the women's lodges Deborah in Cairo and Ruth in Alexandria (both 1939) as well as the youth lodge A.Z.A. (Aleph Zade Aleph, 1943).

The B'nai B'rith adopted the ideals of humanism and philanthropy from the Freemasons, but not their ritual and critical attitude toward religion. They defined themselves as a Jewish organization active on behalf of charity and communal reform, cultural revival, and the defense of Jewish interests in general. By the turn of the century, the lodges of the B'nai B'rith, which were largely made up of members of the rising commercial and professional middle class, were actively working for democratic and social reform within the Jewish community, establishing schools, workshops, and charitable institutions of all kinds. They also supported the movement of spiritual and political Zionism.[7] Finally, the Zionist movement of Egypt at various intervals had a countrywide organization as well, though it was only effective between 1944 and 1948.

THE DEBATE ON PERSONAL STATUS LAW

In the mid-nineteenth century, the Islamic laws regarding non-Muslim (*dhimmī*) minorities, which were based on the so-called Pact of 'Umar, were abolished in the Ottoman Empire (of which Egypt was a part until 1914). The reform decrees known respectively as the Hatt-ı Şerif of Gülhane of 1839 and the Hatt-ı Humayun of 1856 granted equality before the law to all subjects of the sultan regardless of their religious and ethnic backgrounds. However, in the area of personal status law, the personality system characteristic of Islamic law was retained, and hence a central pillar of the *millet* system as well. Indeed, it was only in the nineteenth century that the *millet* system developed into a well-defined institution of Ottoman administration. After the British declared Egypt a protectorate in December 1914, definitely ending Turkish suzerainty, the Egyptian government in its Law number 8 of 1915 confirmed Ottoman practice with regard to the non-Muslim communities. The Egyptian constitution of 1923 did not change existing personal status law. As a result, all matters of marriage, divorce, adoption, guardianship as well as inheritance continued to be settled by the religious courts of the communities concerned. Religious jurisdiction in matters of personal status served to preserve the influence of the clergy among their respective communities, and to uphold religious particularism even in a period of increasing secularization of (urban) culture and political life.[8]

In the 1930s and 1940s, the Egyptian government made repeated attempts to unify personal status law and to eliminate all religious (*shar'ī*) courts. In their place it intended to establish special family courts (*majlis ḥasbī*) to be presided over by both Muslim and non-Muslim judges. If the abolition of religious courts would not have completely broken the authority of the religious hierarchies, the Sunni Muslim community included, it would nevertheless have greatly reduced it. The non-Muslims showed considerable apprehension lest these family courts be based primarily on Islamic (Ḥanafī) law at the expense of their own, Christian or Jewish, codes, and their leaders offered coordinated resistance whenever the Egyptian government tried to move in this arena. Until the 1950s, they were indeed strong enough to prevent any changes in this vital field of communal autonomy and religious influence. It was only in 1955 that the new leadership of the Free Officers succeeded in finally dissolving the religious courts and in replacing them with the new family courts that the previous governments had in vain tried to establish.[9]

It seems, however, that at least in the 1920s and 1930s, Chief Rabbi Haim Nahum was less concerned about an eventual abolition of religious autonomy in personal status matters than were the patriarchs of the Greek Orthodox and the various

Coptic churches. At that time, quite a few members of the Europeanized middle and upper classes of the Alexandria community considered religious legislation obsolete, arguing in favor of unified secular codes. According to them, they were able to count on the tacit support of Haim Nahum Efendi himself. In 1929, Robert S. Rolo, an influential businessman, who in general was not active within the community, approached the British consul general in order to inform him that:

> [T]he community generally speaking was exceedingly dissatisfied with the provision that Jews in matters of personal status were to be treated under Jewish law, which in their opinion was, especially in matters of inheritance, of testamentary powers and matrimonial relationships, unsuited to modern conditions.... I was further given to understand that the Chief Rabbi of Cairo was really in favour of the change though I did not suppose he was in a position to say so openly.[10]

Even though the religious hierarchy had suffered a serious loss in power and authority in the course of the nineteenth and twentieth centuries, the "modernists" did not succeed in taking the last stronghold of rabbinical power. The actual state of secularization was not formally sanctioned. Religious jurisdiction in matters of personal status was only abolished after communal structures had already more or less dissolved.

ALEXANDRIA

In the twentieth century, Cairo and Alexandria, the two major Egyptian cities, were still clearly different from each other. In the interwar period, Cairo numbered about 40,000 Jews among an overall population of 1 to 1.5 million, while Alexandria had an estimated 30,000 Jews out of a total population of 600,000 to 750,000. Cairo was the capital of the country, the seat of government and central administration, much more influenced by immigrants from the countryside who were constantly moving into the city than was Alexandria, a Mediterranean seaport traditionally dominated by Europeans and Levantines, where even in the nineteenth century foreigners had accounted for over one-third of the population. Most noticeable among the cosmopolitan crowd of foreigners and local minorities, portrayed so vividly by Lawrence Durrell in his *Alexandria Quartet*, were the Greeks and the Italians. It was only in the twentieth century that French replaced Italian as the lingua franca of the Jewish community, and in the early 1920s, 25 percent of its notables still carried Italian passports. As a result, Jews were highly influential within the local Italian colony.[11] In the Alexandrian community, which was made up of immigrants from the entire Mediterranean region, and, to a lesser degree, from Eastern Europe, the influence of the Egyptian Arab environment was weaker and Arabic-speakers fewer than in Cairo. Nonetheless, over 30 percent of the Jewish notables registered there in the early 1920s had Egyptian nationality. From 1881 to 1915, the community and its president, Yaʿqūb de Menasce, enjoyed Austro-Hungarian protection, and the share of families with Austro-Hungarian protection or nationality was strikingly high. After the collapse of the Habsburg Empire in 1918, the community was registered as stateless.[12]

Although even in the 1940s a considerable number of Alexandrian Jews were poor and little educated, the community was, generally speaking, more homogeneous socially and culturally than was the Cairo community. But in 1904, a teacher of the Alliance school lamented the degree of internal diversity characteristic of Alexandrian Jewry:

> [I]n Alexandria, where the mounting flood of immigrants becomes more noticeable every day. A cosmopolitan environment par excellence, our city hosts a most heterogeneous population, where individuals of the most diverse origins cross paths, who are fundamentally different in their natural qualities and who seem to have nothing in common except—let us mention it in passing—this love of money, which all seek to gain with equal zeal.... Our institutions [i.e., the Alliance schools] thus offer the spectacle of a little world of the strangest diversity. The indigenous Arab and Syrian element has been joined by the European element, made up largely of Spaniards, Italians, and Rumanians. Each group has a character of its own, special features that make it easily distinguishable from the rest.[13]

By the late 1920s, these distinctions had not been completely obliterated. Yet the differences between the rich and the poor on one hand and the Sephardim and Ashkenazim on the other seemed less marked than in Cairo, even to foreign observers, who usually were extremely critical of local conditions. In 1925, Julius Berger, a representative of the Zionist Executive, reported from Alexandria:

> In Alexandria conditions are different from Cairo, and, it seems to me, [they are] better. There, too, you have the separation between Sephardi and Ashkenazi Jews—the Arabic-speaking element is of no importance there—but relations are much better there and the differences have been significantly reduced under the influence of the seaport, which on the whole gives you a much more European impression than Cairo. The Ashkenazim are more actively engaged in communal leadership and institutions. Social intercourse, too, is more highly developed, even intermarriage is more frequent and does not have the diffamatory character attached to it in Cairo.[14]

The middle class, temporarily weakened by the stock market crisis of 1907, was able to recover and during World War I firmly established its position in Alexandrian society. The great families of the de Menasces, Rolos, Aghions, Goars, and Tilches were in no way inferior to the Cairo élite in wealth, prestige, and influence, nor did they lack the latter's sense of superiority, or outright snobbery.[15]

Among the leading families mentioned by Berger, the de Menasces were undoubtedly the most prominent. The Sephardi Menasce family seems to have come to Egypt via Palestine and Morocco, with the earliest records of their presence in the country dating back to the eighteenth century.[16] Like Yaʿqūb Qaṭṭāwī and Mūsā Mosseri, Yaʿqūb (de) Menasce (b. Cairo 1807, d. Alexandria 1887) began his career as a money changer (*ṣarrāf*) and banker in the Cairo *ḥāra* and eventually became the private banker and *ṣarrāf başı* of the khedive Ismāʿīl. He was one of the earliest businessmen in the country to recognize the opportunities offered by European trade, and together with Yaʿqūb Qaṭṭāwī opened the banking and trading house of J. L. Menasce et Fils with branches in Manchester and Liverpool, followed later by London, Marseille, Paris, and Istanbul. With the support of Ismāʿīl (whose brother Muṣṭafā he had helped through financial difficulties), he also established the Banque Turco-Egyptienne. In 1872–73, he was granted Austrian protection and in 1875, probably because of his services to Austro-Egyptian trade, was given the title of baron of the Austro-Hungarian Empire together with Hungarian citizenship. According to Makāriyūs he was president of the Cairo Jewish community in 1869 (with Ya'qūb Qaṭṭāwī?). In 1871, he moved to Alexandria, where he caused a serious rift and set up a separate community. In 1873, he built the Menasce synagogue as well as the Menasce cemetery and the Ecoles (Fondation) de Menasce. In 1878, the feuding notables were reconciled, and the reunited community elected two presidents, Béhor David Lévi de Menasce (1830–85), Ya'qūb's eldest son and successor, and Béhor Moché Aghion, who remained in office until 1890.

Béhor Lévi's eldest son, Baron Jacques Béhor de Menasce (1850–1916), moved from banking to the profitable cotton and sugar business, acquiring extensive landholdings in Upper and Lower Egypt. In 1890, he followed his father as president of the Alexandria community and held this office for almost a quarter of a century until the outbreak of World War I, when, as a Hungarian citizen, he was treated as an enemy alien by the British authorities. The Baron was a dominant figure, imposing on council, chief rabbi, and community alike, and in spite of his many services to the community was heavily criticized for his autocratic style. To his six children he left land, real estate, and company shares at an estimated value of £E 300,000–500,000.[17]

His younger brother Félix Béhor (1865–1943) studied in Vienna and established the London branch of J. L. Menasce et Fils. In later years, he showed great interest in the Jewish national movement, which his second wife Rosette actively supported. A personal friend of Chaim Weizmann, Félix de Menasce presided over the Egyptian Pro-Palestina Committee, founded in 1918, and in 1920 and 1921 represented the Egyptian Zionist movement in London at the World Zionist Congress Carlsbad.[18] After directing numerous communal organizations for many years, he succeeded Alfred Tilche as president of the Jewish community of Alexandria in 1926, and held the office until 1932. The Menasce family, rich, cosmopolitan, and European-educated, linked by marriage to the best Jewish families, gave the Alexandria community three presidents, who together held office for thirty-four years.

The Rolos, who like the Menasce, Cattaoui, Suarès, and Mosseri families were Sephardi immigrants, and who must have come to Egypt at some point before 1850, provided the Alexandria community with only one president, Robert J. Rolo (1934–48). The Rolos did, however, play a major rôle in the Egyptian economy and society.[19] In the early nineteenth century, Ruben Rolo directed a prosperous trading company, which imported mainly indigo. In 1870, his son Giacomo (Jacob, 1847–1917), together with his eldest brother Simon and several other partners, opened the trading and banking house of Ruben Rolo, Figli et Compagnie, which later cooperated with the Suarèses and Cattaouis in the various projects initiated by the Cassel consortium (*al-dā'ira al-sanīya*, Ḥulwān railways, Crédit Foncier, National Bank of Egypt). During the economic crisis of 1907, Jacob Rolo dissolved the company and with his three sons founded the firm of J. Rolo et Compagnie, which combined banking with the wholesale coal, cotton, rice, sugar, jute, and coffee trade. They also acquired large shares in various major land companies such as the Société de la Domaine du Cheikh Fadl, the Sucreries, and the S.A. du Wadi Kom Ombo. When Jacob Rolo died in 1910, he left land and real estate valued at £70,000 to his eight children.

His eldest son, Robert J. Rolo (1876–?), a British-educated banker and entrepreneur (the Rolos were British citizens), was elected president of the Jewish community of Alexandria in 1934. A convinced anti-Zionist, he resigned in April 1948, just before the outbreak of the first Arab-Israeli War, in a conflict with the pro-Zionist chief rabbi of Alexandria, Dr. Moise Ventura.[20] It was, however, his cousin Robert S. Rolo (1869–?) who gained the strongest influence in Egyptian economic and social circles. He studied law in Paris and practiced for a few years but eventually went into business, assuming a number of directorships on the boards of the companies his father, Simon Rolo, helped create (Crédit Foncier, National Bank of Egypt, S.A. du Wadi Kom Ombo). He also served as a legal adviser to Crown Prince Fu'ād, and was later regarded as a close confidant of the king and a major link between the court and the British Residency. This position seems to have been largely due to the influence of his wife, Valentine, who until her death in 1920, was first lady-in-waiting to Queen Nazlī. Robert S. Rolo, who was made Sir Robert in 1938, was a leading member of the British colony in Egypt and lived in Cairo, but took no part in the affairs of the local Jewish community.[21]

The Aghions, who in the nineteenth and twentieth centuries were mainly engaged in the cotton trade, banking, and land development and who had extensive landholdings in Lower Egypt, were the social equals of the Rolos and de Menasces. Related to all leading Jewish families in the country, they provided one president to the Alexandria community, Béhor Moché Aghion (1878–90).[22] The Tilches, another of the presidential families, were one of the very few élite families to be able to trace their presence in Egypt back to the sixteenth century.[23] Described as the wealthiest trading house in early nineteenth-century Egypt, they had made a fortune in trade with Italy, and, as early as the eighteenth century, moved into banking. Under Muḥammad ʿAlī they imported gold and silver to embellish military uniforms, engaged in the wheat trade, and then turned increasingly toward cotton growing and ginning. Listed as notables of the Alexandria community in 1840, they also played a prominent rôle in the local Italian colony. Alfred Tilche, a lawyer by profession, was president of the Alexandria community in 1925–26 and its vice-president in the early 1930s.

In the nineteenth and twentieth centuries, Alexandria was generally considered the best organized of all Jewish communities in Egypt. In 1913, Somekh, the director of the Cairo Alliance school, described Alexandria as "a model of order and organization," and the reformers in Cairo pointed to it as an example to be emulated. Zionist observers commented favorably on the low level of social and religious tension, and even harsh critics such as Hans Kohn gave credit to Alexandria saying that things were much worse in Cairo.[24] Many of the communal institutions that were created in Alexandria in the nineteenth century, including aid to marriageable girls from poor families (Mohar ha-Betulot,

1867), assistance to destitute travelers ('Ezrat Aḥim, 1885) and support for school children ('Amele Torah, 1894), were adopted in Cairo only at a later date. The Menasce hospital, established in 1890 by the three Menasce brothers Jacques, Félix, and Alfred, enjoyed a very high reputation and was used by both Jewish and non-Jewish patients.[25] The constant arrival of immigrants without sufficient means of support proved a serious challenge to communal leaders, who tried in vain to stop, or at least redirect, this wave of immigration. By selling real estate owned by the community in 1904—during the height of speculation in land and real estate—they were able to build a new school in 1907. But the treasury was empty again after the economic crisis of 1907, and poverty on the increase. The situation improved when World War I brought such high profits in trade and industry that the community was able not only to cope with the sudden arrival of the 11,000 Ashkenazi refugees expelled from Palestine, but also to open new communal institutions.

Education was less well supported. The communal school, which opened in 1907, uniting under its roof a kindergarten and a primary school, and the private Ecoles Fondation de Menasce were attended by children of the lower-middle and the lower classes only. The Alliance school, which demanded a fee, served the middle class until 1919, when the Alexandria community was regarded as too prosperous to require outside help. In the late 1920s, almost 3,000 pupils attended the various community schools. Meanwhile children from the upper-middle and upper classes were sent to European, notably Italian and French, schools such as the Lycée Français, if they were not instructed by private teachers. Enrollment in foreign, that is, non-Egyptian and non-Jewish schools, was closely linked to the availability of good secondary Jewish schools, which were first introduced to Alexandria in 1925. In 1907–8, 80.3 percent of all Jewish students in Alexandria attended foreign schools, in 1912–13, their numbers declined to 77.2 percent, fell further to 47.5 percent in 1924–25, and to an all time low of 40.5 percent in 1930–31. In 1945–46, enrollment rose again to to 59.6 percent.[26]

The occasion that stirred the community to take more direct responsibility for educating its youth was an unhappy one. Around Easter/Passover of 1925, teachers at the Catholic missionary school of Ste. Cathérine, which was attended by a large number of Jewish students, shocked the community by distributing anti-Semitic material repeating the traditional blood libel accusations. The B'nai B'rith immediately responded and established a Union Juive pour l'Enseignement, which the very same year was able to open a Jewish secondary school, the Lycée de l'Union Juive pour l'Enseignement, in the suburb of Muḥarram Bey. In 1928, it had about 450 students, most of them "of rather modest backgrounds."[27] In 1943, the community opened another secondary school, Maimonides, which followed the Egyptian curriculum that the other community schools had already adopted in the 1930s. The primary language of instruction in the schools was hence Arabic rather than French.[28]

In spite of the world economic crisis of 1929–32, which was strongly felt in Egypt, the 1930s brought a new spate of building and philanthropic activity. The Menasce hospital was replaced in 1932 by a larger hospital built by the community. Private philanthropists opened a kindergarten, an orphanage, a pensioners' home, two private schools, and another synagogue. In 1938, a severe financial crisis forced the community to reduce its welfare program for the poor. Violent protests erupted and about thirty unemployed stormed the welfare (*bienfaisance*) office demanding relief.[29] Communal leaders responded, and in the early 1940s, welfare services were again expanded. Alexandria was still regarded as a model community, even though there was, as usual, no lack of criticism. Hans Kohn from the Keren Hayesod summed it up when he wrote in 1928:

> The Sephardim of Alexandria are entirely under the influence of the French [*Franzosentum*]. They imitate the life-style of Parisian high society, leading a totally superficial life, showing no deeper interests, [they] make a lot of money and spend a lot of money—but have no sense of social work and national responsibility. Things are even worse in Cairo.[30]

In organization, the Jewish community of Alexandria was very similar to that of Cairo, except that in Alexandria all Jews living in the city regardless of rite and origin were considered part of the community. The Ashkenazim, who in 1904 (before the arrival of the refugees from Palestine) are reported to have made up 10 percent of Alexandrian Jewry, demanded a more prominent rôle in communal affairs. The Sephardi notables reacted by passing an amendment to the community statutes in 1907 restricting the right to participate in the general assembly to those who had paid their *'arikha* dues for four full years. This effectively excluded even those newcomers who were prepared to pay a higher *'arikha* than prescribed. It was only in 1930 that the Ashkenazim established a charitable society (Société de Bienfaisance) of their own.[31]

The community statutes of 1872 (written in Italian) still seem to have been the basis of communal organization in the 1930s. At that time, about nine-hundred dues-paying members were entitled to vote in the general assembly, with their fees ranging from £E 1 as the most common sum to £E 10 (7 members), £E 15 (5 members), and £E 25 (4 members) per annum. Five members of the Rolo family contributed a total £E 75; seven Menasces, £E 64; fifteen Aghions, £E 55; and four Goars, £E 31.[32] The council acted as the highest communal body. Its fifteen members were elected for six years, and they in turn elected the president, vice-president, and treasurer as well as their alternates. Their responsibilities were broadly defined. The 1872 statutes stated that the council: "Directs, administers, and represents the community ... corresponds with the local government and the consulates in this city ... regulates the relations between the Rabbinate and the community." In the 1930s, these responsibilities were distributed among a number of committees, covering (1) chancellery, finance, and *gabelle* (meat tax), (2) welfare, (3) synagogues and cemeteries, (4) marriage and divorce, (5) schools, (6) hospitals, (7) real estate, (8) *'arikha*, (9) *matsot*, and finally, (10) lawsuits.

In the twentieth century, the paid-up members came mainly from the middle and upper classes, Sephardim and Oriental

Jews active in trade, banking, industry, and the professions. The council was dominated by certain families—de Menasce (Jacques Elie, Félix, Alfred), Rolo (Robert J., Ibram, Max), Aghion, and Tilche—and wealthy entrepreneurs such as the Goar brothers, Raphael Toriel, Benvenuto Campos, Raphael Nahman, Joseph Elie de Picciotto or Félix bey Padoa. Edwin and Jack Goar, to give a few more examples illustrating the rise of Jewish families in Egyptian society, belonged to a family long established in the country, whose name still betrayed its Arab origin (Gohar = *jawhar*, jewel).[33] Edwin N. Goar (1875–?), a banker and one of Alexandria's largest import-export merchants, who sat on numerous company boards and business associations, was educated in Switzerland and married to a member of the merchant family of Piha. A former president of the Eliahu ha-Nabi lodge, he served for many years as vice-president of the Alexandria community before becoming its president from 1948 to 1956. His brother Jack (1887–?), who was educated in Italy and married to Hélène Adès, a member of one of the richest Jewish families in Egypt, served as a colonel in the British army during World War I, and later, as a stockbroker, entered into a close relationship with Ismāʿīl Ṣidqī Pāshā. He was also a personal friend of both King Fu'ād and King Fārūq. An ardent sportsman, he served as vice-president of the exclusive Royal Automobile Club of Egypt and the Jewish World Organization Maccabi. Raphael Toriel, a prominent businessman and member of a family of cotton exporters with extensive landed property (over 5,000 *faddān* in the 1930s), served for more than thirty years as a city councilor, and in the late 1930s was made honorary secretary of the Jewish community.[34]

The career of Joseph Elie (bey) de Picciotto (1872–1938) offers another example of the successful businessman who played such an important rôle in the Egyptian economy, as well as in the local Jewish community. Alexandria-born to a Sephardi family from Aleppo, Joseph Picciotto began as an employee in a trading firm.[35] In 1895, he married Judith Curiel, the daughter of a well-to-do Jewish banker, set up his own business in 1896, and founded a company for importing cotton textiles in 1917. He was elected president of the Association du Commerce d'Importation in 1920 and two years later his success was recognized by an appointment to the prestigious Economic Council of Egypt. An early sympathizer of the Egyptian national movement of the Wafd, he was also a loyal supporter of the king, and was made a senator in 1924. At the same time Picciotto was actively involved in communal affairs, served as president of the Eliahu ha-Nabi lodge from 1917 to 1925 and as vice-president of the Pro-Palestina Committee in 1918. He directed the Alexandria school committee until he resigned over the scandal at the Ste. Cathérine School in 1925. As late as 1933, he was active in the local anti-Nazi movement.

Even immigrants were not excluded from communal leadership. Examples abound, but a few will suffice. Haim Dorra (1898–?) arrived from Damascus and made a fortune in the textile trade; Tunis-born Alfred Nessim Cohen (1881–?) began his career as a teacher with the Alliance Israélite Universelle, later worked as a stockbroker, and, in 1914, together with Haim Perez and Ovadia Salem established the trading company Société d'Avances Commerciales with branches in Cairo, London, and the Sudan. Both were among the most active and prominent council members. Nor were Ashkenazi immigrants excluded: Marco Nadler, a wealthy industrialist, and Dr. Hermann Schlesinger, a medical doctor, who had arrived from Rumania in 1907, were also long-term council members. Incidentally, all of these self-made businessmen and professionals, with the exception of Dorra, sympathized with the Zionist movement from an early date.[36]

Within this circle of wealthy families, which was open to newcomers provided they had the means and upbringing to share their tastes and life-style, communal office circulated more freely than in Cairo. None of the old families had a monopoly over any of the leading positions in the council, not even the de Menasces and Rolos. Jacques Béhor de Menasce, who presided over the community for more than twenty-five years, was the only one to be reproached for his autocratic style. The council members, most of whom were related to him by blood or marriage, or belonged to his circle of friends, were said to behave like a docile "family council," lorded over by the patriarch.[37] Jacques Béhor de Menasce was succeeded by Edgar Suarès (1914–17), Félix bey Tuby (1917–25), Alfred A. Tilche (1925–26), Félix de Menasce (1926–34), Robert J. Rolo (1934–48), and Edwin N. Goar (1948–56). With the one exception of Alfred Tilche, they were all wealthy bankers, entrepreneurs, and businessmen. This was no hereditary monarchy, then, but rather a plutocracy, which outsiders nonetheless tended to view as a "closed shop."[38]

The rabbinate, which headed the Alexandria community until the mid-nineteenth century, was subordinated to the lay body of the community council as early as 1872. The chief rabbi and his deputies were elected by the general assembly upon designation by the council, and their authority was restricted to the religious domain proper. Constant interference of the council caused at least one rabbi, Jacob Toledano, the acting head of the rabbinical court of Alexandria, to resign in 1938.[39]

Those chief rabbis, like Raphael Della Pergola (1910–23), David Prato (1927–36), both from Florence, and Dr. Moise Ventura from Izmir (1937–48), who tried to follow an independent course, sooner or later clashed with the council. Della Pergola and Prato at first tried to promote Italian influence within the Jewish community. More in keeping with their office, they made great efforts to revive Jewish values and traditions, openly supporting Zionism. Because of a serious conflict with the council, Prato almost resigned in 1933. The lingering crisis finally came to a head in 1948, when the council tried to censor all public pronouncements made by Chief Rabbi Moise Ventura, who was well known for his Zionist sympathies. In January 1948, when Ventura would have preferred to resign, his supporters turned to the general assembly, which elected some of them into the council. In the fierce conflict over election the entire council as well as its president, Robert J. Rolo, resigned. An electoral committee that was designated in a general assembly attended by over seven-hundred community members confirmed Ventura as chief rabbi of Alexandria. Ventura, however, decided not to remain in office and in May 1948 left for Paris. As a result of this rift, the Alexandria community was without a chief rabbi, council, and president, when the first Arab-Israeli war broke out on 15 May 1948. While a new council headed by Edwin N. Goar was soon elected, no agreement was reached as to who should succeed Ventura at this difficult moment. Finally Ventura's former deputy, Aaron Engel, an Ashkenazi rabbi as the name would indicate, was designated provisional chief rabbi of Alexandria. Haim Nahum, the chief rabbi of Cairo and Egypt, assumed the presidency of the rabbinical court of Alexandria, further proof of his position as leader of Egyptian Jewry in those years of crisis.[40]

CAIRO

It was only in the late 1940s that Cairo finally assumed the leading rôle among Egyptian Jewry. In the nineteenth century, Alexandria was still the more important center of Jewish life. In the twentieth century, the Cairo community grew more rapidly, but it continued to lag behind in communal integration and organization. Since the massive wave of immigration starting in the 1860s, the Cairo community had been particularly marked by internal fragmentation. Although according to its statutes, the Communauté Israélite du Caire comprised all Jews domiciled in Cairo for at least one year, in actual fact, the Ashkenazim and the Karaites had been able to preserve their independence. Out of a total 40,000 Jews living in Cairo in the interwar period, an estimated 30,000 were of Sephardi and Oriental origin, some 5,000 were Ashkenazim, and another 6,000 to 7,000 (and here figures are particularly hard to establish) were Karaites. With the exception of the Karaites, all these groups were in turn divided along the lines of origin, language, culture, social class, and hence, to a certain extent, of identity as well. In 1912, a teacher of the Cairo Alliance school commented on the diversity of language and culture among his students: "The majority of our children are made up of indigenous Jews, indolent and lazy, who speak Arabic; of a great portion of Ashkenazim with a lively intelligence who are the jewel of our schools and who insist on retaining their German dialect [*jargon*, i.e., Yiddish]; and of a minority of Spanish Jews, lively and alert, who have almost all come from Turkey and who at home speak Ladino."[41]

In 1925, Julius Berger, from the Zionist Executive in Jerusalem, wrote a lengthy report on his visit to Egypt, in which he also described the Cairo community:

In Cairo the Jewish community, which numbers about 30,000 individuals [*Seelen*] is divided into three parts: (1) the Arabic-speaking part long established in the country, which has been partly enlarged by immigration from the North African countries, and which constitutes the proletariat of the Jewish population; (2) the Spanish [*spaniolisch*] Jews, who over a period of several centuries have immigrated from Spain, Italy, etc.; (3) the Ashkenazi Jews, who have settled in Cairo over the last two decades only and who all in all number at best 2,000 individuals.

The most important of these parts is group no. 2, which is at the helm of communal affairs, ruling the community and its institutions, [and which is] in large part wealthy, to a small part very wealthy, and even extremely wealthy, and whose real language is French. Compared to them the Arabic, or as they say, Egyptian-speaking Jews are of much lesser importance; but they together with the Spanish Jews form one united bloc vis-à-vis the Ashkenazi Jews. The latter, some of them medical doctors, dentists [and] also many employees, are by and large looked down upon. They are spoken of as the "Schlechtes," they are not regarded as being socially equal; marriages between Ashkenazi and Sephardi Jews are very rare and are considered a *mésalliance* by the Sephardim.[42]

Under these circumstances, it must have been extremely difficult to establish communal institutions capable of absorbing the large and ever growing numbers of immigrants arriving in Cairo. Before World War I, the community maintained a considerable number of synagogues, but only a few communal and charitable institutions, among them the Ecoles gratuites de la Communauté, which developed out of the Alliance school that opened in the *ḥāra* in 1896. In 1902, it was transferred to ʿAbbāsīya and then taken over by the community in 1912.[43] The same year, the first community statutes were adopted. The community was dominated by a small circle of families who distributed communal office among themselves: a Cattaoui was elected president, a Mosseri vice-president, and their younger relatives presided over the various communal committees and institutions. It was only after World War I that their monopoly came under growing attack, a process gradually leading to wider participation in communal affairs.

The rise of the Cattaoui family to their position of prominence among Egyptian Jewry began in the mid-nineteenth century.[44] The Cattaouis (Qaṭṭāwī) were a Sephardi family, who may have come to Egypt via Holland, but who may have lived there as early as the Fāṭimid era. The earliest documents available refer to the late eighteenth century only. Their name seems to be derived from a village called Qaṭṭā, located in the area of present-day Zamālik. The seventeenth-century historian Joseph ben Isaac Sambari (1640–1703), who was claimed as an ancestor by some members of the family, allegedly took his name from a small village close to Qaṭṭā. The first Qaṭṭāwī emerging as a historical figure is Ya'qūb Menasce Qaṭṭāwī (1801–83), who under 'Abbās (1845–54) was director of the mint and together with several partners held the farms of customs and fisheries. The khedive Ismā'īl (1863–79) made him *ṣarrāf başı*, head of the money changers, an office later assumed by Ya'qūb Levi Menasce, whose career resembled Ya'qūb Qaṭṭāwī's in many ways. Together they established the banking and trading house of J. L. de Menasce et Fils, which proved very successful and was soon able to open branches in Liverpool, Manchester, Marseille, and other cities. When his four sons grew up, Ya'qūb Qaṭṭāwī separated from Ya'qūb Menasce and founded the banking and trading firm of J. M. Cattaui Figli et Compagnie with offices in Cairo, Alexandria, and Paris. Ya'qūb Qaṭṭāwī, who was still living in the tradition of Oriental Jewry, eating local food, dressing in the Arab way, and speaking Arabic and Hebrew only, was, together with Ya'qūb Mosseri, one of the first Jews to leave the *ḥāra* and to settle in Shubrā, which at the time was still a rural suburb. In spite of this move, he served as lifelong president of the Cairo Jewish community. He was also the first Egyptian Jew to be granted the title of *bey*, and in the early 1880s was furthermore made a baron of the Habsburg Empire. As Austro-Hungarian citizens and aristocrats, the Qaṭṭāwīs henceforth called themselves "von Cattaoui," and only changed to "de Cattaoui" after the outbreak of World War I.

Ya'qūb's eldest son, Aslān bey Ya'qūb Qaṭṭāwī (1824–83), focused his attentions on the family business, and together with the Suarès family helped to create the local sugar industry. In the twentieth century, his ten children constituted the most prominent branch of the family. Moise de Cattaoui Pasha (1849–1924) was the youngest and most prominent of Aslān Ya'qūb's four sons.[45] As a partner in the family firm, he married Ida Rossi, daughter of Dr. Elia bey Rossi, the personal physician of the khedive, in 1874. After a brief interval in Naples, where the couple fled during the 'Urābī revolt of 1881–82, they moved to a palacelike villa surrounded by a large park in the Ismā'īlīya quarter of Cairo in 1883. The same year Moise Cattaoui was elected president of the Austrian Welfare Organization and served, with his brother Joseph, as president of the Cairo Jewish community. He remained in this office for forty years until his death in 1924. Although vehemently attacked for his authoritarian style, he was also remembered for his rôle in founding and maintaining the private Ecoles Moise de Cattaoui. While he was a practicing Jew, he rejected the Zionist movement, which his wife viewed with much more sympathy. As numerous as his many responsibilities in the community were—in 1904 he was also elected honorary president of the Egyptian B'nai B'rith lodges—Cattaoui did not neglect the family business. In conjunction with the Suarèses, Rolos, and Menasces, he became involved in railroad construction, the Ṭanṭā waterworks, and public transport. Moreover, he sat on the board of the Crédit Foncier and the National Bank of Egypt, and as late as 1923 helped establish the Egyptian Delta Land and Investment Company, which built the suburb of Ma'ādī on its estates. Yet after his death, communal leadership did not pass to his sons, who devoted their energies to business and the liberal arts, but to his nephew Joseph Aslan Cattaoui, a son of his brother Aslan, and later to Joseph Aslan's younger son René.

Compared to the Cattaouis, who in spite of their French education and European business contacts emphasized their

Egyptian-Jewish identity and maintained excellent contacts with the Egyptian élite, even the Mosseris, while possibly wielding greater economic influence, had to step back into the second line of communal leadership.[46] In the contest for the presidency, the Mosseris consistently lost to the Cattaouis, and were left with the vice-presidency and the chair of various communal committees. The first of this line of vice-presidents coming from the Mosseri family was Nissim J. bey Mosseri (1848–97), a wealthy banker and the son-in-law of Yaʿqūb Qaṭṭāwī. He was followed by his son Joseph N. bey Mosseri, Jr. (1869–1934), a merchant banker married to Jeanne Aghion. His younger brother Elie (1879–1940), despite his marriage to Laura Suarès and great influence in Egyptian economic and political circles, lost against Joseph Aslan Cattaoui, when they competed for the presidency in 1924, and had to content himself with the vice-presidency. The same happened to his younger brother Maurice (1886–?), who was elected vice-president in 1941, but lost to Joseph Aslan's son René when he stood for president in 1943.

Supported by the chief rabbi of Cairo, the Cattaoui and Mosseri families ruled the community largely unobstructed until the 1920s. By the end of World War I, Moise de Cattaoui Pasha had been president for over thirty years, and one Mosseri had followed the other as vice-president. In violation of the statutes, the council did not give any account of its financial dealings. In 1918, the Mosseris, in whose bank the community funds were deposited, were even accused of embezzling £E 18,000.[47] Criticism of the Cattaoui and Mosseri rule was growing. In a sarcastic letter to a friend written in 1897, the Bulgarian Zionist Marco Barukh had already mentioned all the problems that were later to become the stock in trade of criticism directed against the communal establishment: the absenteeism and indifference of the all-too-busy bankers, who nevertheless were anxious to ward off all attempts at reform; the impotence of the well-meaning lawyers; the materialism of the rising middle class; and finally the material and the spiritual misery of the poor.[48] The teachers of the local Alliance school, headed by the indefatigable S. Somekh, did not tire of attacking the dictatorship of Moise Cattaoui Pasha. In 1908, the Société pour la Renaissance Juive en Egypte (Jam'īyat al-Nahḍa al-Adabīya al-Isrā'īlīya), which had just formed in the *ḥāra*, published a pamphlet titled *Tayaqquẓ al-umma al-isrā'īlīya* (Awakening of the Jewish Nation), which was directed against Cattaoui and called for school reforms.[49] At that time, the community schools were so poor and inadequate that many children were left with no instruction whatsoever. A teacher of the Alliance reported in 1908:

> The indigenous Jews are still rather backward. They have only one little school, situated in a dirty quarter [i.e., the *ḥāra*], where instruction of a most elementary kind is given. The notables of the community, who are very rich and highly educated, do not want to do anything to raise the moral level of their coreligionists. We therefore see with sadness a large number of children roaming the streets all day instead of going to school.[50]

The situation seems to have improved when, in 1912, the community opened its new school in 'Abbāsīya, which, in spite of its name (Ecoles gratuites), was not free. In 1913, approximately 1,200 students were enrolled; 200 students attended the Alliance school, and another 100 to 200 went to private schools. At the Lycée Français, 240 of the 760 pupils enrolled were Jewish; in the Jesuit schools, 760 out of 2,700; in the Italian schools, 180 out of 540; and in the British missionary institutions, 80 out of 370.[51]

During World War I, the Sephardi Cairo lodge of the B'nai B'rith, founded shortly before in 1911, renewed its efforts on behalf of communal reform, particularly in the fields of welfare and education. When a letter to the Egyptian prime minister, Ḥusayn Rushdī Pāshā, in March 1917 produced no effect, it published a declaration in April 1917 entitled "On the Rôle of the Béné Bérith in the Affairs of the Jewish Community in Cairo," which called for the dissolution of the council, limitation of the term of presidential office, wider authority for the chief rabbi and the rabbinical court, equal distribution of the *'arikha* among all community members, creation of more welfare organizations in general, and of a hospital in particular.[52] The reformers organized in the lodges of the B'nai B'rith were members of the commercial and entrepreneurial middle class of Sephardi and Oriental origin. Many of them were recent immigrants and their sons, who had prospered in the period of economic expansion between the 1880s and the early 1900s and, after the temporary setback of 1907, during World War I. Now they demanded a greater share in communal affairs. S. Avigdor of the Alliance viewed these "upstarts" with unveiled suspicion, reporting in 1918:

> One thing is clear, and that is the success of the methodical campaign that for the last two years has been run by what I will call the new party, called that of the foreigners, [which is] recruited particularly among those bourgeois who got rich during the war, the *nouveaux riches*, whose strength of cohesion, intellectual and financial resources are concentrated in the Lodge of the Béné Bérith. This lodge, whose existence was hardly known before the war, has become influential in Cairo ever since its members enlarged their fortunes in an inconceivable manner, or created for themselves lavish positions. It is these new bourgeois, these *nouveaux riches*, who previously had been kept by their Egyptian coreligionists from any function, participation or position in the management of communal affairs, who have exposed to daylight the evils of communal administration under the leadership of Cattaui Pasha; and their campaign has been crowned with success.[53]

That many of the reformers were immigrants was indeed used against them by advocates of the established order, as the Cairo lodge mentioned in its open letter to the Jewish public of April 1917, which denounced theses efforts as a: "clumsy maneuver to present us as foreigners [who are] trying to eliminate the Egyptian from the council in order to rule there as masters.... We have shown by our indefatigable zeal in this struggle to get communal services somewhat organized that the management of these 'Egyptians' has led to a state of complete disorganization."[54]

A look at the group of reformers who were elected into the council in November 1916 largely confirms Avigdor's description.[55] Among this group of eleven, only two, Robert Rolo and Jacques Green, came from wealthy Jewish families long established in the country. Salomon Cicurel, son of the immigrant

Moreno Cicurel, Albert Haym from Istanbul, Albert Najar and Albert Harari from Syria, Maurice Gattegno, Isacco Benaroio, Elie Gallico, Marcetto Mattatia, and Ugo Morpurgo were all successful merchants, bankers, and businessmen very active in welfare. And they were all of foreign nationality. Confronted with the "systematic obstruction of the directorate" (i.e., Cattaoui and the Mosseris), the young guard of reformers, who at the time must have been in their mid-thirties or early forties, resigned en bloc in March 1917. Moise de Cattaoui, by contrast, refused to resign from his office as president of the community, and after the forced resignation of his nephew Jack Mosseri, who for many years had headed the school committee, took over this position as well. When those who had paid their *'arikha* refused to pay their contribution to the schools, the number of students declined dramatically, until at the end of 1918 a mere five hundred remained. When the Alliance, too, closed its school, a large number of children were left without instruction. Those who could afford to do so sent their children to foreign schools, be it the secular Lycée Français or the Christian missionary establishments.[56]

As the community was not lacking in means but in organization—according to Somekh the number of millionaires could no longer be counted after the war, and the treasury of the community positively bursted with gold, the members of the Cairo lodge decided to take independent action.[57] In 1917, Isacco Benaroio and some of his friends founded a welfare organization called La Goutte de Lait. Under its auspices, an orphanage was opened in the Tawfīqīya quarter housing three-hundred children. In 1918, the Société Israélite des Oeuvres de Bienfaisance, established by Abramino Menasce, another member of the commercial middle class, opened a polyclinic in Garden City, which in 1926 was replaced by a hospital in 'Abbāsīya. In 1923–24, several private primary and vocational schools opened in the *ḥāra* to provide the poorest section of the community with some elementary instruction. At the same time, the formal organization of the community slowly disintegrated. A general assembly held in June 1921 was attended by only seven of over three-hundred paid-up members. When Moise de Cattoui died in 1924, the community for a time had neither a president, nor a council or chief rabbi. The last incumbent, Rabbi Raphael Aaron ben Simon, had already resigned a few years earlier over a dispute with the council.[58]

In 1924–25, the Jewish community of Cairo elected new leadership. Moise de Cattaoui Pasha was replaced as president by his nephew Joseph Aslan de Cattaoui Pasha, and the uncharismatic Raphael Aaron ben Simon was succeeded by Haim Nahum Efendi, both of them strong personalities with considerable influence in the community as well as in Egyptian society.

When Joseph Aslan de Cattaoui Pasha (1861–1942) defeated Joseph N. Mosseri to become the fourth in his family to serve as president of the Cairo community, he was already a well-known man with far-reaching connections in Egyptian business and political circles.[59] After studying engineering in Paris at the prestigious Ecole des Ponts et Chaussées, he worked at first with the Egyptian Ministry of Public Works and then went into private business as an adviser and partner in various companies of the Suarès-Cattaoui-Rolo-de Menasce group. This link was reinforced when he married Alice Suarès, a daughter of Félix Suarès. In 1912, he was made a pasha; in 1914, he was elected to the Legislative Assembly and in 1916 joined the Committee on Trade and Industry. Between 1919 and 1922, he seems to have sympathized with the national movement of the Wafd, for in 1920–21, he was sent to London as legal adviser to the Egyptian delegation. In 1920, he became one of the original founders of Bank Misr, an exclusively Egyptian enterprise aimed at stimulating industrial growth independent of European capital and intervention, and in the mid-twenties served as its vice-president. At the same time he sat on the boards of the Kom Ombo Company, the Sucreries, and a considerable number of other major enterprises in the agricultural, transport, banking, and industrial sectors.

After leaving the Wafd and joining the Liberal Constitutionalist Party of ʿAdlī Yeghen Pāshā, which represented the interests of large landowners, Joseph Aslan Cattaoui entered Parliament in 1922 as deputy of Kom Ombo (it will be remembered that his family had extensive interests in the S. A. du Wadi Kom

Ombo). The same year he was appointed to the Constitutional Commission preparing the new constitution of April 1923. He reached the pinnacle of his political career when in November 1924, he became minister of finance in the anti-Wafdist cabinet of Aḥmad Zīwar Pāshā, formed after the murder of Sir Lee Stack, who was the governor-general of the Sudan and *sirdār* of the Egyptian army. Although Cattaoui soon after switched his political loyalty to the royalist Ittiḥād Party, he was demoted to the less influential portfolio of minister of communications in March 1925. In early May 1925, he resigned from office. Rumor had it that a telegram he had sent to Sa'd Zaghlūl, the leader of the Wafd party and foremost political rival of Aḥmad Zīwar, on the occasion of the Little Bayram (*'īd al-fiṭr*) celebrations, had upset his colleagues who regarded it as a breach of cabinet conduct. Moreover, it was thought that he had actually acted on behalf of the king, with whom Cattaoui was then rather close, who sought some kind of rapprochement with Zaghlūl. In recognition of his service, King Fu'ād made him a member of the Egyptian Senate in 1927, where between 1931 and 1935 he chaired the finance committee. His wife Alice, née Suarès, was first lady-in-waiting to Queen Naẓlī, a position previously occupied by Valentine Rolo. She was also the first Jewish woman to receive a high Egyptian decoration.[60] After Joseph Aslan Cattaoui suffered a stroke in July 1938, his son Aslan took over his seat in the Senate; yet he did not resign from his office as president of the Jewish community in Cairo until his death in May 1942.

Despite his French education, Joseph Aslan Cattaoui saw himself as an Egyptian of Jewish faith, who at all times stressed the loyalty to king and country of the community he represented. He did so in his dealings with the Egyptian authorities just as much as he did with his Zionist critics. He rejected political Zionism as a national movement that aimed to establish a national home, or possibly even a Jewish state, on Arab territory.[61] But he was a practicing Jew, and in 1935 served as vice-president of the honorary committee of the Paris-based Confédération Universelle des Juifs Séfardim. His influence in Egyptian economic and political circles was thought to be considerable, and it was only some British diplomats who dismissed him as nice, but "in the political arena very weak," always anxious to please the king. In spite of his conscious efforts to emphasize his Egyptian identity, John Murray from the British Residency wrote in 1925, after Cattaoui's resignation from his cabinet post: "Jusef Cattaoui Pasha, a French educated local Jew, is a charming and intelligent man but is really looked on as more than half a foreigner and politically he is of no importance."[62]

But this disparaging comment must have referred to Egyptian politics at large. When it came to the interests of the Jewish community, Joseph Aslan Cattaoui Pasha, because of his close links with members of the Egyptian and local foreign élite as well as European diplomats, was well suited to act as spokesman and intermediary. His preferred style was to intervene discreetly with the authorities rather than airing grievances in public or bringing conflicts to the open. This low-profile approach, which was shared by the new chief rabbi, Haim Nahum Efendi, could be observed in all major conflicts either within the community or between the community and other groups of Egyptian society, ranging from the anti-Semitic incident at Ste. Cathérine in 1925 over German anti-Semitic and Jewish anti-Nazi activities in the early 1930s to the conflict over Zionism in the late 1930s and the 1940s.

The new chief rabbi, Haim Nahum Efendi (1873–1960), was a man of unusual erudition and political experience, very well connected in diplomatic and political circles in the former Ottoman Empire, France, and the United States.[63] Born in Magnesia near Izmir, he studied law in Istanbul and then went to Paris to attend the Rabbinical Seminary and to study Oriental languages. At that time he also established ties to the Committee of Union and Progress in which the Young Turk reform movement had organized. Upon his return in 1908, he was made chief rabbi (*ḥākhām başı*) of Istanbul, but continued to serve the new Turkish government in a variety of functions. In 1918–19, he joined the Turkish delegation attending the armistice negotiations at The Hague, unofficially represented his country in Washington in

1920–22, and in 1923 served as adviser to the Turkish delegation at the Lausanne Peace Conference. His involvement in Turkish diplomacy and his political ambitions, which, according to his critics, made him neglect the interests of his community and the spiritual responsibilities of his office, also brought him into open conflict with local Zionists. While he saw the Zionists, who were mainly Ashkenazim, as tools of German interests, they described him as a "type of purest mendacity," a "serpent" spinning vile intrigues and, at the very least, a "true Oriental."[64] The conflict became so sharp that in March 1920, Nahum finally resigned, ostensibly for the reason that the Turkish authorities refused to allow Jews of foreign nationality to vote in the elections for the Jewish National Assembly (*meclis umumi*). Had the reason really been this dispute, he would hardly have chosen to represent this very government in his subsequent assignments in Washington and Lausanne.

It was this man, who had gained a reputation as a diplomat and Orientalist rather than a spiritual guide to his flock—"the best rabbi of the diplomats and the best diplomat of the rabbis" as an observer was later to say of him—that the Jewish community of Cairo chose to have as its new chief rabbi in 1925.[65] The moving forces behind this choice appear to have been Moise and Joseph Aslan Cattaoui, who in his career, style, and outlook had much in common with Nahum on one hand and the Cairo lodge of the B'nai B'rith on the other, which Nahum was soon to join. As the candidate of the Oriental and Sephardi middle and upper classes in general and the Cattaouis in particular, he was opposed by certain rival élite factions (notably the Mosseris) and sympathizers of Zionism. Doubts were also voiced in religious circles, both inside and outside the *ḥāra*, where he was thought to be too liberal, if not quite simply too lax in his religious belief and practice.[66] Haim Nahum had excellent relations with King Fu'ād, whom he had known before the latter's accession to the throne, thereby securing his direct access to the palace. Fu'ād made him chief rabbi of Egypt and the Sudan in 1925, granted him Egyptian nationality in 1929 and appointed him a senator in June 1931 and a member of the Egyptian Academy in

November 1933.[67] The president of the Cairo community and its chief rabbi, therefore, maintained close contacts with the palace, the liberal parties, and leading economic circles in the country. They saw themselves as Egyptian patriots, and as champions of a policy of integration, and considered Zionism a potential danger to the security and well-being of the Egyptian Jewish community.

The decision in favor of Joseph Aslan Cattaoui in April 1924 led to tumultuous scenes in the general assembly of July 1924, when the entire council resigned. The decision in favor of Haim Nahum created a heated debate on the career and personality of the new chief rabbi. Calm was finally restored when a new council was elected in February 1925, and Haim Nahum assumed office in March 1925. Nahum immediately ordered a reorganization of the Cairo rabbinical court, and in November 1926 the community adopted new statutes modeled on the Alexandria statutes of 1872, which realized at least some of the demands for communal reform.[68]

According to the new statutes, the community was directed by a council elected by the general assembly for a period of three years. Only those male members of the community who had paid the *'arikha* for three consecutive years were given the right to vote. Unlike Alexandria, at least one-third of the eighteen council members had to be Egyptian citizens. One major demand of the reformers was met when the presidential term was restricted to one year. However, this did not change actual practice: Joseph Aslan Cattaoui remained in office, ill and partly paralyzed, until his death in 1942. The responsibilities of the council were defined in a comprehensive manner (Art. 9): "The Council is invested with the most extended powers to manage the affairs and interests of the community as well as to safeguard the rights and privileges enjoyed by this community *ab antiquo*." The responsibilities of the chief rabbi, by contrast, who at that time seems still to have been too new and too weak to assert himself, were strictly limited, and his dependency on the council in matters of finance and administration expressed even more clearly than in Alexandria (Art. 28): "The powers of the chief rabbi are exclusively religious. He is president of the rabbinical court whose regulations are laid down by the community council. He signs all documents of personal and civil status.... [All] administrative questions related to all services of the community including those of the rabbinate are exclusively decided by the community council."

In the mid-twenties, the council was still dominated by wealthy businessmen and professionals, but many of them represented the reform movement of 1916–17. Among them were self-made men, immigrants or the sons of immigrants such as Abramino Menasce and Albert Haym, who have been mentioned before; Isaac Nacamuli, Abramino Acher, Isaac Amiel, and Ezra Rodrigue, whose careers resembled closely those of Moreno Cicurel and Joseph Picciotto; or Haim Barcilon, Salvatore Iscaki, and Victor Zagdoun, who belonged to established middle-class families.[69] The old complaints were still heard, but were now voiced mainly by foreign observers and local representatives of the Zionist movement. In 1925, Julius Berger lamented the absence of Jewish life in Egypt and the lack of communal institutions. Two years later, in November 1927, his colleague Grünhut reported that:

> In contrast to the Ashkenazi community, the "Arab-Jewish community" occupies an important place, the more so since it is presently headed by the former minister of finance, Cattaoui Pasha. It has been not more than fifty to sixty years since the forefathers of Messrs. Cattaoui, Mosseri, Menasce, etc., lived crowded together in the Jewish quarter [*ghetto*]. They were mostly money changers, small-scale bankers, etc., who, because of British influence, were able to rise on the social scale. They acquired great wealth and moved from the ghetto into the most wonderful palaces conceivable. They have been completely modernized in their life-style and the sons of the old generation today occupy the most prominent positions in Egypt, some of them in government, to a much larger extent, however, in business. They have not extended this modernism to the community to the degree that might have been expected. It is easy to see that the rich have not done very much for their own people who live in poverty and misery. This is not to say that Egyptian Jews do not engage in charity, but they do so in the traditional

way. Even today we can find hosts of beggars [sitting] in front of the offices of a Cattaoui, Mosseri, etc., who are not sent away empty-handed. There is no systematic approach [*Planmaessigkeit*] at all.

The immigration of Sephardi Jews from Turkey and the Balkans, as well as of the Jews of Aleppo has had a positive influence on the [overall] standard [*Niveau*] of the community. Some of the immigrants have brought money with them, and, much more important, they brought their abilities, language, and business skills, and contributed significantly to the upsurge of trade and commerce in Egypt.[70]

Hans Kohn, a representative of the Keren Hayesod, was even more critical of local conditions, and after a brief visit to Alexandria reported from Cairo in 1928:

Things are much worse still in Cairo. There all power is placed in the hands of twenty to twenty-five old families, who only in the last years could be moved to do anything at all for the needs of the community, but who are still very far from seeing that one should also do something for matters outside Cairo. The Jews there, and even more so in the provincial towns, are completely Arabized and have assimilated precisely the bad qualities of the people in whose midst they live. They have become mean and without any sensitivity to the necessity of [doing] tasks that are not directly linked to pleasure.[71]

Yet even Zionist observers had to admit that these very same circles spent over £80,000 on a new Jewish hospital and a school, and that in the course of the 1920s and 1930s, a large number of organizations, associations, and clubs were founded to satisfy the material and spiritual needs of the community. In 1925, a Société d'Etudes Historiques Juives presided over by Cattaoui and Nahum was established, which among other things took an active interest in the Cairo Geniza materials. In 1925–26, a group of Jewish women founded a branch of the Women's International Zionist Organization (WIZO). Although they may have cared little for Zionism, they were active in relief work in the *ḥāra*, where they opened a polyclinic and an office dealing with questions of health, hygiene, and family planning.[72]

In spite of the economic crisis of the early thirties, which affected the Jewish commercial middle and upper classes, too, communal institutions were further expanded. In the mid-thirties, 2,500 children, (still less than one-third of the 8,500 Jewish children between the ages of six and fifteen), attended communal schools, which included the two Ecoles gratuites in ʿAbbāsīya, the Moise de Cattaoui School for boys, and the Marie Suarès School for girls (which both charged a fee), a kindergarten and a vocational school established by Salvator Cicurel. Another 20 percent were sent to other Jewish schools, 40 percent to French and Italian secular, 4 percent to (religious) Christian and 3 percent to Egyptian state schools.[73] While the Cairo branch of the Union Universelle de la Jeunesse Juive, founded in the early 1920s, had to close down in 1935 because of declining participation, a new Association de la Jeunesse Juive Egyptienne was formed the same year. Its aim was to spread the knowledge of Arab-Jewish history and tradition and at the same time to work for a gradual Egyptianization of the Jewish community. In 1935, Egyptian Jewry celebrated the eight-hundredth anniversary of the birth of Moses Maimonides. A new synagogue named after him opened in 1936. The 1930s also saw intense activity among the lodges of the B'nai B'rith, which from 1933 headed the local anti-Nazi movement and in 1934 established the Grande Loge du District d'Egypte et du Soudan to coordinate activities among the various local Jewish communities.[74]

In May 1942, Joseph Aslan Cattaoui died after having been partially paralyzed by a stroke in 1938. The candidates for succession once again came from the Cattaoui and Mosseri families, Joseph Aslan's younger son René and Maurice Mosseri, a younger son of Joseph N. Mosseri. Only the third contender, Isaac Nacamuli (1869–1945), was an outsider, a self-made businessman, who had established one of the largest paper stores in Egypt and had married into the Cattaoui family. Nacamuli had served as vice-president of the community but did not know any Arabic. *Al-Shams*, the platform of the Association de la Jeunesse Juive Egyptienne described the election as a choice between the cosmopolitan *haute bourgeoisie* and the reformers inspired by Egyptian patriotism.[75] They called upon the assembly to increase the number of council members from eighteen to twenty-four with a majority of Egyptian nationals and to include representatives of the younger generation and the intelligentsia. French was to be replaced by Arabic and Hebrew as the official languages of the community. The president was to be of Egyptian nationality, Arabic-speaking, and wearing the tarboosh (rather than the European hat), who would be elected by the general assembly and not just by the council. In short, the reformers wanted to make the community more democratic and at the same time more Egyptian. The only suitable candidate, according to *al-Shams*, was René bey Cattaoui, scion of a respected Jewish family, long established in the country and well connected within its ruling circles. In the analysis of Israel Wolfensohn, one of the mentors of the Association de la Jeunesse Juive Egyptienne, most Jews in the *ḥāra* and in 'Abbāsīya, voted for Cattaoui; the rich families of the Suarès, Mosseri, and Green, including several members of the Cattaoui family itself, voted for Mosseri, while the immigrants from the Mediterranean area and Europe supported Nacamuli, who, after all, was one of their own.

In April 1943, René bey Cattaoui was indeed elected president of the Cairo Jewish community, the fifth member of his family to occupy this position in uninterrupted succession. Isaac Nacamuli was elected honorary president, Salvator Cicurel and Dr. Isaac Lévi vice-presidents, Albert Haym secretary, and Emile N. Adès treasurer, all of them highly successful businessmen and managers. Only Maurice Mosseri, the main loser in this contest, was left without representative office.[76] The council once again included Abramino Acher, Haim Barcilon, Salvatore Iscaki, Ezra Rodrigue—the reformers of 1916, Jacques Lévi-Garboua, and the lawyers Charles Chalom and Clément Harari, most of them in their late sixties and seventies. Ovadia Salem and Aslan Vidon, two of the most prominent Jewish businessmen and philanthropists, also entered the council. Ovadia Salem (1888–?) immigrated from Salonika in 1903 and in 1914, after having worked for some time as a banking clerk, joined Alfred N. Cohen and J. H. Perez in founding the Société d'Avances Commerciales, which soon developed into one of the largest companies in the field. Salem contributed generously to charitable works, engaged in the lodges of the B'nai B'rith and was close to the local Zionist movement, but appears not to have been an active member.[77] Aslan Vidon (1882–?), like Nacamuli, Acher, Rodrigue, and Salem, worked his way up in a commercial firm and in 1917 opened a highly successful company, which supplied the government, army, and hospitals with clothing and tents. At an early stage, he turned to philanthropy, establishing, together with his wife, a school in 1933 and an orphanage in 1934.

René bey Cattaoui (1896–?), the new president, was educated in Lausanne and married to Céline Goar. After working for a number of years with the Egyptian Ministry of Agriculture and the Sucreries, he became director general of the S. A. du Wadi Kom Ombo in the late 1920s. A member of the Economic Council and the Institut d'Egypte, he entered Parliament as deputy of the Kom Ombo district in 1938, while his elder brother Aslan replaced their father in the Senate. René was reelected to Parliament in 1945. In 1936, he was for the first time elected a member of the community council, and sat on the school committee for several years before becoming one of the vice-presidents of the community. In 1941–42, he helped establish the Jewish Society for Social Reform, to improve the living conditions of the poor in the *ḥāra*.[78]

The newly elected council was still faced with the same problems as its predecessors: education and the urgent rehabilitation of the *ḥāra*, where the effects of poverty and the lack of housing, hygiene, medical care, and education were growing ever more serious. A youth club, al-'Ushsh (The Nest), was founded to promote more constructive occupations among the *ḥāra* youth, whose favorite pastime seems to have been to race through the quarter on motorcycles. In 1947, the community together with the Jewish Society for Social Reform opened a social center in the *ḥāra*, which included a polyclinic, public baths and showers, a ritual bath (*miḳwe*), a kitchen, which served between 100 and 120 free meals daily, a workshop, and a documentation center on family and health conditions in the quarter. The center was run by women from middle- and upper-class families and directed by André Jabès, who also helped to expand a cheap housing program for *ḥāra* inhabitants.[79]

Education was still the subject of fierce debate. In 1944, a committee formed with the aim of establishing a new secondary, and possibly also a vocational school. Aslan Cattaoui, however, the chairman of the school committee, was firmly opposed to this project. He suggested that parents send their children to the Egyptian government schools or other non-Jewish institutions in town.[80] In spite of his opposition, the secondary school opened in 1945, and Cattaoui resigned from office. In 1947, the community sold the Moise de Cattaoui and Marie Suarès schools in Daher, integrated the boys' school into the Ecoles gratuites in 'Abbāsīya (al-Sabīl), and expanded the vocational Fondation Cicurel school. In 1948, a total 1,750 students were registered in the Sabīl complex and the new community school in the *ḥāra*, 750 less than a decade earlier. In addition, there were three talmud torah schools (*yeshivot*) in the *ḥāra*, 'Abbāsīya and the center of town, which were attended by about 400 students.[81]

At the same time, a radical reform of the welfare system was considered. The idea was to replace the traditional system whereby wealthy families supported certain *ḥāra* families, supplemented by food and money distributed by the community on the Jewish high holidays, by a modern system of cards entitling the owner to a fixed and regular allowance rather than making him the recipient of alms. The old system of individual charity was, however, preserved until the 1950s, and so one could still see the "family poor" coming to the house of their patron on the eve of the Shabbath and the high holidays, or the patron going to the *ḥāra* to distribute his donations in the synagogue there.[82] Poverty, unemployment, illiteracy, and begging were not eliminated in the *ḥāra* and continued to be debated in the assembly and commented upon in the pages of *al-Shams*.

In the years during and after World War II, when conditions were becoming more difficult not only for Jews, but for local foreign minorities in general, the reformers also intensified their efforts to improve coordination among the various Jewish organizations in the country. Since the 1920s, there had been calls for a merger between the Oriental/Sephardi and the Ashkenazi communities in Cairo. In 1945, a committee formed that was to dissolve the Ashkenazi community organization, adopt a number of Ashkenazi representatives into an "Egyptian Council" (*al-majlis al-miṣrī*) and convene a joint general assembly. The Ashkenazi minority, however, was not prepared to merge with the Oriental and Sephardi majority. Nor were they willing to contribute to the relief of the poor in the *ḥāra* and in Daher at a time when they had at last reduced poverty within their own community, previously so much despised by the Sephardim. Their financial contribution was, therefore, limited to the school committee.[83]

All attempts to promote unity between Cairo and Alexandria failed. A joint committee established for this purpose in the summer of 1943 seems to have achieved as little as its successor in May 1948, when coordination between the communities would have been desirable.[84] Efforts to achieve greater coordination among the various associations and clubs within the (Sephardi) community of Cairo itself were more successful. In February 1945, the community formed a committee to deal with this issue. A few months later, in October 1945, the government issued a decree placing all associations of a religious or charitable nature under the supervision of the chief rabbi. All other associations were to be registered with the Ministry of Social Affairs. While the chief rabbi was never able to assert his control over all charitable associations, this was nonetheless a limited success for the champions of unification.[85]

Some progress was also made in the important fields of Egyptianization and democratization of community structures. In the early 1930s, the community schools were placed under the supervision of the Ministry of Education and adopted the Egyptian curriculum. Arabic was henceforth the main language of instruction, particularly in the senior classes. But it was only the children from lower and lower-middle class families who attended community schools, which charged either a moderate fee or none at all. The middle and upper classes continued to send their children to European institutions, where the language of instruction was French, Italian or English. The assembly and council held their meetings in French, and their reports were not translated into Arabic until the mid-forties. The majority of assembly and council members were not Egyptian nationals, nor were they able to read and write Arabic. The council was thus never transformed into a *majlis millī* composed of Arabic-speaking Egyptian citizens, representing "true" Egyptian Jewry, as the reformers of the 1930s had hoped it eventually would.[86]

The reformers were more successful in their attempt to make communal structures more democratic. In the thirty years since World War I, the old families had been obliged to share some of their power with the rising middle class, mostly immigrants and the first generation of their children, many of whom had acquired great wealth. The lodges of the B'nai B'rith, which they had introduced into the country, wielded considerable influence in their communities and the provincial towns. But as much as the new or nouveau riche middle class may have dominated communal life in the interwar period, it had been unable to reach the highest office. In 1943, Isaac Nacamuli, who represented this class, was elected honorary president, Salvator Cicurel and Isaac Lévi attained the posts of vice-president. But the presidency had rested with a Cattaoui.

The last bastion fell in August 1946, when René Cattaoui, who had been ill for some time, resigned for health reasons. As his successor, the council chose Salvator bey Cicurel (1894–?), head of the great family firm Les Grands Magasins Cicurel, *bey* of second degree, *chevalier* of the French Légion d'Honneur and the Order of the Crown of Italy, a businessman highly influential in Egyptian economic circles and an ardent sportsman, president of the Jewish Maccabi sports club, and for many years active in communal affairs—but he was not a Cattaoui. Society was shocked. Unofficially it was surmised that René Cattaoui, sensing his isolation within the community and fearing for the policy of conciliation and integration that his family stood for in these years of escalating tension between Jews and Arabs, had given up before becoming even further entangled in this conflict. It was also surmised that the Zionists in the council and assembly had worked toward replacing him by Cicurel, who, although not himself a Zionist, was at least not as openly opposed to their aims as Cattaoui had been.[87] The election of Salvator bey Cicurel marked the final achievement of the middle class, which for many decades had proved its dedication to communal welfare and reform.

Shortly thereafter, the council decided to change the community statutes. A committee headed by André Jabès, the secretary general of the community, submitted a draft to all communal organizations for discussion, which was then taken to the council in March 1948. The council rejected the proposition granting voting rights to all members who had paid their dues for two rather than three years, as had been the practice so far. The idea was clearly to prevent newcomers from gaining too much influence in too short a time. However, active voting rights were extended to women, though not without lengthy debate. While Chief Rabbi Haim Nahum supported the proposition, Dr. Isaac Lévi, the new vice-president, argued that women were too busy in the family to be able to actively participate in communal affairs, suggesting that they devote themselves to the issues of welfare and education. *Al-Shams* encouraged women, who had always been very active in the various charitable works, to establish a women's council parallel to the all-male community council, but was unable to win a majority of council members over to its views. At the same time, women were refused the right to elected office, and hence remained excluded from the council.

It was further decided to establish a council of notables (*majlis al-wujahā'*) to assist the community council in these difficult years. Most importantly, Chief Rabbi Haim Nahum saw his position finally recognized, when the new statutes made him, together with the council, the official representative of the community in all dealings with the authorities and other non-Jewish bodies. In a disagreement between the council and the chief rabbi, the final decision was to reside with the general assembly. The problem was that when this revision of the statutes was finally adopted in 1948, Haim Nahum was already in his mid-seventies, almost blind, and heavily burdened with the many responsibilities of his office.[88]

THE PROVINCES

In the interwar period, there were still several small Jewish communities in the major trading centers of the Delta and the Suez Canal Zone. Upper Egypt, by contrast, had no significant Jewish population outside of Gīza, which was slowly turned into a suburb of Cairo. The various communities were placed under the jurisdiction of the chief rabbinates of Cairo and Alexandria, but had their own council or at least an acting head recognized by the local community. The smaller centers of Jewish life were, however, caught in a vicious circle. Because income was higher and life much more attractive in Cairo and Alexandria, the commercial middle class and the younger generation joined in the general migration to the big cities. Sometimes they left a branch of their business in the provinces, which was run by an agent. The less prosperous, and perhaps less dynamic, members of the lower-middle and lower classes, who were largely of indigenous or Oriental origin, were left behind. Lacking the means to maintain the more expensive communal institutions—synagogues, schools, and cemeteries—or to pay a rabbi, butcher (*shoḥeṭ*), and teacher, they were unable to provide the basic communal services. This made life in the provinces even less attractive, and migration to the big cities ever more alluring. Schools had to close, the synagogues were hardly attended, and communal life gradually disintegrated.

Ṭanṭā was one of the few provincial cities to escape such a fate. At the turn of the century, Ṭanṭā was the major marketplace of a large cotton growing area and was linked to all centers of the country by a close network of railway lines. After thirty years of continuous immigration, its population stood at

75,000 inhabitants in 1909. Among the immigrants, there were also a considerable number of non-Muslims, mainly Greeks and Jews. Before the economic crisis of 1907, the local Jewish community was considered very prosperous and was even able to delegate two members to the city council that had been created in 1905. Raphael Suarès obtained the concession for the Ṭanṭā waterworks in 1897–98, and the Société Electrique de Basse Egypte was financed by Jewish bankers from Cairo and Alexandria. Some of the immigrants such as the Benzakein family, who had arrived from Morocco around 1865, and Mūsā Cohen Dwek, who came from Baghdad, made a fortune within a few years. The Benzakeins had about F700,000 before World War I, and Mūsā Dwek nearly 6 million. But the large majority of the Jews in Ṭanṭā, who had come mainly from Morocco and Algeria, lived in abject poverty, "wallowing in misery," as a teacher of the local Alliance school wrote in 1905.[89] To another of his colleagues they appeared ignorant, narrow-minded, fanatical, and superstitious:

> The Jewish population of Ṭanṭā is thus made up of Syrians, Moroccans, Algerians, and Spaniards. In their majority they are still steeped in ignorance and one would hardly think oneself in the proximity of two centers of almost European character. The Jews of Ṭanṭā, like the Christians, still have a narrow mind and are fanatical and superstitious as in all small provincial towns. They even preserve some Muslim customs. The women are very apathetic, very careless and, though honest, frivolous and exceedingly proud.[90]

In Ṭanṭā, the exodus of the middle and upper classes started after the crisis of 1907, earlier than in most other provincial towns. Their place was taken by poor Oriental and Ashkenazi immigrants, as described in another Alliance report:

> Unfortunately, times are bad; since 1907, Egypt has been undergoing a terrible financial crisis, which increases yearly; our coreligionists in Ṭanṭā have been hit particularly hard, almost all Jewish merchant houses have submitted their balances or have been declared bankrupt. Several well-to-do or rich families have left our town in order to settle in Cairo or Alexandria. On the other hand, many poor families have come to live in Ṭanṭā, attracted by the facilities offered by our community [such as] free instruction for their

children and other advantages. As a result, the Jewish community of Ṭanṭā, which some years ago was regarded as very rich, is today in greatly reduced circumstances.[91]

The situation improved during World War I, but this did not stop the exodus of the commercial middle class to the bigger cities. In 1924, Isaac Farhi from the Alliance described how the merchants and entrepreneurs, whom the war had made rich, fled the provincial atmosphere of Ṭanṭā, leaving behind a few traders, commercial agents, and one medical doctor, many peddlers and even more beggars. He also noted that Jews did not engage in the local cotton business, as they found Ṭanṭā quite simply too boring.[92] In 1936, yet another teacher of the Alliance described the same situation. According to him, a "profound transformation" had taken place between 1918 and 1928 so that in the mid-thirties the community found itself in a "deplorable state," where seven-eighths of the Jewish population lived off the charity of the remaining one-eighth. Two or three traders had stayed on, about fifty employees, several half-starved peddlers, and a large number of unemployed, among them many young people. Fargeon reported in the late 1930s that most of the Jews in Ṭanṭā were employees in banks, shops, and local firms. Many of them must have been commuters who only spent their workdays in Ṭanṭā, returning to their families in Alexandria or Cairo for weekends and holidays.[93]

In spite of this exodus of the middle and upper classes, the Ṭanṭā community, numbering between 700 and 1,000 individuals in 1927, was relatively well organized. It had its own council and president as well as statutes, which, unlike those of Cairo and Alexandria, were written in Arabic. It also disposed of considerable funds amounting, according to Fargeon, to £E 6–7 million in 1938. The close link between Ṭanṭā, Alexandria, and Cairo was reflected in the fact that several communal leaders—Rahmin Chemla, Emile Suarès, Albert Hazan or Maurice Lagaris—came from prominent Cairo or Alexandria families; only Abraham Benzakein and Mūsā Cohen Dwek had made their fortune in Ṭanṭā itself. Ṭanṭā fell under the jurisdiction of the chief rabbinate of Alexandria, but had its own rabbi, two synagogues, and a cemetery. Several philanthropic associations and a Maccabi sports club had been active since the early 1900s. In 1921, the B'nai B'rith opened a local lodge, Ohel Moché, which soon numbered twenty-one members, and the Zionist movement, which for many years had been active, established a club (ha-Mo'adon ha-'Ivri) to teach Hebrew evening courses.[94]

In 1905, the Alliance Israélite Universelle together with the community opened the first Jewish school in Ṭanṭā. In order to lessen the financial burden, in 1920, some community members suggested merging with Alexandria and dissolving the local community organization altogether. The idea was rejected by the local notables, who nevertheless placed the expensive schools under the supervision of the Alexandria community. Among the 200 to 250 students attending the local Jewish school in the 1920s, about 20 to 25 percent were Muslims and another 12 to 15 percent Christians. The Jews of Ṭanṭā, therefore, met their non-Jewish neighbors not only at work and, since there was no separate Jewish quarter in Ṭanṭā, in their living areas, but also at school. The language of instruction was French, but the students were also fluent in Arabic. The few remaining wealthy families continued, "for reasons of class consciousness," to send their children to the local Ecole des Frères or to Alexandria.[95]

The Jewish community of Port Said, which only developed after the opening of the Suez Canal in 1869, grew rapidly with the continuous flow of Oriental and Ashkenazi immigrants. It had some 400 members in 1907, 600 in 1917 and over 1,000 in 1927. Then the numbers decreased again, partly because many of the Yemeni and Adeni Jews left, having only interrupted their journey, and now proceeded to Palestine, their original destination. After the exodus of the middle class, the community was made up of Sephardi and Oriental immigrants from Turkey, Yemen, and Aden on one hand and of Ashkenazi immigrants on the other. Of the 70 families registered by S. Somekh in 1908, 25 were Sephardi and Oriental immigrants from Turkey, 21 Ashkenazim from Russia and Rumania; 16 families had arrived from Yemen, 2 from Italy, and 1 from Algeria; 5 were of Egyptian origin. In 1928, a delegate of the Jewish National Fund registered 135 families with a total 300 to 350 individuals. At that time, the majority of 70 to 75 families had come from (Yemen and) Aden; 30 to 35 were Eastern European, and 20 to 25 Sephardi (and Oriental). According to Fargeon, 75 percent of the Jews living in Port Said in 1938 had come from Yemen and Aden.[96] The large majority of immigrants was very poor, and a teacher of the Alliance described them as "mostly very backward and fanatic." But there were also a considerable number of employees and a small, but wealthy class of businessmen, managers, and professionals.[97]

The community was divided into two groups, which were also separated by residence. While the Ashkenazi and Sephardi Jews lived in the European quarter, the Yemeni and Adeni Jews inhabited a separate area with their own synagogue and school. Both were built by Menaḥem Mūsā Benin, a millionaire who, together with his large family, controlled the local Yemeni community. Both subgroups were, however, united in the Jewish community of Port Said, which had its own president, council, and assembly of 120–30 dues-paying members (in 1938), two rabbis and two synagogues for the Sephardim and the Yemenites respectively (the Ashkenazim accordingly had no synagogue of their own), as well as a cemetery. The council was dominated by the Ashkenazim, who in the 1930s also provided the president, Max Mouchly, a partner in the Simon-Arzt-Stores, the largest store in town. The local schools were inadequate, particularly after the school built by Menaḥem Mūsā Benin closed in 1934. As a result, a large number of children were either sent to non-Jewish institutions or left to roam the streets.

Organizational life was better developed, although even here the Zionist observers found much amiss. Some associations had already been active in the nineteenth century. By the 1920s, their number had been increased by a women's, a youth, and a Maccabi sports club, the Israël lodge of the B'nai B'rith as well as local branches of the Zionist Organization, the Jewish National Fund, and the revisionist New Zionist Organization. During World War II, an emissary of the leftist ha-Shomer ha-

Tsa'ir arrived in Port Said to organize *'aliya* to Palestine; and in 1944, the newly established Zionist Federation opened an office in town. All Zionist and non-Zionist activities came to a standstill in 1948, and only the council continued to function. It seems remarkable that in Port Said, which in the nineteenth and early twentieth centuries had seen a considerable number of ritual murder accusations, which only subsided in the mid-twenties—Somekh once called it "the classic ground of ritual murder [acccusations]"—relations between the Jews, the Muslims, and the Christians were, at least until the late 1930s, said to be excellent on the whole.[98]

The Jewish community of al-Manṣūra, the capital of the Daqhalīya province, shared the fate of the other provincial towns. At the turn of the century, there were 150 Jewish families living there, who engaged mostly in the trade in cotton, textiles, and so-called Manchester goods. By the end of the 1920s, most of these families had left al-Manṣūra for Cairo and Alexandria, where they played an active rôle in communal affairs. By then the Jews had also left their old quarter, the *rub' al-yahūd*, and dispersed throughout town. Of the 500 to 600 Jews who lived in al-Manṣūra in the late 1920s, only 50 families totaling 150 to 200 individuals remained in the late 1930s. After years of serious internal tension, the community adopted its first statutes in 1918, but continued to be directed by those members of the old families who had remained in al-Manṣūra. After the small talmud torah school closed its doors, only the two synagogues and the Jewish cemetery, neither of them much used, were left. The Sephardi rabbi assumed all tasks pertaining to ritual and religious service. A women's club looked after the needs of the poor. The middle class and what remained of the local élite were organized in the Maghen David lodge; the youth frequented the Maccabi club for sports and literature. In the 1930s, the Zionist movement and the Jewish National Fund were represented by the president of the community, Sédaka Lévy, who also served as vice-president of the Grande Loge du District d'Egypte et du Soudan of the B'nai B'rith. Virtually no reports are preserved from the 1940s and 1950s, when the Jewish community of al-Manṣūra seems to have gradually dissolved.[99]

The story repeats itself in the Delta towns of al-Maḥalla al-Kubrā, Damanhūr, and Zaqāzīq. The Jewish population in al-Maḥalla al-Kubrā was rather large and prosperous at the turn of the century, but later lost most of its four-hundred families to Alexandria, Cairo, and even Ṭanṭā. The ten families that remained in 1938 were still able to pay a rabbi, but not to maintain a school or a cemetery, in spite of the additional income derived from the pilgrimage to the Torah scroll of Rabbi Ḥayyim al-Amshāṭī, which was kept in the al-Ustādh synagogue.[100] The Jewish community of Damanhūr, the capital of the Buḥayra province, also profited from a pilgrimage. The tomb of Rabbi Abū Ḥaṣīra of Morocco attracted large numbers of pilgrims, both Jewish and non-Jewish, and the festivities marking the pilgrimage closely resembled the birthday of Muslim saints and the Prophet Muḥammad himself as celebrated in Egypt. The Jewish community of Damanhūr, having only been established in the 1880s, was reduced to a mere fifty to sixty members after 1917, most of them commuters between Damanhūr and Alexandria. In 1930, they nevertheless formed a communal council to look after the interests of the small community and to maintain the local synagogue and cemetery.[101]

The Jewish communities in the Suez Canal Zone were equally of recent origin. At the turn of the century, the city of Suez witnessed a large influx of foreigners, among them many Jews from Yemen. But after a short period of prosperity during World War I, it receded again into insignificance. Most immigrants went to Alexandria, Cairo or Palestine. In 1927, the Egyptian census registered 127 Jews in Suez, and in 1937 and 1947 a mere 80. There was no communal life and no institutions except an old cemetery. Conditions were no better in Ismā'īlīya. Here, too, the Jewish population had grown during World War I, when the Allied forces stationed there attracted large numbers of merchants and traders. They left with the troops as soon as the war was over. A few employees and shopkeepers stayed behind, two Ashkenazi watchmakers, and the family of the director of the Electricity and Ice Supply Company, Simha Ambache, a wealthy immigrant from Palestine. While the community had neither a school nor a cemetery, it did have a *dayyan* and a *shoḥeṭ* and a prayer room, which seems, however, to have been little frequented.[102]

There were also Jewish communities in the Delta towns of Zaqāzīq, Ziftā, Banhā, Mīt Ghamr, and Kafr al-Zayyāt as well as in Ḥulwān, Asyūṭ, and Aswān in Upper Egypt. Zaqāzīq, the capital of the fertile Sharqīya province and a center of the cotton and wheat trade, attracted a considerable number of foreign traders at the beginning of the century. In 1917, 250 Jews lived there. By 1927, their number had dwindled to 150, who showed little interest in communal life. While the community boasted a magnificent synagogue and a cemetery, it had no rabbi after 1926, and no school. The other Jewish communities were generally headed by a notable, but maintained no communal institutions and, Asyūṭ excepted, no cemetery. In the late 1930s, only Mīt Ghamr had a rabbi; the Banhā community tried to find one in 1948. Throughout the interwar period, the Jews living in the provincial towns, most of whom had assimilated into their Egyptian environment, seem to have lived in close proximity and basic harmony with their Muslim and Coptic neighbors. None of these towns except Port Said had a special Jewish quarter, and no disturbances in intercommunal relations are reported in the period after World War II outside the sphere of anti-British and anti-Zionist agitation.[103]

3

Socioeconomic and Political Change, 1914–1948

In the interwar period, relations between the Muslim majority of the population and the local Jewish minority were generally harmonious though never very close. In the late 1930s, intercommunal relations began to deteriorate. The deterioration was not so much caused by new conditions or behavior within the Jewish minority itself as by a gradual shift in the political climate in Egyptian society at large. A number of factors contributed individually and in conjunction to alter the sociopolitical fabric of society and the position of the minorities linked to it. These factors included the effects of "modernization" as initiated in the nineteenth century, the rise of nationalism in its various forms, and the resurgence of (political) Islam—all of them factors that worked directly or indirectly against the dominance of non-Muslim minorities and foreigners in the country. Therefore they did not affect the Jews alone. To them were added the influence of fascist propaganda on nationalist youth and the impact of the Palestine conflict on the general Egyptian public, which affected the Jews more specifically.

WORLD WAR I AND ITS AFTERMATH

Before 1952, over 70 percent of the Egyptian population lived in the countryside.[1] The rural population included *fallāḥīn* owning or cultivating plots of land between 0.1 and 2 *faddān*, with a minority cultivating up to 5 *faddān*, who made up about 15 percent of the general population and 93 percent of all landowners; landless peasants who rented land; permanently employed agricultural laborers; and migrant workers (*tarāḥīl*) who were only hired for the season—all "virtually of no consequence" as far as direct influence on national politics was concerned.[2] At the other end of the social scale was the landowning élite of Turko-Circassian or genuinely Egyptian origin, who had obtained large tracts of land under Muḥammad 'Alī and his successors, which they were able to enlarge in the period of rapid agricultural development in the late nineteenth and earlier twentieth centuries. As large landowners owning at least 30 *faddān*, as merchants, high government officials, deputies, senators, and ministers they combined wealth and power.[3]

Most members of this class left the administration of their estates (*'izba*) to local agents and lived as absentee landlords in the larger cities. Between the élite and the mass of small peasants and agricultural laborers, was the rural middle class of families owning plots of land ranging from 5 to 30 *faddān*, whose members frequently also served as village heads (*'umda*). Appointed by the government, they acted as intermediaries between their village communities and the authorities. Many of the leading figures of the interwar period, like Sa'd Zaghlūl, William Makram 'Ubayd, 'Abbās al-'Aqqād, and Ṭāhā Ḥusayn, who belonged to this rural middle class of village notables, and were able to provide their children with the higher education that would pave the way to a career in business, civil administration or the military.[4]

Urban society was broadly split into the landowning élite of absentee landlords, merchants, and high officials of diverse origin at the one end, and the mass of the urban poor at the other. This lower class included a high percentage of recent immigrants from the countryside, many of whom were only temporarily employed, or not at all. Between the élite and the lower class ranged the lower-middle class of petty bureaucrats, craftsmen, office workers, teachers, and shopkeepers, who comprised about 10 percent of urban society, and the upper-middle class of well-to-do merchants, higher officials, and professionals, a "nascent bourgeoisie," which was largely recruited from either the urban élite of Turko-Egyptian origin or the rural middle class of village notables.[5] Links between the rural and the urban population were thus still strong. It was the newly evolved urban middle class, headed by university and high school students, which from the turn of the century became increasingly involved in politics previously controlled exclusively by the British and the landowning élite.

Between 1897 and 1927, the number of industrial workers increased from a very low level to about 273,000, corresponding to about 10 percent of the urban and 3 percent of the total population. In the interwar period, industrial workers could no longer be included in the lower-middle class employed in traditional crafts and occupations.[6] These new industrial jobs, requiring as they did organized and regular work at fixed hours promoted communication within the workforce. As a result, there developed within this social group a specific way of life and a political awareness based on common interest. By the 1940s, the process of class formation, which could also be observed within the *haute bourgeoisie*, implying not only "objective" aspects of status and ownership, or control, of the means of production, but also the "subjective" factor of class consciousness, was far advanced. Yet as the experience of communist and trade union activists would show, barriers and resentment based on ethnicity and religion were preserved even among industrial workers, one of the most modern sectors of urban Egyptian society.

The tensions underlying this system of highly uneven distribution of power, wealth, and prestige had already emerged before World War I. They grew considerably during the war, which brought forced recruitment and requisitions to the countryside, and inflation and a scarcity of food and goods to the towns. Landless peasants and agricultural workers as well as salaried employees and officials were most affected by these developments. Landowners, by contrast, had benefited from the steep rise in the price of land and agricultural products, notably of cotton. Merchants had profited from the demand of the Allied forces and entrepreneurs from the opportunities offered when the country was cut off from European competition. Under these conditions, Jewish employees suffered and Jewish entrepreneurs prospered as did everyone else.[7]

After the war, the accumulated tension erupted in the national uprising of 1919, which was directed primarily against the British, who in December 1914, declared Egypt a protectorate, thereby ending Ottoman suzerainty. The intensity and vehemence of this revolt seem to have taken not only the British administration by surprise, but also Egyptian nationalist leaders.[8] While it was primarily a national uprising against foreign domination, it also led to a series of local revolts against the state authority in general and individual landowners in particular. What was called a revolution by the nationalists was in fact a highly heterogeneous movement, encompassing the most diverse groups and strata of society with their specific aims and purposes. Economic grievances caused by the British wartime measures combined with religious resentment against the non-Muslim occupier and its supporters within the local foreign communities. To these was added a genuine desire for political independence, which was further nourished by President Woodrow Wilson's Fourteen Points of January 1918. In spite of its Islamic coloring, the uprising witnessed unprecedented unity among Muslims and Copts, in which even some members of the Jewish minority participated.[9] That the movement did not bring about, or even aim at, fundamental changes in the socioeconomic set-up of Egyptian society, and that it did not achieve immediate independence, led many observers to deny it the quality of a real revolution. And yet the uprising of 1919 did set off a process of Egyptianization, and hence did contribute to a marked, albeit gradual, change in the political and economic life of the country. The issue of national independence, focused on Anglo-Egyptian relations, was to dominate national politics until the new age after the revolution of the Free Officers.

It was perhaps inevitable that in the years following the events of 1919, the national front began to show growing signs of strain and conflict. After another upsurge in the early 1920s, nationalist activity gradually subsided in the countryside, and was largely confined to the urban centers. On the political stage there was a constant rotation of the same political and social forces in varying rôles. The situation only changed in the mid-thirties when a non-parliamentary opposition of Islamic militants and paramilitary youth movements entered the political arena.

In November 1918, a group of politicians met to represent the Egyptian people as a delegation (*wafd*) in London and at the peace negotiations following the collapse of the Ottoman Empire.[10] For the parliamentary elections of 1924 that came after the formal end of the British protectorate in 1922, this delegation, the Wafd, organized as a Western-style political party. However, the Wafd did not relinquish its claim as the sole legitimate representative of the Egyptian people, as a national movement rather than a political party representing the specific interests of one section of the nation only. Until the late 1930s, the overwhelming majority of the population did indeed support the Wafd, even after leadership had passed from the charismatic Saʿd Zaghlūl (1860–1927) to his less forceful successor Muṣṭafā al-Naḥḥās Pāshā (1879–1965). In spite of general support, personal ambitions and rivalries soon created friction and rifts within the party, resulting in successive splits and the establishment of new parties.

These parties resembled cliques of personal friends and relatives grouped around individual personalities rather than Western-style parties with a clearly defined program, registered membership, and permanent organization. The so-called minority, that is, non-Wafdist, parties such as the Liberal Constitutionalists, Ittiḥādists, Saʿdists, and Shaʿbists, differed with regard to specific points of their program such as their position vis-à-vis the king and parliamentary democracy, or their concept of national independence. But they hardly differed in their actual politics and social base. The upper-class families of large landowners, high officials, merchants, and professionals controlled the minority parties. From the late 1930s onward, they gained increasing influence within the Wafd as well, and as a result, continued to control the government and Parliament.[11]

When elections were relatively free, the Wafd was certain to win a majority. But the British and the king were strong enough to manipulate the rules and procedures and to bring the minority parties to power whenever they wished. Because of their weakness, the smaller parties showed themselves more "moderate" than the Wafd, more prepared to accept less than the full independence (*al-istiqlāl al-tāmm*), which the Wafd demanded.

In lengthy negotiations, successive Egyptian governments tried to improve their status and enlarge their freedom of action vis-à-vis the British Residency. Reacting to widespread nationalist activity, the British in 1922 unilaterally declared the end of the protectorate, and Sultan Fu'ād ascended the throne as king of Egypt. However, the British reserved for themselves four spheres of control, which were to be excluded from Egyptian sovereignty: imperial connections, that is, the Suez Canal; defense; the Sudan; and, last—but highly important in the context of the position of the Jewish minority—the protection of foreigners and local minorities. This last point was of particular significance as it implied equal status and shared interests of foreigners and minorities, which included not only immigrant Greeks and Italians, but also the native Copts. If they enjoyed special protection under barely disguised British rule, they also ran the danger of being associated with the foreigners protected by the colonial power.

The August 1936 Anglo-Egyptian Treaty of Alliance marked an important step toward full independence. The treaty abolished the four reservations of British control established in 1922. The Convention of Montreux that followed in May 1937 provided for an end to the Capitulations and the Mixed Courts, which were eventually abolished in 1949. But the treaty did not end British military presence in the country.[12] The national aspirations of the Wafd, radical youth groups, and the Islamic movement, therefore, still remained to be fulfilled. Egypt's relations with Britain, which retained much of its influence on Egyptian politics, therefore continued to absorb the political energies of the government and opposition up to the 1950s.

In view of this preoccupation with national politics, which was also reflected in the programs and activities of the major parties, the social question was relegated to second rank. It was hoped that social justice and equality would be achieved in the golden age after British presence and European influence had come to a definite end. The landowning élite had a definite interest in gaining national independence, thereby reducing foreign influence in the economy and society of the country. But like the upper-middle and upper classes of foreign or minority origin, they tried to prevent any fundamental changes in the socioeconomic and political order of society.[13] Common economic interest was complemented by growing homogenization in culture and life-style, which combined to make of the local *haute bourgeoisie* a class in the Marxist sense of the term.[14] When it came to the question of national independence, certain differences remained, as many members of the foreign colonies and the local minorities continued to regard the British as their main protectors against Egyptian nationalist aspirations.[15] Even with regard to economic issues, the rising class of Egyptian entrepreneurs was gradually forced to abandon the aim of full independence as they entered into ever closer cooperation with the foreigners and minorities dominating the local economy.

Bank Misr, which was founded in 1920 in order to reduce Egyptian dependence on foreign capital and to lay the foundation of an independent Egyptian industry, is a prime example.[16] While Bank Misr did succeed in creating a whole complex of industrial companies in the fields of food processing, textiles, and transportation, its financial basis was so restricted that by the late thirties, it saw itself compelled to cooperate with the very circles of foreign business and capital whose dominance it had initially set out to reduce or, if possible, to eliminate altogether. In this context it should be recalled that among the founders of the bank there were also two Jews of Egyptian nationality, Joseph Aslan Cattaoui and Joseph Cicurel, who later represented the bank at its Paris office. By joining this effort to create an independent Egyptian banking system and industry, Cattaoui and Cicurel demonstrated that in spite of the fact that much of their economic success was based on close links with foreign business and capital, important sections of the Jewish bourgeoisie did in fact identify with local economic interests.[17]

The situation was quite different for the Muslim and Coptic lower and middle classes. Even though the introduction into Egyptian agriculture of the (labor intensive) cultivation of cotton and sugar cane meant a growing demand for human labor, this was not sufficient to meet rapid population growth. Caused partly by the improvement in health and hygiene, the Egyptian population rose from 9.6 million in 1897 to almost 13 million in 1927, and to 16 million in 1937. The pressure resulting from this rapid increase drove large numbers of peasants into the cities, most of all to Cairo.[18] The immigrants from the countryside came to the cities hoping for work and a general improvement in their living conditions. Yet traditional crafts and industrial workshops, which as a rule employed a maximum of ten workers, were too few and too small to provide a sufficient number of jobs. Modern industry developed slowly. While the British enforced the principles of economic liberalism and free trade, the local entrepreneurs preferred investment in land and real estate offering quick returns and high prestige to less secure, though equally profitable investment in industry. The companies established by local industrialists such as Aḥmad ʿAbbūd, Amīn Yaḥyā, and the Miṣr concern were not yet able to absorb the immigrant labor force. The firms controlled by foreigners and members of the local foreign minorities generally tended to favor members of their own communities, particularly when it came to leading positions in management and administration. Foreigners and local minorities tended, moreover, to be better paid than their Muslim colleagues.[19]

The world economic crisis of 1929–32 seriously affected Egyptian industry, as well, although the government of Ismāʿīl Ṣidqī Pāshā (1930–33), who as president of the Federation of Industries was closely linked to local and foreign business, worked actively toward protecting and promoting local industry—largely at the expense of Egyptian workers. The measures taken included holding down wages, restricting social legislation, and repressing labor demands, as well as introducing higher import duties, which did in fact help to improve conditions for local industry. Yet in spite of these protective measures, industry still employed a mere 10 percent of the workforce in 1952, creating 15 percent of the gross domestic product.[20] As a result of rapid population growth and limited employment opportunities, the problems of overpopulation and unemployment were partly transferred from the countryside to the cities, where under different living conditions and increased chances of communication and organization they assumed immediate political relevance.

THE LIBERAL AGE, 1919–36

The central preoccupation of Egypt's political community in the interwar period was nationalism, aiming at complete liberation from colonial rule, foreign control, and influence. In the late nineteenth and early twentieth centuries, two major currents of thought had evolved, one based on the (pan-)Islamic reform movement often referred to as Salafīya, and the other on the "liberal" concept of territorial nationhood. By contrast, pan-Arabism as a nationalist movement based on language and ethnicity did not evolve as a major political force until the early forties.[21]

The liberation movement of the late nineteenth century was still firmly rooted in Islam. It was only from the 1890s on that, under the influence of European nationalist thinking, attachment to Egypt was gradually transformed into a concept of territorial nationalism. An Islamic thinker and reformer like Rifā'a Badawī Rāfi' al-Ṭahṭāwī (1801–73) saw himself as an Egyptian patriot, but not as a nationalist in the modern sense. The same holds true for the leaders of the 'Urābī revolt of 1881–82, who, because they raised the slogan "Egypt for the Egyptians," were later reclaimed as modern-style nationalists.[22] Incidentally, one of the first advocates of the new idea of territorial nationalism was a local Jew, James (Ya'qūb) Ṣanū' (1839–1912), also known by his Arabic pen name, Abū Naḍḍāra.[23] In 1907, two of the most important parties of "liberal" Egyptian nationalism were founded: the Ḥizb al-Waṭanī, with its newspaper *al-Liwā'*, led by Muṣṭafā Kāmil (1874–1908) and Muḥammad Farīd (1868–1919), and the Ḥizb al-Umma, a group of politically minded intellectuals and landowners, with its newspaper *al-Jarīda*, edited by Aḥmad Luṭfī al-Sayyid (1872–1963).[24]

Both parties shared a common enemy, British colonialism and its foreign dependents, and their view of Egypt as a distinctive historical and political entity within the wider Islamic *umma*. But while the Ḥizb al-Waṭanī propagated a pan-Islamic strategy of liberation transcending the national boundaries of Egypt that demanded loyalty to the Ottoman Empire as the main power pitted against Britain and France, the Ḥizb al-Umma advocated a rather secular concept of purely Egyptian nationalism. In the twenties, this line was adopted by many of Egypt's most influential writers, journalists, and politicians.

The nationalist leaders of 1919 wanted to abolish British rule and to create a sovereign Egyptian nation state devoid of formal ties to larger religious or ethnic entities. The leader of the Wafd, Sa'd Zaghlūl, himself a student of the eminent Muslim reformer Muḥammad 'Abduh, stressed the principle of unity among all children of the fatherland irrespective of religion or ethnicity. Although formally rejecting the notion of secularism, this concept nevertheless went a long way toward promoting the separation of religion and politics. In a press interview, Zaghlūl thus declared in May 1919 that: "The present movement in Egypt is not a religious movement, for Muslims and Copts demonstrate together, and neither is it a xenophobic movement or a movement calling for Arab unity (*jāmi'a 'arabīya*)."[25]

While the national movement also voiced resentment of foreign dominance in religious terms, it nevertheless united in its ranks Muslims and Copts, among whom serious tension had erupted only a few years earlier. A number of prominent Copts, such as William Makram 'Ubayd, Wīṣā Wāṣif, Georges Khayyāṭ, Sīnūt and Murquṣ Ḥannā, and Wāṣif Buṭrus Ghālī joined the Wafd and played a prominent rôle in its leadership until the 1940s.[26]

Given the liberal orientation and policies of the Wafd and the so-called minority parties, it is easily understood that they attracted not only Copts, but also a number of Egyptian Jews. Félix Benzakein, Vita Sonsino, and David Hazan joined the Wafd at an early date. Hazan, a former member of the Ḥizb al-Waṭanī, was even condemned to death in absentia by the British because of his nationalistic agitation.[27] In 1921, the lawyer Léon Castro, a personal friend of Sa'd Zaghlūl, directed Wafdist propaganda in Europe, and in 1922 he founded the Wafdist journal *La Liberté*, which, however, was bought up by the royalist Ittiḥād Party as early as 1925. Joseph Aslan Cattaoui, who had sat on the Legislative Assembly with Sa'd Zaghlūl, initially sympathized with the Wafd, but joined the Liberal Constitutionalist Party in 1922 and the Ittiḥād Party in 1925. Joseph Elie de Picciotto, a businessman from Alexandria, organized an opulent reception for Zaghlūl when he returned from his exile on the Seychelles in 1923. The lawyers Moise Dichy, Isidore Feldman, and Zaki Orebi were actively engaged on behalf of Egyptian independence. In the 1930s and 1940s, the Association de la Jeunesse Juive Egyptienne demonstrated its solidarity with the Wafd. Still, these were just individuals, of whom only Cattaoui and Castro exerted any significant political influence.[28]

The group of liberal politicians, writers, journalists, and artists, members of the intellectual élite strongly influenced by European political thought, followed a concept of national identity based on territory, culture, and history that was essentially secular. 'Alī 'Abd al-Rāziq (1888–1966), a shaykh at al-Azhar, even attempted to conceptualize, and to legitimize in Islamic terms, a separation of the state, or of politics, and Islam, which in Islamic theory are inseparably linked together.[29] Aḥmad Luṭfī al-Sayyid, Ṭāhā Ḥusayn (1884–1974), and Tawfīq al-Ḥakīm (1899–1987) propagated the idea of a specific "Egyptian character," which, they said, was shaped by its Arab-Islamic heritage, but was essentially rooted in pre-Islamic, pharaonic tradition linking Egypt to the Mediterranean European culture rather than the Arab-Islamic one. The pharaonism of the 1920s and 1930s, which was further stimulated by the discovery, in

1922, of the tomb of King Tutankhamen in the Valley of the Kings, found its main expression in literature and the visual arts.[30]

If the concept of pharaonism based on pre-Islamic Mediterranean tradition was essentially the domain of a limited circle of Westernized artists and intellectuals, the principle of liberal territorial nationhood was also reflected in legal and political reality. In the field of foreign policy, the Egyptian government kept out of general Arab affairs unless they touched directly on Egyptian interests, including the Arab-Zionist conflict over Palestine. It even rejected the ambition of the king to re-establish the caliphate, which had been abolished in 1924 by the Turkish republican government.[31]

The principle of national unity over and above all ethnic and religious boundaries found its clearest expression in the Egyptian constitution of April 1923.[32] In its first article, the constitution declared Egypt a sovereign, free, and independent state, without any reference to the country's links to the wider Islamic *umma* or the Arab nation. However, the rôle of religion in domestic affairs was left ill-defined. Article 149, (the number alone indicates its low priority) declared Islam to be the religion of the state and Arabic its official language. At the same time, Article 12 laid down the absolute freedom of conscience (which runs strictly counter to the Islamic ban on apostasy), and Article 13 guaranteed the free practice of religion "in accordance with the established customs of Egypt." Articles 23 through 28 based legislation on the will of the people, and not the principles of Islamic law, the *sharīʿa*. In view of so much ambiguity, future conflict about the actual rôle of Islam in politics and society was literally prescribed.[33]

The majority of the commission that had been formed to work out the new constitution rejected the principle of proportional representation of the various ethnic and religious groups, which had been applied in the Legislative Assembly of 1912 as well as in selecting the commission members themselves.[34] Proportional representation was suggested by the Coptic lawyer Tawfīq Doss (Daws) and was supported by, among others, the patriarch of the Coptic Orthodox Church and the president of the Cairo Jewish community, Joseph Aslan Cattaoui. It was, however, rejected by most spokesmen for the Coptic and Jewish communities, who saw the dangers of such a policy at a time when the British reserved for themselves the protection of foreigners and local minorities, virtually excluding them from the Egyptian nation, and placing them in dangerous proximity to the colonial power. The Wafd as well as the majority of commission members understood this well enough. They therefore rejected the idea of proportional representation on the grounds that it was liable to cast doubt not only on Egyptian tolerance, but also on the very possibility of peaceful coexistence of the various religious communities. Even without specific legal provisions, Copts and Jews were regularly represented in Parliament until the 1950s. The Jewish representatives included Joseph Elie bey de Picciotto, Moise and Joseph Aslan de Cattaoui Pasha, Aslan bey de Cattaoui and Haim Nahum Efendi in the Senate, as well as Félix Benzakein and René bey de Cattaoui in the Chamber of Deputies. While non-Muslim minorities such as the Greeks, the Armenians, and the Jews were generally not regarded as genuine Egyptians, they were treated as full members of the Egyptian nation enjoying equal rights and duties, provided they supported the demand for independence, learned Arabic and adapted, to a certain extent, to local customs and traditions.[35]

A TEST CASE: NATIONAL-SOCIALIST PROPAGANDA AND THE LICA

The early 1930s witnessed a first attempt to single out the Jews from the heterogeneous group of local foreign minorities, making them the target of specific attacks and accusations. It did not originate with the Egyptian nationalist and Islamic movements, but with local members of the National-Socialist German Workers' Party (NSDAP). This first attempt to export to Egypt the brand of anti-Semitism specific to modern Europe provides an interesting test case with regard to the reactions of both the local Jews and the Muslim and Coptic majority of the population. It, therefore, deserves close examination, even though the events as such were of limited relevance in an era when the issue of Anglo-Egyptian relations and the search for national identity dominated all else.

When Adolf Hitler took power in Germany in January 1933, local groups (*Ortsgruppen*) of the NSDAP under the direction of its Foreign Organization (Auslandsorganisation) had already been active in Cairo and Alexandria for a number of years. The German colony in Egypt was insignificant, numbering about 1,200 individuals in the mid-thirties, of whom about 450 lived in Cairo. There was a German Club, which was founded in 1853 in Alexandria and in 1927 in Cairo, and a United German-Austrian Chamber of Commerce, established in 1928. A number of medical doctors of German-Jewish origin excepted, most of the Germans were salaried employees or merchants, who had returned to Egypt in the early 1920s after their fortunes had been sequestered by the British during World War I.[36] A very few succeeded in gaining wealth and prestige, among them the cotton merchant Hugo Lindemann. The family of the Führer's deputy, Rudolf Hess, by contrast, which came from Alexandria, had lost all their property in World War I. It was Rudolf's brother Alfred who in 1926 founded the Ortsgruppe Cairo and in 1933 the Country Section (Landesgruppe) Egypt. He left Egypt in early 1934, when he was appointed deputy director of the Foreign Organization in Germany. By 1937, 214 of the 1,178 Germans (*Reichsdeutsche*) registered in Egypt by this organization had joined the NSDAP, most of them (197) after January 1933.[37]

The Jewish community in Egypt, whose middle and upper classes were, thanks to their close links to Europe, very well informed about developments there, reacted quickly to the Nazi takeover in Germany. A circular containing the major points of the NSDAP program, which was distributed by the head of the Cairo Ortsgruppe, Dittrich, in February 1933 caused "great alarm" among the Jewish members of the German colony.[38] Concern quickly spread to the entire Jewish community. In March and April 1933, mass meetings organized by the lodges of the B'nai B'rith were held in Cairo, Alexandria, Port Said, al-Manṣūra, and Ṭanṭā, which were attended by thousands of community members including Chief Rabbi Haim Nahum Efendi, and spokesmen of the community councils, as well as representatives of several non-Jewish minorities living in Egypt. The associations of stockbrokers in Alexandria and of commercial clerks also expressed their solidarity with Jewish protests against German anti-Semitism.[39] The participants in the mass meetings sent protest telegrams to General von Hindenburg, the president of the German Reich, to the Human Rights' League in Paris, and the League of Nations in Geneva. They furthermore decided to create the Ligue contre l'Antisémitisme Allemand, Association Formée par Toutes les Oeuvres et Institutions Juives en Egypte in order to defend local Jewry against Nazi propaganda and activities on Egyptian soil. They elected a committee of six including Léon Castro, Simon Mani, Raphael Toriel, and Abramino Menasce, who represented the commercial and professional middle class, but not a single member of the Jewish élite. The committee, in turn, founded the Ligue Contre l'Antisémitisme Allemand, which in September 1933 joined the Ligue Internationale Contre l'Antisémitisme Allemand (LICA), that had formed in Amsterdam a few months earlier with Léon Castro as its vice-president.[40]

The LICA thus formed part of a worldwide movement. Within Egypt, its specific goal was to inform the local Jewish as well as the non-Jewish public about the objectives of German National-Socialism and, as far as possible, to restrict German propaganda in the region. The LICA developed very fast, and in 1935 numbered about 1,500 members. Headed by a Comité d'Action, which included Léon Castro, the journalist Jacques Maleh of the journal *L'Aurore*, and the businessman Raphael Sakkal, it formed a number of sections to deal with, among other matters, the press and the boycott of German goods and products. A youth section, LISCA (Ligue Internationale Scolaire Contre l'Antisémitisme), was founded in September 1933 and by December 1934 had attracted about 650 members.[41] As the Alexandria branch began to show open Zionist sympathies, a rival non-Zionist organization called Jeunesse Internationale Contre l'Antisémitisme (JICA), and led by Castro's son, Raymond, was formed in August 1935, which adopted the slogan "Liberty, Fraternity, Peace." The anti-Nazi youth movement also included activists of the socialist and communist left.[42]

The press and information campaign of the LICA was made easier by the fact that Jewish journalists worked not only with Jewish papers such as *L'Aurore*, *Israël*, *La Tribune Juive*, and *al-Shams*, but also with the big French and English papers, which were read not only in Egypt but in other Middle Eastern countries as well. Through large advertising agencies such as the Société Orientale de Publicité and the Cairo Advertising Company, Jewish businessmen exerted additional influence on the press. These facts were frequently pointed to when German and Egyptian sources wanted to brandish the issue of "Jewish influence" on the press. Some simply classified the French and English newspapers in Egypt as being Jewish.[43]

In May 1933, local Jews circulated a publication in French entitled *Anti-Semitism in Germany*, which was immediately seized by the Egyptian authorities. A supporter of the NSDAP, who seems to have acted at the instigation of the German chargé d'affaires, Pilger, reacted by distributing a publication in both German and French entitled *On the Jewish Question in Germany*, which dealt with the alleged links between international Jewry, Marxism, and Bolshevism.[44] He was sued for libel and incitement of racial hatred by a Jewish businessman of Italian nationality, Umberto Jabès, who was supported by the B'nai B'rith and the LICA. The case was rejected by the Mixed Court of Alexandria in January 1934 on the grounds that, from a legal point of view, Jabès could not, as an individual, regard himself as being insulted by a publication that attacked the Jewish community in general. Jabès appealed, but to no avail. The Mixed Court of Appeal in Alexandria confirmed the judgment in May 1935.[45]

Neither Jabès nor the German publisher of the pamphlet, Van Meeteren, were concerned with the value of £E101 for which

Jabès had sued the latter. The primary aim of the LICA was to draw attention to the program and propaganda of German National-Socialism. The German side decided after some hesitation to turn the lawsuit into a major attack on the campaign of "slander and hatred" (*Hetz- und Greuelpropaganda*) that "international Jewry" had initiated against the German Reich. A German lawyer was sent to Cairo from Essen after the Jewish side had tried (in vain) to persuade two prominent French lawyers to defend its cause. Wolfgang Diewerge, a member of the NSDAP Struggle Association of the Commercial Middle Class (Kampfbund des gewerblichen Mittelstandes, Gau Groß-Berlin), who was in charge of directing the lawsuit in the German Ministry of Propaganda (Reichsministerium für Volksaufklärung und Propaganda), arrived from Berlin to work out the German strategy. In September 1933, he submitted a memorandum on how to deal with the Cairo Jewish Trial.[46]

Apart from the press campaign and the lawsuit, the most important weapon in the hands of the LICA was the boycott of German goods and services. Even before the B'nai B'rith and the LICA, the Zionist paper *Israël* had, on 24 March 1933, appealed to the Egyptian Jewish public to boycott Germany. Between 18 and 20 April 1933, Léon Castro published the boycott call in various local papers:

> Jews of Egypt.... As Germany cynically proclaims its contempt for all that is Jewish, you cannot, without failing in your own eyes, without betraying your history and your collective and individual dignity, continue to have any kind of relations whatsoever with Germany or with Germans: you have to break all material, intellectual, and social links to them. The Germans hate you, despise them. The Germans reject you, reject them.[47]

The LICA called upon Jewish businessmen to break off relations with their German partners whenever possible and to neither order nor sell German products. It called upon the Jewish public not to buy German goods. When the appeal was not universally followed, delegates of the boycott committee went to the shops to speak to the owners and their customers, and in certain instances, even posted picketers to keep the public away by force. The large department stores, such as Cicurel, Chemla, Adès, and Lévi-Benzion, initially observed the boycott. The boycotters were particularly successful in the case of German films, as a large part of the audience tended to be Jewish. By systematically interrupting film showings, the LICA succeeded in almost completely banning German films from the Egyptian market.[48] The German anti-boycott committee, formed in April 1933, was unable to stop these activities, and while the boycott movement gradually declined over the thirties, it was maintained until the outbreak of World War II.[49]

It was, of course, impossible for Egyptian Jews to have any significant impact on German industry and commerce. In 1930, Germany ranked fourth among Egypt's foreign trade partners, and in 1932 its share in Egyptian foreign trade amounted to 7 percent. In spite of the Jewish boycott, German exports to Egypt even increased slightly in 1933–34 and 1934–35.[50] Nevertheless, exports of pharmaceuticals, cosmetics, cloth, beer, and, as mentioned above, of films were sufficiently affected for the German minister in Cairo, Dr. Eberhard von Stohrer, to protest repeatedly to the Egyptian government.[51] Prompted by von Stohrer, the Association of German Cotton Spinners threatened in October 1933 to cancel their orders for Egyptian cotton—Germany ranked third among the importers of Egyptian cotton in 1930—if the Jewish boycott movement was not ended. The Egyptian government reacted with considerable concern and von Stohrer, who claimed to have been unpleasantly surprised by the threat of the association, took care to have it withdrawn immediately. But he also succeeded in obtaining a pledge from the Egyptian government that in the future it would act more efficiently to prevent further anti-German activity on its territory.[52]

At the same time, the boycott movement was faced with opposition from quite a different quarter as well. In August 1933, representatives of Zionist organizations in Palestine concluded a secret agreement with the German Ministry of Economy, which was to enable German Jews wanting to emigrate to Palestine to transfer part of their property out of the country.

The so-called Haavara (Transfer) Agreement provided that German Jews wishing to emigrate to Palestine had to deposit their capital with a special account of the Haavara Organization. Specific German export products difficult to sell on the open market were to be purchased out of this fund and then sold to Jews in Palestine. Once the sales quota was met, the German emigrants were reimbursed part of their deposits out of the profits Haavara had made.[53]

The Haavara Agreement could not be held secret for long. Once it became known, it was severely criticized from various quarters, ranging from certain NS-organizations such as the Auslandsorganisation and the European competitors of German trade, to the Zionist revisionist movement in Palestine. After the terms of the agreement were extended to cover Egypt and Iraq in 1935, it was also fought by the LICA, whose boycott campaign ran directly counter to the intentions of the Haavara Agreement. In November 1935, the Zionist revisionist paper *ha-Yarden* disclosed that in January 1935, the Haavara had begun to extend its activities to these Arab countries through a company called Nemico (Near and Middle East Commercial Corporation). In the following years, Haavara made about 10 percent of its profits in the Middle East outside Palestine.[54]

Egyptian Jews saw the agreement, which was meant to safeguard the particular interests of German Jewry, as a betrayal of the interests of world Jewry in general. *L'Aurore* called it "a masterpiece of treason" that had caused an "enormous scandal" among Egyptian Jews.[55] Representatives of the Haavara reputedly succeeded, in April 1935, in convincing the leaders of the local Jewish boycott movement, many of whom were close to Zionism, to cease their campaign. Officially, however, the boycott of German goods and services continued until the outbreak of the war.[56]

In cooperation with the British Residency, the Egyptian government tried to contain the German-Jewish dispute carried out on its territory. In the spring and summer of 1933, it called upon Jews and Germans alike to end their quarrel and banned all open-air meetings staged by either side. As a result, the boycott movement had to be carried on silently from the early summer of 1933.[57] A special warning was given to the editor of *L'Aurore*, Jacques Maleh, who firmly backed the protest and boycott movement. The acting high commissioner, Walter Smart, drew Maleh's attention to the wider repercussions of the German-Jewish quarrel, when he summoned him in October 1933: "I admonished him suitably on the basis that the Jews were fouling their own comfortable nest in Egypt by stirring up this trouble as their action is resented by their Egyptian hosts. It was not in the interest of the Jews to create in Egypt anti-Jewish feeling similar to that in Palestine."[58]

It was certainly not in the interest of the Egyptian government to get into trouble with its German trading partners. But neither was it in its interest to tolerate attacks on one of the local minorities at a time of intense negotiation with Great Britain, particularly since the minority concerned was the Jews persecuted abroad and quite influential in business and press circles at home. The German chargé d'affaires in Cairo, Pilger, therefore complained in June 1933: "The [Egyptian] government probably does not view the Jewish movement with favor, either. However, considering the great influence the Jews exert, especially in Egypt, because of their dominant position in finance, it has so far been impossible to get the government to issue an official declaration against the boycott apart from its promise not to tolerate any more mass meetings."[59]

In August 1933, the Egyptian government issued a circular against the boycott, and the minister of foreign affairs, Ṣālib bey Sāmī, condemned the boycott publicly. At the same time, the Germans were sharply admonished by the government after anti-Semitic songs such as "Death to Juda" (Juda verrecke) had been sung at a so-called German meeting on 20 April 1934.[60] On the Jewish side, Maurice Fargeon, for example, was taken to court and convicted for attacking the Führer in his book *The Modern Tyrant: Hitler or the Truth about the Life of the Führer (A New Brown Book)* published in French in September 1933. A group of Jewish youth who assaulted the German consul in Alexandria were arrested.[61] The Egyptian government firmly resisted efforts made by the local Jewish community to facilitate the immigration of a large number of Jewish emigrants from Germany. Many of the prospective immigrants were professionals, notably medical doctors, and the local professional unions protested against their competition. Egyptian Jews, therefore, had to restrict themselves to collecting money for a colony of German Jewish emigrants in Palestine.[62] On the other hand, the Egyptian authorities were unable to restrain Jewish journalists, many of whom had foreign nationality and hence were protected by the Capitulations, even though the British, French, and Italian consuls were prepared to cooperate to some extent.[63]

In their joint effort to contain the Jewish anti-German campaign, the Egyptian government, the British Residency, and the German chargé d'affaires were able to secure the good offices of prominent community members including Joseph Aslan Cattaoui, Elie Mosseri, Victor Harari, Maître Alexander, Charles Adès, and Haim Nahum. They saw the activities of the LICA as dangerous to the harmonious coexistence of Jews and Muslims, and they regarded Léon Castro and his collaborators as unreliable and radical elements who put their private ambitions above the interests of the Jewish community as a whole. As early as April 1933, Eberhard von Stohrer reported from Cairo that the boycott was not directed from above but rather, as he had learned during occasional meetings with local Jews, the communal leaders distanced themselves from it. Chief Rabbi Haim Nahum openly condemned the boycott in November 1933. In December 1933, a contact of the German legation reported after a meeting with the personalities named above that the latter would have liked to end the boycott and the lawsuit, which they regarded as being "extremely stupid and harmful," but that they did not want to follow openly a divergent course (*eine Extratour tanzen*).[64] It was not that the official leaders of the community were passive. Rather they saw public restraint, private intervention, and quiet diplomacy, the classic instruments of cabinet politics, as the best ways to achieve positive results.[65]

The Egyptian public at first took little notice of the German-Jewish conflict carried out in their midst. The English, French, and the Arabic press reported on developments inside the German Reich and the reactions of Egyptian Jewry to them, and at least until the summer of 1933, even showed clear sympathies for the Jewish cause.[66] From the beginning, however, both the German and the Jewish sides tried to influence the press by paying money to leading journalists and by promoting news and statements favorable to their points of view. The German legation successfully contacted selected journalists from the Arabic newspapers. The French minister in Cairo, Gaillard, suspected, moreover, that King Fu'ād's pro-German sympathies had influenced the attitude of the press, which initially had been critical of the German government's anti-Semitic policies.[67] In May and June 1933, *al-Balāgh*, *Rūz al-Yūsuf*, and *al-Jihād*, *al-Muqaṭṭam* and *al-Ṣabāḥ* published a series of articles in which they criticized Jewish anti-Nazi activities in Egypt as selfish and harmful to Egyptian national interest. On 5 May 1933, after Jewish boycotters had broken up a German film showing, *al-Balāgh* wrote that the Jewish boycott movement was a reactionary Zionist enterprise reminiscent of the Crusades and that the Jews had to choose between Egypt and Palestine. After a similar incident, *al-Ṣabāḥ* warned its Jewish brothers (*ikhwānanā al-isrā'īlīyīn*) in moderate tones not to harm Egypt and reminded them of the possibility that the problem between the Jews and Germany might turn into a problem between the Jews and Egypt.[68]

In September 1933, Wolfgang Diewerge from the NSDAP in Berlin submitted a memorandum entitled "Press Support of the Cairo Jewish Trial," which had been commissioned by the German Ministry of Propaganda. He suggested that German propaganda should expose, through interviews with Egyptian politicians and "sensational reports" on the "international Jewish conspiracy in Egypt," the evil character of Léon Castro and his collaborators as well as the danger (*Gemeingefährlichkeit*) the Jews presented to the Germans, and the rest of the world.[69] In a comment on Diewerge's memorandum, a German lawyer practicing in Cairo, Dahm, warned the German authorities not to overestimate the influence of public opinion in a country like Egypt and to concentrate rather on winning over members of the Egyptian government. He argued that it was not so much through "love declarations" that this was to be achieved, but rather through signs of a certain huffiness (*gewisse Verschnupftheit*) in order to counter Jewish influence, which he felt was so strong that: "[N]ewspapers simply are not prepared to publish any articles that might be in any way offensive to the Jews. You always have to keep in mind that Jewish influence is much greater than German influence, and that here much more so than anywhere else where material interest alone decides."[70]

Diewerge, Dahm, and the NSDAP group in Cairo realized that the Jewish campaign against Nazism in itself was not enough to create the kind of conflict between Jews and Arabs the German side was hoping for. Dahm stated with regret that: "The educational level of the broad masses is not advanced enough for them to understand racial theory. The awareness of the Jewish danger has not been roused here as yet."[71] In view of this unfavorable position, Diewerge and the Ortsgruppe advised that German propaganda should be extended to include the conflict between Jews and Arabs over Palestine. In his memorandum of September 1933, Diewerge suggested that the German side elaborate on the conflict between Jews and Arabs in Palestine and "counter the view that National-Socialist Germany regarded the Arab race as inferior." The Cairo Ortsgruppe summed up the strategy by writing that the press campaign was of limited value in creating "anti-Jewish feeling in the Arab population," and that: "[O]ne has to start with the issue where real conflicts of interest exist between Arabs and Jews: Palestine. The antagonism between Arabs and Jews existing there has to be transplanted to Egypt."[72]

As the later years were to show, it was indeed not so much the endeavors of Nazi propagandists or of paramilitary youth groups influenced by the fascist model as the Palestine conflict itself, in which Egypt was becoming increasingly involved, that jeopardized the position of the Jews in Egyptian society.

PARAMILITARY YOUTH MOVEMENTS, ISLAMIC RESURGENCE, AND THE PALESTINE CONFLICT, 1936–39

In the late 1920s and early 1930s, militant youth and Islamic groups emerged, which, by the end of the thirties, would be able to challenge the Wafd and the minority parties in the intellectual as well as the political spheres. Though their rise was not directly linked to the Palestine issue, they soon began to show much more interest in Palestine than did the traditional parties. During the world economic crisis of the early thirties, the idea of a boycott of imported goods, especially British, in order to protect domestic industry against foreign competition, was gaining ground among the Egyptian middle class. The Wafd supported such a boycott, and in 1932–33 a group of nationalist high school and university students made a fresh attempt to promote Egyptian industry. The immediate result of their Piaster Plan (*mashrūʿ al-qirsh*) was not very impressive. Its promoters collected just enough money to open a factory to produce tarbooshes, which as opposed to the European hat, were regarded as symbols of the real Egyptian.[73]

However, out of this group of nationalist students developed one of the political movements that was to exert considerable influence on Egyptian youth and the future élite of the country. In October 1933, Aḥmad Ḥusayn, one of the student leaders, founded the Young Egypt Society (Jamʿīyat Miṣr al-Fatāt), which in December 1933 was transformed into a political party.[74] Under the slogans "God, Fatherland, the King" and "Egypt above all," Miṣr al-Fatāt propagated a new and militant brand of Egyptian nationalism that was directed against any kind of foreign interference, and against the adoption of immoral and "un-Islamic" customs of foreign origin. At the same time, it called for the unity of the Nile Valley, that is, Egypt and Sudan, and for a strong Egypt uniting Muslims and Copts that was to become the leader of the Arab Islamic world. With its paramilitary Green Shirts, Miṣr al-Fatāt was the first political organization in Egypt to be modeled in part on the fascist movements of Italy and Germany whose hierarchical structure, uniforms, demonstrations, and marches it imitated and whose emphasis on continuous struggle and strong leadership it adopted. The Wafd was soon to follow with its Blue Shirts and the Muslim Brothers with their Rovers (*al-Jawwāla*) and Battalions (*al-Katā'ib*).[75] Its paramilitary exercises and active rôle in the press gave Miṣr al-Fatāt much more publicity than was warranted by its small membership, which amounted to a few hundred. There was a surge in membership in 1937, but it never exceeded a thousand.[76]

Miṣr al-Fatāt was of minor importance compared to the Islamic organizations that in the 1930s began to expand in the political sphere previously dominated by nationalist parties of various persuasion.[77] In the late nineteenth century, Muslim reformists around Jamāl al-Dīn al-Afghānī (1839–97, in Egypt 1871–79) and his Azhar-trained student Muḥammad 'Abduh (1849–1905, mufti of Egypt from 1899) propagated the idea that only Islam purified of abuse and based on the Qur'ān and Sunna, that is, the practice of the Prophet and his Companions (*al-salaf al-ṣāliḥ*), would bring about the desired renewal of Muslim society and its liberation from foreign rule. The intellectual school of the Salafīya, as it was further developed by 'Abduh's student Rashīd Riḍā (1865–1935), already contained the basic lines of thinking that were later adopted by the political Islamic movement.[78] While originally it did not reach beyond the limited circle of religious thinkers and Azhar students centering around the journal *al-Manār*, it was rooted in the religious beliefs of the overwhelming majority of the population and hence had much greater potential appeal than the territorial, essentially secular, frame of reference of the liberal nationalists.

One of the most active and influential Islamic groups was the Young Men's Muslim Association (Jam'īyat al-Shubbān al-Muslimīn), founded in 1927 by a number of former members of the Ḥizb al-Waṭanī and adherents of the Salafīya movement such as shaykh Jāwīsh and Muḥibb al-Dīn al-Khaṭīb, who were later joined by Ṣāliḥ Ḥarb Pāshā.[79] By the late thirties, both the nationalist Miṣr al-Fatāt Party, which took on an increasingly Islamic coloring, and the Young Men's Muslim Association had been overshadowed by the Muslim Brotherhood, which was to remain by far the strongest Islamic organization in the country. The Society of the Muslim Brothers (Jam'īyat/Jamā'at al-Ikhwān al-Muslimīn) was founded in 1928 by a young teacher, Ḥasan al-Bannā (1906–49) in Ismā'īlīya, the headquarters of the Suez Canal Society, one of the most potent symbols of foreign presence in the country. After modest beginnings, the society quickly expanded, particularly after al-Bannā was transferred to Cairo in 1932. By the 1940s, the Muslim Brotherhood had developed into a political force second only to the Wafd. In 1939, it had over 500 branches in all parts of Egypt as well as a wide network of contacts and branches in neighboring Arab countries, notably Syria, Iraq, Palestine, and Yemen. After World War II, its membership comprised hundreds of thousands—500,000 according to one estimate and just as many sympathizers.[80]

The main aim of the Muslim Brothers was to realize in twentieth-century Egypt the ideal Islamic society envisaged by the founders of the Salafīya movement. The Muslim Brothers stood for the integral vision of Islam as the basis and guide for all aspects of life. The mission was truly comprehensive in that it aimed at fulfilling the spiritual as well as the material needs of the Muslim community and its individual members. Ḥasan al-Bannā accordingly characterized the aims and rôles of the Brotherhood as "a Salafiyya message, a Sunni way, a Sufi truth, a political organization, an athletic group, a cultural-educational union, an economic company, and a social idea."[81]

A strong element of social criticism, inspired by the ideal of social equality as it is firmly rooted in Islamic tradition, rendered the Brotherhood increasingly critical of the political establishment and the parliamentary system dominated by it. The Brotherhood supported the nationalist call for economic independence and a reduction of foreign interference in Egyptian politics and society. But it also demanded basic reforms in agriculture and industry. Unlike the other political groups, the Muslim Brothers did not merely talk about reform, but acted as well, creating social centers, clinics, evening schools, welfare associations, and meeting clubs. Their program and activities gained them widespread respect, particularly among the urban lower and middle classes, which included not only high school and university students active in all political movements but also teachers, government officials, and private employees, traders and shopkeepers, craftsmen, and workers who had, until the mid-thirties, been regarded as the mainstay of the Wafd. By contrast, the Muslim Brothers were less well represented in the countryside.[82]

Regarding Egyptian nationalism, the Muslim Brothers did not see national liberation as an end in itself, but only as a first step on the way to the restoration of the Islamic *umma* transcending all boundaries of nation, state, and ethnicity.[83] Their position on minority rights in the Islamic *umma* was ambiguous: while Ḥasan al-Bannā advocated freedom, justice, and equal rights for all citizens irrespective of race, origin, and religion, he demanded that the Islamic laws—laws implying the inequality of *dhimmīs* in crucial areas of social and political life—be reintroduced.[84] In an Islamic Egypt modeled on Muslim Brother ideas, non-Muslim minorities would clearly have fewer chances of integration and participation than in the liberal, essentially pluralist nation state propagated by the Wafd. From 1936 on, complaints were increasingly heard that Copts were being discriminated against, a development generally ascribed to religious agitation against the dominance of non-Muslims in an Islamic country.[85]

Virtually all aspects of social and political change have been offered to explain the rise of paramilitary youth organizations and militant Islamic groups in the Egypt of the 1930s. At their root was the destruction of the traditional village and urban communities resulting from the capitalization of agriculture, incipient industrialization, and economic liberalism. Rapid population growth led to overpopulation, large-scale migration to the cities, slum formation, and unemployment, which grew even more serious during the world economic crisis of the early thirties. Suffering and discontent engendered protest against the luxury of the upper class and disappointment with the "liberal," but corrupt, parliamentary party system, which seemed unsuited to local conditions. The misery and social inequality were particularly felt by high school and university students who, in their search for orientation, meaning, and identity, were driven ever further into political activism as the main outlet for their frustrations and creative energies.[86] This search for orientation and identity was also reflected in intellectual circles. In the mid-thirties, prominent writers like 'Abbās al-'Aqqād, Muḥammad Ḥusayn Haykal, and even Ṭāhā Ḥusayn were turning to Islam as the essence of cultural authenticity.[87]

In the second half of the 1930s, the framework and climate of political action in Egypt changed significantly. The death of King Fu'ād I in April 1936 gave ambitious politicians and political groupings promoted by them more room in which to maneuver. The Anglo-Egyptian Treaty of August 1936 and the Convention of Montreux of May 1937 reduced British control over Egypt, provided an end for the Capitulations, and opened the way to Egypt's admission to the League of Nations. From 1936 on, the Egyptian government enjoyed much more freedom of action in dealing with foreigners and minorities at home and with its Arab neighbors abroad. This was Egypt's first chance to become actively involved in foreign policy. In the preceding years, fascist regimes had come to power in Europe, offering alternative models of political ideology and organization to the liberal European democracies that the Middle East had known as colonial powers. The outbreak, in 1936, of the Arab revolt in Palestine, for the first time, raised genuine interest in wider Arab affairs among the Egyptian public.

Under the new conditions of the late thirties, the pattern and methods of political contest were also beginning to change. To the classic triangle of the king, the Wafd, and the British, which had so far monopolized the political arena, were added the paramilitary youth groups and the Islamic movement with their base in the urban middle class. Even though King Fārūq in 1938 dissolved the paramilitary organizations of the Wafd, Miṣr al-Fatāt, and the Muslim Brotherhood, their ideological outlook was not changed. The activist groups continued to stress the values of strong leadership, struggle (*jihād*), and martyrdom, the art of dying (*fann al-mawt*) idealized by Ḥasan al-Bannā, which drew its inspiration not only from Islamic tradition, but also from contemporary European models of authoritarianism. While the Wafd had already mobilized the masses, if only on a temporary basis, and while political conflict in the years after 1919 had also involved demonstrations, strikes, and boycotts, street action and violence increased significantly in the second half of the 1930s.

The outbreak of the Arab revolt in Palestine in 1936 greatly strengthened the idea of Arab unity, which in the 1940s and 1950s would gradually supersede territorial Egyptian nationalism. Until the mid-thirties, the Palestine problem had hardly played any rôle in Egyptian politics. The only groups to take an active interest were Syrian and Palestinian exiles, Azhar students, and Islamic organizations such as the Young Men's Muslim Association.[88] Neither the press nor the parties represented in Parliament, not to mention the general public, took more than a passing interest in the developments in neighboring Palestine, and the government abstained from any kind of active involvement. Until well into the 1920s, certain politicians and writers, including the noted Muslim reformer and editor of the journal *al-Manār*, Rashīd Riḍā, even showed respect for the achievements of the Zionist settlers. And while Islamic circles represented the conflict in religious terms as one involving Jews and Arab Muslims, the leading nationalist parties and their press still distinguished between Jews and Zionists. Pinning their hopes on a peaceful solution, they pointed to the dangers of religious strife, which to them seemed incompatible with the spirit of the age.[89]

The reaction in Islamic circles to the Wailing Wall incidents of August 1929, and reports on the alleged intention of the Jews to desecrate the Muslim holy places in Jerusalem, notably the

Aqṣā Mosque, caused some concern among Jewish community leaders in Egypt. They told the political groups active in the community, among them first and foremost the Zionists, to keep absolutely quiet. At the same time, they contacted the Egyptian authorities and European diplomats to obtain protection should the Jews be attacked by pro-Palestinian "fanatics." The Egyptian government did, indeed, take special security precautions in order to protect Jewish institutions and establishments. However, no serious incidents were reported.[90]

By the mid-thirties, Egyptian politicians such as Muḥammad 'Alī 'Allūba, 'Alī Māhir, William Makram 'Ubayd, and 'Umar Ṭūsūn had recognized the centrality of the Palestine question to the issues of national independence, Arab strength, and Islamic unity. In Egypt, as in the other Muslim Arab countries, the Palestine question promised to activate energies based on religion, patriotism, and Arabism, and to give political prominence to its advocates. The Muslim Brotherhood in particular would be able to profit from, and literally cash in on, growing involvement in the Palestinian cause, which it supported in close cooperation with the Arab Higher Committee led by Ḥājj Amīn al-Ḥusaynī, the mufti of Jerusalem.[91]

In the early summer of 1936, the Arab Higher Committee sent its first emissaries to Egypt in order to mobilize the government, the court, the press, and the religious authorities (*'ulamā'*) for the Palestine cause. Their campaign still focused on the claim that the Jews intended to desecrate and destroy the Muslim holy places in Jerusalem, and it did meet with some success. The year 1936 was the point at which widening circles of the Egyptian public were drawn into the Arab-Zionist conflict over Palestine. By the end of the decade, they had begun to demonstrate their involvement not only in words, but also in deeds. Islamic propagandists declared that it was the religious duty of every Muslim (*farḍ 'aynī*) to engage in a holy war (*jihād*) on behalf of Palestine. Mosques were turned into propaganda and mobilization centers. Friday prayer offered excellent opportunities for communication and organization. Activities were no longer restricted to Islamic circles and to verbal protest and fund-raising. Solidarity committees were organized, demonstrations staged, mass meetings and congresses held. For the first time, the nationalist parties and the press began to show genuine interest in the Arab-Muslim cause centered on Palestine.[92]

As a result of this growing involvement in the Palestine question, the second half of the 1930s witnessed the first attacks on local Jewry as the fifth column of Zionism. In some cases the Jews were also accused of exploiting their Egyptian hosts and were attacked as members of a people whose moral deficiencies combined with financial power, made them a menace not only to the Arabs and the Muslims but to all human society. Starting in 1936, a newly established Palestine Arab Information Office, which the French legation suspected of cooperating with the Nazis, published a daily bulletin and distributed what the French classified as anti-Semitic material throughout French North Africa.[93] In May 1936, the Muslim Brotherhood called for a boycott of Egyptian Jews.[94] In September 1936, the first anti-Jewish graffiti appeared on the walls of the Jewish quarter in Port Said after a visit there of the president of the Islamic Youth Organization of Palestine. The recommendation made by the British Peel Commission in July 1937 in favor of partition, which, for the first time, implied the establishment in Palestine of a Jewish state as opposed to a mere national home, was universally rejected by Palestinians and Egyptians.[95]

In 1938, attacks on local Jews increased noticeably. In the course of violent student demonstrations in Cairo, Alexandria, and Ṭanṭā in April and May 1938, voices were heard shouting "Down with the Jews" and "Jews get out of Egypt and Palestine." In May 1938, during the celebrations of the Prophet's birthday (*mawlid al-nabī*), the police had to prevent violent demonstrators from entering the Cairo Jewish *ḥāra.* During the World Parliamentary Congress for the Defense of Palestine held in Cairo in October 1938, anti-Zionist and openly anti-Semitic material was distributed, including Arabic translations of Hitler's *Mein Kampf* and the *Protocols of the Elders of Zion.*[96] Pamphlets were distributed calling for a boycott of Jewish goods, shops, and department stores, and in July 1939 Miṣr al-Fatāt even created a special boycott committee, which published three blacklists of Jewish merchants.[97] For the first time, bombs were placed in a Cairo synagogue and in private Jewish homes in al-Manṣūra, Asyūṭ, and al-Maḥalla al-Kubrā in June 1939, though no serious damage was done. Jewish owners of department stores such as David Adès received personal threats.[98] Time and again, Egyptian Jews were called upon to state their position with regard to Palestine and to dissociate themselves from Zionism.

In the publications distributed by militant nationalist and religious organizations as well as by Syrian and Palestinian emigrants grouped around the Arab League (al-Rābiṭa al-'Arabīya), Egyptian Jews were denounced as sympathizers with Zionism, exploiters of the Egyptian masses, and elements dangerous to their host peoples. A pamphlet distributed in Cairo in October 1938, which was immediately seized by the police, ran:

O Young Men:

Towards the revolution.... In Palestine today monstrous slaughterings are being carried out by the English and the Jews the enemies of Islam.... The English soldiers and the Jewish police are violating the Mosque of Omar ... and they are destroying its dome and walls. The Arabs are threatened with extinction in the Holy Land as a result of this savage torture and mutilation for which humanity can show no precedent....

O Moslem and Christian youths alike:

The *jihād* on behalf of Palestine has become a sacred and holy obligation.... Your duty in this severe affliction is to make of the Palestine revolution a general revolution whose flames will spread to Egypt and burn up the English and the Jews, the opponents of the Arabs and Islam.

O Youth of the University:

Proclaim an implacable strike until the Moslems in Palestine shall be victorious over the hungry hounds who seek to lap up the blood of her spotless sons....

O Merchants:

Boycott the English and the Jews....

O Politicians:

Tear up the unjust treaties.... Compare democratic England in Palestine with dictatorship Germany in the Sudetenland, and know that the foremost enemies of Islam are the English, the catspaws of the Jews, the lowest race on earth.

O Egyptians:

To the Palestinian arena, where your brethren, the fighters in the *jihād* are raising the standards of God in striking and majestic manner.

O Youths:
TO THE REVOLUTION
Either a victory which will raise up God's word, or a martyrdom for which there is an immortal reward.[99]

In their attacks on the Jews, the Muslim Brothers and Miṣr al-Fatāt offered a complex blend of arguments and images. Religious sentiment against the Jews as enemies of the Prophet and Islam combined with adaptations of the anti-Semitic stereotypes of European provenance to create an image of the Jew as enemy, which was, however, based on political and economic factors rather than on religious or racist grounds. Leading Egyptian politicians were well aware of the potential implications of this course. As early as 1936, the Wafdist leader Muṣṭafā al-Naḥḥās warned that the conflict over Palestine might lead to anti-Jewish outbursts in Egypt. Muḥammad Maḥmūd, from the Liberal Constitutionalist Party, who succeeded al-Naḥḥās in the office of prime minister, in September 1938 pointed to the possibility that anti-Jewish pogroms in the Arab world might occur if the religious aspects of the conflict were not kept under control. With different emphasis Muṣṭafā al-Marāghī, the head of al-Azhar University, emphasized the danger Zionism presented to the Jews of the Arab world. The participants in the World Parliamentary Congress for the Defense of Palestine, who met in Cairo in October 1938, repeated this same argument, warning of anti-Jewish incidents in the Muslim Arab countries.[100] Muḥammad 'Alī 'Allūbu, by contrast, a well-known supporter of radical nationalist and pan-Arab movements, and one of the organizers of this congress, declared that his primary aim was, on the contrary, to involve Egyptian Jews in the conflict in order to make "things as hot as possible for the Jews in Egypt and elsewhere in the Near East."[101]

Local Jewish leaders were seriously disturbed by the rising tide of anti-Zionist and anti-Jewish feeling in nationalist and Islamic circles. They reacted exactly as they had a decade earlier, when the Palestine conflict produced its first repercussions in Egypt, and as they were wont to do in all crises involving a potential threat to the safety and well-being of Egyptian Jewry. They used their extensive contacts with Egyptian politicians and foreign diplomats in order to have the authorities stop, or at least restrain, anti-Zionist and anti-Jewish propaganda and activities. Considerable sums of money were paid to certain Arab papers to complement the diplomatic approach.[102] At the same time, they put pressure on local Jewish associations, notably the Zionist ones, to end all overt activities that might cast doubt on the loyalty of the Jewish citizens to the state of Egypt. Their foremost concern was to prevent the emergence in Egypt of a Jewish question. The best tactic seemed to them to remain as inconspicuous as possible, keeping a low profile in order not to draw undue attention to the existence of a Jewish minority in the country, let alone a national movement active in its midst.[103] In a report titled "The Jewish Milieu in Alexandria," S. Avigdor from the Alliance Israélite Universelle reported in December 1937:

> "Here in Egypt, the Jewish community [*milieu juif*] and in particular the one in Alexandria wants to avoid speaking publicly about the burning question of anti-Semitism. It wants to systematically prevent Egyptian journals and [public] circles from provoking or rousing feelings hostile to the Jews in a country where, in spite of the proximity to Palestine, they have lived and continue to live in good understanding with the Muslim and Coptic Egyptians."[104]

In a telegram dated 2 November 1938 (Balfour Day), Joseph Aslan Cattaoui as president of the Cairo community appealed to Chaim Weizmann to work on behalf of moderation and cooperation between Jews and Arabs: "As Egyptians [we] urgently appeal to you [to] recommend moderation all around and [a] spirit of conciliation; with firm determination [we] realize [that] loyal union alone [is] capable of assuring [a] durable future peace and concord among populations made to understand each other and already united in [a] common origin and by long-standing fraternal feelings."[105]

The community leaders were by and large successful with their two-tiered strategy. The Zionists suspended most overt activities, and the Egyptian government tried to curb anti-Jewish agitation and action, seizing pamphlets and publications, and offering police protection to Jewish homes and institutions. Muṣṭafā al-Marāghī even banned all anti-Jewish propaganda among Palestinian students at al-Azhar University.[106] It was not in the interest of the Egyptian government to tolerate attacks waged by their political opponents on the non-Muslim minorities living in the country, be they Jews or Copts. The Wafd preserved its concept of a pluralist nation state uniting all religious communities even in these years marked by an upsurge of Islamic feeling and activism. An increasing number of articles appeared in the local Arab press calling for calm and tolerance and defending the Jews against all accusations of treason and corruption. After the demonstrations of April 1938, the Wafdist paper *al-Balāgh* wrote: "Our Jewish brethren have experienced some concern following yesterday's demonstrations.... May our Israelite compatriots be reassured. Egypt's sympathy for Palestine contains no offense and no desire to hurt them. They, too, are children of Egypt. As such, they carry the same rights and the same obligations. Their conduct in Egypt has always been excellent. Egyptians feel for them nothing but affection and loyalty [*fidélité*]."[107]

The wider Egyptian public and the press did not take part in the campaign against Zionism and Egyptian Jewry waged by nationalist students and Islamic activists. Nevertheless, involvement in the Palestinian-Arab cause increased steadily in the late 1930s. Local Jews and foreign observers were particularly concerned about the simultaneous spread of Italian and German propaganda, which since the fascist takeover in Italy and Germany had increased significantly. From 1932, Italy broadcast news and propaganda via Radio Bari, including Arabic programs beginning in 1934. In 1933, the German Reich established a special Arab press service and in 1935 opened a branch of the German News Office (Deutsches Nachrichtenbüro) in Cairo.[108] Members of the local Jewish community kept the foreign diplomats informed about German activities in Egypt and the neighboring Arab countries.[109] It was generally assumed that Miṣr al-Fatāt, the Young Men's Muslim Association, and the Muslim Brotherhood had contacts with the Italian and German regimes. Ḥājj Amīn al-Ḥusaynī, who had close links to the Muslim Brotherhood, did in fact support the fascist powers during World War II and never concealed the anti-Semitic side of his enmity toward Zionism and the Jews. Ḥasan al-Bannā, by contrast, the leader of the Muslim Brothers, rejected racial theory as utterly incompatible with Islam.[110]

Involvement in the Palestine cause was so closely linked to the struggle against the British presence in Egypt and the Middle East at large that many outside observers saw it merely as one symptom of xenophobia, of general hostility to all things British or foreign. They were led to believe that the Palestine issue in general, and anti-Zionism in particular, were merely tools in the hands of cynical and ambitious politicians struggling for power. Such a view, if it was not totally unfounded, nevertheless neglected the genuine alarm with which Egyptian intellectuals and politicians watched the establishment, and rapid expansion, of a Zionist settlement supported by the Western colonial powers. To them, the Jewish national home was not only a serious obstacle on the path to Arab and Islamic unity, but also a direct threat to the economic, military, and cultural interests of Egypt itself.[111]

Having, for the first time, gained some room to maneuver in foreign policy, Egyptian politicians began to develop a growing interest in regional politics. Leadership in the Arab world, a "political caliphate" to replace the religious one, as the French minister in Cairo, de Witasse, called it, seemed to come naturally to Egypt as the most populous Arab state and the seat of the prestigious Azhar University.[112] As late as July 1937, the Wafdist prime minister, Muṣṭafā al-Naḥḥās, still refused to formally involve his country in the Palestine conflict. Egypt was only represented at the Bludān Conference of September 1937 by six politicians participating in a private capacity. But in September 1938, the new Egyptian prime minister, Muḥammad Maḥmūd, offered Egyptian mediation in the Palestine conflict, and in February 1939, Egypt was officially represented at the London Round Table Conference by four of its leading politicians. After a lengthy period of refusal and hesitation, Egypt was at last officially involved in the Palestine question, which was before long to implicate it even militarily.[113]

There had been previous attempts to mediate in the Arab-Zionist conflict involving Egyptian politicians, Syrian emigrants, and representatives of the Zionist Executive. In many instances, these encounters were arranged through the good offices of local community members and Zionist activists. They had always worked toward a negotiated settlement and peaceful coexistence of Jews and Arabs in Palestine and the Middle East at large, but did not wish to draw the community as such into the dangerous confrontation between Arabs and Zionists. Their hopes and expectations were aptly expressed in an article published in January 1936 in the pro-Zionist periodical *Hatikvah*:

> In this country of extraordinary liberty, where so many races and cultures come together in fraternal harmony, under the auspices of an intelligent, just, and good sovereign [King Fu'ād I], who proclaims and desires peaceful coexistence among his subjects, Egyptian Jewry, [as a] connecting link between Palestine, the North African countries, and Europe ... can and must play the special rôle of spiritual and cultural mediator between Eretz Israel and Mediterranean Jewry, in close collaboration with Jewish France and Italy and all Jewish forces dispersed in the various countries of Roman language.

As early as 1913, a first meeting had been held between members of the Syrian Decentralization Party and the Zionist Federation of Egypt. Chaim Weizmann met again with representatives of this party in 1918, and in 1922 was able to win over to a negotiated settlement of the Palestine issue the grand master of the National Grand Lodge of Ancient Free and Accepted Masons in Egypt.[114] In the 1920s and 1930s, Colonel Kisch from the Zionist Executive in Jerusalem had several meetings with Egyptian politicians, which were arranged by his Jewish friends in Egypt.[115] Mediation efforts were stepped up in 1937–38, when tension began to rise in Egypt. In February 1938, Chaim Weizmann came to Egypt to meet Prince Muḥammad ʿAlī, a prominent member of the royal family, and the British ambassador, Sir Miles Lampson. In March 1938, Muḥammad ʿAlī visited Sir Herbert Samuel, the British high commissioner in Palestine. In June, Lampson consulted with Victor Harari and Maître Alexander from the Alexandria Jewish community, and in April 1939, Chaim Weizmann met the Egyptian prime minister, the foreign minister, and ʿAlī Māhir. In spite of the hopes the Jewish side attached to these mediation efforts, they came to nothing.[116] The British government was not prepared to welcome an Egyptian rôle in the search for a comprehensive settlement of the Palestine conflict. The British ambassador to Cairo, Sir Miles Lampson, explained in June 1938:

> Maître Alexander's plan was that some such solution might be engineered through the influence of notable Muslims outside Palestine and that Egypt might play the part of an honest broker in the matter. This, he knew, would be a part which the Egyptian Government would very much like to play and in fact Nahas Pasha had offered to play such a rôle but for various reasons His Majesty's Government had not deemed it politic to pursue the matter. He [Lampson] did not think that at the moment His Majesty's Government would welcome any further proposals of this sort.... At the present moment the Arab-Jewish Problem in Palestine had got inextricably involved in Mediterranean and European politics and the enemies of Great Britain were fishing in troubled waters.[117]

In spite of the negative attitude taken by the British, the dialogue between Egyptian politicians, Zionist representatives, and local Jews was continued during World War II.

WORLD WAR II AND ITS AFTERMATH

World War II sharpened the internal tension that had built up in the interwar period. On the political level, however, all overt activities had to cease after the government declared a state of siege and introduced strict press censorship in September 1939. The successive governments of ʿAlī Māhir (August 1939–June 1940), Ḥasan Ṣabrī (June–November 1940), Ḥusayn Sirrī (November 1940–February 1942), Muṣṭafā al-Naḥḥās (February 1942–October 1944), Aḥmad Māhir (October 1944–February 1945), and finally of Maḥmūd Fahmī al-Nuqrāshī (February 1945–February 1946) tried to maintain Egypt's neutrality within the limits of its obligations under the Anglo-Egyptian Treaty of Alliance of 1936. While the government did intern or expel all German citizens in the country, with the exception of German Jews, and while it did break off diplomatic relations with the Reich, it tried to avoid declaring war on the Axis powers. After Italy entered the war in June 1940, many of the estimated 60,000 Italian citizens living in Egypt were interned, again with the exception of Italian Jews and known antifascists.[118] But it was not until February 1945 that the Egyptian government saw itself obliged to declare war on Germany and Italy. The prime minister, Aḥmad Māhir, was shot dead while reading the declaration of war in the House of Deputies.[119]

After the outbreak of the war, the German government decided to step up its propaganda in the Middle East. For the first time, the Germans made use not only of written publications and pamphlets but also of radio broadcasts which, it was hoped, would reach the illiterate masses. Yet the effectiveness of this propaganda remained limited. As long as Germany followed the policy of leaving the Mediterranean to its Italian ally and of seeking a peaceful settlement with Britain, German propaganda had to confine itself to slogans directed against the British and the Jews without giving any pledges of material support to the Arab nationalists. It was only in 1940–41, after its Blitz victories in Western and Northern Europe, that Germany began to adopt a new strategy. While keeping up the official line of respecting, at least for the sake of outward appearances, Italian prerogatives in the area, and of avoiding conflict with Great Britain, Germany became increasingly involved in the Arab liberation struggle against French and British colonial rule. The most noticeable instance was the revolt of Rashīd ʿAlī al-Kaylānī in Iraq in spring 1941.[120]

In Egypt, the Axis powers—Germany more so than Italy, which had, after all, occupied Libya and Abyssinia—could count on the sympathies of King Fārūq and of nationalist circles among the youth, and the junior officer corps. These pro-German elements were brought into loose contact by a number of politicians close to the royal court, among them ʿAlī Māhir, Ṣāliḥ Ḥarb, and ʿAzīz ʿAlī al-Miṣrī.[121] Their fascination with Nazi Germany was not based on the racial theory of the Führer who, incidentally, did not think highly of the Arab race.[122] Only a few years earlier, the Nuremberg Laws of September 1935 had roused strong emotions in Egyptian political circles, when it became known that Egyptians, too, were to be regarded as racially inferior to Aryan Germans. Unlike the Turks and the Persians, the Egyptians had little chance to establish their racial credentials as a Nordic people. Calm was only restored after Berlin granted a special dispensation to mixed marriages between Germans and Egyptians who were, thereby, classified as belonging to the "Mediterranean group of Aryans."[123] The German side also attempted to elaborate on the common principles allegedly shared by National-Socialism and Islam, notably the principles of strong leadership and of hostility to the Jews.[124] The fascist model of political and social organization with its emphasis on unity, leadership, and struggle unto death indeed seemed to offer new hopes of strength and glory to the colonized nations of the Third World. But it was Germany's rôle as the most powerful opponent of Britain and France that mattered most. Egyptian sympathies with, and support of, the Axis powers therefore closely followed the course of military events in Europe and the Middle East.

When in 1941–42, the German Africa Corps under Field Marshal Erwin Rommel advanced toward Libya, King Fārūq sent a telegram to the Führer expressing his highest respect and offering the support of "90 percent" of the Egyptian people. He added that: "He was filled with highest respect for the Fuehrer and the German people, whose victory over England he was fervently wishing for. He knew himself united with his people in the wish to see German troops victorious in Egypt as liberators from unbearable, brutal English yoke as soon as possible."[125]

As long, however, as the British had their army in Egypt, and as long as they were able to influence the selection of political and military leaders in the country, the secret sympathies of the king and the nationalist opposition were of little practical use. German diplomats in Berlin were well aware of this state of affairs and noted that, even though the king was pro-German "through and through," the mass of the Egyptian population was uncritical and not interested in politics.[126] When in early 1942, Rommel marched toward the Egyptian border, young demonstrators took to the streets of Cairo protesting against the British and the Jews and shouting "Advance Rommel! " (*ilā 'l-amām yā Rūmīl*). The British ambassador reacted to the rising tide of pro-Nazi sentiment, and on 4 February 1942 forced the king to install a Wafdist cabinet headed by Muṣṭafā al-Naḥḥās, which, it was hoped, would be more sympathetic to the British cause. King Fārūq could do nothing but send another secret cable to Berlin assuring the Führer of his respect and sympathies.[127]

The Jewish community felt seriously menaced by the German advance in North Africa. As early as August 1940, members of the Alexandria community began to flee south. Their numbers increased greatly after the German air attacks on Cairo and Alexandria in June and September 1941. In June 1942, the German Africa Corps took Ṭubrūq, and in July 1942, Marsā Maṭrūḥ. Thousands of Jews fled to Cairo from Alexandria, though even there the community was afraid of a massacre. By the summer of 1941, some 90,000 people, not all of them Jews, were reported to have left Alexandria, and a year later another 35,000 had left Cairo.[128] In collaboration with Chief Rabbi Haim Nahum, the local Zionist organizations prepared lists of known antifascists and Zionists whom the British embassy promised to evacuate from Egypt. A certain number of them were indeed temporarily taken to Palestine.[129] In spite of some threats against the Jews and foreigners, however, the Egyptian population remained calm. The prime minister assured the chief rabbi that even if the Germans did invade Egypt, the Jews had nothing to fear and that no discriminatory measures would be introduced. Anxiety subsided after the British victory at al-ʿAlamayn in November 1942. In February 1943, the German capitulation at Stalingrad broke the German offensive on the East European front. Among the Egyptian nationalists, the hopes pinned on German military support in the struggle against Britain faded.[130]

The Jewish community had sided with the Allies in the war against the Axis powers. Many local Jews of British, French or Greek nationality fought with their armies on various fronts. Wealthy members of the community donated large sums of money to the British war effort and established clubs for Jewish soldiers in the British army stationed in Egypt. Some Jews collaborated in the Egyptian branch of the France Libre movement led by General de Gaulle, which was founded in July 1940 and numbered about four-hundred members.[131] Individual members of the local Zionist movement including Léon Castro and Albert Staraselski, the head of the revisionist New Zionist Organization, continued to inform the British authorities about German and Italian activities in the area.

Among Italian Jews, who for many years had shown themselves particularly patriotic in their feelings for Italy, quite a few had initially sympathized with the fascist regime. Some of them began to reconsider their attitude when Italy occupied Abyssinia in 1935. Prominent Jewish businessmen such as the Pinto brothers and Elie Mosseri who, up to then, had played a major rôle in the local Italian colony, transferred some of their money out of Italy and registered their firms in Egypt.[132] In September 1938, when Mussolini introduced anti-Semitic legislation in Italy, they threatened to withdraw their remaining deposits from Italian banks, to boycott Italian goods and services, and to adopt Egyptian nationality.[133]

In the spring of 1940, antifascist committees were formed in the Italian Jewish colony to fight the fascist influence, which continued to be strong within its ranks. In 1935, a British report had registered about 2,000 party members in the local Italian colony. The initiative to actively combat fascist influence seems to have come from Masonic circles, notably from within the Garibaldi lodge, which at the time numbered about 50 members, and which in July 1940 founded a new lodge called Cesare Battisti.[134] By the end of 1940, they had organized into the Antifascist Action Group, which in 1941 merged with the Free Italy group in the Gruppo d'Azione Antifascista Italiani Liberi. By December 1941, this organization had 45 Italian and 115 members of other nationalities.[135] But their efforts met with only limited success. As Jews and Freemasons, many of them, moreover, known for their leftist sympathies, and as collaborators with the British who supported their endeavors, they were easy to discredit in the eyes of the other Italians. Local fascists prepared lists of their opponents in order to take their revenge after the war, supposing, of course, that it would be won by the Axis. Even within the Jewish community, certain prominent individuals remained loyal to fascist Italy.[136]

The effects of World War II on Egyptian society and politics in general were in many respects similar to those of World War I. Tension increased between the landowning and entrepreneurial upper-middle and upper classes on one hand and the salaried lower-middle and lower classes on the other, which included not only Egyptian nationals but also foreigners and stateless people. Provisioning the Allied troops stationed in the country gave a fresh impetus to local industry at a time when Egypt was again cut off from foreign imports. Many new companies sprang up and new branches of industry developed, thereby increasing the

Egyptian proportion of local industry. As a result, ever-growing numbers of peasants and agrarian laborers were attracted to the cities, first and foremost to Cairo and Alexandria. During the war, the Allied troops employed some 200,000 to 245,000 persons, who were laid off after the war. This massive discharge of workers and employees further aggravated the problem of unemployment, which persisted despite the remarkable industrial growth that lasted until 1949, and the social, cultural, and political problems resulting from it.[137]

The gap between the upper and upper-middle classes and the lower-middle and lower classes, who suffered from inflation, the scarcity of goods, and a high rise in prices (between August 1939 and late 1944 the index of consumer goods rose by almost 300%) was particularly glaring in Cairo. The upper class displayed their wealth quite openly. The Allied soldiers, so hungry for pleasure and dissipation, created added resentment. The dispossessed strata were all the more aware of the situation because the late 1930s had witnessed a growth of social consciousness and criticism, which no longer accepted social inequality as natural and inevitable. During the war, the trade union and leftist movement in Egypt experienced a new upsurge, particularly when, after the defeat of the fascist Axis, the Soviet Union was left as the only serious opponent of the Western powers. The Wafdist government of Muṣṭafā al-Naḥḥās sought to restrict communist influence among students and workers by introducing new labor legislation. In 1942, trade unions for industrial workers were legalized and the minimum wage for agricultural laborers was raised from 2–3 to 5 piasters per day. But these belated measures were not enough to stem the tide of labor unrest and political protest that erupted after the war.[138]

Added to the economic and social crisis was the obvious inability of the political leadership to challenge the British, who did not hesitate to use military force when intervening in Egyptian affairs. Economic hardship, growing awareness of social inequality, and political criticism thus combined to discredit the political and economic system established under British control.

The so-called minority parties, having never had a broad popular basis, had relatively little to lose. The king, by contrast, who was still young, but inefficient, fat, and notoriously pleasure-seeking, had lost the enormous popularity he had enjoyed upon his accession just a few years earlier. The Wafd, which had already lost some ground to the new militant nationalist and Islamic groupings, was further weakened by a series of splits and defections. One of the most serious blows to its reputation came when it was made public that the Wafd owed its comeback in February 1942 to the military intervention of the British. Its image was tarnished further, when in 1943, William Makram ʿUbayd, one of its most prominent leaders who had just been expelled from the party, took his revenge by disclosing in his *Black Book* the rampant corruption and nepotism within the Wafd.[139]

Under these circumstances it was only natural that the opposition was gaining ground. In the process of agitation, repression, relaxation of control, fresh agitation, and new repression that unfolded under the successive governments of the postwar era, the Muslim Brotherhood emerged as the strongest popular force in the country besides the Wafd. In spite of almost continuous repression, the Brotherhood under its charismatic supreme guide (*al-murshid al-ʿāmm*), Ḥasan al-Bannā, was able to keep up its campaign against the British, the Jews, the party politicians, and the king himself, who had lost the favor he initially enjoyed with the Brothers. In 1942–43, some members built up the so-called secret apparatus (*al-jihāz al-sirrī*), which was to play a crucial rôle in the violence of the late 1940s. By 1946, the Brotherhood had about one million members and supporters.

Political life in the period between 1945 and the 1952 revolution was dominated by two major camps: the Wafd, which had effectively split into a right and a left wing, and the Islamic camp. The Wafdist right wing under Fu'ād Sirāj al-Dīn Pāshā, a lawyer and large landowner, who was appointed secretary general in 1948, was prepared to cooperate, to a certain extent, with the Muslim Brothers in the common fight against the communists. The smaller left wing of the Wafdist Vanguard (al-Ṭalīʿa al-Wafdīya), by contrast, cooperated with the leftist student and workers' committees that formed in 1946. The Wafd was challenged by the strictly anticommunist Muslim Brothers and other Islamic groups, including Miṣr al-Fatāt, which in the course of the 1940s, had adopted a distinctly religious coloring.[140]

The restrictions imposed under martial law had hardly been lifted when the tension accumulated during the war erupted in violent demonstrations. From 1943–44 on, foreign observers had noted increasing agitation against foreigners and non-Muslims. In the spring of 1943, Azhar students and deputies in Parliament protested against the admission into the country of Jewish refugees from Europe and Palestine.[141] In the summer of 1944, the Muslim Brothers stepped up their campaign against the Zionists in Palestine and their alleged Jewish sympathizers inside Egypt who were urged to dissociate themselves from Zionism not only in words, but also in deeds. Participants in special training courses were instructed on how to "heat up public opinion with regard to the Palestine question."[142] The Kutla Party of Makram 'Ubayd formed a special anti-Zionist committee, which issued violent pamphlets against the Jews and the Zionists. In the press and radio, appeals were made to fight against the Jews and the Zionists and to boycott the Jews living in Egypt.[143]

The local Jewish leaders were extremely concerned about the rise of anti-Zionist propaganda, which in certain circles took on a decidedly anti-Jewish note. Their concern increased when in November 1944 members of the extremist Zionist Stern Gang (Leḥi) assassinated the British minister resident in the Middle East, Lord Moyne, in Cairo.[144] They tried once more to convince the local Zionists, who had shown unprecedented activity during the war years, to suspend all overt activities. But unlike the late 1920s and mid-1930s, the communal leaders were no longer obeyed. In order to seek a solution to the dangerous conflict over Palestine, which threatened to implicate all Jews regardless of their personal convictions, both Zionists and non-Zionists continued with their mediation efforts. During the war, they had arranged a number of meetings of Egyptian politicians with prominent representatives of the Zionist Executive, such as Moshe Shertok and Eliahu Sassoon, who came to Egypt quite frequently. But no breakthrough was achieved.[145]

The Egyptian authorities also took the rise of anti-Zionism with its anti-Jewish overtones seriously. They tried to prevent the demonstrations announced for 2 November 1945 (Balfour Day), which it was feared, might develop into a mass outburst against the British and possibly against other foreigners and non-Muslim minorities as well. In late October 1945, the British embassy received a confidential report from Fitzpatrick Pasha, the assistant commandant of the Cairo city police, stating that there could be no doubt that "there is considerable ill-feeling in Cairo against Jews." He noted that "if any move is made by the Jews in Palestine against the Arabs, there will certainly be a reaction in Egypt." And while he was not "unduly worried," he nevertheless ordered that special security precautions be taken and police protection was given to all Jewish establishments in Cairo and Alexandria.[146]

Government protection proved to be insufficient when on 2 November 1945 the Balfour Day demonstrations did indeed deteriorate into anti-Jewish riots.[147] The radio and the press, including the papers of the Wafd, which at the time was out of government, the Muslim Brothers, Miṣr al-Fatāt, and the Young Men's Muslim Association had called for massive demonstrations to protest British policy in Palestine. Their appeal was followed by thousands of people—20,000 according to some estimates—who on the morning of Friday, 2 November, gathered in the Azhar Mosque at the center of old Cairo. When they marched to a mass rally in the square of 'Abidīn Palace, the king's residence, they were joined by all sorts of dubious elements, who in the previous hours had already plundered a large number of shops owned by Jews or Europeans in the city center and the Mūskī area. It appears that non-Jewish shopowners had been given previous warning to keep their shops closed. Against Ḥasan al-Bannā's express appeal to disperse after the meeting, crowds of people continued their march through the major shopping areas, broke into the Jewish quarter, looting shops and private homes and assaulting its inhabitants, vandalized the nearby Ashkenazi synagogue and then set it afire. The destruction was not limited to Jewish establishments, for the Greek-Orthodox Patriarchate, Catholic churches, and a Coptic school were equally damaged. Though the Egyptian police were quick to respond, they were unable to prevent the violence and destruction, as they had been ordered not to use their firearms. The riots left four hundred injured, one policeman killed, and an estimated £1 million in property damage.

New demonstrations planned for the following day were largely suppressed. Jewish youth in the Cairo *ḥāra* formed self-defense (*hagana*) units and built road blocks. The authorities took some three-hundred looters to court, but were unable to trace the organizers of what apparently had been a planned attack. The Egyptian prime minister put the blame on the "mob" and the Zionists themselves who, according to him, had provoked such violent reactions.[148] In Alexandria, the demonstrations turned even more violent, leaving at least five people dead. A member of the British embassy noted—to his great relief—that the passions of the demonstrators were clearly directed against the Jews, and not the British. Smaller demonstrations were staged in al-Manṣūra, Port Said, and Ṭanṭā.[149]

The Cairo community council in collaboration with the local Zionist Organization—itself a remarkable phenomenon—prepared a mildly worded note of protest, which Chief Rabbi Haim Nahum sent to Prime Minister Fahmī al-Nuqrāshī Pāshā on 6 November. King Fārūq expressed his deepest regrets concerning these incidents, when he received the chief rabbi the same day. The government also offered to pay for the reconstruction of the Ashkenazi synagogue, destroyed during the attacks.[150] But on 6 and 7 November, the head of the Sufi brotherhoods in Egypt and the head of al-Azhar University called upon the chief rabbi to publicly repudiate Zionism. Haim Nahum initially refused to do so. Allegedly pressured by the court, the government, and René Cattaoui, the president of the Cairo community, he changed his mind and on 9 November sent a second note to the Egyptian prime minister. Referring to a declaration that the communal councils of Cairo and Alexandria had sent to the World Jewish Conference in America in the summer of 1944, he expressed in this note the desire of Egyptian Jews to be recognized as loyal citizens of the Egyptian homeland:

> to form an integral part of this noble nation.... They [Egyptian Jews] do not only consider this a sacred duty, but hope to make their feelings the conduct to be followed in the entire world in settling the Jewish question, supported and reinforced by a demand to the Allies to find the homeless Jews [*sans patrie*] a refuge other than narrow Palestine. With regard to the Palestine issue, there is, as they have [already] recommended, no other solution but close cooperation between Arabs and Jews, in an atmosphere of complete agreement, imbued with confidence and mutual understanding.[151]

According to Haim Nahum, the Jews of Egypt, therefore, hoped that the Allies would find for their persecuted and homeless coreligionists a homeland other than "narrow" Palestine—a declaration amounting to the first public repudiation of Zionism on the part of an official representative of Egyptian Jewry. In their dismay, the local Zionists considered starting a large-scale press campaign in Britain and the United States denouncing this declaration as the "result of terror, blackmail, [that] they link up with the oppression of the Christians in Syria and are one great wave of fashism [*sic*]."[152]

On 9 February 1946, anti-British demonstrations organized by the nationalist, leftist, and Islamic opposition, which were largely unrelated to the Palestine issue, came to a head when twenty students were killed in the so-called massacre of the ʿAbbās bridge in Cairo. In the second half of the 1940s, the series of demonstrations, strikes, and assassinations escalated further. The central theme of the conflict was still total liberation from British control, including the complete withdrawal (*jalāʾ*) of British troops, and the unity of the Nile Valley. Compared to this central issue, the Palestine conflict once more receded into the background.

After World War II, the anti-British struggle unfolded under rapidly changing conditions. Great Britain itself had lost prestige and power compared to the new global powers, the United States and the Soviet Union. Egypt, by joining the initiative to create the Arab League, adopted the pan-Arab line propagated by key political figures such as 'Alī Māhir and 'Abd al-Raḥmān 'Azzām. The participation of an official Egyptian delegation in the London Round Table Conference on Palestine of February 1939 indicated the beginning of practical involvement in Arab affairs. It may be that the Arab card was played by 'Alī Māhir, 'Abd al-Raḥmān 'Azzām, Makram 'Ubayd, and the king primarily for reasons of personal power and aggrandizement. They were indeed anxious to secure for Egypt and its ruling dynasty leadership in the Arab world, for which the Hāshimites and other aspirants to the caliphate were competing. The Wafd and the British, too, pursued their separate interests in supporting the establishment of the Arab League.[153] Yet pan-Arabism was not merely the game of ambitious politicians. The Arab line, if it was rooted in Islam, was already implied in the way most Arab Muslims, and the followers of the Salafīya movement in particular, saw the relationship between Arabism and Islam. In their view, it was the Arabs to whom Islam had first been revealed in their own language and who had founded its glory. Its decline had only set in under the Persians and Turks who were insufficiently assimilated into the superior culture inherited from the Arabs. It was, therefore, the Arabs from whom the rebirth of the *umma* was to be expected. For Muslim Egyptians, therefore, the transition from Egyptian patriotism to pan-Islam and pan-Arabism was not so difficult provided Egypt was not defined in terms of Mediterranean-European but of Arab-Islamic culture. Once this point was agreed, Egypt was the country to which, because of its historic achievements and present potential, leadership in the Muslim Arab world came quasi-naturally.[154] A strong and united Egypt was a precondition of all further unification attempts be they ethnic (pan-Arab) or religious (pan-Islamic). Under changed conditions, Egyptian strength and unity could very well become the ultimate objective again.

For the non-Muslim minorities, the new Arab-Islamic line of foreign and domestic policies created much greater problems of identity and integration than the concept of the territorial nation state advocated by the Wafd and the liberal intellectuals in the 1920s and 1930s. In other parts of the Arab world, Oriental Christians, who had played such a prominent rôle in the Arab renaissance of the preceding decades, tried to compensate for their not being Muslim by stressing their Arab credentials. Oriental Jews faced the same situation. Their dilemma was described by a French diplomat, who wrote in late 1943:

> Among the Egyptians, there is a nationalist, xenophobic fermentation with a strong dose of Islamic fanaticism. Pan-Arab sentiment does not manage to rid itself of this confessional character. As a result, Oriental Christians feel threatened by the advance of pan-Arabism, although they speak Arabic. But the majority regard its success as certain, they do not dare struggle against destiny, they are afraid, and they cry with the wolves in the hope that they will nonetheless be forgiven for not being Muslim if they make themselves as much like Arabs as possible [*arabissime*].[155]

With all their conscious display of Arabism, Christians and Jews could not change the fact that they remained non-Muslims, *dhimmīs* of inferior rights and status, if the Islamic movement should ever succeed in establishing in Egypt an Islamic order modeled on the age of the Prophet.

4

Jewish Reactions to Political Change

Many members of the Egyptian Jewish community were keen observers of the changing political climate in the 1930s and 1940s. They realized that the Jewish minority had to respond to the new challenges. This would mean defining their specific identity, be it as Egyptians of Jewish faith or as Jews from Egypt, as members of the Egyptian or of a separate Jewish nation. With their low-profile strategy, Jewish community leaders had always avoided making a definite stand on political issues other than calling for harmony, cooperation, and mutual understanding, referring to the statutes that did not give them a political mandate.[1] In the 1930s and 1940s, they were forced to confront the issues of nationalism, Islam, Arabism, and Palestine.

In a community so ethnically and culturally diverse, it could hardly be expected that the search for identity and political orientation would follow any single line. In fact, three major trends of varying weight and impact can be distinguished that were, to a certain extent, linked to regional origin and social class: Egyptian patriotism; involvement in the local socialist and communist movement; and Zionism. Responses thus ranged from an attempt to adapt to local conditions and to participate in Egyptian politics—be it in the form of Egyptian nationalism or the struggle against the established order in the country—to ethnic and/or religious particularism, which ultimately, could lead to emigration. The large majority of local Jews, however, remained indifferent to this search for identity. They did not see any grave danger to their security and well-being, and they therefore continued to lead their private lives, hardly involved in the debate about political and cultural change that was going on around them.

EGYPTIAN PATRIOTISM

In the interwar period, only the less well-educated lower and lower-middle classes spoke Arabic as their native tongue, and only about one-fourth of the Jews living in Egypt had Egyptian nationality. As early as 1912, S. Somekh, the director of the Cairo school of the Alliance Israélite Universelle, had lamented the indifference of most Jews to the history and politics of their host country:

> Because of the totally different orientation of their culture, our coreligionists play no rôle whatsoever in the destiny of the country, where they live as strangers. They hold no official function; the administration and the native bar are completely inaccessible to them, and with good reason. They have neglected the Arab culture and language, some because of their exotic origin, the majority out of contempt for all things native.... It would take a national preparation to make them ready for integration into the mass of the natives.[2]

His view was confirmed in later years by numerous local and foreign observers. Some saw abstention from politics as an advantage, which protected local Jews from entanglements in political conflicts that they were too weak to determine in any case. Others, like Somekh, deplored their indifference and apathy, which was frequently combined with a marked sense of superiority over the "natives" and their political preoccupations.[3] Egyptianization in language, nationality, and ultimately in general culture could, moreover, possibly serve a double purpose: to help integrate Jews into Egyptian society, and at the same time to unify a community internally divided along multiple lines of origin, language, and culture. Politically, it was simply expedient to stress national solidarity and Egyptian-Arab identity at a time of intense Egyptian nationalism and rising pan-Arabism.

A number of local Jews had been engaged in the Egyptian national movement of 1919 and had joined the Wafd Party, among them David Hazan, Vita Sonsino, Félix Benzakein, and the ubiquitous Léon Castro. They seem to have remained loyal to the Egyptian cause well into the interwar period. The radical nationalist groups such as Miṣr al-Fatāt with their strong criticism of foreign influence, for obvious reasons, held much less attraction for members of the local foreign minorities. Consequently they do not seem to have had any Jewish members. It is worth mentioning that at least until the late 1930s, even local Zionists supported the national aspirations of the Egyptian people. It was by no means rare to find Egyptian Jews who, like Léon Castro, sympathized and collaborated with both the Egyptian and the Jewish nationalist movements.

In the Senate and the Chamber of Deputies, the Jewish community was represented by several of its leading personalities including Joseph Aslan, and René and Aslan Cattaoui, Joseph Elie Picciotto, Félix Benzakein, and Chief Rabbi Haim Nahum, who emphasized their loyalty to king and country. In 1924–25, Joseph Aslan Cattaoui even served in two successive cabinets, first as minister of finance and later as minister of communications. Murād Faraj, the eminent Karaite lawyer, poet, and writer, composed poems in classical Arabic style (*qaṣā'id*), which dealt with the common heritage of Jews and Arabs. At the same time, he worked actively on behalf of closer cooperation between Karaite and Rabbanite Jews.[4]

Until the mid-thirties, these personalities remained essentially isolated. It was only in September 1934 that a group of Jewish writers and journalists around Sa'd Ya'qūb Mālkī, a teacher and former writer with the Zionist paper *Israël*, began publishing *al-Shams*. It was the first Arabic Jewish paper of any importance in Egypt and was published weekly until June 1948.[5] A few months later, in July 1935, the same group founded a youth club in the Cairo Jewish *ḥāra* called Association de la Jeunesse Juive Egyptienne (Jam'īyat al-Shubbān al-Yahūd al-Miṣrīyīn). Their slogan was "Fatherland, Faith, and Culture," and *al-Shams* was their press forum. Besides Mālkī himself, the group included Dr. Alfred Yallouz (1898–?), a journalist, Dr. Hilāl Farḥī (1867–1940), a medical doctor and writer, and Dr. Israel Wolfensohn (Ben Ze'ev) (?–1980), a professor of literature and former student of Ṭāhā Ḥusayn. All three were former members of the Société d'Etudes Historiques Juives founded in 1925, who had written scholarly works on the history and literature of the Arab world and Middle Eastern Jewry.[6]

It was the declared aim of the association and its weekly to make the local Jews aware of their Jewish heritage and at the same time to promote a sense of Egyptian identity and patriotism.[7] To a certain extent, they shared the aims of the local Zionists, and it is no coincidence that Wolfensohn, Yallouz, and Castro were actively involved in both movements. The distinction was mainly one of emphasis: the Egyptian patriots wanted to turn their coreligionists into Jewish Egyptians, whereas the primary aim of the Zionists was, of course, to educate Egyptian Jews in the spirit of Jewish nationalism. Patriotic clubs and unions were popular at the time among other groups such as the Greeks. The association met with some response among Jewish youth, but had attracted a mere fifty members by 1941.[8]

The champions of Egyptianization found influential allies among communal leaders in Cairo. As mentioned earlier, Joseph Aslan Cattaoui saw himself as an Egyptian of Jewish faith, who took an active part in the economic and political life of the country. Chief Rabbi Haim Nahum, too, emphasized his loyalty to the Egyptian nation and called upon local Jews to adopt Egyptian nationality.[9] The weekly *al-Shams* and the association went one step further in proclaiming their solidarity with the Wafd Party. In December 1935, they sent a delegation to meet Muṣṭafā al-Naḥḥās in order to declare their support for the national front, which had been formed to negotiate a treaty with Britain. Moreover, they stressed once again that the Jews did not desire any British guarantees for their position, since Egypt had neither a majority nor minorities, but only citizens who were all equal before the law. In the 1940s, the association joined the universal call for the evacuation of British troops from Egypt and for the unity of the Nile Valley. After the violent demonstrations of February 1946, religious services were held in all synagogues to commemorate the Egyptian "martyrs"; the association collected £E 800 for their families, and in March 1946 participated in a general strike against British military presence.[10]

Regarding the Palestine question, the association advocated cooperation and peaceful coexistence between Jews and Arabs. It stressed not only the cultural traditions shared by both peoples, but also the racial affinities, which, according to this view, united them as Semites (*al-jins al-sāmī*). This cultural and racial affinity of Jews and Arabs was also claimed by members of the Zionist movement, who propagated the theme of "the Jews as Orientals" returning to their ancestral home in Palestine to live in harmony with their Arab brothers.[11] The association welcomed the establishment in Palestine of a national home for the Jews (from other parts of the world), and *al-Shams* reported extensively on the progress of Zionist settlement there. However, it also emphasized the fact that regardless of what was going to happen to Palestine, Egyptian Jews would always continue to be loyal Egyptian citizens.[12]

The appeals to local Jews to fully integrate (*indamaja*) into Egyptian society, to participate in its cultural and political life, to learn Arabic and to wear the tarboosh, met with only limited success. In the elections of 1936, not a single Jew stood for Parliament, and when in 1938, Rabbi Jacob Toledano called upon local Jews to contribute to a project on the history of Egyptian Jewry, he received no response. The Société d'Etudes Historiques Juives was completely inactive by the late forties.[13] Egyptianization of the community, which was largely defined in terms of adopting Arabic as the official language at school and in council meetings, advanced with difficulty. While an Egyptian curriculum was introduced in the community schools of Cairo and Alexandria in the early thirties, French, Italian or English remained the chief languages of instruction in the private schools attended by the middle and upper classes.[14]

When Joseph Aslan Cattaoui, the active supporter of Egyptianization, died in 1942, *al-Shams* mounted a campaign to elect his younger son, René Cattaoui, whom they promoted as the only representative of "true" Egyptian Jewry. The association used the occasion to call for comprehensive reforms in community organization, which was to be transformed from a group of French-speaking notables into a real communal council (*majlis millī*) made up of Arabic-speaking Egyptian nationals. René Cattaoui was indeed elected in April 1943, but resigned in the summer of 1946 without having realized these objectives. When his successor, Salvator bey Cicurel, was elected, the question of Egyptianization and Arabization seems no longer to have been an issue.[15] The patriotic movement never attracted more than a few dozen registered members and a number of sympathizers in literary and intellectual circles. In spite of the support of prominent communal leaders, it failed to reach its ultimate aim, to Arabize, Egyptianize, and homogenize the Jewish community in Egypt.

COMMUNISM

Involvement in the local communist movement could also be seen as an attempt to participate in the political life of the country, and to integrate into Egyptian society. But it implied a much more radical approach to the dilemmas facing non-Muslim minorities in a society under colonial rule. It was an attempt not to adapt to the sociopolitical order, but to transform it so as to make possible peaceful coexistence among Muslims, Christians, and Jews. This attempt brought its advocates few gains. In fact, the prominent position of Jewish activists in the local communist movement was frequently used to discredit both the communists as being dominated by foreign (Zionist) elements, and the local Jewish community as being a hotbed of communism and a danger to the established sociopolitical order in the country. In September 1948, the Egyptian prime minister, Maḥmūd Fahmī al-Nuqrāshī Pāshā, told a British diplomat that the mass arrest of Zionists, communists, and other enemies of the regime served a double purpose, because: "[S]olely as a result of Egyptian armed intervention in Palestine he, Noqrashi, had been able to round up and intern the most dangerous communists here. Not only that but there had been intensified research here on the subject and this had revealed that the Jews as a whole were so much involved in, or on the fringe of, Communism as to be indistinguishable as a general rule from Communists whether overt or suspect." And that:

"[A]ll Jews were potential Zionists, but that anyhow all Zionists were Communists, and he looked at the matter as much from the point of view of Communism as from the point of view of Zionism.... This Zionist/Communist combination in connection with the Palestine affair was a danger to all non-Communist states etc. etc."[16]

Sir Ronald Campbell, to whom these revelations were addressed, had good reason to be surprised. Even in the 1940s, when the leftist movement had won over large sections of educated Jewish youth, communists and Zionists were still a minority among Egyptian Jewry. Individual Jews had been prominent in the local labor and communist movements since the late-nineteenth century, but these were isolated cases. Soon after the first Russian revolution of February 1905, a small group of Ashkenazi immigrants, members of the socialist Jewish Bund, arrived in Egypt. They settled in the Ashkenazi quarter of Cairo, the Darb al-Barābira, where they propagated socialist internationalism and fought against the local Zionists. Their activities, however, remained largely restricted to the Russian- or Yiddish-speaking Ashkenazi minority living in this enclave.[17]

Of much greater importance to the communist movement was another immigrant of Russian origin, Joseph Rosenthal, a well-to-do jeweler born in Beirut in 1867, who, since his arrival in Alexandria in the 1890s, became active in the local trade union movement.[18] He began by acquainting members of the foreign colonies with Marxist ideas, and in 1920 joined a number of leftists in founding the first socialist organization in Egypt, the Groupe d'Etudes Sociales. Together with a small group of Egyptians including Salāma Mūsā, Muḥammad 'Abd Allāh 'Inān, and Ḥusnī al-'Arabī, he founded the Egyptian Socialist Party (al-Ḥizb al-Ishtirākī al-Miṣrī) in August 1921, which followed a nationalist, moderately socialist course until it joined the Third International (Comintern) in 1922–23. Before being admitted, though, it had to adopt a clearly defined communist program, change its name accordingly, and expel Rosenthal, who was accused of harboring anarchist sympathies. His daughter Charlotte, however, who was married to one of the delegates of the Comintern in Egypt named "Avigdor," was elected to the central committee in 1924. Rosenthal himself was readmitted in 1924–25, and seems to have died in 1927.

The Egyptian Communist Party, which throughout the 1920s was very active in the local labor and trade union movement, claimed about 1,500 adherents in March 1923, and, according to Comintern figures, had 700 members in 1924. It maintained its contacts with the Comintern mainly through a number of local Soviet trade agents and was linked to the stronger communist movement of Palestine through Ashkenazi Jewish activists, who were also prominently represented within the party itself. As a result of frequent arrests, its cadres were severely reduced, and by the late 1920s, the party had ceased functioning.[19]

The striking presence of Jewish activists of foreign origin in the Egyptian communist movement had negative effects on the movement itself as well as on the local Jewish community. Inside the Egyptian Communist Party, Egyptian activists headed by Ḥusnī al-'Arabī, who in 1922–23 had been active in ousting Rosenthal, conducted a campaign against the presence of foreigners in general and Jews in particular, which it was felt discredited the movement in the eyes of potential (Muslim and Coptic) Egyptian sympathizers.[20] At the same time, the Egyptian and British authorities were gravely concerned about Soviet ("Bolshevic") influence on the local communist and labor movements. They tried to restrict the entry and transit of Russian Jews, or of Jews of Russian origin, arriving from Palestine, including representatives of the Zionist movement such as David Ben Gurion and Yitzhak Ben Zvi. In February 1929, the British high commissioner in Palestine, Sir John Chancellor, reported to London that the Egyptian government seemed "to refuse visas for Egypt to Palestine citizens of Russian origin, solely because of their previous nationality or provenance" as it assumed that "the terms Russian, 'bolshevic' and 'communist' are synonymous."[21] To this the British high commissioner in Cairo, Lord George Lloyd, replied that: "It should be made clear ... that it is not only in the case of 'Palestine citizens of Russian origin' that special procedure is applied but to all persons of Russo-Jewish origin whatever may be their present national status. The Ministry of the Interior ... justify their action by the fact that of 81 foreigners who since 1923 have come under their notice in connection with communist propaganda no fewer than 35 have been of Russo-Jewish origin."[22]

However, in the 1920s the local Jewish community was not yet in danger of being identified with communism, and linked to a foreign power regarded as hostile by both the Egyptian and the British authorities. The communist movement was still too small to be perceived as a threat to Jewish life in the country. Indeed it was hardly noticed by the overwhelming majority of local Jews, who were, after all, not of Ashkenazi, but of Oriental and Sephardi origin.

Under the impact of the world economic crisis and the rise of fascism in central Europe, the leftist movement became increasingly more active in the mid-thirties. Like the early labor movement, leftist activism originated with the local foreign colonies, Greeks, Italians, Armenians, and Jews. Together with a number of Western-educated Egyptian intellectuals, these foreigners founded Marxist study circles that published journals such as *Les Essayistes* (1931), *L'Effort* (1930s, both directed by Léon Castro), *La Gerbe* (Isaac Lévi), and *Art et Liberté* (1939, Georges Henein). In those years, the leftist movement was, at least as far as its foreign members were concerned, closely linked to the antifascist struggle and its attention was primarly focused on European events. In 1935, a Swiss journalist, Paul Jacot-Descombes, founded the Ligue Pacifiste, which was affiliated with the Rassemblement Universel pour la Paix (Universal Peace League). Its membership was made up almost exclusively of foreigners, most of them Greek or Jewish, but it also cooperated with the Egyptian Women's Movement and leftist circles within the Wafd. Relations with the Italian antifascist groups were also close. The Jewish anti-Nazi organization of the LICA, by contrast, was closer to Zionism. The main contribution of the antifascist movement consisted of acquainting local intellectuals with Marxist thought, some of whom were later to break out of the European ghetto to build a communist movement among Muslim and Coptic Egyptians.[23]

Within the Muslim and Coptic majority of the population, socialism and communism only began to gain ground during World War II. Economic hardship and international shifts in power, including notably the decline of the fascist Axis and the rise of the Soviet Union, combined to create much more favorable conditions for leftist thought and action. Among foreigners and local minorities, the antifascist struggle had created widespread interest in socialism. In 1941–42, members of the antifascist organizations and of the older debating clubs, some of them ancient cadres of the Egyptian Communist Party, established new Marxist study circles, which operated among foreign and Egyptian intellectuals. The Groupe d'Etudes, which was founded by Jacot-Descombes in 1939 to succeed the Ligue Pacifiste, for a short period included among its twenty to thirty members virtually all the Jewish activists who were to direct the communist movement in the 1940s. The Union Démocratique, which was formed in the same year, recruited its members mainly among Italian antifascists and had a large following in the French lycées in Cairo and Alexandria, which were attended by Jewish middle-class youth. By contrast, its membership included few Muslim Egyptians. The membership lists of these groups read like a who's who of the communist movement of the forties and fifties, including Marcel Israël, Henri and Raoul Curiel, Hillel Schwartz, Raymond Aghion, and Ezra Harari, to name only some of the most prominent Jewish activists. But the wide range of personalities, ideas, and convictions united in the Union Démocratique were a constant source of conflict and division. During the course of the 1940s, internal dissension was to drive the communist movement into a confusing cycle of coalition, split-up, reconciliation, merger, new conflict, and new rupture that is impossible to describe here in adequate detail.[24]

Internal debate and conflict, if it was not simply based on personal rivalries, generally revolved around three issues: national versus social struggle, Egyptianization (*tamṣīr*), and proletarization (*ta'mīl*). Under the impact of Arabism and the Palestine issue, the question of priorities (national versus social struggle) was hotly debated. In the evaluation of the communist movement at large, and of its individual members, their stand on Arab nationalism and Palestine turned out to be as important as their achievements in social struggle. Egyptianization and proletarization referred to the question of whether in a nonindustrialized country like Egypt communist activity ought to focus on the intelligentsia, among whom foreigners and minorities were heavily represented, or whether it ought from the beginning to work among Egyptian peasants and industrial workers. All three issues were of special relevance to Jewish activists. It should be mentioned that Jews were to be found in all camps.

In 1942–43, several groups formed around certain former members of the Union Démocratique—Henri Curiel, Marcel Israël, Hillel Schwartz, and Aḥmad Ṣādiq Sa'd—that represented the various currents of leftist thought. They included in the first place the Mouvement Egyptien pour la Libération Nationale (MELN, al-Ḥaraka al-Miṣrīya lil-Taḥarrur al-Waṭanī) headed by Henri Curiel (1914–78). Curiel came from a wealthy Sephardi family; his father was a banker of Italian nationality and he himself was French-educated. He joined a variety of Marxist study circles and in 1941 opened a stationery and bookshop (Le Rond Point) in Cairo, which became one of the meeting places of leftist and antifascist circles. Through this bookshop and a cadre seminar, Curiel succeeded in training a considerable number of (Muslim and Coptic) Egyptian and Jewish activists. Curiel advocated a strategy of Egyptianization, and MELN did, in fact, include only a limited number of foreigners among its five-hundred to six-hundred members, who were organized in a separate section. According to Curiel himself, students made up 16 percent and workers 50 percent of a total of five-hundred members in June 1947.[25] However, workers seem to have been underrepresented at the leadership level. Egyptianization was also the aim of the Popular Liberation Organization (Taḥrīr al-Sha'b), headed by Marcel Israël, which published a number of widely read papers such as *al-Majalla al-Jadīda*, *al-Usbū'* and *al-Taṭawwur*, and of the New Dawn group (al-Fajr al-Jadīd), headed by Aḥmad Ṣādiq Sa'd, Yūsuf Darwīsh, Raymond Douec, and Aḥmad Rushdī Ṣāliḥ. New Dawn saw itself as part of the Egyptian national movement, cooperated closely with the Wafdist left and admitted only a small number of foreigners.[26]

The opposite line was advocated by a group formed by Hillel Schwartz known as Iskra/al-Sharāra (The Spark). Iskra's aim, which it propagated through its newspaper *al-Jamāhīr*, was to increase training and education of intellectuals, foreigners, and minorities. Its membership was recruited primarily from students and foreigners, and in 1945, foreigners alone accounted for 40 percent of its nine-hundred members. Because of its focus on training the intellectual cadres of a future communist mass movement, and the Western life-style of its members, its female cadres in particular, Iskra was heavily criticized by the rival communist organizations.[27]

After World War II, the communist organizations were at last able to go beyond the limited circle of foreigners and local foreign minorities and to reach wider sections of the urban Muslim population. The formation of student and workers' committees in February 1946 gave them added weight in the political arena. In July 1946, when the government of Ismā'īl Ṣidqī Pāshā adopted a hard line to suppress the emerging communist movement, arresting its leading cadres, suspending its publications and dissolving its organizations, the leftist activists went underground. In the new alliances that were formed, the major rivals, MELN and Iskra, merged to become the Mouvement Démocratique pour la Libération Nationalc (MDLN, al-Ḥaraka al-Dīmuqrāṭīya lil-Taḥarrur al-Waṭanī, HADITU). Membership quickly rose to several thousand and its weekly *al-Jamāhīr* attained relatively wide circulation. However, HADITU survived only until shortly after the wave of arrests of May 1948, when it split into several rivaling factions.[28]

HADITU was organized into a number of sections—students, workers, intellectuals, women, the army, Sudanese, and foreigners, among whom Jews were strongly represented—and inherited from Iskra and MELN the high percentage of students, intellectuals, and foreigners (about 60%) and a corresponding dearth of (Muslim) Egyptian workers (28%). In spite of this membership bias, it was actively involved in the labor movement of the late forties. HADITU also inherited the controversy over the appropriate rôle of foreigners, or to be more precise: of non-Muslims and Jews in particular, in the communist movement. Moreover, HADITU, which viewed itself as part and parcel of the Egyptian national liberation movement, had to define its position with regard to Palestine. Following the Soviet line, it called first for the creation of a secular democratic state in Palestine uniting Jews and Arabs (the binational solution), but later had to reverse its stand in favor of partition and the establishment of two separate states for the Jews and Arabs respectively. By first opposing Zionism as a bourgeois movement allied to imperialism, and later endorsing its central aspiration, the establishment of a Jewish state in Palestine, HADITU and the other communist groups adopting the Soviet position became isolated from Egyptian and Arab nationalist circles.[29]

That Jews were among the most prominent communist activists was bound to cast additional doubt on their motives. It, therefore, seemed almost inevitable that the presence of so many Jews in conspicuous leadership positions would be regarded as highly compromising by many Egyptian party members. Criticism of the Jewish rôle in the movement increased markedly during the Arab-Israeli war of 1948. A small number of Jewish activists like Aḥmad Ṣādiq Sa'd, Yūsuf Darwīsh (a Karaite), and Raymond Douec sought the solution in conversion to Islam.[30] Others tried to establish their credentials by actively combating Zionism among the local Jewish community.

In 1945, several young people led by Ezra Harari, a member of the central committee of Iskra, formed a cultural section within one branch of the Maccabi sports club in Cairo. In April 1947, they challenged the Zionist candidates in the elections for the Maccabi board, and when, as a result of manipulation, the Zionists were elected, violence erupted. The new leadership called in the police, who immediately arrested the communists—the element that seemed to pose a greater threat to public security than the Zionists. After their release, the communists reported the incident to the Wafdist paper *Ṣawt al-Umma*, which published a series of articles attacking local Zionists, Egyptian Jews, and the Egyptian authorities for allowing the Zionists to operate openly. Harari's group also formed the Ligue Juive contre le Sionisme "Egypte" (al-Rābiṭa al-Isrā'īlīya li-Mukāfaḥat al-Ṣahyūnīya) with branches in Cairo and Alexandria. Their main objective was to fight Zionist activity and to make the public realize that not all Jews living in Egypt were Zionists.[31] In May 1947, this Anti-Zionist League distributed an appeal in Arabic and French to all Jews in Egypt, which condemned Zionism as a tool of British imperialism:

Appeal to the Jews of Egypt

Jewish Brothers!

The Zionists pretend to solve the Jewish problem. They pretend to defend the interests of our community. [What a] lie....

Jewish Mothers!

We want to prevent your children becoming the victims of the TREACHEROUS ILLUSIONS of Zionist propaganda, which wants to send them to Palestine to live in the midst of the hostility of the majority of the population and under a regime of pogromlike oppression.

Jewish Men! Jewish Women!

Zionism wants to throw us into a dangerous and hopeless adventure. Zionism contributes to making Palestine uninhabitable. Zionism wants to isolate us from the Egyptian people. Zionism is the enemy of the Jewish people.

Down with Zionism!
Long live the brotherhood of Jews and Arabs!
Long live the Egyptian people![32]

A similar manifesto calling on the Jews to participate in the national liberation struggle was seized by the police in June

1947. The Anti-Zionist League was disbanded ("for reasons of public security"). But Harari did not give up. By December 1947, he had founded the Forum group, a new anti-Zionist organization within the Iskra faction of HADITU, which, according to a British report, had "a considerable following among the Jewish community in Cairo." In fact, its influence seems to have been limited to the Jewish left and did not reach the majority of the Jewish community or the communist movement, let alone the general Egyptian public.[33]

During the 1940s, many middle- and upper-class Jewish students of French secondary schools, notably those of the Mission Laique Française, became interested in Marxism. After World War II, progressive ideas were rather fashionable even among the gilded youth of Jewish high society. Members of the Zionist movement, which remained largely restricted to lower and lower-middle class youth, who as a rule went to community schools and tended to be less well educated, scorned the verbal radicalism (*Salonkommunismus*) of the high school students.[34] But they ignored the fact that many of these communists went to prison in the successive waves of arrests, as the Egyptian government took the communists much more seriously than their Zionist opponents. The Jewish community in general risked being identified not only with Zionism allied to imperialism as the major external threat to national security, but also with communism as the gravest danger to internal security and the ruling order. Prime Minister Fahmī al-Nuqrāshī clearly expressed these suspicions, and leftist activists paid dearly for them in 1948.

Jews remained active in the communist groups that formed after the Arab-Israeli war of 1948, even though by that time most of their rank and file as well as their leadership were Muslim Egyptians. In spite of a series of defections, HADITU remained the largest communist organization; its membership rose from 100 to 200 in February 1950 to 2,000 to 3,000 in late 1952. At the time, its activities were no longer limited to students and workers, but also reached into the villages of the Egyptian countryside.[35] In December 1948, a number of activists headed by Odette Hazan, who dismissed HADITU as too moderate and too ineffective, decided to create a new communist organization, dedicated to completing Egyptianization and proletarization ("100% workers"). Ironically, it was made up almost exclusively of foreigners, university graduates, and professionals, most of them Jews. Within a year it had lost its initial 500 adherents. In September 1949, Hillel Schwartz formed yet another group called Toward an Egyptian Communist Party (Naḥwa Ḥizb Shuyūʿī Miṣrī), but its leadership including Schwartz himself was arrested as early as March 1950.

By the autumn of 1949, all communist activists interned because of the war had been released. The new Wafdist government expelled several stateless or foreign activists including Henri Curiel (August 1950). Marcel Israël, Hillel Schwartz, and a number of other prominent Jewish cadres also left the country. From the beginning of 1950, HADITU, which continued to be the largest communist organization in the country, as well as the new Communist Party of Egypt that was formed in January 1950 and the National Peace Committee (Ḥarakat Anṣār al-Salām), which followed suit in February 1950, had a purely Egyptian leadership. While Jews were still active in these groups, they no longer occupied any exposed leadership positions.[36] In spite of this, several court cases of the early 1950s were still labeled "Zionist-Communist trials," showing once again how difficult it was for the press and the general public to separate the Jews, and the anti-Zionist communist Jews in particular, from the Zionists.[37]

ZIONISM

By the 1940s, Zionism had a rather long, but not very distinguished history in Egypt. Up to World War I, its influence was confined to lower and lower-middle class immigrants of Ashkenazi and, to a lesser extent, of Oriental origin, who were held in rather low regard by their Sephardi coreligionists. In 1897, Marco Barukh (1872–99), a young activist from Bulgaria, founded the first Zionist association in the Ashkenazi Darb al-Barābira quarter in Cairo. The Bar Kokhba Society numbered some three-hundred Ashkenazi and Sephardi members in 1901, but was disbanded shortly after in 1906. It was followed by a number of equally short-lived groups in Cairo, Alexandria, Port Said, Ṭanṭā, and al-Manṣūra. Most of them were rendered ineffective because of tensions among their members, who, while they were all young, poor, and inexperienced, differed widely in their origin, language, and cultural background.[38] Yet in 1913, S. Somekh, who in general was highly critical of Zionism, had to concede that Zionist educational activities had created a definite religious revival within the local community. In 1913, there were over eight-hundred regular contributors to the Zionist fund Keren Kayemet le-Yisra'el, but only eighty subscribers to the largest Zionist paper of the prewar era, *La Renaissance Juive* (1912–14). The spread of Zionism in Egypt was hampered not only by the poverty and inexperience of its activists, but also by the indifference of the Sephardi majority, and by the condescending hostility of its leaders, who saw Theodor Herzl, the founder of the Zionist movement, as a mere *Shnorrer* (money grubber).[39]

World War I brought the Zionist movement its first major flowering. In April 1915, the Zionist leader Vladimir Jabotinsky was able to recruit 600 men for a Zion mule corps, which fought with the British army at Gallipoli.[40] Between 1914 and 1918, more than 11,000 Ashkenazi Jews expelled from Palestine found refuge in Alexandria and Cairo, where their educational and cultural activities made an impression on the local Jewish population. While most of the refugees returned to Palestine or Eastern Europe after the war, quite a few remained to become active in the local Zionist movement.[41] In 1917–18, the calls for urgent relief for the Jewish settlers in Palestine were answered by the Special Relief Fund in Cairo, which had Zionist sympathies, and a rivaling non-Zionist Jewish relief fund in Alexandria.[42] The groundwork of educating the public about Zionist aspirations had already been accomplished, when in November 1917 the Balfour Declaration was issued. At Chaim Weizmann's insistence, Egypt's first mass Zionist rally was held in Cairo on 28 October and was attended by over 3,000 community members, who "enthusiastically" welcomed the forthcoming declaration.

Weizmann received the telegram he had asked for: "This Mass Meeting of Jews of Egypt unanimously favours reconstitution of Palestine as National Home of Jewish People and trusts that His Majesty's Government will use its best endeavours to facilitate achievement of this object."[43]

A similar meeting was held in Alexandria on 11 November 1917, which attracted between 7,000 and 8,000 community members. These enthusiastic scenes were repeated in 1918, when the newly formed Jewish Legion and the Zionist Commission headed by Chaim Weizmann passed through Egypt to be cheered by thousands in the streets of Cairo and Alexandria.[44]

The mass participation of the Jewish public in national meetings seemed to augur well for the Zionist movement in 1917–18. After all previous attempts to centralize the movement had failed, the Comité d'Action in Copenhagen made a fresh effort in June 1917 and created the new Zionist Federation of Egypt (Fédération des Sionistes d'Egypte). Its committee included a number of lawyers, medical doctors, and businessmen, most of them Ashkenazim. The committee was headed by Jack N. Mosseri (1884–1934), a member of the influential Mosseri family, who was one of the very few Sephardi élite members to sympathize with political Zionism.[45] It was hoped, therefore, that as a man of means, prestige, and connections he would be able to make Zionism more acceptable to his circle of friends and relatives, who dominated the Jewish communities of Cairo and Alexandria.

In January 1918, the first issue of *La Revue Sioniste* (1918–24) was distributed, which was to serve as the official organ of the federation. It was followed, in July 1920, by an independent Zionist paper *Israël*, which was edited by Albert D. Mosseri (1868–1933), a medical doctor, cousin of Jack Mosseri, and early convert to Zionism. Of the three original editions in French, Hebrew, and Arabic only the French continued after his death. It was published by his Palestinian-born wife, Mazal Mathilda (née Mani), until 1939, when she returned to Palestine.[46] In August 1918, a group of Alexandrian notables sympathetic to the Zionist movement, including Félix de Menasce, Joseph Elie de Picciotto, Alfred N. Cohen, and Léon Nacmias, founded the Pro-Palestina Committee. While they declared it was to be a "purely humanitarian," meaning, nonpolitical and non-Zionist organization, they cooperated with the Zionist Organization of Alexandria. Together with the lodges of the B'nai B'rith, they helped to finance an information office of the Zionist Organization of Alexandria, which between 1920 and 1927, assisted in settling some 12,000 European Jews in Palestine.[47] Public meetings again took place in May 1920 to celebrate the decision of the San Remo Conference to recognize the British Mandate over Palestine. The Alexandria meeting passed a resolution stressing both the assembled's deep attachment to Egypt and their joy at this event, which would guarantee a haven of refuge for their dispersed coreligionists.[48]

A delegation of notables representing the communities of Cairo and Alexandria called on the British high commissioner, Sir Edmund Allenby, to express their warmest thanks and congratulations. At the same time, the first Zionists were elected to the community councils of Alexandria and the Ashkenazi community in Cairo, which even formed a special Commission for Zionist Affairs.[49] The British Residency, to whom the Zionist Federation had offered, as early as August 1917, "any service that the Authorities might ask of them," did little to restrict Zionist activity in Egypt. The British did, however, control the spread of news regarding Palestine, both anti-Zionist and pro-Zionist, if it were deemed liable to "harm Arab susceptibilities."[50]

And yet the favorable conditions existing under benevolent British surveillance were not in themselves sufficient to keep the Zionist Federation alive. Because of personal tensions and rivalries, Jack Mosseri resigned from the federation and the *Revue Sioniste* to join Chaim Weizmann's Zionist Commission in April 1918. The federation lost control over its two major branches in Cairo and Alexandria, where the local Zionist organizations and various other Zionist groups continued to work independently and without much coordination. A series of reshuffles within the Zionist Organization of Cairo, which was torn by internal dissension, could not halt the process of disintegration. Membership declined from three hundred in April 1923 to one hundred in March 1924 and a mere eighty in 1927. Conditions were hardly any better in Alexandria.[51] The *Revue Sioniste*, which had had four-hundred subscribers in 1918, but was suspended several times, ceased publishing in 1924.[52]

Activities centered mainly on organizing lectures, balls, and soirées, distributing information in French, Arabic, and Hebrew, assisting non-Egyptian *'olim* (immigrants to Palestine), and collecting the *sheḳel* (membership fee in the Zionist Organization), as well as contributions to the Jewish national funds. But contributions were never as high as might have been expected from a community with as prosperous a middle and upper class as that of Egypt. Between 1901 and 1943, the Keren Kayemet le-Yisra'el had received 26,000 Palestinian pounds, roughly equaling £E 25,000.[53] Enough *sheḳalim* were collected, however, so that the Egyptian movement could be represented at the various World Zionist congresses. In 1925, one-hundred members of the Egyptian community attended the inauguration of the Hebrew University in Jerusalem, and with them came the head of Cairo University, Aḥmad Luṭfī al-Sayyid. At about the same time, a cultural center, Bet ha-'Am, was opened in Alexandria and a group of upper-class women founded an Egyptian branch of the Women's International Zionist Organization. All efforts to resuscitate the Zionist Federation, however, were doomed to failure.[54]

In the summer of 1929, when news of the Wailing Wall incidents in Jerusalem reached Egypt, the leaders of the Cairo community intervened with the Egyptian authorities to stop Palestinian propaganda against Zionism and the Jews. At the same time they urged the local Zionists to suspend all overt activities. The latter obliged, and the Zionist organizations, whose influence had been on the wane for a number of years, went into hibernation.[55] In a letter to the Keren Kayemet le-Yisra'el dated 19 December 1929, representatives of the Cairo Zionist Organization wrote: "You will understand that the concern to preserve intact the longstanding friendship between the Arabs and Jews of Egypt has obliged our chiefs to stop all Zionist work here, all public references to the unfortunate events in Palestine, all festivities in favor of Zionist funds."[56]

In spite of a total ban on fund-raising for the Palestine *yishuv* passed by Chief Rabbi Haim Nahum in February 1930, collections for the national funds were carried out secretly and under various guises.[57] But there was opposition in the community against such activities, which seemed liable to compromise the Jews in their country of residence. A Zionist activist reported from Alexandria in March 1930:

> It is not only that people are frightened, but a decided animosity and antipathy to Zionist aims has sprung up. They look upon it as something that threatens their own peace and must be discouraged. The doors have been completely shut, with a solid determination not to allow anything to be done.[58]

Hitler's rise to power in Germany definitely strengthened the concern among Egyptian Jews for Jewish affairs in general and for Palestine in particular. In May 1933, Jewish notables in Cairo and Alexandria formed (separate) committees to help German Jewish emigrants settle in Palestine. These were organized on strictly humanitarian, that is, non-Zionist lines.[59] The LICA and the local Jewish press covered events in Germany and Europe in great detail. But the Zionist movement proper did not profit much from this growing interest in Judaism and Palestine, even though quite an impressive number of Zionist clubs sprang up in Cairo and Alexandria. Most were cultural in orientation, but some, for the first time, engaged in pioneer work and *'aliya*, notably ha-'Ivri ha-Tsa'ir (founded in Cairo in 1932) and he-Ḥaluts (Cairo, June 1933 and Alexandria, July 1934).[60] All these organizations remained small, with membership ranging between fifteen and thirty. The pioneer groups excepted, they were all short-lived. The Zionist Organization of Alexandria had three-hundred paying members in 1937, and its Cairo counterpart an estimated one hundred to two hundred.[61]

One of the groups most active at the time was the revisionist movement, affiliated with Vladimir Jabotinsky, who in 1935 separated from the General Zionist Organization. The revisionists, led by the journalist Albert Staraselski, were particularly influential among Italian Jews in Alexandria, some of whom were moreover suspected of harboring fascist sympathies. According to a later activist, members were mostly Sephardim (i.e., Sephardi and Oriental Jews) of lower- and lower-middle class background, including many workers and a few professionals, but no students. Between 1931 and 1934, Staraselski even edited his own Zionist revisionist paper *La Voix Juive*.[62]

During the Arab revolt of 1936–39, Egypt, for the first time, became involved in the Palestine conflict. Members of the radical nationalist and Islamic opposition began to attack Egyptian Jews in general as Zionism's alleged fifth column. In 1938–39, anti-Zionist and anti-Jewish agitation rose sharply, and Jewish fears of local reactions to the Palestine conflict increased accordingly. The community leaders responded precisely as they had under less serious circumstances in 1929, and as they did in all situations involving a potential threat to Jewish security in Egypt. They intervened privately with the Egyptian authorities and leading politicians, enlisted the support of the British embassy and other foreign representatives, paid high sums of money to the local Arab press, and asked the local Zionist leaders to stop all open activities. Once again the Zionists concurred.[63] Funds destined for the Jewish settlers (*yishuv*) in Palestine continued to be collected in secret with improving results.[64] But of the many Zionist groups established in the early 1930s, only ha-ʻIvri ha-Tsaʻir in Cairo and he-Ḥaluts in Alexandria were still active in 1939. By the outbreak of World War II, the Zionist organizations had almost ceased to exist.[65]

There are many reasons for the relative weakness of Zionism in Egypt throughout the interwar period, and beyond. Among them was the language problem. From the outset there had been a lack of Zionist material in the locally spoken languages, notably French and Arabic, and it remained scarce until the end.[66]

Certificates permitting legal immigration to Palestine were also scarce. The authorities in Palestine gave preference to Jewish immigrants from areas of persecution, that is, Europe, and to those who were physically able and properly trained to do manual work. This regional and occupational bias went against Egyptian applicants, most of whom belonged to the commercial and white-collar middle class. The small number of certificates allocated to Egypt, never exceeding fifteen to twenty per year, failed to meet the demand of the pioneering youth movements. Motivation to engage in Zionist activity consequently suffered.

However, as Zionist activists themselves stated, Egyptian Jews did not show much inclination to go to Palestine in the period before 1948. According to the Israeli census of 1961, 890 Jews immigrated from Egypt and the Sudan in the period up to 1931; 1,145 followed between 1932 and 1939, and another 1,985 between 1940 and 1947.[67] Many of these *'olim* were Oriental Jews from Yemen, Aden or Morocco, or Ashkenazi Jews from Eastern Europe, who, for various reasons, had been forced to interrupt their journey to Palestine. They proceeded on to Palestine as soon as conditions permitted.[68]

Far more important than the lack of information about Zionism, immigration certificates, and forceful speakers attracting large audiences were several internal factors that limited Zionist success among Egyptian Jewry. One of these, always mentioned by both Zionist and non-Zionist observers, was truly basic: the security and material comfort enjoyed by the broad middle and upper classes of Egyptian Jewry, and the absence of anti-Jewish or anti-Semitic feelings in the general Egyptian public. Militant groups like Miṣr al-Faṭāt and the Muslim Brotherhood were, until the late 1930s, dismissed as the radical fringe, not to be taken seriously so long as they were not backed by influential politicians or the government. There was no Jewish question in Egypt in the interwar period, and Egyptian Jews had not developed the specific sense of suffering known to their Eastern European coreligionists. As a consequence, they did not regard Zionism as an issue relevant to their own situation.

When aid and investment were provided to build up the national home in Palestine, it was primarily for humanitarian and economic reasons, and they were suspended in times of crisis. Financial and press support of the Jewish settlers, which their Arab-Muslim critics classified as political Zionism, have thus primarily to be seen in terms of philanthropy. Palestine was seen as an indispensable refuge for persecuted Jews from other parts of the world, notably from Europe, not for the Jews of Egypt.[69]

What Jewish visitors from Europe and Palestine, most of them Ashkenazim, deplored most was the apparent lack of Jewish life—as they knew it; the pervading sense of materialism; the absence of any superior cultural or spiritual interests in this Oriental environment, in short, the basic indifference of most Jews in Egypt to things specifically Jewish. At the turn of the century, Rudolf Nassau did not spare Egyptian Jewry in his "Letters from Cairo": "Egypt today is still the freest country in the world.... And yet there is probably no other country with a Jewish material [*Judenmaterial*] as inferior intellectually and politically. Without comprehension, stupidly even, the Jews here in their overwhelming majority face all questions of Jewish culture or nationhood.... Saison morte in permanence."[70]

In the late 1920s, a teacher from the Alliance Israélite school in Ṭanṭā reported from her community:

> The characteristic trait of this Jewish community [*Judaisme*] is its difference from that of the other countries. It [the community] has nothing of Oriental or Occidental Jewry. It lacks the ardent piety and sincerity that distinguishes the latter. It is completely special.... The Egyptian is a Jew in name only. He has no idea of being a descendant of the people who have given religion and morals to the world. It is true that the Egyptian Jew always says his prayers, and observes all the rites, but he lacks the Jewish soul ... the Egyptian Jew cares about nothing.... Having never suffered, the Egyptian Jew feels no emotion when faced with someone else's misery.... Our Egyptian coreligionist acts for nothing but glory and snobbism.... Two reasons of equal importance—prosperity and the lack of a Jewish education—have brought the Egyptian Jew to this detachment from all that does not concern him personally.... It is therefore vanity and the enviroment

that have extinguished the love of [their] race in our coreligionists; which have brought them to this indifference toward their distant brethren.[71]

And from a Zionist point of view, Richard Lichtheim wrote in 1937:

The problem is that it is a lazy, Oriental, un-intellectual [*ungeistiges*] environment. One must not measure it by European standards. And yet most [local Jews] are, in their special way, "good Jews," but they are not Zionists in the proper sense. They lack the struggle against Europe, against assimilation. Today there are tendencies toward assimilation in Egypt, but they are all superficial, because [they are] impossible from a cultural point of view.... The poor are pro-Zionist in a natural way—somewhat like the Oriental Jews in Jerusalem—and easy to influence in the direction of [Zionist] revisionism.[72]

The modern reader might be tempted to dismiss such criticism as an expression of European arrogance and ignorance of local ways of life and thinking were it not for the fact that within the local community the indifference, materialism, and superficiality of Egyptian Jewry were harshly criticized as well.[73] Egyptian Jews were "good Jews" in the sense that most of them kept the basic rules of Jewish law. However, they did so out of tradition rather than of conviction. Jacob Weissman, a Zionist activist who had come from Palestine, wrote in December 1943:

In Egypt there is no Jewish life in the proper sense, each of us is a Jew on special occasions only, but nothing in everyday life calls him to himself.... The waves of intense Jewish life that I reconstruct in Egypt were caused by [special] events, such as the ... exodus of some 12,000 Russian Jews from Palestine to Alexandria, the events of Hitlerism, etc."[74]

The strongest emotional attachment to Jewish tradition was found among the poor, indigenous Egyptian, Ashkenazi, and Yemeni Jews living together in special quarters in Cairo and Port Said. However, faith was frequently so intermingled with superstition that both orthodox and enlightened observers found little to be pleased with. In the 1930s and 1940s, there were only five or six *yeshivot* (religious schools) in the whole of Egypt, and the rabbis all came from outside the country. Hebrew was known only by an insignificant minority.

Among the poorest segments of the community and among its Western-educated middle and upper classes, who sent their children to non-Jewish, preferably Christian missionary, schools, conversions to Christianity occurred in sufficient numbers to alarm both the religious and secular hierarchies. The motives for conversion differed between classes. For poor families, economic reasons were involved when marriageable girls who had inadequate dowries could not find Jewish husbands. The various associations founded to provide dowries to marriageable girls (Mohar ha-Betulot) could not solve the problem, and the surplus of women after World War I must have further aggravated the situation.[75] The basic difficulty, however, was not so much economic. It was the lack of Jewish education among girls and women, who in the best of cases were trained to be good mothers and housewives, but had no deeper knowledge of Jewish tradition and history.[76] The children attending Christian missionary schools were frequently exposed to systematic attempts at conversion, which in a number of cases were successful.[77] The greatest scandal occurred in 1932, when Jean Cattaoui de Menasce (1896–?), the son of Félix Béhor and Rosette de Menasce, not only converted to Catholicism and joined the Dominican order, but also insisted on celebrating mass and preaching publicly in his native city of Alexandria.[78]

Efforts to revive Jewish life and traditions were intensified during the twenties and thirties, and not in Zionist quarters alone. The Egyptian-Jewish press informed its readers about contemporary Jewish and world affairs, Jewish history and religion, and Jewish contributions to the cultures of Western Europe and the Islamic world. The chief rabbis of Cairo and Alexandria made great efforts to encourage Jewish learning, open *yeshivot* and clubs, edit papers, and give frequent lectures. While Haim Nahum generally viewed political Zionism with diplomatic restraint, and with open hostility in times of crisis, the chief rabbis of Alexandria, David Prato (1927–36) and Moise Ventura (1937–48) openly supported Zionism provided it was religiously based.

Nevertheless, they failed to rouse the community, and especially the youth, from its indifference and apathy.[79]

A considerable portion of Zionist work consequently had to be devoted to educational purposes with a strong emphasis on the cultural rather than the political aspects of Zionism. The statutes of the Zionist Organization of Alexandria of 1937, for instance, declared that the principles of Zionism were based on Jewish tradition and that Jerusalem as the ancient seat of Jewish culture was to be rebuilt. Its principal objective was to "develop within the community the sense of Jewish national consciousness." Its Programme d'Action included creating a cultural center, organizing excursions to Palestine, and carrying out "serious, intelligent, and rational" propaganda for the Jewish national funds. No mention was made of *'aliya*.[80]

What most Zionist observers failed to sufficiently take into account was that despite the lack of deep religiosity and Jewish solidarity—as expressed in generous contributions to the Palestine *yishuv*—most Jews in Egypt were traditional enough to reject the secular, if not openly antireligious attitude of certain representatives of socialist Zionism. In the interwar period, socialism and communism were not yet as popular among educated Jewish youth as they were to be after World War II. The older generation seems to have had as much difficulty as the Egyptian and British authorities in separating Bolshevism, atheism, and Zionism, all of which were represented by Ashkenazi immigrants from Europe and Palestine.[81] The stricter notions pertaining to family life and, most of all, to the conduct of girls and women caused many parents to look with horror on the "promiscuity" reigning in the Jewish youth clubs in Egypt, not to mention in the kibbutsim in Palestine/Erets Yisra'el itself.[82]

An additional problem came to the fore in the late 1920s, when representatives of the Sephardi minority in Palestine maintained that Sephardi and Oriental Jews were being discriminated against by the predominantly Ashkenazi Zionist leadership. The Sephardi middle class and élite of Egyptian Jewry were considerably disturbed by the Sephardi question, which remained an issue throughout the 1930s and 1940s.[83]

These misgivings regarding the Ashkenazi character of the Zionist movement were, of course, closely related to a fundamental problem besetting not only Zionist activity, but any kind of unified action on the part of Egyptian Jewry. It consisted in the sociocultural barriers separating various groups of differing regional origin, rite, education, and social status. All the Zionist emissaries commented on the snobbery and arrogance of the class-conscious Sephardi élite and middle class toward the Ashkenazi newcomers, even when the latter lacked neither money nor culture. The mutual disdain seriously hampered cooperation among Ashkenazi, Sephardi, and Oriental activists up to the mid-forties.[84]

Before as well as after World War II, the rank and file of the Zionist organizations, the fund-raising committees, and the various youth movements were made up of lower-middle class wage earners, salespeople, schoolteachers, and students, most of them young. The proportion of women was high. The early Ashkenazi activists were joined by more and more Oriental and Sephardi sympathizers until in the 1940s, the latter comprised the majority of the youth movements.[85] Hardly any members were recruited from the indigenous Jews in the Cairo *ḥāra* and the provincial towns. The Karaites seem to have viewed Zionism, if based on religion, with favor, but took virtually no part in organized activity.[86] On the other hand, there was little to attract the Sephardi élite to this predominantly lower-middle class movement of Ashkenazi origin. In the late 1930s, the Alexandria élite still considered Zionism "very unchic," the petty affair of "honest but terribly insignificant people," as put by an upper-class supporter of Zionism.[87]

The logical conclusion for Zionist leaders to draw was that in order to make a greater impact on the Sephardi and Oriental majority, they had to win over its élite.[88] This strategy met with some success in Alexandria, where internal divisions were less marked than in Cairo, and where the chief rabbis actively supported Zionism.[89] Generally, however, the goal was not reached, for even though the Zionists did win over a few members of the élite—Jack and Albert Mosseri, Félix and Jacques Elie de

Menasce, Felix Green, and Ralph Harari—they were usually too busy to devote much time to Zionist ends. Moreover, they were absent in Europe throughout the summer months, and withdrew from active participation as soon as it seemed to involve personal risk. Interestingly, they were almost all married to women with strong, if generally loosely defined Zionist sympathies. These upper-class women usually acted on philanthropic rather than on strictly political grounds and frequently lacked any clear notion as to what exactly Zionism implied. But they were among the most generous contributors to Zionist funds and institutions. The most influential group to sympathize with Zionist aspirations, cultural but also political, were the lodges of the B'nai B'rith. Yet in the 1930s and 1940s, even the B'nai B'rith avoided being associated with Zionism, although many members such as Léon Castro, Simon Mani, Alfred N. Cohen or Jacob Weissman continued to cooperate individually.[90]

There were no more mass demonstrations of support for the Jewish national movement after the mid-twenties. By that time it had become quite clear that the king, Fu'ād I, though anything but anti-Jewish, was opposed to Zionism as a political movement aiming at the establishment of a Jewish national home in Palestine. It also seemed that the British Residency was adopting a more reserved stand.[91] The Cairo community council headed by Joseph Aslan Cattaoui took a clear anti-Zionist position. Chief Rabbi Haim Nahum, who tried to avoid antagonizing either the authorities or the Zionists, counseled caution and moderation. Even in Alexandria, where conditions were generally more favorable to the Zionists, the community leaders succeeded in restricting the activities of their pro-Zionist chief rabbis, both of whom left their posts after long and bitter quarrels with the lay council. The councils were, of course, motivated by the fear that the Egyptian public might react against the Zionists in particular and Egyptian Jews in general. Their response was to try to be as inconspicuous as possible.[92]

The potential dangers of Zionist propaganda and activity in Egypt were not lost on those in charge of the movement. Their idea, however, was to make use of Egypt's growing regional rôle and the wide circulation of its press in order to influence public opinion in Egypt itself and in the Arab world at large. Certain themes, which had been expressed as early as 1913 by a member of the Zionist Executive, Dr. Ya'aḳov Thon, ran through Jewish contributions to the Egyptian press, and were later taken up by the local Jewish press. These included a strong emphasis on the Oriental origins of the Jews, on the close cultural and racial affinities between Jews and Arabs as brothers in the "Semitic race" (*al-jins al-sāmī*), and on Jewish contributions to the common Middle Eastern civilization. On a different level, they referred to the economic, cultural, and political benefits to be derived from unrestricted Jewish immigration to Palestine and from close cooperation between Jews and Arabs in the area.[93]

When it proved necessary to explain the undeniable conflicts between Jews and Arabs in Palestine, perfidious Albion, that is, British imperialism, the source of all evil in the area, was brought into play. Britain, it was argued, thwarted all efforts to achieve cooperation in order to keep the Middle East under its exclusive control.[94] Attemps were also made to use the excellent contacts of local Jews to reach leading Arab politicians. Local Jewish leaders, who were greatly alarmed by growing tension in Palestine and upset by the way the Zionist Executive was handling, or, in their eyes, mishandling, the situation, strongly endorsed all moves toward understanding with the Arabs. But they were in no position to bridge the existing differences.[95]

When in September 1939, the Egyptian government introduced martial law and strict press censorship, anti-Zionist as well as Zionist activities came virtually to a standstill. And yet the war was to bring Zionism its first upsurge of lasting effect. The impending abolition of the Capitulations, the rising tide of Islamic feeling, the drive to Egyptianize business and the administration, coinciding with wartime scarcity and inflation followed by postwar unemployment, sharpened the sense of insecurity among the non-Muslim minorities. The growing impact of the Palestine conflict affected the Jewish minority in particular, and so did the advance of the German Africa Corps, which was only halted by the British victory at al-'Alamayn in November 1942.

In a striking parallel to World War I, these internal developments were accompanied by an influx of Jews from neighboring Palestine. Among the Allied armies stationed in Egypt there were also thousands of Jewish soldiers. Special clubs were opened for them by members of the Jewish élite, the B'nai B'rith, and the Zionist organizations of Cairo and Alexandria. In these clubs, the Jewish soldiers met members of the local communities and, by way of personal contact, reached individuals who had hitherto been unimpressed by Zionist propaganda. The soldiers, moreover, visited the schools and *yeshivot* to talk about Zionism and Palestine, to teach Hebrew, and to form the first nuclei of the various youth groups affiliated with the Palestine branches of the Zionist movement.[96]

Organized work began in the summer of 1943, when the first three emissaries (*sheliḥim*) from the Palestine *yishuv*, who had been selected and trained by the Jewish Agency and the Mossad for 'Aliya Bet (illegal immigration), arrived in Egypt under false names, wearing British uniforms.[97] The dispatch of these emissaries marked a turning point in the attitude of the Zionist leadership toward Middle Eastern Jewry in general and Egyptian Jewry in particular. Up to World War II, all eyes had been turned on Europe and the destruction of the Jewish communities there. The focus now shifted to the Middle East, where under wartime conditions communications were relatively easy, particularly so in the case of British-occupied Egypt. In the Middle East urgently needed funds could still be collected. At the same time, anti-Jewish moves were, rightly or wrongly, expected even here, notably in countries such as Iraq.[98]

The *sheliḥim* arrived in Cairo, Alexandria, and Port Said to build up pioneer movements among Jewish youth, whom they regarded as the only section of the community amenable to Zionist ideals and practical work. Young people of both sexes between the ages of ten and twenty-six, many of them enrolled in the communal schools, were given theoretical and, to a lesser extent, practical instruction. They were then taken by various legal and illegal means to Palestine. The language used was mainly French, or Arabic in the Cairo *ḥāra*, where one group of twelve to fifteen members was recruited. Only a single group, the ḳevutsa Bar Kokhba, was able to use Hebrew in its daily activities.[99]

By November 1943, about 500 young people had joined the various Zionist youth groups in Alexandria, the ha-ʿIvri ha-Tsaʿir excepted, which did not cooperate with the other organizations. By 1947, 300 to 400 were still members. In Cairo, the combined membership of all groups, again excepting ha-ʿIvri ha-Tsaʿir, was 500 to 600 in 1944, and about 400 in November 1947. In Port Said, the he-Ḥaluts ha-Tsaʿir numbered about 60 in June 1944. Another 500 to 600 young people had joined the independent ha-ʿIvri ha-Tsaʿir in Cairo and Alexandria. Overall membership should have reached about 1,500 between 1944 and 1948, but because of constant fluctuation may well have been somewhat lower.[100]

All efforts to create a unified youth movement for the whole of Egypt failed. By 1944, there were four major organizations working more or less independently of each other: he-Ḥaluts ha-Tsaʿir, ha-ʿIvri ha-Tsaʿir, the Bene ʿAḳiva, and the Egyptian branch of the New Zionist Organization. The nonpolitical Ḥaluts ha-Tsaʿir was affiliated to the worldwide Ḥaluts (Zionist pioneering) movement. The Cairo branch with its 400 to 500 members formed part of the Jewish Boy Scout movement of the Maccabi, which in 1938 joined the Egyptian Boy Scout movement and was officially registered with the Egyptian Ministry of Social Affairs. The Alexandria branch of 250 to 400 members was also registered as a scouting movement (Les Eclaireurs Israélites), but operated independently of the purely sportive, non-Zionist Alexandria Maccabi.[101] Around 1947, he-Ḥaluts ha-Tsaʿir split into two rival groups: ha-Bonim, which continued the previous nonpolitical line, and Dror, which adopted the line of the leftist Aḥdut ha-ʿAvoda.[102]

Ha-ʿIvri ha-Tsaʿir with 500 to 600 members, founded in Cairo in 1932, was reorganized by *sheliḥim* in 1942–43 and was affiliated with the leftist ha-Shomer ha-Tsaʿir. In Egypt, it refused to recognize the authority of the *sheliḥim* of he-Ḥaluts ha-Tsa'ir and cooperated on an informal basis only on the committees organizing clandestine *'aliya*. Ha-'Ivri ha-Tsa'ir, which was more openly political than he-Ḥaluts ha-Tsa'ir, advocated a socialist, binational solution to the Palestine conflict and established good contact with the leftist youth in the Wafd and the local socialist groups. However, it seems to have avoided making public the nonreligious, socialist stand of its mother organization in Palestine, whose name it did not adopt. This was done in order not to alienate potential supporters from among the Egyptian community, which, if not religious in a narrow sense, was still largely traditional.[103] The small Bene 'Aḳiva group numbering 120 to 150 members was affiliated with the religious Mizraḥi Zionists and cooperated with the others on *'aliya*.[104]

There was no cooperation at all between these three organizations and the fourth, the Egyptian section of the revisionist New Zionist Organization led by Albert Staraselski, which had about one-hundred members in 1944. The general Zionists strongly objected to the activities of Irgun (Irgun Tseva'i Le'umi) and Leḥi (Loḥame Ḥerut Yisra'el) in Egypt, involving mostly arms smuggling to Palestine. After the murder of Lord Moyne in November 1944, which forced all *sheliḥim* to leave Egypt at least temporarily, the larger Zionist groups began to supervise revisionist activities more closely. While there had been some sympathy for the assassins not only within the Jewish community, but also in Egyptian nationalist circles, particularly among Muslim Brothers, most community members and its leaders condemned the murder. Staraselski himself was arrested and expelled from Egypt in May 1945, and revisionism, which had been quite strong among Italian Jews in the 1930s, ceased to play a rôle in Egypt.[105]

Although these groups differed from each other in their political outlook, it seems that as a rule it was less political conviction that made young Jews join any one of them than rather nonpolitical motives such as friendship or quite simply the wish to get away from home and to meet young people. These personal motives seem to have been particularly true for girls, who made up 10 to 20 percent of the pioneering movements, but only 5 to 10 percent of the *'olim*, and for whom this provided one of the few acceptable ways of escaping close parental supervision.[106]

Zionist leaders in Egypt and Jerusalem felt that the work for *'aliya* among the young was not enough and that a new central organization was needed to coordinate activities. In late 1943, there were only a few activists of the old guard left, most of them Ashkenazi businessmen from Palestine. The situation in Cairo was considered a catastrophe.[107] In January 1944, the Zionist Executive, therefore, appointed Léon Castro president of the Comité Provisoire de la Fédération Sioniste d'Egypte with full power to reorganize and coordinate Zionist work in Egypt. Castro, a lawyer and journalist, veteran member of both the Egyptian national and the Zionist movements, former head of the LICA and prominent member of the B'nai B'rith, recommended himself by his wide political experience, even though his private life was not beyond reproach.[108] By November 1946, an estimated 1,000 members had joined the Zionist Federation branches in Cairo, Alexandria, and Port Said. To the great confusion of the Egyptian and the British authorities, the federation presented itself as the Egyptian office of the Jewish Agency for Palestine in Cairo, and as he-Ḥaluts in Alexandria. The Central Committee under Castro and the lawyer Emile Najar, and the Grand Comité d'Action under Jacob Weissman, a businessman from Palestine, were elected at the First Territorial Conference of Egyptian Zionism in Alexandria on 7 January 1945. The latter included among its forty members a considerable number of wealthy businessmen, some of them quite influential in the community councils of Cairo and Alexandria.[109]

The Zionist Federation as well as the youth movements were able to work legally, if discreetly, without being seriously hindered by the Egyptian authorities, at least until November 1947.[110] In 1944–45, the Egyptian undersecretary of state, Ḥasan Rif'at Pāshā, consulted the security officer at the British embassy regarding Zionist activities in Egypt, which he wished to curtail, without necessarily closing the offices of the federation in Cairo and Alexandria. The Foreign Office, however, instructed its local staff on 14 March 1945 "if possible [to] keep out of any Zionist-Egyptian squabbles," and so no steps were taken.[111] Throughout the war, Zionist leaders from Palestine visited frequently to consult with local activists. Delegates were sent to the World Zionist Congresses in 1946 and 1947. However, the local leadership thought it inadvisable to hold open elections for the federation.[112] Funds officially destined for various charitable institutions, which, according to Léon Castro, amounted to £100,000 in 1943–44, were secretly transferred to Palestine.[113] In response to the riots of 2 November 1945, Zionist youths formed self-defense (*hagana*) units in the Cairo *ḥāra*. They were even provided arms from British supplies to defend Jewish quarters and institutions against further attacks.[114]

Opposition to Zionist activities came from two separate camps within Egyptian Jewry, the communal leadership on one hand and the communist movement on the other. Communal leaders feared more than ever that Zionist activities, carried on in a country becoming ever more deeply involved in the Palestine conflict, could hardly fail to compromise the entire community, Zionists and non-Zionists alike. Since the late 1930s, attacks on local Jews as the fifth column of Zionism, backed by British and American imperialism, had been on the increase, and were spread by the Arabic press ranging from the Wafdist *Ṣawt al-Umma* to the journal of the Muslim Brotherhood, *Jarīdat al-Ikhwān al-Muslimīn*. The presidents of the Alexandria and Cairo communities, Robert J. Rolo and René Cattaoui, were strongly opposed to political Zionism. In a "Note on the Jewish Question," which they sent to the World Jewish Conference in America in the summer of 1944, both men clearly distanced themselves from the central objective of Zionism, the establishment in Palestine of a Jewish national home or state, suggesting that a refuge outside Palestine be found to absorb Jewish refugees and displaced persons. As always, they called for a peaceful solution to the Palestine conflict and stressed the loyalty of the Jews to their respective Arab homelands:

For some, PALESTINE has seemed an insufficient outlet. It is therefore essential to select a country other than Palestine.... It would be most desirable (and we think it is possible) that the Palestine question be solved as a result of Jewish-Arab collaboration in an atmosphere of mutual understanding between the parties [concerned] on the basis of perfect harmony imbued with sincerity and loyalty.[115]

In October 1944, René Cattaoui wrote a letter to Léon Castro calling upon him to close the preparation (*hakhshara*) camps in which boys and girls were given practical training for *'aliya* and kibbuts life. According to Cattaoui, these camps were "liable to undermine paternal authority and to do great harm to the sacred institution of the family" and to "seriously compromise the official relations between our community and the national authorities, which have always been excellent." The council, he continued, could not tolerate activities that stood "in flagrant opposition to the currents of opinion among official circles and the overwhelming majority of the Egyptian nation to which this community belongs."[116]

Castro sent a cool reply stating that as honorary delegate of the Jewish Agency he was not responsible for the youth movements and *'aliya*. On 1 January 1945, Cattaoui warned Castro that the council would see itself obliged to "solicit, in the public interest, the intervention of the Egyptian authorities," if his previous demand were not met. It was not, and nothing happened. The Zionist movement even proceeded to hold its First Territorial Conference on 7 January.[117] René Cattaoui, who faced a strong Zionist faction within the Cairo community council, declared his resignation in October 1945, withdrew it shortly afterward, but made it final in August 1946. His Zionist opponents, on the other hand, could not prevent Chief Rabbi Haim Nahum from issuing an anti-Zionist statement on behalf of Egyptian Jewry after the incidents of November 1945. In Alexandria, the pro-Zionist chief rabbi, Dr. Moise Ventura, finally resigned in January 1948 and left for Paris shortly before the outbreak of the first Arab-Israeli war in May 1948.[118]

Neither the communal leadership nor the Jewish left, whose anti-Zionist activities have already been referred to, were able to restrict Zionist propaganda and operations in Egypt. But in December 1947, when the United Nations' decision in favor of partition sparked anti-Zionist demonstrations and renewed attacks on foreign-owned stores, Jewish firms, institutions, and residential areas, the Zionist leaders, who knew that they were under surveillance, began to consider going underground. Early in 1948, he-Ḥaluts ha-Tsa'ir closed its office in Alexandria, and at the beginning of May, the Cairo office of the Jewish Agency for Palestine followed suit. By the time martial law was declared and the first local activists were interned, all *sheliḥim* had returned to Palestine. Zionism as an organized movement came to an end in May 1948. By contrast, large-scale operations to transfer Jews to Israel started only in 1949 and continued well into the 1950s.[119]

Zionism, thus, played an ambiguous rôle in Egypt, in some respects similar to communist activism. At first it looked like an imported solution to imported problems—Western-type nationalism, the Palestine conflict. Yet that Western-style nationalism and concern for the Palestine cause were new and imported did not prevent them from having considerable impact on Egyptian politics and society, particularly from the mid-thirties on. In the 1940s, Islamic activism and Egyptianization restricting the rôle of non-Muslim minorities could no longer be seen as alien, or transient, elements of Egyptian politics. Still, up to at least 1948, most Egyptian Jews did not view Jewish nationalism as an alternative, and a solution to their predicament. *'Aliya* to the Promised Land was insignificant. If Zionism was the strongest political movement in both numbers and impact—much stronger than Egyptian nationalism and communism—it nevertheless did not win over the majority, and was opposed by significant sections of the élite. It was only after the Arab-Israeli wars of 1948 and 1956 that Egyptian Jews left the country in great and ever-growing numbers. The conclusion is evident: in Egypt as in the other Middle Eastern countries, the aim and outcome of political Zionism, the creation of a Jewish state in Palestine, was a major factor in creating the very problem which, under different historical circumstances, it was meant to solve—that of anti-Jewish feeling and activity preventing peaceful coexistence of Jews and non-Jews in one country. But Zionism was not the only element to undermine coexistence, and not the sole cause of the end of Jewish life in Egypt.

5

The Beginning of the End

Sections of Jewish youth and the middle class became increasingly politicized in the late 1930s and the 1940s. Among the youth, French-educated students largely adopted leftist ideas, whereas many middle- and lower-middle class children attending the community schools leaned toward Zionism. There were Egyptian patriots in both camps, including the Zionists, who tried to combine solidarity with the national aspirations of the Egyptian and the Jewish people. The question is, of course, whether there was still a chance, in the 1940s, to integrate the Jews, or any other non-Muslim minority except the Copts, into Egyptian society as it became increasingly defined in terms of religion and ethnicity. Even if the Jews had all become Egyptian patriots, learned Arabic, and applied for Egyptian nationality, it would still not have changed the basic fact that they overwhelmingly were not of Egyptian origin, not "real Egyptians," and not Muslim. In the 1940s, these facts began to carry increasing weight.

EGYPTIANIZATION

With the Montreux Convention of 1937, the process of Egyptianization, for which nationalist and Islamic circles had long been pressing, began to take shape. In 1938, the Alexandria Conseil Sanitaire, Maritime et Quarantenaire was nationalized, and in

1940 the Caisse de la Dette abolished and the National Bank of Egypt transformed into a central bank under Egyptian direction. As already mentioned, unemployment was becoming a serious problem especially among highly politicized high school and university graduates. There was, therefore, an urgent demand for more jobs. Despite constant protests from European businessmen and diplomats, the Egyptian government began taking the first tentative steps in that direction. In 1942–43, Arabic was made obligatory in all business dealings, and in 1946, shop signs had to be written in Arabic. Shop owners and businessmen unable to read and write Arabic were thus forced to take on additional Egyptian personnel.[1]

In May 1945, the Egyptian government proposed a bill to increase the Egyptian share in the personnel, management, and capital of joint stock companies, which went far beyond the previous legislation passed in 1923, 1927, and 1936. According to British reports, it took effect even before being officially passed in July 1947 as Law number 132 (Company Law). The new law fixed the Egyptian quota at a minimum 75 percent of all salaried employees, 90 percent of the workers, and 51 percent of paid-up capital of joint stock companies, and obliged all firms concerned to submit detailed lists specifying the nationality and salary of their employees.[2] As a result, foreign observers expected massive discharges from the companies concerned—up to 60,000 according to one British source—affecting Greeks, Maltese, Levantines, and Jews.[3] But there was no specific anti-Jewish bias implied in the law, even though *al-Shams* claimed that certain companies required proof of Egyptian nationality of their Jewish staff only. On the other hand, *La Tribune Juive* reported that many of the companies affected were run by Jewish managers who knew how to get around the legal restrictions.[4] Given that the Egyptian economy was still largely controlled by foreign or non-Muslim capital and management, and given the politically explosive issue of unemployment, particularly among educated youth, government action was long overdue. The problem, however, was in the actual execution of the law, which in itself contained no discriminatory passages. The question was more specifically who exactly were the "Egyptians" intended to benefit from Egyptianization.

British and French diplomats repeatedly charged the authorities with discriminating not only against local foreign minorities, but also against the indigenous Copts, accepting only Muslims as "real Egyptians." Their suspicions were not only based on complaints by the minorities concerned, but also on statements of Egyptian officials, including the minister of trade, who declared in May 1945: "that in order to protect 'real Egyptians' ... they had put the percentage of Egyptian staff high: they were sure that a large proportion of the nominal Egyptians would turn out not to be 'real Egyptians.'"[5]

A French report had already noted in May 1944 that the minorities were being "practically eliminated from public functions" and that former Ottoman subjects were not readily recognized as Egyptian nationals. In recent years, only a few Muslims of North African origin had been granted Egyptian nationality. The nationalist policy, it continued, which had a distinctly Islamic tinge, was still "on the surface" only, and did not seem very grave as yet. The report went on to warn, however, that nationalist policy should not be underestimated because the problem was precisely that the strategy was not expressed in formal legislation, but in "practical discrimination."[6]

After the Allied forces had withdrawn, unemployment was just as high among the Jewish lower and lower-middle class as among Muslims and Copts. In view of the imminent discharges, applications for naturalization rose dramatically. In November 1947, the Cairo community alone registered 1,000 applications per week. The Egyptian authorities were very slow in dealing with them, and in 1948–49, hundreds of decisions were still pending, with many applications having already been rejected.[7] As the Egyptianization drive coincided with strikes directed primarily against foreign-owned companies and with campaigns against the Copts, the Greeks, and the Jews, a sense of insecurity and anxiety began to spread among the local non-Muslim minorities, the Jews included.[8]

Yet in spite of the Balfour Day riots of November 1945 and some isolated incidents occurring in their wake, the mass of the Egyptian population did not show signs of anti-Jewish feeling.[9] The anti-Zionist campaign of militant nationalist and Islamic groups with its anti-Jewish overtones did not seem to affect the general public, nor did it lead to any government action directed against Egyptian Jews. The government even admitted a considerable number of expatriate Jewish professionals into the country. In *al-Ahrām* of 13 November 1946, Chief Rabbi Haim Nahum, therefore, denied reports published by several Jewish papers in Palestine that Egyptian Jews were being oppressed and that because of the bad economic conditions they were forced to leave the country.[10] There was only one major area in which government discrimination against Jews could be discerned: from 1946 on, Jews had increasing difficulty obtaining Egyptian travel documents for Palestine, be they exit visas for travel to Palestine for Jews living in Egypt, or entry and transit visas for Jews arriving from Palestine. The reason for this policy is obvious: the Egyptian government could hardly be expected to openly tolerate Jewish migration to Palestine at a time when the newly created Arab League was constantly calling for its instant stop.[11] And yet a little later, after the war of 1948, the Egyptian authorities did nothing to stop massive Jewish emigration leading, at least indirectly, to Palestine.

In the autumn of 1947, public interest turned again to the Palestine question which was being discussed at the United Nations, where a majority seemed to seriously consider partition. Within the Egyptian Jewish community, ha-'Ivri ha-Tsa'ir, *al-Shams*, and the communist groups had at last come to support this solution, which was, however, categorically rejected by the Arab side. The head of the Egyptian delegation to the United Nations, Muḥammad Ḥusayn Haykal from the Liberal Constitutionalist Party, took up the warnings of Egyptian politicians, Islamic religious authorities, and other members of the Arab League when he warned the Palestine Commission that a decision in favor of partition could lead to an unprecedented wave of anti-Jewish feeling in the Arab world, and that the spilling of Arab blood in Palestine would inevitably lead to the spilling of Jewish blood in Arab countries.[12]

Leading Egyptian-Arab newspapers had already dropped all distinctions between Zionists and Jews, emphatically declaring that all Jews were Zionists. The press launched an offensive against Egyptian Jews denouncing them not only as Zionists and communists, but also as capitalist exploiters and dealers in arms and women—a destructive element corrupting all states and societies.[13] Egyptian Jewry as a community suffered because its internal structure was so complex and political opinion so varied. These ranged from the close connections of its élite to the colonial system established and maintained under British control, to the anticapitalist, leftist tendencies of its academic youth and the Zionism of the middle class. For the anticommunist Islamic opposition there could hardly be a case better suited to their propaganda than that of Henri Curiel, the son of a wealthy banker of Sephardi origin and Italian nationality, a Jew and a communist, who combined virtually all the negative aspects the opposition could want. Religious sentiment, in a narrow sense, against the Jews as enemies of the Prophet and Islam was used as propaganda in the mosques and in Islamic circles but seems to have been less powerful than accusations based on economic and political motives.

Even in these tense times, the Egyptian government continued to show itself well-disposed toward the local Jewish population, though not always very effectively so. In July 1947, it banned all demonstrations against the British and the Jews that were to be staged in connection with the Palestine hearings at the United Nations. It imposed a state of emergency on Balfour Day of November 1946 and 1947, and offered intensified police protection to Jewish institutions, which did, indeed, prevent some isolated incidents.[14] In December 1947, the government officially denied rumors that the Jews had caused the raging cholera epidemic by poisoning the fountains with microbes. In March 1948, it issued a blanket order prohibiting all propaganda that might upset intercommunal relations.[15] But it proved either unable or unwilling to prevent the serious riots that occurred between December 1947 and September 1948. From 2 to 4 December 1947, large-scale demonstrations were staged in all major cities to protest the United Nations' decision of 29 November to partition Palestine. Demonstrators rallied against the British, the Zionists, and the Jews, and attacked, and in some instances destroyed, shops and establishments owned by Europeans, Jews, Greeks, and Copts. The incidents were strikingly similar to the riots of November 1945, which also included demonstrations against the British, the Zionists, and the Jews in general and were equally led by Islamic and nationalist groups and students. Acts of vandalism were committed by an anonymous mob ("riff-raff" as it was called by British observers) bent on destruction rather than on any identifiable political motive. All this was tolerated with a surprising degree of patience by the police, who only stepped in when violent demonstrators were about to enter the Jewish *ḥāra* in Cairo. On 5 December, the government proclaimed a state of emergency in Cairo and prohibited further demonstrations planned for 14 December.[16]

The Muslim Brotherhood, which was involved in a bitter power struggle with the government of al-Nuqrāshī Pāshā, has to bear at least the moral responsibility for much of this violence. In December 1947, the Muslim Brotherhood, Miṣr al-Fātat, and the *'ulamā'* of al-Azhar called for a holy war (*jihād*) on behalf of Palestine and urged Egyptian Jews to contribute to the Palestine funds. The propaganda and donations campaign was coordinated by the Nile Valley Committee for the Defense of Palestine headed by 'Alī Māhir and 'Alī 'Allūba Pāshā, veteran advocates of a pan-Arabism.[17] In January 1948, a member of Parliament proposed a bill declaring Zionism illegal and placing Egyptian Jews under stricter surveillance. The minister of justice, however, opposed the bill declaring that a formal prohibition of Zionism was unnecessary.[18] Coptic leaders, who, like their Muslim compatriots, wanted to preserve the Arab character of Palestine, nevertheless defended their "Jewish brothers," "Egyptians like ourselves," against the charges of treason.[19]

Noting the signs of heightened tension, the local Zionist organizations began to adopt greater security measures in November 1947. But it was very difficult for the pioneering youth movements to go underground. At the beginning of 1948, the British consulates in Egypt stopped granting travel visas for Palestine, a step that included everybody, but for obvious reasons mainly affected Jews. The youth movements thus lost their last legal means of organizing *'aliya* from Egypt. The police repeatedly searched the offices of the Zionist Federation and the Jewish Agency in Cairo and Alexandria—though not without giving previous warning to its leaders.[20] It infiltrated the youth groups and compiled lists of their members and of participants in Zionist meetings, and in April 1948 arrested an emissary and his group who were taking photographs in the harbor of Alexandria.[21] The Zionist Federation in Alexandria (he-Ḥaluts) closed its offices in early 1948, while the Cairo branch (Jewish Agency) held out until May 1948.[22]

THE ARAB–ISRAELI WAR

Even before the State of Israel was proclaimed on 14 May 1948, the government of Fahmī al-Nuqrāshī Pāshā declared a state of emergency on 11 May followed by martial law on 15 May. On the night of 15 May, "for reasons of public security related to the present situation," hundreds of Zionists and communists, mainly Jews, were arrested, as well as numerous Muslim Brothers, who were then interned in separate camps.[23] The Palestine campaign offered the perfect opportunity to eliminate the most dangerous oppositional elements, regardless of their attitudes on the Palestine issue itself. The Muslim Brotherhood, which in the postwar period had become the strongest challenger to the regime in power, was banned in early December 1948.[24] The arrested Zionists and communists presented a simple case from Prime Minister al-Nuqrāshī's point of view: both groups were represented by Jews so they must be identical. According to Sir Ronald Campbell, the British ambassador in Egypt, al-Nuqrāshī repeatedly declared that: "[A]ll Jews were potential Zionists, but that anyhow all Zionists were Communists, and he looked at the matter as much from the point of view of Communism as from the point of Zionism;" and that: "Speaking of the continued exercise of the emergency powers ... he was still using them to defeat Communist efforts. These were directed exclusively by Jews, which made things easier for the Egyptian Government."[25]

The Zionist emissaries from Palestine, who through certain channels had learned of the decision of the Arab League to mobilize the Arab armies to enter Palestine, left Egypt.[26] It was, therefore, only local Zionists who were arrested in the first wave of May 1948. Members of ha-'Ivri ha-Tsa'ir, whom Jays Pāshā of the Alexandria City Police declared to be Boy Scouts and hence nonpolitical, were not included, and neither were prominent Zionist activists such as Léon Castro, while others like Jacob Weissman, Roger Oppenheim, and Dr. S. Zuckerman were only arrested months later. Arrests were, therefore, far from comprehensive. By contrast, they included a number of well-known businessmen such as Ovadia Salem and Aslan Vidon, who, without being members of the Zionist Federation, were generally known for their Zionist sympathies, as well as businessmen like Isaac Vaena who had no connections with Zionism.[27] The first wave of arrests on 14–15 May was followed by further government action in June, July, and September 1948, which was by and large directed specifically against local Zionist and communist activists. According to British reports, 554 Jews were still interned in June 1948 after many of those initially arrested had already been set free.[28]

The treatment of the internees at Huckstep (Cairo), Abū Kīr (Alexandria) and at the respective women's prisons was, generally, satisfactory, partly because of the intervention of the Jewish communities, which was helped by generous payments to the officials in charge. The prisoners were allowed to receive visits and food from their relatives and were even able to celebrate the Jewish holidays.[29] The European diplomats protested the measures taken by the Egyptian government against the members of a religious minority that had no formal relations to the State of Israel, a state Egypt did not recognize, but against which it was waging a war. Sir Ronald Campbell compared this conduct to the British government interning its Catholic subjects in the hypothetical case of a war against the Vatican. Yet Prime Minister Fahmī al-Nuqrāshī showed himself perfectly unimpressed by these remonstrances, and repeated his favorite theme on the identity of Zionism and communism.[30]

The companies owned by those interned and their private fortunes were placed under the supervision (*gestion*) of a special government body. From a legal point of view, they were, therefore, neither seized nor sequestered, but merely "administered." Included were several large companies such as the Société d'Avances Commerciales (Alfred N. Cohen, J. H. Perez), the companies of Isaac Amiel, Chemla, Adès, and Gattegno (but not Cicurel), the firms of communist and Zionist activists (Curiel on one hand, Weissman, Kahanoff, Matalon, Oppenheim, and Dwek, on the other), and finally, on 20 December, all the companies owned by the Muslim Brotherhood.[31]

In this dangerous situation, which, for the first time, seemed to directly affect, and threaten, the position of the Jews living in the country, Jewish communal leaders made every effort to affirm their loyalty to Egypt, which King Fārūq had indeed formally acknowledged on 11 May 1948 in a declaration made before the outbreak of hostilities. In August 1947, Chief Rabbi Haim Nahum, as the highest representative of Egyptian Jewry, had already sent a letter to the United Nations expressing the support of his community for the national aspirations of Egypt, and in January 1948, leaders of the Cairo and Alexandria communities, René Cattaoui and Edwin Goar, had called upon Egyptian Jews to show their solidarity with the Palestinians.[32] On 16 May 1948, *al-Ahrām* published a letter from René and Aslan Cattaoui, both of whom by that time had resigned from communal office, to Haim Nahum, in which they wrote that "their religion was Judaism, their homeland Egypt, and their nationality Egyptian."[33] The Jewish community of Port Said sent a letter to the governor of the Canal Zone confirming their loyalty to the state of Egypt and condemning Israel. The Jewish lawyer Zaki Orebi sent articles to the Egyptian press denouncing Zionism as a tool of imperialism. *Al-Shams*, which as late as March 1946 had published an article on the importance of creating a Jewish state in Palestine, did not mention the establishment of the State of Israel; and *al-Kalīm*, which in July 1945 was still calling for *'aliya* to Palestine, dissociated itself from Zionism and "vehemently" condemned the establishment of the "so-called state" of Israel.[34]

The Wafdist *Ṣawt al-Umma* meanwhile called for more determined action against local Jews, Zionism's alleged fifth column. In May and June 1948, the paper published blacklists of Jewish businessmen, who were urged to prove their loyalty, and to expiate for their previous acts of exploitation by contributing to the Palestine cause, if not with arms in hand and the blood of their children, then at least with their money. When Jewish contributions for the Palestine fund amounting to £E40,000 were received in June 1948, *Ṣawt al-Umma* wrote that this ridiculously low sum had been rejected by the Egyptian government.[35]

In spite of the agitation of the Muslim Brothers, Miṣr al-Fatāt, the Nile Valley Committee, and the Kutla Party headed by the former Wafdist leader Makram 'Ubayd, no organized outbursts of violence or outright pogroms against local Jews occurred during the first weeks of the war. In early June 1948, the British described the situation as tense, but quiet:

> The Jewish community in Egypt lives without molestation by the Egyptian authorities, and Jews, both rich and poor, carry on their normal activities in satisfactory conditions. In view of the recent Egyptian tendency to xenophobia and extreme nationalism, the Jews are apt to be nervous of their position, as are the Copts and other minorities in Egypt; but no drastic measures have been taken against them. Those who are Egyptian subjects are apt to emphasize that their temporal loyalty is not affected by their religious beliefs. The liberality of the Egyptian attitude is creditable not only in view of the fact that Jews are amongst the leading Communists in Egypt, but of course in view of Palestine and Zionism.[36]

From Alexandria, reports came in that there was "no active vendetta" against the Jews there, but "how the situation will develop is another question."[37]

These misgivings were not unfounded. But it was only after Israeli air raids on Cairo and Alexandria that Egyptian Jews suffered acts of violence. On 20 June 1948, over twenty people were killed when a bomb exploded in the Karaite quarter of Cairo. A note attached to the bomb claimed that it had been placed there by the Rabbanite Jews, an assertion that met with general disbelief among both Karaites and Rabbanites. On 15 July, the Israeli air force bombed heavily populated quarters of Cairo and Alexandria, and on 16 July, the Muslim Brothers declared during Friday prayer that it was "not only the Zionists" who were responsible for these attacks. Jews, Europeans, and even Egyptians who "looked Jewish" were attacked in the streets. Between 19 July and 2 August, bombs were placed in a number of Jewish-owned cinema houses and department stores. Again, the authorities tried to put the blame on the Zionists or on intra-Jewish quarrels.[38] August was generally quiet except for a number of assaults on individual Jews and Europeans. In the second week of September, a number of Jewish families were evacuated from sensitive zones (i.e., areas close to the royal palaces in Cairo and Alexandria, the Ministry of War, and military barracks). On 22 September, several bombs exploded in the Cairo Jewish *ḥāra* killing twenty-nine people. In reaction to these explosions, Prime Minister al-Nuqrāshī had fifty inhabitants of the *ḥāra* arrested, against whom nothing more specific could be charged than that after these attacks they had shown themselves "inexplicably stubborn, even aggressive."[39] Two months later, on 12 November 1948, a bomb devastated the offices of the Jewish-owned Société de Publicité, whose influence on the press had for many years been offensive to radical nationalists.[40] Then calm was restored. In 1949, Jews again met with difficulties in obtaining visas for Palestine. Between July 1949 and February 1950, the Zionists and most of the communists who had been interned over the preceding months were released and their firms and fortune returned by the government. The foreign nationals and stateless persons among them were expelled from Egypt.[41]

As was to be expected, Egyptian Jewry suffered from the repercussions of the Arab-Israeli war. They had seen the destruction of homes, shops, department stores, and cinema houses, and even random assaults on individuals. But there had been no organized persecution, let alone persecution ordered by the government. The primary source of the attacks and accusations, all observers agreed, was the Muslim Brothers, who with their large membership and secret apparatus had the necessary men, means, arms, and ammunition to lead the fight against the Jews, the British, and the government.[42] The ban on the organization in early December 1948 escalated the confrontation. In the same month, a member of the secret apparatus assassinated Prime Minister Fahmī al-Nuqrāshī Pāshā; in February 1949, Ḥasan al-Bannā was killed by the secret police. The Muslim Brothers, who in their propaganda never distinguished between Jews and Zionists, provided the necessary justification for the attacks on local Jews, and it was their supporters who placed some of the bombs and called for further action. Their call was answered by a mob, which made no distinctions between the Jews, the Zionists, and the non-Muslim foreigners in general.

The government was again reproached for acting too late and too ineffectually to prevent these acts of violence, be they spontaneous or organized. Sir Ronald Campbell did not miss the opportunity to point out, in his very British manner, to the Egyptian prime minister that: "It could be unfortunate ... if foreign representatives here were to report that the Egyptian Government were unable by their own efforts to protect their nationals." He added that "His Excellency took the hint."[43]

The government had, indeed, failed to prevent the mass riots and had not enforced the ban on propaganda spreading religious hatred. But it had not passed any anti-Jewish legislation either, even though the evacuations and arrests were, Muslim Brothers excepted, directed primarily against Jews, whether they were Zionists, communists or totally uninvolved in politics. It was only in September 1950 that the Nationality Law was amended to include a paragraph providing that Egyptian nationality could be withdrawn from any person involved in actions in favor of states that were at war with Egypt or with whom Egypt had broken off diplomatic relations. But it was not until six years later, in November 1956, immediately after the Suez War, that a new amendment to the Nationality Law was passed defining these persons as Zionists.[44] Until then, discriminatory measures against Jews had never been codified in formal legislation. The restrictions regarding exit visas, for instance, applied to all citizens irrespective of religion and political conviction. It was mainly the pettiness of poorly paid minor officials that made these restrictions particularly harsh for Jews, who were generally regarded as being rich and difficult to distinguish from the Zionists, communists, and foreign oppressors in general.[45] Yet compared to what would take place in Egypt during and after the wars of 1956 and 1967, suffering was still relatively mild in 1948. The community emerged from the first Arab-Israeli war without heavy losses in human life and property.

This view was borne out by the reaction of the Egyptian Jews themselves. It is certainly true that a sense of insecurity was spreading, and that the communities tried to protect themselves by emphasizing their loyalty to Egypt and donating to the war fund. But the commercial and entrepreneurial middle and upper classes—committed Zionists excepted—still did not consider leaving Egypt for Europe, the Americas or Israel. They clearly did not see their economic and social position jeopardized by developments, which were, in their view, solely linked to the war and hence temporary. Events up to 1956 seemed to prove them right.[46] However, the situation looked quite different from the perspective of the lower and lower-middle classes, who, even before the war, had seen their position undermined by widespread unemployment, which was rendered even more serious by the drive to Egyptianize Egyptian business and administration. In the years between 1949 and 1951, members of the Jewish lower and lower-middle class did, indeed, leave Egypt in large numbers. But they seem to have done so mainly for economic reasons, even though in this case it is particularly difficult to separate political from economic motives. The move toward Egyptianization was, after all, equally motivated by economic and political factors. Unless they carried a foreign passport, Jewish emigrants had little choice regarding their destination, again suggesting political motives of a decision (in favor of Zionism and Israel), which in actual fact may have been less clear-cut and premeditated.

The emigration of lower-middle class Jews from Egypt in the period 1949–51 was organized from Israel, jointly financed by international Jewish organizations and the local Jewish community—and it was tacitly tolerated by the Egyptian government. In spring 1949, new emissaries of the Israeli Mossad arrived in Egypt. They opened "travel agencies" in Cairo and Alexandria, such as American Express, Paltours and others, through which the departure of Egyptian Jews to Europe and from there to Israel was openly arranged.[47] The travel agencies prepared lists of applicants for emigration, providing them, by a variety of legal and illegal means, with the required travel documents for France or Italy. They were able to count on the cooperation of certain employees of the French, Italian, and British consulates, who issued passports, visas, *laissez-passers* or simple *feuilles de route*. They also secured, largely through bribery, the cooperation of certain Egyptian officials. Money was provided partly by the local Jewish communities, which also paid for the required health checks at the communal hospitals. Their motives must have been mixed; but it is to be assumed that the opportunity to get rid, in a discreet way, of the poorer sections of the community was included among them. The journey to Marseille or Genoa was paid for by the Jewish Agency, the Joint Distribution Committee, and several other international Jewish organizations. Once they had arrived in Marseille or Genoa, the emigrants were taken to preparation (*hakhshara*) camps and from there to Israel.

Those members of the middle and upper classes who decided to leave the country, too, did so at their own expense. They, for the most part, preferred to go to Western Europe, the Americas or Australia rather than Israel, which, apart from the many problems besetting life there, was also more alien on the cultural and social levels. The total number of immigrants to Israel from 1949 to 1951 was estimated at 15,000 to 20,000, corresponding to about 20 to 25 percent of the Egyptian Jewish population.

The Israeli census of 1961 registered 14,895 immigrants from Egypt and the Sudan in the period from 1948 to 1951, and the Israeli census of 1972 gave their total figure as 15,872 for the years 1948–54.[48]

The Egyptian government could not but have noticed the sudden, but very marked desire of local Jews, who had previously not even been able to afford Alexandria, to spend their holidays in Mediterranean seaports. Yet it did nothing to prevent their departure. The head of one travel agency in Alexandria was being observed because he was suspected of dealing in drugs. It can be assumed that government inaction was based on a number of considerations. These included the fear of appearing intolerant and undemocratic to foreign observers; the assessment that the Zionists were not concerned with changing the existing order in Egypt and that it was, therefore, better to leave the ground to them rather than to their communist rivals; the realization that the overwhelming majority of local Jews could not be integrated or assimilated into Egyptian society, once it defined itself primarily in Arab-Islamic terms; and finally the sober calculation that the departure of thousands of clerks, salesmen, and managers would make room for that many "real" Egyptians.[49] As far as the government was concerned, it was regrettable that these emigrants went to Israel of all countries. But when it became a question of choosing between general Arab interest and more narrowly defined Egyptian national interest, the latter clearly won—Egypt first.

THE BURNING OF CAIRO

By 1950, public interest had again returned to the central concern of national politics: liberation from British control. Beginning in October 1951, the struggle against the British military presence on the Suez Canal developed into a guerrillalike Canal war. It culminated in Black Saturday on 26 January 1952, when in reaction to the killing of forty Egyptian policemen in the city of Ismāʿīlīya large parts of the modern quarters of Cairo were burned down by violent demonstrators and an unspecified mob.

It was only in the late afternoon after the riots had passed their climax that the police finally intervened. The extent to which the Muslim Brothers, Miṣr al-Fatāt and other groups were involved in preparing and organizing the violence was never officially established. It is quite possible that the government no longer dared to name or punish those responsible.[50] The riots were directed against the British presence in the country, and foreign influence in general. Jews were only marginally involved in so far as they were included among the non-Muslim minorities that had benefited from British rule and protection. The riots were also aimed at the ruling élite, the king, the parties, and the military leadership. All had been discredited by the war against Israel, which had revealed the extent of corruption and incompetence rampant among the military and political leadership. In this respect, the burning of Cairo can indeed be seen as a prelude to the takeover by the Free Officers in July 1952. It had demonstrated very clearly that the majority of the urban population was no longer prepared to support the ruling élite and the sociopolitical system it represented.

By the early fifties, Egyptian Jews had largely returned to their regular occupations, business, family life, and recreation. They were no more affected by the events of 1952 than were the other non-Muslim minorities and Europeans living in the country. After the revolution of July 1952, the Free Officers took great pains to make foreigners and local minorities, Copts and Jews in particular, feel at ease. General Muḥammad Najīb visited Jewish schools and synagogues, and Chief Rabbi Haim Nahum attended national celebrations as he had under the monarchy.[51] While Zionism as an organized movement had come to an end in May 1948, and while large-scale emigration to Israel between 1949 and 1951 was organized from abroad, the Zionist youth movements continued to operate as private debating clubs. It was from these clubs that the members of a sabotage and espionage group were recruited to undermine a potential rapprochement between the new Egyptian government and the United States. The so-called Lavon affair that disrupted Israeli political life when in 1953–54 the group was caught and tried for high treason, strained not only Israeli politics but also damaged relations between the local Jewish community and the Egyptian authorities.[52]

Yet the decisive blow against Egyptian Jewry did not come until October 1956, when the coordinated attack, or tripartite aggression, by Israel, France, and Britain on Egypt seemed to finally prove the old theory of the alliance between Zionism and imperialism. Popular reaction and the measures taken in connection with the war affected Egyptian Jewry in a much more serious and pervasive way than in 1948. Mass arrests included Zionists as well as non-Zionists, and the expulsion of all British and French nationals was extended to include thousands of stateless Jews. Legal changes finally made Zionism a criminal offense without, however, providing a clear-cut definition of what exactly that implied.[53] The nationalization decrees of 1961–62, marking the beginning of the regime's newly adopted "socialist course," affected all private business in the country, Jewish as well as non-Jewish. While it was thus by no means specifically directed against the Jews, it definitely deprived the Jewish middle and upper classes of their livelihood.[54] Emigration, which had sagged in the early fifties, surged during and after the war of 1956. Of the 50,000 to 55,000 Jews who had remained in Egypt after the first Arab-Israeli war, another 40,000 to 50,000 left the country in 1956–57, either of their own accord or by force. The remaining 5,000 to 10,000 were then subjected to the nationalization measures. In 1967, an estimated 2,500 to 3,000 Jews were still living in the country, and by the eighties, their numbers had dwindled to a mere 300 to 400.

Conclusion

In the interwar period, Jews occupied a secure and respected place in Egyptian society. No restrictions were imposed on their economic activities or on their religious, cultural, social, and political life, Zionism included. The Jews were considered to be highly influential in the Egyptian economy, where, according to a former member of the community, they had the final say or, to put it in French as seems more appropriate, "ils faisaient la pluie et le beau temps."[1] But Egyptian Jewry did not act as an organized pressure group wielding economic and political power. Economic power and political influence were indeed exerted by individual members of the community, but they did not represent Egyptian Jewry as a whole for the simple reason that there was no such unified and homogeneous entity. Large-scale immigration, social differentiation, and cultural change together had created a fragmented community divided along lines of regional origin, rite, language, nationality, social class and, within the limits of a basic sense of Jewishness, of identity as well.

In the nineteenth century, Jews had occupied a well-defined position as a non-Muslim *millet*, which may have been viewed by Muslims with suspicion, or even contempt, but which nevertheless implied "toleration within the framework of discrimination," as Siegfried Landshut put it. In the words of Nehemiah Robinson it was "enlightened from a medieval, not a modern, perspective."[2] By the turn of the century, their status had improved markedly. But the situation had also become a great deal more complicated. After the Islamic laws regarding *dhimmīs* were abolished in the second half of the nineteenth century and all citizens declared equal before the law, the different ethnic and religious communities were, at least in principle, free to step out of their traditional enclaves. British control gave the non-Muslim minorities a greater sense of security. Rapid economic expansion provided them with unprecedented opportunities for social advancement. After World War I, increased mobility and the spread of higher education among Muslims and Copts gradually began to blur the lines between the previously autonomous groups. Intensified interaction brought new contact and acculturation, but also sharpened competition and resulting friction.

During the entire period under consideration, the Jews remained just one of several non-Muslim minorities living in the country, and not the most important or potentially threatening one. This basic fact can hardly be stressed enough. In Egypt as in most parts of the Middle East, Jews never had the highly conspicuous rôle of the major or only religious minority that they played in many parts of Europe. The Copts were by far the most important non-Muslim minority and even among the so-called local foreign minorities, the Greeks rivaled the Jews in numbers, economic power, social prestige, and cultural influence. The Syrians and Armenians, though fewer in number, also played an important part. Jews were affected by interwar developments only in as much as they formed part and parcel of this group of local foreign minorities, which included all those who by their regional (ethnic) background, language, culture, and education were not Egyptian. That there was also a sizeable number of indigenous, that is, truly Egyptian Jews, was widely ignored. The community as a whole was identified with its majority of more or less Westernized immigrants and their children, and their image was projected upon the rest.

Nominal nationality was regarded as secondary compared to these criteria of culture and, at least implicitly, of political identification based on religion and ethnicity. Jews consequently were included in one group not only with the Greeks, the (Christian) Syrians, and the Armenians, who may or may not have held Egyptian passports, but also with the British, the French, and the Belgians living in Egypt. There is no indication of any hostility toward Jews as such in the years between World War I and the outbreak of the Arab revolt in Palestine in 1936. The hostility that manifested itself after that date was linked to the Palestine issue and for many years limited to small groups of militant nationalist and Islamic activists.

The absence of manifest hostility or open aggression in the interwar period does, of course, tell very little about latent prejudice or resentment harbored against Jews in the non-Jewish population, particularly so in a situation of foreign domination. But as always it is extremely difficult to make any assumptions regarding the real feelings of the population in general concerning Jews or any other minority. It should be kept in mind that almost all Jews in Egypt lived in the large cities, and that the hostility displayed toward them in the 1940s and 1950s was a purely urban phenomenon. While it would, therefore, be interesting to learn about the attitudes of Egyptian peasants toward the Jews, it would be of little practical relevance. The attitudes of the peasants had an impact only when they moved to the cities and participated in political activity there. But even for Cairo and Alexandria, there is very little evidence indicating that there was serious conflict between Jews and non-Jews in general, and between Jews and Muslims in particular.

In the nineteenth century, travelers and foreign observers reported tangible signs of "contemptous hatred" and discrimination against local Jews who were still living their separate existence, as expressed in residential segregation, occupation, and dress. But travel accounts are valuable mainly in the absence of more systematic material. They are usually too random and frequently too personal to be taken at face value. When it comes to popular images and self-images, these reports should be treated with extreme caution. One has difficulty reconciling a British report from the late 1880s that speaks of the local Jews as one of the most hated minorities in the country, with

Elkan Adler's statement that these same Jews were "respected," "hard-working," and "not unpopular."[3] It may be well to adopt a middle course and to assume that in the late nineteenth century, Jews were neither particularly liked nor particularly hated. They may simply not have been conspicuous enough to create a specific image. There is, at any rate, no evidence to support a persecutionist view.

For the early twentieth century, the reports of the Alliance Israélite Universelle, though written by outsiders whose *mission civilisatrice* was foremost in their minds, provide much valuable information on communal affairs, but little on relations between local Jews and Muslims. S. Somekh, the director of the Alliance school in Cairo, describes one incident of sectarian violence involving Jews and Muslims in 1904, which was caused by a funeral procession through the adjoining Muslim and Jewish quarters of the Cairo Mūskī area. Yet he ascribed the physical violence that erupted to the fanaticism of both groups, without drawing any general conclusions from this single, and it would seem, isolated incident.[4] With the exception of a very limited number of ritual murder (blood libel) accusations raised against local Jews by Muslims (rather than Greek, Syrian or Coptic Christians) in the period between 1870 and 1925, there are no indications of manifest popular aggression and hostility until the 1940s.

That it was possible in later years to activate religious sentiments against the Jews, when the antagonism was basically of a political and economic nature, suggests that these sentiments may have been latent even before. Indeed, it is well known that the Qur'ān, and the *ḥadīth* even more, contain a sufficiently large number of references denouncing the Jews as enemies of the Prophet and Islam to make it possible for every moderately educated Muslim to quote at least some of them.[5] However, this fact remained irrelevant until the late 1930s, when the Qur'ān and *ḥadīth* began to be cited in the context of the Palestine conflict. Until then, these references simply do not seem to have been quoted in order to legitimize hostile action against the Jews. And even in the late 1930s, religious arguments against the

Jews were restricted to opposition groups in the nationalist and Islamic camps. It was almost a generation later that anti-Jewish propaganda based on the Qur'ān and Sunna were actively spread by the government and the state-controlled media. The use of the epithet *yahūdī* (Jew) is also quite instructive. When employed by Muslim Cairenes living in the traditional city quarters, it carried with it the connotation of suspicion, miserliness, and self-imposed segregation. To be a *yahūdī*, then, was clearly negative, particularly when contrasted with the qualities ascribed to "real" (urban) Egyptians, the *abnā' al-balad* as described by Sawsan El-Messiri. But it remained an image of the Jew in the abstract, largely unrelated to the real Jews living among urban Muslims and Copts. It is reported by former members of the Egyptian Jewish community that it was never directed against them personally, not even in the 1940s. While it would thus be desirable to have a detailed treatment of the image of the Jew, both local and foreign, as reflected in the Egyptian literature of the time—and it cannot be stressed enough that the time factor is crucial here—this literary image may not have been reflected in daily life.[6]

Nevertheless, it remains revelant to ask to what extent Jews were integrated into Egyptian society in these years of economic success, social rise, and peaceful coexistence—under British control. Integration is, of course, an elusive phenomenon, as difficult to define as the related concept of assimilation. Here it will be understood as a two-sided process, implying the intention on the part of the minority concerned to participate not only in the economic, but also in the social, cultural, and political life of the host society. At the same time, there must be a certain degree of openness and tolerance on the part of the majority, which presupposes, at the very least, the absence of deep-seated prejudice, overt discrimination, and a fundamental clash of values and styles of behavior. All these concepts are in themselves vague and notoriously difficult to define, but then integration may be looked upon as a process, denoting a certain willingness to participate and to accept rather than the end result of it.

In dealing with the issues of integration, segregation, and identity, it is again necessary to distinguish between the various subgroups of local Jewish society. As has been shown above, the Jews of the small cities in the Delta and along the Suez Canal, who were predominantly of Oriental or indigenous origin, were the most thoroughly assimilated into the language and life-style of their Egyptian environment; and, with a few exceptions, they were no longer segregated in their living areas. Special quarters, to the extent that they still existed in the nineteenth century, were abandoned in the early twentieth century. Moreover, there was constant interaction between the various ethnic and religious groups in the economic sphere. But even with regard to the minority of Jews living in the provincial cities, one will have to point to the symbols of a separate, or, as Jacques Hassoun calls it, a double identity, as it was best expressed in dress, which combined the Egyptian *jallābīya* with the European jacket.[7] According to him, even the poorest Jews claimed membership in two societies and two cultures, the Egyptian and the European, even if the latter was more an aspiration than a fact.

The case of the Jews of the Cairo *ḥāra*, a much more significant segment of Egyptian Jewry, shows that cultural assimilation and spatial proximity must not be equated with close interaction. While the Jews in the Cairo *ḥāra* did come into daily contact with their Muslim and Coptic neighbors, whose culture and life-style they shared to a high degree, they nevertheless maintained spatial segregation. Separateness was further reinforced by the fact that the Jewish poor rarely attended Egyptian institutions, but were educated at Jewish communal or private schools. Because of their poverty and lack of education they were much more dependent on communal services than were their middle- and upper-class coreligionists. They were, therefore, of necessity more oriented toward their own community, highlighting the importance of vertical as opposed to horizontal links and cleavages. The Jews of the *ḥāra* may thus be seen as one of the last remnants of the *millet* system, combining acculturation with separateness, as expressed in residence, education, and social intercourse. Yet they clearly had the potential for integration into Egyptian society. That they were not was the result of political developments linked to the Palestine conflict.

The Ashkenazi lower and lower-middle classes, which mainly continued to live a traditional life modeled on the Eastern European Jewish *shtetl*, are, of course, not included here. Grouped together in the Cairo Darb al-Barābira and the Daher areas, the Ashkenazim preserved their distinctive language, dress, and customs, which set them apart not only from Egyptian society at large, but also from Oriental and Sephardi Jewish society. Origin, rite, and residence, then, continued to have considerable influence on the degree of integration, acculturation, and assimilation to (Muslim) Egyptian society.

This applies to the Jewish middle class as well, which was possibly even more heterogeneous than the lower class of the provincial towns and the ethnic quarters of Cairo. While some members of the commercial and professional middle class preferred to stay in their traditional districts, where they were able to preserve their Jewish customs and life-style, the large majority moved to middle-class areas, which were inhabited mostly by other local foreign minorities, and where they adopted the cosmopolitan culture largely influenced by Greeks and Italians. The various minorities were educated together in French, Italian, British or Greek schools, mixed frequently at work and in social life, and shared certain economic and political interests with regard to the British and the Egyptian public. By no means did this preclude intercommunal rivalry based on economic competition and religious resentment, which, in some cases, was even reinforced by a sense of racial superiority.[8] Even if one does not rank this kind of resentment and hostility as anti-Semitic, there was an undeniable element of ambivalence in the relations between local Jews and the Greek, Armenian, and Syrian Christians, which was not completely superseded by their common interests regarding outside threats. Local (non-Coptic) Christians had, after all, been the main source of ritual murder accusations, which subsided only in the 1920s. Passions still latent came once more into the open when, in 1925, the anti-Semitic incident occurred in Alexandria at the French missionary schools of Ste. Cathérine and Sacré Coeur.

Contacts between middle-class Jews and Muslims seem to have been largely restricted to the sphere of business. As the example of the Egyptian Jewish youth club reveals, only a minority of middle-class Jews showed any desire to integrate into Arab-Egyptian society and to participate in Egyptian social, cultural, and political life. Contacts in the social and private spheres were further restricted by a number of factors operating independently of the individual's wish to integrate and participate. One of these factors was religious personal status law, which made intermarriage as the ultimate symbol of close interaction very difficult. In the Egyptian censuses, no more than twenty-five to thirty-five mixed marriages (5–6% of all marriages contracted by local Jews) were registered annually. Nonetheless, the journal *al-Shams* saw itself obliged, in 1944, to point to the number of mixed marriages and the predicament of marriageable Jewish girls from poor families, who, for lack of a genuinely Jewish education as much as for lack of an adequate dowry, were tempted to consider marrying non-Jews or even to convert.[9] Another factor concerned the seclusion of Muslim women, which made it difficult for foreigners and non-Muslims in general to include Muslims in their social activities. Interaction was, therefore, largely restricted to female circles meeting for tea, bridge or charity on one hand and all-male clubs and shooting parties on the other. In addition, it was precisely the Muslim and Coptic Egyptian middle class that resented most intensely the preponderance of foreigners and local foreign minorities, the Jews among them, in the Egyptian economy and society; and it was they who worked to reduce or, if possible, to eliminate it altogether.

Interaction seems to have been closest at the highest level of society, that is, among the élites of the various communities. The Jewish élite families were linked to their Muslim, Coptic, Levantine, and European peers by common interest, education, taste, and life-style. Robert Tignor has illustrated this process of cultural assimilation of the Egyptian *haute bourgeoisie*, and the evolution of a distinctive class consciousness that went with it. Close cooperation in business, as manifested in the increase of ethnically mixed boards of joint stock companies, was accompanied by social interaction in clubs and associations of all kinds, bridge evenings, balls, receptions, marriages celebrated in grand style, and summer vacations spent in Europe. Even intimate contacts seem to have been possible, if not outright chic in certain circles of high society. A number of Jewish élite members maintained good relations with the king and the royal family. The fact that two Jewish women, Valentine Rolo and Alice de Cattaoui, served as first lady-in-waiting to Queen Nazlī illustrates the high regard in which their families were held. That inter-communal relations were generally good is evident in the frequency with which wealthy Jews donated large sums of money to Christian and Muslim charitable works or to Egyptian state institutions.[10] Religion and ethnicity as the primary frames of identity and group solidarity thus became increasingly superseded, but never completely supplanted by the horizontal element of social class. A sense of separateness was preserved even among the communal élites, and their relationship remained characterized by a frequently uneasy combination of cooperation and competition.

By adopting, even if superficially, European culture and education, the Jewish middle and upper classes moved away, and became alienated, from both their Jewish background and their Egyptian environment. The adoption of European languages and first names was only the most visible sign of this new orientation and gradual integration into the cosmopolitan subculture, which was particularly strong in Alexandria. On the economic level, the Jewish middle and upper classes were closely linked to, and indeed identified with, the economic system established and upheld by the colonial power. On the political level, the Jewish élite stressed its loyalty to the Egyptian nation and the king, but barely participated in the national struggle. They, therefore, came very close to Albert Hourani's highly unfavorable description of the Levantine bourgeoisie:

The increase of trade with Europe and America led to the rise of a new class of minority-population: the Levantine bourgeoisie of the big towns, Syrian Christian, Armenian, Greek and Jewish, very different in mentality from the Christians of the villages and the old towns, and much more distant than they from the majority. Often very rich and very powerful in the economic and financial spheres, they were slavishly imitative of Europe, at least on the surface, and more often than not despised the Oriental life around them. Often they had no loyalties at all, certainly no political loyalty to the State in which they were living. They tended to attach themselves to one or other of the foreign Governments with interests in the Middle East, to imitate the French or English way of life and serve foreign Governments with a feverish and brittle devotion.[11]

The dynamism and Westernization of the Jewish middle and upper classes, which proved so useful in the economic sphere, maneuvered them into a marginal, and ultimately precarious, position within Egyptian society at large. If this offered them a chance to serve as intermediaries between Egypt and Europe, especially in the economic sphere, it also exposed them as dependents of Britain and the colonial system in general. These ties made them part of the European and Levantine local foreign colonies, regardless of their origin and nationality. But unlike the Greeks and the Italians, they did not have a safe refuge in Europe in the years of crisis, the minority of foreign nationals always excluded. The prevailing sense of superiority toward the (Muslim and Coptic) Egyptians, who appeared mainly as domestic servants, shopkeepers, government officials, peasants or beggars, was, therefore, frequently mingled with a certain sense of anxiety, "this little fear" that Edith Cohen referred to in an interview, or "apprehensive caution" described by Jacob Landau for the nineteenth-century.[12] A search for added security was the natural result of this anxiety, efforts to purchase foreign passports, to maintain close links with the British Residency and the other European powers. The European powers, in turn, did their best to win the Jewish community over by defending their interests with the Egyptian authorities, by paying subsidies to their schools and charitable institutions, and by granting passports and decorations to their élite. The British, it will be imagined, were not altogether unhappy with this situation, as a letter written in 1926 by Sir Neville Henderson, the acting high commissioner, stated so well:

In itself, nevertheless, a little xenophobia is not a bad thing, as it inclines the foreigner to acquiesce more readily in the predomination of British control and influence as their only real safeguard.... That is surely the ideal position: that the Egyptian should regard us as his friend and protector against the rapacious foreign cuckoo and that the foreigner should consider us to be his only safeguard against the injustice and discrimination of the Egyptian fanatic.[13]

Yet until the 1940s, there seems to have been no overriding sense of danger among Egyptian Jews. They did, however, try not to draw attention to their existence and activities, be they economic or political, and to remain as inconspicuous as possible. If this policy of keeping a low profile helped to avoid trouble, it certainly did not solve the question of identity, which under growing outside pressure began to take on more urgency. The question of whether Egyptian Jewry was to regard itself as a minority fully integrated into Egyptian society, possibly preserving features of the *millet* system such as religious jurisdiction in personal status matters, or as a national minority with separate political aspirations, was left unresolved. It was mainly outside pressure, which treated the Jews as a separate community with complex collective features, that was to provide the practical answer to these questions.

In the second half of the 1930s, relations between the Muslim majority and the local Jewish minority began to deteriorate, although this did not lead to any dramatic consequences like open persecution or massive emigration. The full impact of these changes only appeared in 1956–57, several years after the Free Officers had taken over. In the interwar period, rapid population growth, massive migration to the cities, and unemployment aggravated the country's social problems. Socioeconomic change gradually transformed the mechanisms of political conflict as well. "Liberal" territorial nationalism with its secularist tendencies was superseded by (politicized) Islam and pan-Arabism, a search for national unity, if not homogeneity, in which the ethnic factor tended to merge with the religious. The resulting drive to Egyptianize public life and the economy attempted to eliminate, or at least greatly reduce, the foreign presence in the Egyptian economy and society.

These developments concerned all local foreign minorities, and after 1956 the large majority of Greeks, Italians, Belgians, French, and British did, indeed, leave the country as well. Non-Muslim and non-Arab minorities had smaller chances to integrate into the Egyptian nation once it came to be increasingly defined on Arab and Islamic lines. This applied to Jews as well as to Christians. But the Jews had more strikes against them than the others. Not only were they not Muslim, and mainly not of Egyptian origin; most of them did not share the Arabic language and culture, either. Added to these factors was their political diversity. There were among them royalists and capitalists who had profited from the colonial system and the privileges of the Capitulations, but also socialists, communists, and, of course, Zionists—the major enemies, one internal and the other external, of the regime as well as of its nationalist and Islamic critics. The association with Zionism, real and imagined, was, of course, the element that harmed them most. Taken together, Egyptian Jewry presented a combination of attributes that could hardly have been worse in the eyes of committed Muslim nationalists.

In the agitation against the Jews of the late thirties and the forties, diverse elements combined to create a complex image of the Jew as enemy. That such a highly complex stereotype could develop implied that in the mid-twentieth century, Jews were still primarily treated as members of an ethnoreligious community with distinctive traits and objectives rather than as individuals with personal opinions and aspirations of their own. Individual deviation from this collective image, as demonstrated by Jews active in the Egyptian nationalist or the communist movements, tended to be viewed with suspicion: it was regarded as a cunning effort to realize collective "Jewish interest," a sort of family job-sharing, where some members of the family assumed the tasks of capitalists in the service of foreign interest and other members the tasks of pro-Arab "progressives" or Jewish nationalists—all in order to secure a foothold in every political camp.

The situation remained full of contradictions, reflecting the ambiguities inherent in the old *millet* concept, where the religious factor tended to blend with the ethnic one to create separate ethnoreligious communities. These, under different circumstances, might see themselves, or be seen by others, as separate nations in the modern sense. In Egypt and the Arab world at large, the Jews were not recognized as a separate political community with national rights of their own (which would have justified Zionism). And yet, they were attacked as just such a community because of their real or alleged links to Zionism, if not outright identity with it. All individual differences were ignored. The Muslim Brothers, for instance, saw the Jews as a religious minority with guaranteed rights, albeit inferior ones, which they shared with all non-Muslim *dhimmīs* living in an Islamic society. But they actually treated them as a nation with distinctive national characteristics, though a nation defined primarily in religious terms.

In sum, a Jewish question as it emerged in nineteenth-century Europe did not exist in twentieth-century Egypt. Jews were not discriminated against because of their religion or race, but for political reasons. While it was possible to mobilize religious (Islamic) resentment against them—and the Qur'ān and Sunna provide a rich stock of appropriate references—religious resentment was secondary and only came to bear under specific political and economic circumstances. While this is true of Christian Europe as well, where anti-Semitism did not develop autonomously either, but under specific sociopolitical conditions, there still remains a difference in scope and emphasis. In Egypt, hostility was primarily linked to a clearly identifiable political issue, the Palestine conflict. The polemics of Islamic and nationalist militants, which, for obvious reasons, received so much attention, should not tempt one to identify them with the sentiments of the Egyptian population at large. In the period under consideration, there were no signs of anti-Jewish or anti-Semitic feeling among the general public. It should also be remembered that until 1956, the government did not introduce discriminatory legislation against the Jews, nor did it initiate any propaganda or persecution campaigns against them.

To return to general judgments on the situation of the Jews in the Arab world or, even more comprehensively, under Islam, the more extreme interpretations can be safely rejected. The case study of twentieth-century Egypt calls for caution and modesty. There was neither uninterrupted persecution and terror nor undisturbed harmony ended by the sudden appearance of Zionism or Jamāl ʿAbd al-Nāṣir. The assumption that Islam is inherently intolerant, and that anti-Semitism is present at all times and places, is refuted by the economic and social success of the Jewish middle and upper classes in the interwar period, and even more so by the absence of popular anti-Semitism during this period and beyond. But the assumption that it was only Zionism or the evil genius of ʿAbd al-Nāṣir that created problems between the Muslim majority and the Jewish minority in the country is equally unfounded. It ignores the tension resulting from economic competition and cultural difference, which intensified in the period of emancipation from British control, and which, sooner or later, would have greatly reduced the rôle of foreigners and local foreign minorities in Egyptian society and the economy, the Jews included. That the Jews were driven out altogether, a few hundred people excepted, and that the Greeks or the Italians were not, was the result of the Arab-Israeli conflict over Palestine. What one is left with then, as is so often the case, is a complex picture, which allows specific answers for specific groups and periods only. No broad generalizations can be made except the admittedly rather trivial one that historical circumstances change, and that it is not only ideology that changes with them, but also the expression of religion. But then reality has never been simple or historical development unilinear, and "eternal Egypt" is no exception to the rule.

Notes

INTRODUCTION

1. Siegfried Landshut, *Jewish Communities in the Muslim Countries of the Middle East* (London, 1950), p. ix; differing figures in Hayyim J. Cohen, *The Jews of the Middle East, 1860–1972* (New York, 1973), p. 69 (without the Maghreb); for the exodus, see also Terence Prittie and Bernard Dineen, *The Double Exodus: A Study of Arab and Jewish Refugees in the Middle East* (London, n.d.), pp. 20–26.
2. For works emphasizing Muslim-Jewish coexistence, see Ya'qūb Khūrī, *al-Yahūd fī'l-buldān al-'arabīya* (Beirut, 1970); Ali Ibrahim Abdou and Khairieh Kasmieh, *Les juifs des pays arabes* (Beirut, 1971); Qāsim 'Abduh Qāsim, *al-Yahūd fī miṣr min al-fatḥ al-'arabī hattā 'l-ghazw al-'uthmānī* (Cairo, 1987); 'Alī Shilsh, *al-Yahūd wa-l-māsūn fī miṣr. Dirāsa tārīkhīya* (Cairo, 1986); and Maurice Mizrahi, *L'Egypte et ses juifs: Le temps revolu (XIXè et XXè siècles)* (Geneva, 1977), pp. 11ff, who claims that it was only under Jamāl 'Abd al-Nāṣir that problems emerged. For highly differentiated views, see Norman A. Stillman, *The Jews of Arab Lands: A History and Source Book* (Philadelphia, 1979); Shmu'el Ettinger, ed., *Toldot ha-yehudim be-artsot ha-islam* (Jerusalem, 1981); and Bernard Lewis, *The Jews of Islam* (Princeton, 1984). For works emphasizing Islamic intolerance, see Martin Gilbert, *The Jews of Arab Lands: Their History in Maps* (Oxford, 1975); and the studies of Bat Ye'or/Yahudia Masriya [pseudonym].

CHAPTER ONE

1. For contemporary attitudes toward the "native" Egyptians, see, e.g., Anthony M. Galatoli, *Egypt in Midpassage* (Cairo, 1950), p. 65.

2. On the foreign colonies, see Marius Deeb, "The Socioeconomic Role of the Local Foreign Minorities in Modern Egypt, 1805–1961," *International Journal of Middle East Studies* 9 (1978): 11–22; and Ṣāliḥ Ramaḍān Maḥmūd, "al-Jālīyāt al-ajnabīya fī miṣr fī 'l-qarn al-tāsi' 'ashar," Ph.D. diss. (Cairo University, 1969), pp. 14-48; Athanase G. Politis, *L'Héllénisme et l'Egypte moderne*, 2 vols. (Paris, 1929–30); Angelo Sammarco, *Gli Italiani in Egitto: Il contribuo italiano nella formazione dell'Egitto moderno* (Alexandria, 1937); Albert Hourani, "The Syrians in Egypt in the Eighteenth and Nineteenth Centuries," in *The Emergence of the Middle East* (London, 1981), pp. 103–23; and Thomas Philipp, *The Syrians in Egypt, 1725–1975* (Stuttgart, 1985).
3. *AS* 1917 (Cairo, 1918), p. 22; similar results from the census of 1927 (*AS* 1935–36 [Cairo, 1937], p. 21).
4. AIU, Egypt, II.B.27, Grunberg, Cairo, 5, 11, 20 December 1893. AIU, Egypt, II.E.35.d, Danon, Alexandria, 27 March 1903, reported that "In order to cover the growing budget deficit, a deficit caused by the influx of Jewish immigrants, the community council had decided to ask the authorities to push back every Jew who could not prove he had sufficient means of support."
5. S. D. Goitein, *A Mediterranean Society*, 4 vols. (Berkeley and Los Angeles, 1967–83), 2:1–40; and Mark Cohen, *Jewish Self-Government in Medieval Egypt: The Origins of the Office of Head of the Jews, ca. 1065–1126* (Princeton, 1980), pp. 287–94.
6. Maurice Fargeon, *Les juifs en Egypte depuis les origines jusqu'à ce jour* (Cairo, 1938), pp. 126ff and 169ff.
7. Fargeon, *Les juifs*, pp. 157ff; Landau, *Jews*, pp. 9–20, and 103–14; Harald Motzki, *Ḏimma und Egalité* ... (Bonn, 1979), pp. 54-56.
8. This estimate is based on the figures given for the inhabitants of the Cairo Jewish *ḥāra*, which, however, are far from precise. According to Landau (*Jews*, p. 30), there were about 3,000 Jews in the *ḥāra* in 1920; the Egyptian censuses of the interwar period register some 4,500 to 5,000 Jews in the quarter of al-Yahūd al-Rabbānīyīn. An unsigned communication of 20 November 1943 (CZA, S6/1982) put their number at 7,000, and *al-Muṣawwar* (no. 1239) at 9,800 (quoted from Landshut, *Jewish Communities*, p. 28)
9. See sources in note 8 above and Edmond Harari, "Quelques réflexions ..." (Paris, 1980), unpublished ms; Jacques Hassoun, "Chroniques de la vie quotidienne," in *Juifs du Nil* (Paris, 1981), pp. 107–92. See also AIU, Egypt, XI.E.182.j, Somekh, Cairo, 27 March 1910.
10. On the problem of begging, see *Israël*, 9 and 16 September 1932; *al-Shams*, 14 November 1942, 3 October 1947; CZA, S5/793, Czernowitz, 6 February 1944.
11. Hassoun, *Chroniques de la vie quotidienne*; AIU, Egypt, XI.E.182.j, Somekh, Cairo, 27 March 1910; AIU, Egypt, XIV.E.206, Douec, Ṭanṭā,

5 March 1909; CZA Z4/3229I, Grünhut, "Bericht über Ägypten," Jerusalem, 29 November 1927.

12. AIU, Egypt, XIII.E.184, de Semo, al-Manṣūra, 19 July 1893.
13. *al-Shams*, 18 January and 22 February 1935; Mizrahi, *L'Egypte et ses juifs*, pp. 32, 61–62.
14. On the Moroccan immigrants, see AIU, Egypt, I.B.9, Goar, Alexandria, 26 September 1907; on the Yemeni Jews, AIU, Egypt, IX.E.182.b, Somekh, Alexandria, 13, 24 June 1898; and CZA, KH4B/450, Czernowitz, 9 January 1939.
15. OH(35)1, Y. Shohet, 10 December 1964; OH(35)6, J. Kahanoff; and OH(35)2, I. Lévy-Romano.
16. Fargeon, *Les juifs*, p. 141; David Siton, *Ḳehilot yehude sefarad we-ha-mizraḥ ba-'olam be-yamenu* (Jerusalem, 1974), pp. 76-80; and Stillman, *The Jews of Arab Lands*, pp. 74–75.
17. Almost all of the eighty-two Jewish lawyers listed as "avocats près la cour" in CZA, KKL5/472, 14 May 1930, were of Sephardi or Oriental origin. On the medical doctors, see Maurice Fargeon, *Médecins et avocats juifs au service de l'Egypte*. Vol. 1: *Les médecins juifs d'Egypte* (Cairo, 1939?).
18. AIU, Egypt, VI.E.87, Benaroya, Cairo, 1 May 1908; AIU, Egypt, I.G.24, Benneys, Ṭanṭā, 25 March 1928; also CZA, Z4/3229I, Grünhut, Jerusalem, 29 November 1927.
19. Arnold Wright, ed., *Twentieth Century Impressions of Egypt: Its History, People, Commerce, Industries, and Resources* (London, 1909), p. 25; and Landau, *Jews*, pp. 26 and 102 for several Ladino periodicals published in the early twentieth century.
20. Landau, *Jews*, pp. 25–27.
21. Sammarco, *Gli Italiani*, p. 43; Landau, *Jews*, p. 25–26. The communal archives in Livorno were partly burned, making it very difficult to either prove or disprove descent from this community.
22. On the Italian colony, see AA, Abt. II, Po3, von Prittwitz, Rome, 1 October 1924; and FO 371/19097, Fitzpatrick, "Intelligence Note," 5 September 1935.
23. Richard Lichtheim, *Rückkehr: Lebenserinnerungen aus der Frühzeit des deutschen Zionismus* (Stuttgart, 1930), pp. 276ff; and Comité d'Assistance aux Réfugiés Israélites de Syrie et Palestine, *Rapport général sur la période entière, 19 décembre 1914–15 juillet 1920* (Alexandria, 1921); also Nurit Govrin, "The Encounter of Exiles from Palestine with the Jewish Community of Egypt during World War I, as Reflected in Their Writings," in *The Jews of Egypt: A Mediterranean Society in Modern Times*, edited by Shimon Shamir (Boulder, 1987), pp. 177–91.
24. In 1881, there were about 200 Ashkenazi families in Cairo (AIU, Egypt, II.B.21, Liechtenstein, Cairo, 16 February 1881); in 1911, their number

was estimated at 3,000 to 4,000 individuals (AIU, Egypt, XI.E.182.j, Somekh, Cairo, 29 August 1911); and in 1927, 300 to 400 families (CZA, Z4/3229I, Grünhut, Jerusalem, 29 November 1927); in 1938, 5,000 individuals (Fargeon, *Les juifs*, p. 231; *The Jewish Chronicle*, 3 June 1938); according to *La Tribune Juive*, 14 April 1948, it was reduced to 1,000 community members in the late forties. For Alexandria, reports differ: while according to a teacher of the Alliance Israélite, Ashkenazim made up 10 percent of the local Jewish community in 1904 (AIU, Egypt, II.E.35.b, Danon, Alexandria, 1 July 1904), Gittelman reports that there were only 20 Ashkenazi families before the massive, but short-lived influx of 1914–15 (*Israël*, 11 September 1935). I have not been able to find any data on the interwar period.

25. Gittelman, *Israël*, 2 April and 20 May 1936; *The Jewish Chronicle*, 3 June 1938; *La Tribune Juive*, 4 February 1948. For German Jews, see CZA, Z4/3229I, Grünhut, Jerusalem, 29 November 1927; and CZA, KH4B/451, Kohn, Jerusalem, 10 December 1928.
26. AIU, Egypt, IX.E.182.c, Somekh, Cairo, 7 September 1899; AIU, Egypt, II.E.35.a, Danon, Alexandria, 21 December 1900; CZA, Z4/3229I, Grünhut, Jerusalem, 29 November 1927.
27. Fargeon, *Médecins*; and CZA, Z4/2051, Berger, Jerusalem, December 1925.
28. AIU, Egypt, J.C.A. 5, "Letter of the Jewish Association for the Protection of Girls and Women to J.C.A.," including a report by A. Phillips (Beirut, 19 April 1903) mentioning a "very large number of Jewish fallen women ... for the most part natives of Russia and Roumania." For numbers of women registered as white slaves in Egypt, see the journal *La Traite des Blanches* 23 (April 1909) and 24 (September 1909). For conditions in general, see Sir Thomas Russell, *Egyptian Service, 1902–1946* (London, 1949). See further AIU, Egypt, III.B.35.k, 30 January 1913; and Marion A. Kaplan, *Die jüdische Frauenbewegung in Deutschland* (Hamburg, 1981), pp. 186–87 and 190–223.
29. *Die Welt* 13 (1904): 3–4, and 20 (1904): 7; see also AIU, Egypt, II.E.35.b, Danon, Alexandria, 1 July 1904; CZA, Z4/2051, Berger, Jerusalem, December 1925; and CZA, Z4/3229I, Grünhut, Jerusalem, 29 November 1927.
30. Landau, *Jews*, pp. 27–28 and 239–41; Gittelman, *Israël*, 2 April 1935 and 27 June 1935; Fargeon, *Les juifs*, pp. 230–31. See also annual reports of the Ashkenazi community in the Jewish press.
31. *Israël*, 27 June 1935; *al-Shams*, 24 August 1942, 26 April 1946, and 2 April 1948; also Fargeon, *Les juifs*, p. 231.
32. *Die Welt* 20 (1904): 4; very similar is AIU, Egypt, X.E.182.e, Somekh, Cairo, 7 March 1902; CZA, Z4/2051, Berger, Jerusalem, December 1925; CZA, Z4/3229I, Grünhut, Cairo, 16 November 1927; CZA, Z4/-3229I, unsigned report, August 1927; *Israël*, 6 June 1935.

33. For example, CZA, S6/1982, unsigned, 20 November 1943.
34. CZA, Z4/2051, Berger, Jerusalem, December 1925; and OH, Gisèle Littman, 10 November 1971.
35. ha-Rav Yusuf al-Gamil, *Toldot ha-yahadut ha-ḳara'it*, vol. 1 (Ramla, 1979) is not always very reliable. I was unable to see Murād Faraj's book on the Karaites and the Rabbanites and Simon Szyszman's study, *Le Karaisme: Ses doctrines et son histoire* (Lausanne, n.d.). The following is mainly based on the entry under "Karaites" in *Encyclopaedia Judaica*, 2d ed. (Jerusalem, 1972), vol. 10, pp. 762–82, whose authors, J. E. Heller and L. Nemoy, did little to conceal their critical attitude toward Karaism; see also Emanuela Trevisan Semi, *Gli ebrei caraiti tra etnia e religione*. Testimonianze sull' ebraismo, vol. 18 (Rome, 1984).
36. Fargeon, *Les juifs*, p. 234; Goitein, *A Mediterranean Society*, 2:7.
37. Cohen, *The Jews*, p. 72; Egypt, Ministry of Finance, Statistical Department, *Population Census of Egypt, 1937* (Cairo, 1942), table 34, p. 292; Fargeon, *Les juifs*, p. 235; and interviews with Ovadia Yūsuf, Cairo, 7 March 1980; and Yūsuf Marzūq, Tel Aviv, 30 June 1980.
38. For 1927, *Kadima* 4 (December 1935): 30; for 1937, Egypt, *Population Census, 1937*, table 34, p. 293. In 1947, 243 Karaites were registered in Alexandria; Egypt, Ministry of Finance and Economy, Statistical and Census Department, *Population Census, 1947* (Cairo, 1954), vol. 16: Muḥāfaẓat al-Iskandarīya, table 5, p. 35.
39. See table 9; further, Fernand Leprette, *Egypte: Terre du Nil* (Paris, 1939), pp. 189ff; and Fargeon, *Les juifs*, p. 235.
40. *al-Ittiḥād al-Isrā'īlī*, 18 May 1924. The Karaite synagogue of Mūsā Dar'ī is still to be found in the Khurunfish quarter, near Maydān al-Jaysh.
41. *al-Kalīm*, 16 March, 1 April 1945, and 1 June 1948; *al-Ittiḥād al-Isrā'īlī*, 15 February 1925.
42. "In their colored cotton dresses, mostly in rosé, which hide nothing of their fat figures, their full bosoms, they give to the quarter, with their natural and careless [*nonchalant*] lack of modesty, an unexpected sense of intimacy" (Leprette, *Egypte*, p. 189). For a less colorful and more critical view of the position of Karaite girls, see *al-Kalīm*, 16 May 1945 and 1 June 1948.
43. *Die Welt* 20 (1904): 7.
44. For 1927 and 1947, see Cohen, *The Jews*, p. 72; for 1937, see Egypt, *Population Census, 1937*, table 34, p. 292.
45. For an excellent analysis see Zvi Zohar, "Lowering the Barriers of Estrangement: Rabbanite-Karaite Intermarriage in Twentieth-Century Egyptian Halakha," in *The Jews of Egypt*, edited by Shimon Shamir (Boulder, 1987), pp. 143–68.
46. On Rabbanite-Karaite relations in general, see Mordecai Roshwald, "Marginal Jewish Sects in Israel, Part 1," *International Journal of Middle East Studies* 4 (1973): 226–29. Landau's statement that in the

nineteenth century, Egyptian Karaites were not recognized as Jews by the local Rabbanites (*Jews*, p. 51), is not confirmed by al-Gamil. But see also Elkan Nathan Adler, *Jews in Many Lands* (London, 1905), p. 25; and Nassau in *Die Welt* 20 (1904): 4. Considerable intercommunal tension is reported in *L'Aurore*, 28 March and 4 April 1924. On Murād Faraj and Ibrāhīm Cohen, see al-Gamil, *Toldot*, pp. 155 and 160ff.

47. FO 921/117, 10 March 1943; and FO 141/1040, file 682, 22 February 1945; Fargeon, *Les juifs*, pp. 235–36.
48. *al-Ittiḥād al-Isrā'īlī*, 15 February 1925; for Alexandria, see Fargeon, *Les juifs*, p. 189.
49. *al-Shams*, 9 July 1936; Sihām Naṣṣār, *al-Yahūd al-miṣrīyūn bayna al-miṣrīya wa-l-ṣahyūnīya* (Beirut, 1980), pp. 51–55; *al-Kalīm*, 16 February, 16 March, and 1 April 1945, 19 July 1946.
50. *Ṣawt al-Umma*, 22 to 26 May 1948; *al-Kalīm*, 1 July 1948.
51. For the use of Italian, see Sammarco, *Gli Italiani*, pp. 36ff; and AIU, Egypt, II.B.10, Suarès, Alexandria, 23 September 1905. For French, see Landau, *Jews*, pp. 80ff; and Fargeon, *Les juifs*, pp. 214–15.
52. *al-Shams*, 28 September 1934; Fargeon, *Les juifs*, p. 215.
53. Landau, *Jews*, pp. 73 and 76; AIU, Egypt, V.E.38, Ezran, Alexandria, 19 January 1912. For the ḳevutsa Bar Kokhba, see CZA, S6/1982, Alexander, 17 February 1944.
54. Willy Heffening, "Die Entstehung der Kapitulationen in den islamischen Staaten," in *Schmollers Jahrbuch* 51 (1927): 97–107; and J. Y. Brinton, *The Mixed Courts of Egypt*, rev. ed. (New York, 1968), pp. 3ff and 197.
55. Brinton, *The Mixed Courts*, pp. 4–5 and 201; Alfred von Kremer, *Aegypten*, 2 vols. (Leipzig, 1863), 2: 167–73.
56. FO 371/5031 of 23 January 1923, including Greg to Lindsay, 8 December 1920.
57. FO 371/5031, including Greg to Lindsay, 8 December 1920.
58. FO 371/5031, including Ingram to Greg, 17 February 1921.
59. MAE, Afrique-Asie, Egypte 9, Gaillard to Briand, 11 March 1921.
60. MAE, Afrique-Asie, Egypte 102, draft letter to the Archbishop of Besançon, 21 June 1930.
61. MAE, Guerre 1939-45, Alger 1314, Leger, "Assainissement du Statut de la Protection et de l'Immatriculation en Egypte," 8 July 1939.
62. Landau, *Jews*, pp. 21-22; von Kremer, Aegypten, 2:101–2; and interviews with former community members.
63. See table 3; also Shimon Shamir, "The Evolution of the Egyptian Nationality Laws and Their Application to the Jews in the Monarchy Period," in *The Jews of Egypt*, edited by Shimon Shamir (Boulder, 1987), pp. 33-67.
64. See table 3; Egypt, *Population Census, 1937*, table 32, p. 264; and *Population Census, 1947*, table 15, p. 433.

65. Décret-loi no. 19 of 27 February 1929, in Umberto Pace, ed., *Répertoire permanent de législation égyptienne* (Alexandria, 1934–), vol. 7: *Nationalité égyptienne*, par. 1–8. For a thorough analysis, see Shamir, "The Evolution of the Egyptian Nationality Laws."
66. Motzki, *D̲imma und Egalité*, pp. 54–56; Landau, *Jews*, pp. 9–10.
67. Hamilton A. R. Gibb and Harold Bowen, *Islamic Society and the West: A Study of the Impact of Western Civilization in the Near East*, 2d ed., 2 vols. (London, 1969), 2:243; Carleton Coon, *Caravan: The Story of the Middle East*, rev. ed. (New York, 1976), p. 162.
68. John W. Livingston, "Ali Bey al-Kabir and the Jews," *Middle Eastern Studies* 7 (1971): 221–28; Philipp, *The Syrians in Egypt*, pp. 30–34.
69. E. Roger J. Owen, *Cotton and the Egyptian Economy, 1820–1914: A Study in Trade and Development* (Oxford, 1969); and E. Roger J. Owen, *The Middle East in the World Economy, 1800–1914* (London, 1981), pp. 122–52 and 212–22; Robert L. Tignor, *Modernization and British Colonial Rule in Egypt, 1882–1914* (Princeton, 1966); Robert L. Tignor, *State, Private Enterprise, and Economic Change in Egypt, 1918–1952* (Princeton, 1984); Eric Davis, *Challenging Colonialism: Bank Misr and Egyptian Industrialization, 1920–1940* (Princeton, 1983).
70. Cohen, *The Jews*, pp. 105–13; Jacob M. Landau, "The Beginnings of Modernization in Education: The Jewish Community in Egypt as a Case Study," in Jacob M. Landau, *Middle Eastern Themes: Papers in History and Politics* (London, 1973), pp. 157–71; André Chouraqui, *Cent ans d'histoire: L'Alliance Israélite Universelle et la renaissance juive contemporaine (1860–1960)* (Paris, 1965). See, e.g., AIU, Egypt, XII.E.182.m, Somekh, Cairo, 20 May 1918.
71. On the Suarèses, see Kurt Grunwald, "On Cairo's Lombard Street," *Tradition* (Berlin) 1 (1972): 13ff; and Mizrahi, *L'Egypte et ses juifs*, pp. 65–66.
72. Edouard Papasian, *L'Egypte économique et financière* (Cairo, 1933), p. 194; MAE, Afrique-Asie, Egypte 70, "Crédit foncier," 13 May 1924.
73. Kurt Grunwald, "'Windsor-Cassel': The Last Court Jew," in *Leo Baeck Institute Yearbook*, vol. 14 (London, 1969), pp. 133–37 and 157; Grunwald, "On Cairo's Lombard Street," pp. 10–11; A. B. de Guerville, *New Egypt* (London, 1905), pp. 51–53; and Jeffrey G. Collins, *The Egyptian Elite under Cromer, 1882–1907* (Berlin, 1984), pp. 43–47.
74. Collins, *The Egyptian Elite*, pp. 174–201, 347–53; Gabriel Baer, *A History of Landownership in Modern Egypt, 1800–1950* (London, 1962), pp. 41, 95–96; Davis, *Challenging Colonialism*, pp. 56ff; list of buyers in ʿAlī Barakāt, *Taṭawwur al-milkīya al-zirāʿīya fī miṣr, 1813–1914, wa-atharuhā ʿalā ʾl-ḥaraka al-siyāsīya* (Cairo, 1978), pp. 476-500.
75. FO 141/485, file 7259/6, 5 August 1918 and 19 January 1922; MAE, Afrique-Asie, Egypte 57, 5 December 1907, and MAE, Afrique-Asie, Egypte 58, 10 August 1908. Chambre de Commerce d'Alexandrie, *La*

renaissance de l'Egypte (Cairo, 1940), pp. 124–27; Wright, ed., *Twentieth Century Impressions*, p. 464.

76. 'Abd al-Raḥmān Zakī, *Mawsū'at madīnat al-Qāhira fī alf 'ām* (Cairo, 1969), p. 132; Wright, ed., *Twentieth Century Impressions*, p. 183; de Guerville, *New Egypt*, p. 28.
77. AIU, Egypt, II.B.31, Najar, Cairo, 25 April 1900; *The Jewish Chronicle*, 21 April 1939.
78. Makāriyūs quoted from Landau, *Jews*, pp. 127–30; "Mosseri" in *Encyclopaedia Judaica*; *Israël*, 27 July 1928.
79. Obituaries for J. N. Mosseri in *The Jewish Chronicle*, 11 May 1934; and *Israël*, 19 January 1934; see also Grunwald, *On Cairo's Lombard Street*, p. 19. Obituary for Elie N. Mosseri in *The Jewish Chronicle*, 11 October 1940. On his marriage and business activities, see FO 371/15426, 29 May and 3 June 1931; and FO 371/21981, 7 September 1938.
80. For all three, see *AJEPO*, and Elie I. Politi, ed., *Annuaire des sociétés égyptiennes par actions, études financières* (Alexandria, 1929–), *Annuaire 1939*; obituary for Victor Mosseri in *Israël*, 27 July 1928.
81. *L'Aurore*, 3 October 1924; and Murray Harris, *Egypt under the Egyptians* (London, 1925), p. 164.
82. Jacques Berque, *L'Egypte: Impérialisme et révolution* (Paris, 1967) p. 250; for the Jewish community, see AIU, Egypt, XI.E.182.h, Somekh, Cairo, 5 July 1907; AIU, Egypt, I.V.10, Suarès, Alexandria, 1 May 1913; and AIU, France, X.F.17, Danon, Alexandria, "Rapport 1907-8."
83. OH(35)1, Y. Shohet (née Chemla), 20 November and 10 December 1964.
84. Wright, ed., *Twentieth Century Impressions*, p. 377; *Israël*, 6 April 1937; Mizrahi, *L'Egypte et ses juifs*, pp. 34 and 64–65.
85. Donald M. Reid, "Syrian Christians, the Rags-to-Riches Story, and Free Enterprise," *International Journal of Middle East Studies* 1 (1970): 358–67.
86. *AJEPO*; *al-Shams*, 2 March 1945; Makāriyūs quoted from Landau, *Jews*, pp. 251–53; FO 372/2305, Loraine to Chamberlain, 13 February 1927.
87. CZA, KKL5/472, 14 May 1930; and Brinton, *The Mixed Courts*, p. 146. On Carasso, Misrahy, and others, see *The Jewish Chronicle*, 30 April 1937, 14 April 1939, and 2 April 1948; also Abdou and Kasmieh, *Les juifs*, p. 73.
88. Fargeon, *Médecins*, provides short biographies of fifty Jewish doctors practicing in Egypt, of whom thirty-five were definitely Ashkenazim.
89. See chapter two; for the Ashkenazi community, see Gittelman, *Israël*, 2 April 1936.
90. Landau, *Jews*, pp. 9-15; AIU, Egypt, IX.E.182.b, Somekh, Cairo, 29 March 1898. The large number of Jewish employees is documented in the business files of DW/'Abidīn. Maṣlaḥat al-sharikāt, 1948-61. On the reputation of Jewish merchants, see Harris, *Egypt under the Egyptians*,

p. 165; Roger Lambelin, *L'Egypte et l'Angleterre vers l'indépendance, de Mohammed Ali au roi Fouad* (Paris, 1922), pp. 191ff; Leprette, *Egypte*, p. 105; CZA, Z4/3229I, Grünhut, Jerusalem, 29 November 1927.

91. *Die Welt* 20 (1904): 7–8.
92. See table 9.
93. *L'Aurore*, 21 March 1924; *al-Shams*, 10 November 1938, 14 November 1941, 3 August 1942, 16 February 1945, and 3 October 1947.
94. Anas Muṣṭafā Kāmil, "al-Ra'smālīya al-yahūdīya fī miṣr," *al-Ahrām al-Iqtiṣādī*, 23 March to 4 May 1981.
95. Robert L. Tignor, "The Economic Activities of Foreigners in Egypt, 1920–1950: From Millet to Haute Bourgeoisie," *Comparative Studies in Society and History* 22 (January 1980): 416–49.
96. Philipp, *The Syrians in Egypt*, p. 137; Charles Issawi, *Egypt at Mid-Century: An Economic Survey* (London, 1954), p. 63.
97. For a tentative analysis of data from Alexandria shortly before the outbreak of World War I, see Tomas Gerholm, "Economic Activities of Alexandrian Jews on the Eve of World War I, according to *le Mercure Egyptien*," in *The Jews of Egypt*, edited by Shimon Shamir (Boulder, 1987), pp. 94-107.
98. Collins, *The Egyptian Elite*, pp. 87-137; Baer, *A History of Landownership*, pp. 124–25.
99. See *Stock Exchange Yearbooks*, edited by Clément Lévy (Alexandria, 1937, 1939, 1942); Papasian, *L'Egypte économique*, pp. 252–57; Kāmil in *al-Ahrām al-Iqtiṣādī*, 31 March 1981, pp. 30–31, and 20 April 1981, p. 14; Egypt, *Egyptian Insurance Yearbook 1949*, pp. 33–34.
100. AIU, Egypt, "Rapport sur l'Egypte. Présenté à M. le Président de l'Alliance Israélite Universelle," 1 July 1901.
101. Cohen, *The Jews*, p. 88, offers widely differing data in percentages, based on the same Egyptian censuses.
102. For details, see Fargeon, *Les juifs*, pp. 271ff; and table 12.
103. On the Yemenis, see CZA, S5/490, Organization Department of the Zionist Organization, Jerusalem, n.d. (1937–38); and Fargeon, *Les juifs*, pp. 296 and 300. On the general trend, see Deeb, *The Socioeconomic Role*, p. 18; *al-Shams*, 18 January 1935, and 16 June 1944.
104. AIU, Egypt, XIV.E.207.a, Farhi, Ṭanṭā, 5 October 1924; also AIU, Egypt, X.V.218.b, Sasson, Ṭanṭā, 22 July 1920; and *L'Aurore*, 20 March 1925.
105. Jacob M. Landau, "Ritual Murder Accusations in Nineteenth Century Egypt," in Landau, *Middle Eastern Themes: Papers in History and Politics* (London, 1973), pp. 99-142; similar cases from other parts of the Ottoman Empire in Chouraqui, *Cent ans*, p. 104, and Stillman, *The Jews of Arab Lands*, pp. 105–6. The last incident I found occurred in Port Said in 1924 (*L'Aurore*, 21 March 1924; AIU, Egypt, XIII.E.185, Lévy, Port Said, 21 July 1924).

106. Leprette, *Egypte*, p. 190; also Goitein, *A Mediterranean Society*, 2: 290ff; Landau, *Jews*, pp. 29ff; Susan J. Staffa, *Conquest and Fusion: The Social Evolution of Cairo* A.D. *642–1850* (Leiden, 1977), p. 58; and Doris Behrens-Abouseif, "Locations of Non-Muslim Quarters in Medieval Cairo," *Annales Islamologiques* 32 (1986): 117–32.
107. Janet Abu-Lughod, *Cairo: 1001 Years of the City Victorious* (Princeton, 1971), pp. 88ff; Collins, *The Egyptian Elite*, pp. 87-137; Zakī, *Mawsū'a*, pp. 199–200; Henri Lorni, *L'Egypte d'aujourd'hui: Le pays et les hommes* (Cairo, 1926), p. 72; OH(35)4, E. Cohen, granddaughter of Moise Cattaoui; OH(35)1, Y. Shohet, 20 November 1964; and OH IV, II, M. Mosseri, 12 August 1964. The residence of the Jewish middle and upper classes is listed in *Le mondain égyptien et du Proche Orient: Egyptian Who's Who*, edited by E.J. Blattner (Alexandria, 1937ff); and *AJEPO*.
108. AIU, Egypt, XI.E.182.j, 27 March 1910; and AIU, Egypt, XII.E.182.k, 15 May 1913; see also AIU, Egypt, II.B.22, Hazan, 4 March 1896; OH(35)2, I. Lévy; Gittelman, *Israël*, 20 May 1936; Lorni, *L'Egypte d'aujourd'hui*, pp. 70–72.
109. Harari, *Quelques réflexions*.
110. Egypt, *Population Census, 1937*, vol. 10: Muḥāfaẓat al-Iskandarīya (Cairo, 1940), table 5, p. 24; Egypt, *Population Census, 1947*, vol. 16: Muḥāfaẓat al-Iskandarīya, (Cairo, 1952), table 5, p. 35. For the turn of the century, see J. Danon in AIU, Egypt, II.E.35.a, 27 December 1902; and AIU, France, X.F.17, 6 September 1904. The "Jewish quarter" of the 1930s and 1940s is described in *al-Shams*, 31 August 1938, and *La Tribune Juive*, 12 April 1948 (Jean Masri).
111. For al-Manṣūra, see Fargeon, *Les juifs*, p. 287. He is also the best source for the other provincial communities. For Port Said see also CZA, KH4B/450, Grünhut, 28 October 1928; and OH(61)30, M. Masri.

CHAPTER TWO

1. Albert Sapriel in MAE, Guerre 1939–45, Alger 1310, 31 May 1944.
2. Gibb and Bowen, *Islamic Society*, 2: 217ff and 285–86; Albert Hourani, *Minorities in the Arab World* (London, 1947), pp. 20ff; and Benjamin Braude, "Foundation Myths of the Millet System," in *Christians and Jews in the Ottoman Empire: The Functioning of a Plural Society*, 2 vols., edited by Benjamin Braude and Bernard Lewis (New York, 1982), 1: 69–88.
3. *al-Shams*, 19 January 1940, 14 January 1944, and 7 September 1945; Goitein, *A Mediterranean Society*, 2: 1–40.
4. Landau, *Jews*, p. 52; Fargeon, *Les juifs*, p. 193; AIU, Egypt, II.B.22, Comité du Caire, Cairo, 20 December 1895.
5. Pace, ed., *Répertoire permanent, Communauté israélite, 1950*. Règlement d'organisation judiciaire des juridictions rabbiniques d'Egypte, p.

35: Letter by Haim Nahum to the Egyptian prime minister, 26 April 1938. Also Fargeon, *Les juifs*, p. 189; and author's interview with E. Dwek, Cairo, 7 March 1980.

6. *al-Shams*, 10 September 1943, and 7 May 1948. For mutual estrangement, see CZA, KH4B/451, Kohn, 10 December 1928.
7. *Hamenora* (1923), nos. 1–10; and (1924), no. 1; Fargeon, *Les juifs*, pp. 171–74, 203–5, and 232, with occasional variations in the dates given; *al-Shams*, 8 February 1943. For Jewish participation in the local Masonic lodges, see Shilsh, *al-Yahūd wa-l-māsūn*, pp. 189–305.
8. Albert Sapriel in MAE, Guerre 1939–45, Alger 1310, 31 May 1944 (addendum to letter of 3 June 1944); FO 921/117, 10 March 1943. For the original formulation of the so-called Pact of ʻUmar (*al-shurūṭ al-ʻUmarīya*), referring to the second caliph ʻUmar ibn ʻAbd al-Khaṭṭāb (634–44), defining the rights and duties of *dhimmīs* in a Muslim society, see Ibn Qayyim al-Jawzīya, *Aḥkām ahl al-dhimma*, 2 vols., edited by Ṣubḥī Labīb (Damascus, 1961), 2: 657–58.
9. Barbara L. Carter, *The Copts in Egyptian Politics, 1919–1952* (London, 1985), pp. 231–39; Nadav Safran, "The Abolition of the Sharʻī Courts in Egypt," *The Muslim World* 48 (January 1958): 20–28.
10. FO 141/751, file 741, Wasey Sterry to Smart, 10 June 1931. Robert S. Rolo must not confused with his cousin Robert J. Rolo, future president of the Alexandria Jewish community (1934–48).
11. The official data on Jews in Alexandria are clearly too low; for more accurate estimates see, e.g., CZA, S5/490, Czernowitz, 9 January 1939. On Alexandrian society, see Laurence Grafftey-Smith, *Bright Levant* (London, 1970), pp. 32–36. For the Italian Jews in Alexandria, see FO 371/19097, Fitzpatrick, "Intelligence Note," 2 and 5 September 1935; CZA, Z4/2051, Berger, Jerusalem, December 1925; MAE, Afrique-Asie, Egypte 11, 27 November 1926.
12. DW/MW, al-Ṭawā'if al-qibṭīya (4) (1922?); MAE, Afrique-Asie, Egypte 34, 21 April 1928; CZA, Z4/2051, Berger, Jerusalem, December 1925; and CZA, KH4B/451, Kohn, Jerusalem, 10 December 1928; see also table 4.
13. AIU, Egypt, I.E.18, Benveniste, Alexandria, 20 May 1904. For the poor, see AIU, Egypt, I.B.10, Suarès, Alexandria, 11 December 1907; *al-Shams*, 19 July 1940.
14. CZA, Z4/2051, Berger, December 1925; see also, e.g., AIU, Egypt, II.B.35.b, Danon, Alexandria, 1 July 1904.
15. AIU, Egypt, V.E.56, Masliah, Alexandria, 30 January 1913; CZA, KH4B/451, Kohn, 10 December 1928.
16. Makāriyūs quoted from Landau, *Jews*, pp. 144–46; "Menasce," in *Encyclopaedia Judaica*; Wright, ed., *Twentieth Century Impressions*, p. 448; FO 141/655, file 11469, 22 July 1920.

17. FO 141/655, file 11469, enclosure II of 12 March 1921 (Amos report). For criticism, see AIU, Egypt, II.E.35.b, Danon, Alexandria, 18 November 1904; and AIU, Egypt, III.B.35, 11 August 1905.
18. Obituaries in *The Jewish Chronicle*, 3 September 1943; and *al-Shams*, 27 August 1943.
19. Makāriyūs quoted from Landau, *Jews*, pp. 156–57; Wright, ed., *Twentieth Century Impressions*, p. 464; Grunwald, *On Cairo's Lombard Street*, p. 16; Owen, *Cotton*, p. 323.
20. *al-Shams*, 9 April 1948; *AJEPO*; Politi, *Annuaire* 1939 and 1945.
21. FO 371/4992, Ingram to Murray, 13 October 1920; Lord Killearn, *The Killearn Diaries: 1934–1946*, edited by Trevor Evans (London, 1972), p. 60; MAE, Afrique-Asie, Egypte 15, Laffon to Foreign Ministry, 24 April 1920; MAE, Afrique-Asie, Egypte 9, Gaillard to Foreign Ministry, 15 March 1923; some society gossip on Valentine Rolo in OH(35)4, E. Cohen.
22. Landholdings in MAE, Afrique-Asie, Egypte 9, 22 March 1921. According to *Ṣawt al-Umma*, blacklist, 19 June 1948, Gustave Aghion (1881–?) owned 10,000 *faddān* in 1948. See also Politi, *Annuaire* 1939, 1945, and 1954.
23. Virginio Giughese, "Gli Italiani per la cognoscenza dell'Egitto sotto il regno di Mohammed Ali," (thesis, Istituto Superiore de Magistero de Piemonte, 1931–32), p. 20; Wright, ed., *Twentieth Century Impressions*, pp. 450 and 452; *The Jewish Chronicle*, 2 April 1937.
24. AIU, Egypt, XII.E.182.k, Somekh, Cairo, 15 May 1913; Fargeon, *Les juifs*, p. 197; CZA, Z4/2051, Berger, December 1925; CZA, KH4B/451, Kohn, 10 December 1928; also *al-Shams*, 10 December 1936, tracing progress in Alexandria to Ya'qūb Menasce's move there in 1871; and *al-Shams*, 3 August 1942.
25. Landau, *Jews*, p. 66; Fargeon, *Les juifs*, pp. 254ff; Bension Taragan, *Les communautés israélites d'Alexandrie: Aperçu historique depuis les temps des Ptolemées jusqu'à nos jours* (Alexandria, 1932), pp. 116–18; for the economic crisis see, e.g., AIU, Egypt, I.V.10, Suarès, Alexandria, 1 May 1913; and AIU, Egypt, V.E.56, Masliah, Alexandria, 7 September 1914.
26. AIU, France, X.F.17, "Egypte: Rapports annuels 1900-1918," J. Danon, Alexandria; MAE, Afrique-Asie, Egypte 34, Gaillard to Briand, 21 April 1928; Cohen, *The Jews*, p. 110.
27. Statistics from MAE, Afrique-Asie, Egypte 34, Gaillard to Briand, 21 April 1928. On the Ste. Cathérine incident, see *L'Aurore*, 16 May, 5, 12 June, 3 July 1925; AIU, Egypt, I.C.16, Mme. Danon, Alexandria, 27 May 1925; and Antébi, Alexandria, 9 June 1925; MAE, Afrique-Asie, Egypte 44, Giriend, 1 June 1925; and Gaillard, 8 June 1925.
28. *al-Shams*, 12 October 1944, and 19 March 1948.

29. On the economic crisis, see Marius Deeb, *Party Politics in Egypt: The Wafd and Its Rivals, 1919–1939* (London, 1979), pp. 222–23; CZA, KH4B/451, Kohn, 19 December 1929; and Bension to Hermann, 18 December 1930; CZA, KKL5/472, Grünhut, 2 July 1930. For communal institutions, see Fargeon, *Les juifs*, pp. 242, 255, and 264–65; on the synagogues, see Rabbi Jacob Toledano in *al-Shams*, 20 July 1938; for the protest of 1938, see *al-Shams*, 10 November 1938.
30. CZA, KH4B/451, Kohn, 10 December 1928. For conflicting statements, see *al-Shams*, 19 July and 9 August 1940 (critical of the community), and 3 August 1942, and 23 April 1948 (favorable to it).
31. AIU, Egypt, II.E.35.b, Danon, Alexandria, 1 July 1904; and AIU, Egypt, III.E.35, 10 May 1907; Communauté Israélite d'Alexandrie, *Rapport général pour l'année 1933* (Alexandria, 1934), p. 33; *al-Shams*, 13 May 1948.
32. Communauté Israélite d'Alexandrie, *Rapport général pour l'année 1933*, Liste des Arikhistes. According to Jean Masri, *Le judaisme égyptien par l'image, présenté par Jean Masri*, vol. 1: *La communauté d'Alexandrie* (Alexandria, 1948), p. 24, the number of those who had paid the *'arikha* had increased to 3,000 by the late 1940s. For the statutes, see Landau, *Jews*, pp. 184–91; Fargeon, *Les juifs*, p. 211; and *al-Kalīm*, 16 January 1948.
33. *AJEPO*; Politi, *Annuaire* 1939 and 1950; Blattner, ed., *Le mondain* 1937 and 1954; FO 141/722, file 352, Heathcote-Smith to Loraine, 1 July 1932; and CZA, S5/793, unsigned, 21 May 1945.
34. *The Jewish Chronicle*, 25 February 1938; Politi, *Annuaire* 1939.
35. *Hamenora* (1924), nos. 4–5, p. 77; *Kadima* 7 (March 1937).
36. For Dorra, see Aḥmad Muḥammad Ghunaym and Aḥmad Abū Kaff, *al-Yahūd wa-l-ḥaraka al-ṣahyūnīya fī miṣr, 1897–1947* (Cairo, 1969), p. 57; and Blattner, ed., *Le mondain* 1954. For Cohen, see *AJEPO*; Ghunaym and Abū Kaff, *al-Yahūd*, p. 58. For Nadler, see Blattner, ed., *Le mondain* 1937; *Egyptian Gazette*, 1 January 1954; and Fargeon, *Les juifs*, p. 251; for Schlesinger, see Fargeon, *Médecins*, p. 45.
37. AIU, Egypt, II.B.35.b, Danon, Alexandria, 1 July, 18 November 1904, 11 August 1905.
38. OH(61)51, R. Dwek, 19 May 1972, who speaks of a "closed community."
39. Toledano, born in Tiberias in 1880, went to Egypt in 1929. In 1943, he became the Sephardi chief rabbi of Haifa, and died there in 1960 (*al-Shams*, 20 July 1938, and a personal interview with Ehud Toledano, Jerusalem, 15 June 1980). On the position of the rabbis of Alexandria in general, see AIU, Egypt, IX.E.182.a, Somekh, Cairo, 25 December 1896; Landau, *Jews*, p. 52; and Fargeon, *Les juifs*, p. 218.
40. On Prato and Italianization, see MAE, Afrique-Asie, Egypte 34, Gaillard to Briand, 21 April 1928; on Prato and Italian fascism, see CZA, KH4B/452, Erlich 1935. For 1933, see *Oriente Moderno* 1934, p. 46;

for earlier tensions, see CZA, KH4B/450, Berger, 9 April, 10 December 1928. A short biography of Prato is in *Kadima* 19 (March 1937). For Ventura, see *al-Shams*, 16 January, 2 April 1948; *La Tribune Juive*, 3 March, 12 May 1948; and *al-Kalīm*, 1 June 1948. According to Dr. Krause (OH[61]35), a former Zionist activist, it was the Egyptian government that really wished to get rid of Ventura, but preferred to act in an indirect way by working through the community council, which was prepared to cooperate.

41. AIU, Egypt, VIII.E.181, Zonama, Cairo, 3 January 1912. On organization, see Commauté Israélite du Caire, *Statuts de la communauté israélite du Caire* (Cairo, 1927), titre I, art. 1.
42. CZA, Z4/2051, December 1925.
43. Fargeon, *Les juifs*, pp. 213–14. On the synagogues, see Fargeon, *Les juifs*, pp. 198–201; AIU, Egypt, XI.E.182.j, Somekh, Cairo, 27 March 1910; and Zakī, *Mawsū'a*, pp. 230–31.
44. Makāriyūs quoted from Landau, *Jews*, pp. 137–43; "Cattaoui," in *Encyclopaedia Judaica*; Grunwald, *On Cairo's Lombard Street*, pp. 16ff; *al-Shams*, 3 August 1942, and 21 May 1943; OH(35)4, E. Cohen.
45. Makāriyūs quoted from Landau, *Jews*, pp. 140–43; OH(35)4, E. Cohen; Grunwald, *On Cairo's Lombard Street*, pp. 14–15; CZA, Z2/373, Hasamsony, Cairo, 21 December 1910; for Ida Cattaoui, wife of Moise de Cattaoui, see *Israël*, 3 February 1938.
46. See Fargeon, *Les juifs*, pp. 193 and 197; *al-Shams*, 23 May 1941, and 22 April 1943.
47. AIU, Egypt, XII.E.182.m, Somekh, Cairo, 2 January, 11 March, and 25 November 1918.
48. Letter titled "What Does Mr. Cattaoui Do?" quoted in Landau, *Jews*, pp. 247–57.
49. Quoted in Landau, *Jews*, pp. 322–24.
50. AIU, Egypt, VI.E.87, Benaroya, Cairo, 1 May 1908.
51. CZA, Z3/1449, Thon, 7 April 1913.
52. Included in Fargeon, *Les juifs*, pp. 192–97; and AIU, Egypt, III.B.37, 4 May 1917.
53. AIU, Egypt, VI.E.80.a, Avigdor, Cairo, 31 December 1918. Similar assessments are to be found in AIU, Egypt, XII.E.182.m, Somekh, Cairo, 20 May 1918; and CZA, Z4/3229I, Grünhut, Jerusalem, 29 November 1927.
54. AIU, Egypt, VI.E.80.a, Avigdor, Cairo, 31 December 1918.
55. Fargeon, *Les juifs*, p. 194; for details on their background, see Gudrun Krämer, *Minderheit, Millet, Nation? Die Juden in Ägypten, 1914–1952* (Wiesbaden, 1982), pp. 175–76.
56. Fargeon, *Les juifs*, pp. 194–95; AIU, Egypt, III.B.37, 4 May 1917; AIU, Egypt, XII.E.182.m, Somekh, Cairo, 20 May, 25 November 1918.

57. AIU, Egypt, XII.E.182.m, Somekh, Cairo, 2 January 1918, and 21 February 1919.
58. AIU, Egypt, XII.E.182.m, 22 July 1921; and AIU, Egypt, III.B.41, 17 July 1924, both Somekh, Cairo; Fargeon, *Les juifs*, pp. 201ff and 221–22.
59. Obituaries in *al-Shams*, 18 May 1942, and *The Jewish Chronicle*, 22 May 1942; see also Grunwald, *On Cairo's Lombard Street*, pp. 17–18; "Cattaoui," in *Encyclopaedia Judaica*; *Kadima* 1 (1 September 1935).
60. AA, Abt. III, Po5-01110, von Mertens, Cairo, 13 May 1925; FO 371/10887, Allenby to Foreign Office, 6 May 1925; and report, registered 8 June 1925; MAE, Afrique-Asie, Egypte 24, Gaillard to Briand, 11 May 1925.
61. On his Egyptian patriotism and anti-Zionism, see *Hamenora* (1924), nos. 4–5; CZA, Z4/3229I, Grünhut, 29 November 1927; FO 141/759, file 306, Smart to Young, 17 January 1933. For the Confederation, see *The Jewish Chronicle*, 31 May 1935.
62. FO 371/10887, 7 May 1925; also the quotation in FO 407/217, 9 January 1933. For the French, and a much more positive view, see MAE, Afrique-Asie, Egypte 10, Gaillard to Briand, 8 November 1927.
63. *AJEPO*; "Haim Nahum," in *Encyclopaedia Judaica*; *al-Shams*, 19 October 1934, and 31 January 1941; on his career in Turkey, see FO 371/5249, de Robeck to Curzon, 10 April 1920; MAE, Afrique-Asie, Levant, Turquie 112, 1919–20.
64. See CZA, Z3/1489, Zloszisti, Constantinople, 25 October 1910; CZA, Z2/10, Jacobson, 30 December 1910; and CZA, Z2/9, Auerbach, Constantinople, 25 June 1910. On the Young Turk movement, see Bernard Lewis, *The Emergence of Modern Turkey*, rev. ed. (London, 1966), pp. 171–233.
65. The writer E. Fleg, quoted in OH(61)23, N. Farhi, 5 May 1969.
66. FO 141/811, file 16866, Henderson to Curzon, 5 December 1923; Fargeon, *Les juifs*, pp. 202 and 204; *L'Aurore*, 16 January 1924, 20 March 1925.
67. Author's interview with E. Dwek, former secretary to Haim Nahum, Cairo, 7 March 1980; *al-Shams*, 19 October 1934, and 31 January 1941.
68. *L'Aurore*, 4 April, 4 July 1924; 30 January, 20 February, 20 March, and 21 August 1925; Fargeon, *Les juifs*, pp. 191ff; Communauté Israélite du Caire, *Statuts de la communauté* (Cairo, 1937).
69. For details, see Krämer, *Minderheit*, pp. 189–92.
70. CZA, Z4/3229I, 29 November 1927; Berger in CZA, Z4/2051, December 1925.
71. CZA, KH4B/451, 10 December 1928.
72. CZA, KH4B/451, Berger, 9 April 1928; OH(35)2, I. Lévy; OH(35)1, Y. Shohet; and OH(35)6, J. Kahanoff; Fargeon, *Les juifs*, p. 215.

73. Fargeon, *Les juifs*, p. 216; for the effects of the economic crisis, see CZA, KH4B/451, Bension to Hermann, 17 January 1931.
74. *Israël*, 21 August 1935.
75. *al-Shams*, 21 May 1943, also 7 February, 13 July, and 3 August 1942; 8, 22 February 1943.
76. *al-Shams*, 22 April, 14 June 1943; for these individuals, see *AJEPO*; Blattner, ed., *Le mondain* 1937; and Politi, *Annuaire* 1939.
77. *AJEPO*; author's interview with Roger Oppenheim, Haifa, 22 June 1980. Salem was, however, included in a list suggesting members for the new Zionist Federation established in 1944; see CZA, S5/793, Shertok to Castro, 11 January 1944.
78. *AJEPO*; *The Jewish Chronicle*, 25 March 1938, 9 July 1943; *al-Shams*, 15 March, 22 April 1943.
79. *al-Shams*, 4 January 1946; 24 January, 14 February, 4 July 1947, and 12, 19 March 1948; Harari, *Quelques réflexions*, pp. 5ff.
80. *al-Shams*, 1 June 1945, 28 February 1947.
81. *al-Shams*, 14 November 1947, 9 January 1948; *La Tribune Juive*, 10 March 1948.
82. *al-Shams*, 7 May 1948; OH(35)6, Kahanoff mémoirs, 18 July 1965.
83. *al-Shams*, 25 June 1943, 26 April 1946.
84. *al-Shams*, 10 September 1943, and 7 May 1948; *La Tribune Juive*, 10 March 1948.
85. *al-Shams*, 9 February, 12 October 1945.
86. *al-Shams*, 28 September 1934, 27 September 1939, 4 May 1945, and 28 March 1947 for the schools; 14 January 1944 for the council.
87. OH(35)4, E. Cohen; OH(61)51, R. Dwek, 19 May 1972; and author's interview with Emile Najar, Paris, 7 September 1980. For the elections, see *al-Shams*, 2, 20 September, and 1 November 1946, 3 January 1947; for Cicurel, see *AJEPO*; Politi, *Annuaire* 1939 and 1950; *The Jewish Chronicle*, 23 May 1945.
88. *al-Shams*, 22 November 1946; 3, 24 January 1947; 5 March 1948; *La Tribune Juive*, 11 February, 3 March 1948.
89. AIU, Egypt, XIII.E.199, Benveniste, Ṭanṭā, 22 December 1905, and 23 February 1906; AIU, France, X.F.17, Sasson, Ṭanṭā, 20 November 1911. On Ṭanṭā in general, see Wright, ed., *Twentieth Century Impressions*, pp. 476–77.
90. AIU, Egypt, XIV.E.206, Douec, Ṭanṭā, 5 March 1909.
91. AIU, Egypt, XIII.E.192, Alphandary, Ṭanṭā, 14 July 1913.
92. AIU, Egypt, XIV.E.207.a, 8 May, 5 October 1924; and AIU, France, X.F.17, January 1924, all Farhi, Ṭanṭā.
93. AIU, Egypt, XIV.E.212, Mizrahi, Ṭanṭā, 12 December 1936; *Kadima* 14 (November 1936); Fargeon, *Les juifs*, p. 281.
94. Fargeon, *Les juifs*, pp. 290–91; *Hamenora* (1923), nos. 4–6; *La Revue Sioniste*, 15 March 1918; *al-Shams*, 16 November 1934.

95. AIU, Egypt, XIV.E.207.b, Farhi, Ṭanṭā, 2 December 1921, and 5 November 1927; Fargeon, *Les juifs*, pp. 279–81.
96. Landau, *The Jews*, pp. 34–37; AIU, Egypt, XI.E.182.i, Somekh, Cairo, 14 August 1908; CZA, KH4B/450, Pazi, 28 October 1928; *Kadima* 14 (November 1936); Fargeon, *Les juifs*, pp. 295–98.
97. Quoted from AIU, Egypt, XIII.E.185, Lévy, Port Said, 25 November 1923; see also CZA, S5/490, Czernowitz, 9 January 1939.
98. Fargeon, *Les juifs*, pp. 297–98; AIU, Egypt, XI.E.182.i, Somekh, Cairo, 14 August 1908; CZA, KH4B/450, Grünhut, 28 October 1928; OH(61)-30, M. Masri.
99. Fargeon, *Les juifs*, pp. 287–89; *Kadima* 14 (November 1936); AIU, Egypt, XIII.E.184, de Semo, al-Manṣūra, 19 July 1893.
100. Fargeon, *Les juifs*, pp. 282–84; on the pilgrimage, see Hassoun, *Chroniques de la vie quotidienne*, pp. 131–34.
101. Fargeon, *Les juifs*, pp. 271–76; Reine Silbert, "Cent quatre vingt pèlerins juifs en Egypte," in *La Tribune Juive* (Paris), 15 February 1979.
102. Fargeon, *Les juifs*, pp. 298–300; *al-Shams*, 16 June 1944, and 1 June 1945.
103. Fargeon, *Les juifs*, pp. 239 and 271ff; *al-Shams*, 16 January 1948.

CHAPTER THREE

1. Mutawallī, *al-Uṣūl*, pp. 322–32; Mahmoud Hussein, *L'Egypte: Lutte de classe et libération nationale*, 2 vols. (Paris, 1975), 1: 8, 21, 28ff; Baer, *A History of Landownership in Egypt*, pp. 71ff; Mahmoud Abdel-Fadil, *Development, Income Distribution and Social Change in Rural Egypt (1952–1970): A Study in the Political Economy of Agrarian Transition* (Cambridge, 1975).
2. Hussein, *L'Egypte*, 1: 30.
3. Collins, *The Egyptian Elite*, pp. 138ff; Samuel Becker Grant, "Modern Egypt and the New (Turco-Egyptian) Aristocracy" (Ph.D. diss., University of Michigan, 1968); 'Aṣim al-Dasūqī, *Kibār mullāk al-arāḍī al-zirā'īya wa-dawruhum fī 'l-mujtama' al-miṣrī (1914–1952)* (Cairo, 1975), pp. 210ff; Barakāt, *Taṭawwur al-milkīya*.
4. Deeb, *Party Politics*, pp. 8–12 and 26–29; Gabriel Baer, "The Village Shaykh, 1800–1950," in *Studies in the Social History of Modern Egypt* (Chicago, 1969), pp. 30–61; see also Afaf Lutfi al-Sayyid-Marsot, *Egypt's Liberal Experiment: 1922–1936* (Berkeley and Los Angeles, 1977), pp. 15–33.
5. Deeb, *Party Politics*, pp. 10–12; Berque, *L'Egypte*, pp. 192–93; Mutawallī, *al-Uṣūl*, pp. 325 and 333ff; Hussein, *L'Egypte*, 1: 16ff.
6. Hussein, *L'Egypte*, 1: 32; Ra'ūf 'Abbās, *al-Ḥaraka al-'ummālīya fī miṣr, 1882–1952* (Cairo, 1968), pp. 45–46 and 70ff.

7. For wartime profits in general, see FO 141/790, file 6130, Brunyate to Residency, 12 February 1918.
8. Nadav Safran, *Egypt in Search of Political Community: An Analysis of the Intellectual and Political Evolution of Egypt, 1804–1952* (Cambridge, Mass., 1961), pp. 103ff; 'Abd al-Khāliq Lāshīn, *Sa'd Zaghlūl wa-dawruhu fī 'l-siyāsa al-miṣrīya* (Beirut, 1975), pp. 205ff; Aḥmad Bahā ad-Dīn, *Ayyām lahā tārīkh*, 3rd ed. (Cairo, 1967), pp. 170ff; for an in-depth study, see Reinhard Schulze, *Die Rebellion der ägyptischen Fallahin 1919* (Berlin, 1981), pp. 139ff.
9. Carter, *The Copts*, pp. 60–65.
10. Deeb, *Party Politics*, pp. 38ff; Janice Terry, *The Wafd, 1919–1952: Cornerstone of Egyptian Political Power* (London, 1982), pp. 71ff.
11. Deeb, *Party Politics*, pp. 43–45, 272, and 348–50; al-Dasūqī, *Kibār mullāk*, pp. 214ff; Yūnān Labīb Rizq, *Tārīkh al-wizārāt al-miṣrīya* (Cairo, 1975); for party programs, see Maḥmūd Mutawallī, *Miṣr wa-l-ḥayāt al-ḥizbīya wa-l-niyābīya qabla sanat 1952: Dirāsa tārīkhīya wathā'iqīya* (Cairo, 1980).
12. The text of the treaty is in al-Sayyid-Marsot, *Egypt's Liberal Experiment*, pp. 253–67.
13. Issawi, *Egypt at Mid-Century*, pp. 170ff; 'Abd al-Raḥmān al-Rāfi'ī, *Fī a'qāb al-thawra al-miṣrīya. Thawrat sanat 1919*, 2 vols. (Cairo, 1966, 1968), 2: 390–92; 'Abbās, *al-Ḥaraka al-'ummālīya*, pp. 132ff.
14. See Tignor, "The Economic Activities of Foreigners."
15. See, e.g., FO 141/816, file 13348, 1 June 1921; FO 371/14646, Turner to High Commissioner, 5 April 1930.
16. Davis, *Challenging Colonialism*; Marius Deeb, "Bank Misr and the Emergence of the Local Bourgeoisie in Egypt," *Middle Eastern Studies* 12 (October 1976): 69–86; Robert L. Tignor, "The Egyptian Revolution of 1919: New Directions in the Egyptian Economy," *Middle Eastern Studies* 12 (October 1976): 41–46; Mutawallī, *al-Uṣūl*, pp. 177–217.
17. Deeb, "Bank Misr," pp. 71 and 85n70; Davis, *Challenging Colonialism*, pp. 93ff.
18. Wendell Cleland, *The Population Problem in Egypt* (New York, 1936), p. 30.
19. Detailed data for the late 1940s and the 1950s will be found in the files of the Egyptian Ministry of Trade and Industry, collected at the DW/'Abidīn, Maṣlaḥat al-sharikāt.
20. Mutawallī, *al-Uṣūl*, pp. 132–62 and 245-46; for Ṣidqī, see al-Rāfi'ī, *Fī a'qāb al-thawra*, pp. 127–206.
21. Among the extensive literature on Egyptian nationalism, Arabism, and pan-Islam, see Jalal Mohammed Ahmed, *The Intellectual Origins of Egyptian Nationalism* (London, 1960); Safran, *Egypt in Search of Political Community*; Albert Hourani, *Arabic Thought in the Liberal Age* (London, 1962); Charles Wendell, *The Evolution of the Egyptian Na-*

tional Image from Its Origins to Ahmad Lutfi al-Sayyid (Los Angeles, 1972); Nabīh Bayyūmī 'Abd Allāh, *Taṭawwur fikrat al-qawmīya al-'arabīya fī miṣr* (Cairo, 1975); Israel Gershoni, "Arabization of Islam: The Egyptian Salafiyya and the Rise of Arabism in Pre-Revolutionary Egypt," in *Asian and African Studies* 13 (1979): 22–57; Israel Gershoni and James P. Jankowski, *Egypt, Islam, and the Arabs: The Search for Egyptian Nationhood, 1900–1930* (New York, 1986). For a concise presentation, see James P. Jankowski, "Nationalism in Twentieth Century Egypt," *Middle East Review* (Fall 1979): 37–48.

22. See Alexander Schölch, *Ägypten den Ägyptern! Die politische und gesellschaftliche Krise der Jahre 1878–1882 in Ägypten* (Zurich, 1972).
23. Irene L. Gendzier, *The Practical Visions of Ya'qūb Ṣanū'* (Cambridge, Mass, 1966).
24. On Kāmil, see Fritz Steppat, "Nationalismus und Islam bei Muṣṭafā Kāmil," *Die Welt des Islams* 4 (1956): 241–341; on Luṭfī al-Sayyid, see Wendell, *The Evolution*, pp. 204–45, 256–93.
25. *al-Muqaṭṭam* of 8 May 1919 quoted from Lāshīn, *Sa'd Zaghlūl*, p. 212; and Samīra Baḥr, *al-Aqbāṭ fī 'l-ḥayāt al-siyāsīya al-miṣrīya* (Cairo, 1979), p. 81; for repeated reference to the sacred union of the Cross and the Crescent see Baḥr, *al-Aqbāṭ*, pp. 11–12 and 148.
26. Baḥr, *al-Aqbāṭ*, pp. 79ff; Carter, *The Copts*, pp. 60–65, 161–81.
27. *AJEPO*; for Hazan (Ḥazzān) also *al-Shams*, 26 March 1948; DW/MW, al-Aḥzāb al-siyāsīya (3), European Department, 2 August 1923, exiles list; for Benzakein, *Kadima* 6 (February 1936); and Mizrahi, *L'Egypte et ses juifs*, pp. 42–43. On Jews linked to the old Ḥizb al-Waṭanī (founded in 1879, not to be confused with the party of 1907), see Harris, *Egypt under the Egyptians*, p. 43n23; and Landau, *Jews*, p. 12.
28. For Castro, see *AJEPO*; for his rôle in the Wafd, Lāshīn, *Sa'd Zaghlūl*, pp. 413–14 and 437n19; AIU, Egypt, XII.E.182.m, Somekh, Cairo, 22 July 1921, and *Aperçu du travail sioniste au Caire pendant les années 1920, 1921, 1922, 1923* (Cairo, 1924), p. 7; for *La Liberté*, see FO 371/10889, Allenby to Chamberlain, 2 February 1925. See also chapter four.
29. See especially 'Alī 'Abd al-Rāziq, *al-Islām wa-uṣūl al-ḥukm*, which caused a scandal when it was first published in Cairo in 1925. On Haykal, see Charles D. Smith, *Islam and the Search for Social Order in Modern Egypt: A Biography of Muḥammad Ḥusayn Haykal* (Albany, 1983).
30. Safran, *Egypt in Search of Political Community*, pp. 143–47; Hourani, *Arabic Thought*, pp. 70ff, 172–77, and 329ff; for the most detailed treatment, see Gershoni and Jankowski, *Egypt, Islam, and the Arabs*.
31. See Thomas Mayer, *Egypt and the Palestine Question, 1936–1945* (Berlin, 1983), pp. 6–40.
32. Ṭāriq al-Bishrī, *al-Muslimūn wa-l-aqbāṭ fī iṭār al-jamā'a al-waṭanīya* (Cairo, 1980), pp. 167–95. The constitution was based on the Belgian

constitution; see Jacob M. Landau, *Parliaments and Parties in Egypt* (Tel Aviv, 1953), p. 60.

33. See, e.g., Safran, *Egypt in Search of Political Community*, pp. 113ff; for the text of the articles, see Marcel Colombe, *L'Evolution de l'Egypte, 1924–1950* (Paris, 1951), pp. 281–304.
34. See Baḥr, *al-Aqbāṭ*, pp. 75ff and 123–46; Carter, *The Copts*, pp. 128–42.
35. Wendell, *The Evolution*, pp. 8–14, 158, and 239–49; Sawsan El-Messiri, *Ibn al-Balad: A Concept of Egyptian Identity* (Leiden, 1978).
36. For Cairo, see AA, Abt. III, Po25, Deutschtum im Ausland: Ägypten, von Stohrer, Cairo, 3 May 1929 and 6 February 1933; Po2-01743, Pilger, 15 May 1933; FO 141/699, file 581, Keown-Boyd to Smart, 2 April 1933; for Alexandria, see AA, Inland II A/B, von Dumreicher, Alexandria, 9 March 1935; on the German colony in general, see Thomas W. Kramer, *Deutsch-ägyptische Beziehungen in Vergangenheit und Gegenwart* (Tübingen, 1974), pp. 190ff.
37. See Hans-Adolf Jacobsen, *Nationalsozialistische Außenpolitik, 1933–1938* (Frankfurt/Main, 1968), pp. 114, 648, 665; von Stohrer and von Dumreicher quoted in note 36.
38. AA, Abt. III, Po25, Deutschtum im Ausland: Ägypten, von Stohrer, Cairo, 6 and 23 February 1933.
39. See *Egyptian Gazette*, 27 March 1933, and 1 January 1934; *Israël*, 7 April 1933; AA, Abt. III, Po2-01100, von Stohrer, Cairo, 30 March 1933; AA, Abt. III, Po2-01397, 19 April 1933, and Po2-01705, 21 April 1933. Wolfgang Diewerge, *Als Sonderberichterstatter zum Kairoer Judenprozeß (1933): Gerichtlich erhärtetes Material zur Judenfrage* (Munich, 1935), pp. 11–16. Jewish members in the local Masonic lodges joined in the protests against German anti-Semitism, see DW/ʿAbidīn, al-Maḥfil al-māsūnī, 21 April 1933.
40. AA, Abt. III, Po2-01100, 30 March 1933; Po2-01210, 3 April 1933; and Po2-01253, 4 April 1933, all von Stohrer, Cairo; AA, Referat Deutschland, 83–63a 24/5, "Fragebogenaktion zum Boykott," von Czibulinski, Alexandria, 24 May 1935; *Egyptian Gazette*, 27 March, and 22, 24 July 1933.
41. *Israël*, 13, 27 December 1934; 6 February, 4 March 1936; *Kadima* 3 (1 November 1935), and 14 (November 1936).
42. Rifʿat al-Saʿīd, *Tārīkh al-munaẓẓamāt al-yasārīya al-miṣrīya 1940–1950* (Cairo, 1976), p. 120; and Aḥmad Ṣādiq Saʿd, *Ṣafaḥāt min al-yasār al-miṣrī fī aʿqāb al-ḥarb al-ʿālamīya al-thānīya, 1945–1946* (Cairo, n.d.), p. 42; on the JICA, see *Israël*, 14 August 1935.
43. AA, Abt. III, Po2-01397, von Stohrer, Cairo, 19 and 27 April 1933. In 1941, Dr. Hanns Eisenbeiß wrote in a special report (AA, Inland II A/B 83–26, 16 October 1941): "The Egyptian press is completely Judaized [*verjudet*]. In Cairo, twenty French papers are published, of which eighteen are Jewish, that is to say, their publisher or editor-

in-chief is Jewish. Four out of the six French papers in Alexandria are Jewish-owned. Out of the four English papers in Cairo three are Jewish. In Port Said both of the French papers are owned by the Jews."

44. Diewerge, *Als Sonderberichterstatter*, pp. 18ff; *Israël*, 9, 30 June 1933.
45. *Israël*, 30 June 1933, 3 May 1935; *L'Aurore*, 23 January 1934; *The Jewish Chronicle*, 25 May and 7 December 1935; FO 141/426, file 106, 1934, passim. See also caricatures in *Kadima* 1 (September 1935); for the German side, see Diewerge, *Als Sonderberichterstatter*, pp. 26ff; and AA, Abt. III, Po2-0123, Dahm, Cairo, 6 February 1934.
46. AA, Abt. III, Po2-03588, Gutachten Diewerge, Berlin, 29 September 1933.
47. *Israël*, 21 April 1933; *La Bourse Egyptienne* and *La Voix Juive*, both 18 April 1933.
48. AA, Abt. III, Po2-02731, Pilger, Bulkeley, 18 July 1933; *Israël*, 11 August 1933. The Zionist revisionist paper *La Voix Juive* published a blacklist of German products to be boycotted on 18 April 1933. On the films, see FO 141/699, file 581, 1933/34, passim.
49. FO 141/574, file 1238, 27 November 1935; Mizrahi, *L'Egypte et ses juifs*, pp. 224–25; CZA, S25/490, unsigned and undated (spring 1938). On the antiboycott committee, see AA, Abt. III, Po2-01743, Pilger, Cairo, 15 May 1933; Po2-04534, von Stohrer, Cairo, 4 December 1933; and *Israël*, 30 June 1933.
50. AA, Abt. III, Po2-02731, Berlin, 8 August 1933; MAE, Afrique-Asie, Egypte 108, Grandguillot, 16 November 1935.
51. FO 141/699, file 581, Loraine to Simon, 23 November 1933; a list of firms and individuals hostile to Germany in AA, Abt. III, Po2-01253, von Stohrer, Cairo, 1, 4 April 1933.
52. AA, Abt. III, Po2-03442, 18 September 1933; Po2-04073, 8 November 1933; Po2-04079, 9 and 10 November 1933; Po2-04235, 13 November 1933, all von Stohrer, Cairo; MAE, Afrique-Asie, Egypte 108, 13 November 1933.
53. For details, see Werner Feilchenfeld, Dolf Michaelis, and Ludwig Pinner, *Haavara-Transfer nach Palästina und Einwanderung deutscher Juden nach Palästina 1933–1939.* Schriftenreihe wissenschaftlicher Abhandlungen des Leo Baeck Instituts, no. 26 (Tübingen, 1972), pp. 24–27; and Edwin Black, *The Transfer Agreement: The Untold Story of the Secret Agreement between the Third Reich and Jewish Palestine* (New York, 1984), pp. 246–50.
54. *ha-Yarden* of 10 and 14 November 1935 quoted from FO 141/574, file 1238, 27 November 1935; for sales, see Feilchenfeld, Michaelis, and Pinner, *Haavara-Transfer*, pp. 54–55, 69, 76; and Black, *The Transfer Agreement*, pp. 373–74.
55. *L'Aurore*, 14 and 21 November 1935; *Israël*, 15, 20, and 29 September 1933; CZA, KH4B/452, Erlich, 1935; *Kadima* 3 (November 1935), 5

(January 1936), and 19 (March 1937). See also MAE, Afrique-Asie, Egypte 108, de Witasse to Laval, 16 and 25 November 1935.

56. MAE, Afrique-Asie, Egypte 108, de Witasse to Laval, 16 and 25 November 1935; FO 141/574, file 1238, 27 November 1935; and FO 371/20139, Lampson to Foreign Office, 25 May 1936.

57. AA, Abt. III, Po2-01100, Cairo, 30 March 1933; Po2-04534, 4 December 1933; and Po2-01278, 2 April 1934, all von Stohrer, Cairo; FO 141/699, file 581, Keown-Boyd to Chancery, 2 April and 6 June 1933.

58. FO 141/699, file 581, part II, 5 October 1933.

59. AA, Abt. III, Po2-02292, Pilger to Chemnitz Chamber of Trade and Industry, 21 June 1933.

60. AA, Abt. III, Po2-04534, von Stohrer, Cairo, 4 December 1933; and Po2-01264, 2 April 1934; *The Jewish Chronicle*, 2 September 1933; FO 141/426, file 106, Keown-Boyd to Smart, 10 May 1934.

61. On Fargeon's book, see *Kadima* 1 (September 1935), 7 (March 1936), and 13 (October 1936); on the youth, see Mizrahi, *L'Egypte et ses juifs*, p. 163; and FO 141/426, file 106, Jays to Anson, 16 December 1934.

62. FO 141/533, file 556, Lampson to Cecil, 9 March and 4 April 1935; CZA, KH4B/452, Samter, Jerusalem, 25 October 1933; on the colony, see CZA KH4B/452, Helfmann, Jerusalem, 28 May 1933; *Israël*, 12 January, 13 April, 27 December 1934; on the medical doctors, see *Oriente Moderno*, 1 and 24 May 1933.

63. AA, Abt. III, Po2-01397, von Stohrer, Cairo, 19 and 27 April 1933; AA, Referat Deutschland, Po5 N.E. adh. 2, vol. 2, von Stohrer, Bulkeley, 19 September 1933.

64. AA, Abt. III, Po2-01264, von Stohrer, Cairo, 12 April 1933; for the quotation, see AA, Abt. III, Po2-0123, 18 December 1933; and Po2-0732, 21 February 1934; on Haim Nahum, see FO 141/699, file 581, Smart to Millar, 17 November 1933.

65. As early as April 1933, the official representatives of the Jewish communities had seen the Egyptian minister of the interior to warn him of German activities in the country; in May 1933, they sent a memorandum of protest to the League of Nations to the same effect; see *Israël*, 21 April 1933; and AA, Abt. III, Po2-01887, Pilger, Cairo, 26 May 1933.

66. FO 141/699, file 581, Keown-Boyd to Chancery, 6 June 1933; AA, Abt. III, Po2-01397, von Stohrer, Cairo, 19 April 1933; Po2-01743, Pilger, Cairo, 15 May 1933; see also *al-Ahrām*, 1 to 4 April 1933.

67. MAE, Afrique-Asie, Egypte 93, 19 May and 19 September 1933.

68. These articles are collected in AA, Abt. III, Po2-02072, June 1933.

69. AA, Abt. III, Po2-03588, Diewerge, Berlin, 29 September 1933.

70. AA, Abt. III, Po2-03778, Aufzeichnung zu dem Gutachten Diewerges, Ortsgruppe Kairo und Dahm, 6 October 1933.

71. AA, Abt. III, Po2-04006, Diewerge to Prüfer, 1 November 1933, containing the copy of an official letter of the Cairo Ortsgruppe of 2 October 1933. The original German reads: "Fuer das Verstaendnis der Rassentheorie ist der Bildungsgrad der breiten Masse nicht fortgeschritten genug. Das Verstaendnis fuer die Gefahren des Judentums ist hier noch nicht geweckt."
72. Included in AA, Abt. III, Po2-04006, Diewerge to Prüfer, 1 November 1933; see also, Diewerge memorandum, AA, Abt. III, Po2-03588, 29 September 1933.
73. Rif'at al-Sa'īd, *Aḥmad Ḥusayn: Kalimāt wa-mawāqif* (Cairo, 1979), pp. 42–49; for the Wafd, see Deeb, *Party Politics*, pp. 261–63.
74. See James P. Jankowski, *Egypt's Young Rebels: "Young Egypt," 1933–1952* (Stanford, 1975), pp. 12ff, 26, and 52ff; al-Sa'īd, *Aḥmad Ḥusayn*, pp. 55ff.
75. Jankowski, *Egypt's Young Rebels*, pp. 14–15, 38, and 58. In March 1938, these paramilitary organizations were declared illegal, but continued to operate; Deeb, *Party Politics*, pp. 373–78.
76. Jankowski, *Egypt's Young Rebels*, pp. 14–20 and 29–32.
77. A number of these organizations are listed in John Heyworth-Dunne, *Religious and Political Trends in Modern Egypt* (Washington, D.C., 1950), pp. 90–91; and Zakariyā Sulaymān Bayyūmī, *al-Ikhwān al-muslimūn wa-l-jamā'āt al-islāmīya fī 'l-ḥayāt al-siyāsīya al-miṣrīya, 1928–1948* (Cairo, 1979) p. 67n1.
78. Malcolm Kerr, *Islamic Reform: The Political and Legal Theories of Muhammad Abduh and Rashid Rida* (Berkeley and Los Angeles, 1966).
79. Heyworth-Dunne, *Religious and Political Trends*, pp. 11–14; Bayyūmī, *al-Ikhwān al-muslimūn*, pp. 68ff.
80. Richard P. Mitchell, *The Society of the Muslim Brothers* (London, 1969), p. 328; Heyworth-Dunne, *Religious and Political Trends*, pp. 15–18, 68.
81. Quoted from Mitchell, *The Society of the Muslim Brothers*, p. 14; *Majmū'at rasā'il al-imām al-shahīd Ḥasan al-Bannā*, n.p., n.d., pp. 147–87.
82. Heyworth-Dunne, *Religious and Political Trends*, pp. 60–68; Mitchell, *The Society of the Muslim Brothers*, pp. 172 and 328ff, where he mentions the "urban, middle-class, effendi predominance among the activist membership" (p. 329); Uri Kupferschmidt, "The Muslim Brothers and the Egyptian Village," *Asian and African Studies* (Haifa) 16 (March 1982): 157–70. On their social and economic ideas, see al-Bannā, *Majmū'at rasā'il*, pp. 228–88.
83. al-Bannā, *Majmū'at rasā'il*, pp. 17–23, 55–78, 112–20.
84. al-Bannā, *Majmū'at rasā'il*, pp. 69–90; Mitchell, *The Society of the Muslim Brothers*, p. 249; Bayyūmī, *al-Ikhwān al-muslimūn*, pp. 311–16.

85. See, e.g., FO 371/20148, Lampson to Eden, 6 April 1936; AA, Inland ID: Kirche in Ägypten 2, Mylius, Berlin, 12 December 1942, "Die kirchenpolitische Lage im heutigen Ägypten"; FO 371/53293, registered 2 May 1946, including a memorandum on the "Christian minorities in Egypt" of July 1944; also Carter, *The Copts*, pp. 273–79.
86. Jankowski, *Egypt's Young Rebels*, pp. 2–8; Berque, *L'Egypte*, pp. 574–78; Raoul Makarius, *La jeunesse intellectuelle d'Egypte au lendemain de la deuxième guerre mondiale* (Paris, 1960). It will be noticed that these are the same factors usually given when trying to explain the upsurge of militant Islam in the Egypt under Sadat and Mubarak; see, e.g., Gilles Kepel, *The Prophet and Pharaoh: Muslim Extremism in Egypt* (London, 1985).
87. Charles D. Smith, "The 'Crisis of Orientation': The Shift of Egyptian Intellectuals to Islamic Subjects in the 1930's," *International Journal of Middle East Studies* 4 (1973): 382–440.
88. See Mayer, *Egypt and the Palestine Question*, pp. 6–40; James P. Jankowski, "Egyptian Responses to the Palestine Problem in the Interwar Period," *International Journal of Middle East Studies* 12 (1980): 1–38; 'Awāṭif 'Abd al-Raḥmān, "Ittijāhāt al-ṣiḥāfa al-miṣrīya izā' al-qaḍīya al-filasṭīnīya, 1922–1936" (Ph.D. diss., Cairo University, 1975), pp. 473ff.
89. Jankowski, *Egyptian Responses*, p. 4–9; James P. Jankowski, "Zionism and the Jews in Egyptian Nationalist Opinion, 1920–1939," in *Egypt and Palestine: A Millennium of Association (868–1948)*, edited by Amnon Cohen and Gabriel Baer (Jerusalem, 1984), pp. 314–31; Sylvia G. Haim "The Palestine Question in *al-Manar*," in *Egypt and Palestine*, edited by Cohen and Baer, pp. 299–313; Mayer, *Egypt and the Palestine Question*, pp. 11–13.
90. CZA, KH4B/451, Kohn, 19 December 1929; and Fonds National Juif, Cairo, 17 February 1930; CZA, KKL5/472, Weissman, Cairo, 29 January 1930; FO 371/13753, Hoare to Henderson, 31 August 1929; Mayer, *Egypt and the Palestine Question*, pp. 15–23; see also CZA, KKL5/324, Grünhut to Ussishkin, 1 November 1928.
91. Israel Gershoni, "The Muslim Brothers and the Arab Revolt in Palestine, 1936-39," *Middle Eastern Studies* 22 (July 1986): 367–97.
92. Jankowski, *Egyptian Responses*, pp. 11ff. Mayer, *Egypt and the Palestine Question*, pp. 41–137, takes involvement as being verbal rather than practical. For statistics on newspaper coverage, see 'Abd al-Raḥmān, "Ittijāhāt al-ṣiḥāfa al-miṣrīya," pp. 475–76.
93. MAE, Afrique-Asie, Egypte 95, de Witasse to Delbos, 8 June 1936; and MAE, Afrique-Asie, Egypte 97, 4 September 1937; Egypte 98, de Witasse to Bonnet, 10 December 1938. For detailed information on German propaganda in Egypt, see MAE, Afrique-Asie, Egypte 98, de

Witasse to Bonnet, 23 August and 16 November 1938; FO 371/21879, Bentinck report, 11 August 1938.

94. Jankowski, *Egyptian Responses*, p. 15.
95. Mayer, *Egypt and the Palestine Question*, pp. 67–82; for the graffiti, see MAE, Afrique-Asie, Egypte 103, Garreau to Delbos, 2 October 1936; and *The Jewish Chronicle*, 23 October 1936.
96. MAE, Afrique-Asie, Egypte 98, 16 November 1938; FO 371/21998, Lampson to Foreign Office, 30 October 1938; and Weizmann to Baxter, 23 June 1938. Another British report contained in FO 371/21998, dated 29 July 1938, stated, however, that these pamphlets had no impact on the attitude of the general public toward the Jews. For Arabic translations of *Mein Kampf*, see Stefan Wild, "National Socialism in the Arab Near East between 1933 and 1939," *Die Welt des Islams* 25 (1985): 147–70.
97. See *AMJY* 5699 (1938), April–June 1938; AIU, Egypt, I.C.26, 4 and 24 June 1938; AIU, Egypt, I.C.27, 29 April 1938, 14 and 15 May 1938, all Nassi, Ṭanṭā; FO 371/21883, Lampson to Foreign Office, 17 October 1938; FO 371/22000, press memorandum, 16 April to 22 May 1938; FO 371/23352, Bateman to Halifax, 14 August 1939; Jankowski, *Egypt's Young Rebels*, p. 39.
98. CZA, KKL5/1143, James, Cairo, 10 July 1939; FO 371/23352, Sterndale-Bennett to Halifax, 26 July 1939; for Adès, see FO 371/23352, Robertson to Smart, 30 July 1939.
99. Quoted from the English translation in FO 371/21998, Smithers to Cadogan, 29 October 1938; I have not seen the original Arabic.
100. FO 371/20035, Kelly to Foreign Office, 22 June 1936; FO 371/21880, British embassy, Cairo to Oliphant, 13 September 1938; FO 371/21798, Bateman to Halifax, 23 August 1938; FO 371/21882, Lampson to Foreign Office, 20 October 1938.
101. FO 371/21883, Lampson to Foreign Office, 7 November 1938, and 31 October 1938. For the reaction of Joseph Aslan Cattaoui to these attempts to involve Egyptian Jewry, see *al-Shams*, 6 July 1938.
102. MAE, Afrique-Asie, Egypte 103, Garreau to Delbos, 2 October 1936; AIU, Egypt I.C.26, Nassi, Ṭanṭā, 18 July 1938; FO 141/630, file 932, meeting between Kelly, and J. A. Cattaoui, 7 December 1937; FO 371/22000, press memoranda, May–June and September–December 1938; FO 371/21878, 11 June 1938; and FO 371/23342, 15 June 1939, both Lampson to Halifax; FO 371/23305 Kelly, 18 April 1939.
103. CZA, S5/490, Lichtheim to Lauterbach, 8 December 1937; and CZA, KKL5/1143, Subotnik, 11 November 1938; CZA, S5/490 Subotnik, April 1939; and unsigned memorandum, CZA, S5/490, dated 5 March 1940, all Cairo.
104. AIU, Egypt, I.C.23, S. Avigdor, "Le milieu juif d'Alexandrie," Cairo, 6 December 1937; see also CZA, KKL5/1143, James, Cairo, 10 July 1939.

105. CZA, Z4/17425; for a similar statement, see CZA, Z4/17425, 30 January 1939. Weizmann replied (CZA, Z4/17425, 28 November 1938, and 30 January 1939) that it was the Arabs, not the Jews, who created difficulties.
106. AIU, Egypt, I.C.27, Nassi, Ṭanṭā, 29 April and 14 May 1938; *AMJY* 1938, 28 April, 13 May, and 16 June 1938; and *AMJY* 1939–40, p. 373; for al-Marāghī, see FO 371/21878, Lampson to Halifax, 16 June 1938; and FO 371/21879, Lampson to Oliphant, 20 July 1938.
107. *al-Balāgh* of 28 April 1938 quoted from *La Bourse Egyptienne*, 30 April 1938; see also *al-Shams*, 17 November 1938; and MAE, Afrique-Asie, Egypte 97, de Witasse to Delbos, 28 March 1938.
108. MAE, Afrique-Asie, Egypte 98, 2 July, 23 August, 16 November, and 10 December 1938; FO 141/21879, Bentinck report, 11 August 1938; FO 371/21878, Lampson to Halifax, 24 June 1938. See also Callum A. MacDonald, "Radio Bari: Italian Wireless Propaganda in the Middle East and British Countermeasures 1934–38," *Middle Eastern Studies* 13 (May 1977): 195–207. As already mentioned, the NSDAP Ortsgruppe Cairo had, in the context of the anti-German campaign of the LICA, suggested including the Palestine conflict in German propaganda against the Jews and the British.
109. See, e.g., FO 141/630, file 932, Kelly, 7 December 1937; FO 371/21998, Weizmann to Baxter, 23 June 1938; FO 371/21998, memorandum by Sir Robert Rolo to Lord Lloyd, 12 November 1938; FO 371/23342, 1939, passim.
110. Jankowski, *Egypt's Young Rebels*, pp. 20ff and 33–34; al-Sa'īd, *Aḥmad Ḥusayn*, pp. 91–131; for Ḥājj Amīn see Heinz Tillmann, *Deutschlands Araberpolitik im Zweiten Weltkrieg* (East Berlin, 1965), pp. 128, 324, 354–55; Lukasz Hirszowicz, *The Third Reich and the Arab East* (London, 1966), pp. 218–19 and 312–13; and his speeches on Radio Bari in *Oriente Moderno* 1943, pp. 4 and 275; and *Oriente Moderno* 1943–46, p. 2. For al-Bannā, see *Majmū'at rasā'il*, pp. 21–22 (Da'watunā).
111. 'Abd Allāh, *Taṭawwur fikrat al-qawmīya*, pp. 132–33; Jankowski, *Egyptian Responses*, pp. 21–28; for a different view, see Mayer, *Egypt and the Palestine Question*, pp. 301–8.
112. MAE, Afrique-Asie, Egypte 97, de Witasse to Delbos, 17 July 1937.
113. For a detailed analysis, see Mayer, *Egypt and the Palestine Question*, pp. 104–25.
114. For 1913, see CZA, Z3/114, Hochberg, Constantinople, 17 May 1913; and Neville Mandel, *The Arabs and Zionism before World War I* (Berkeley and Los Angeles, 1976), pp. 149ff; for 1918 and 1922, see FO 141/802, file 4759, Clayton, 16 June 1918; FO 371/7773, Allenby to Curzon, 13 May 1922; and memorandum, 18–19 March 1922.
115. Frederick H. Kisch, *Palestine Diary* (London, 1938), pp. 168 and 391–92.

116. See FO 371/21878, Lampson to Halifax, 16 June and 19 July 1938; CZA, Z4/17048, Weizmann to Alexander, 26 June 1938; CZA, Z4/14651, 28 September 1939; and *The Jewish Chronicle*, 21 April 1939; for hopes, see, e.g., *La Bourse Egyptienne*, 29 October 1937, and CZA, S25/5218, Ben Ascher, Alexandria, January 1939.
117. FO 371/21878, Lampson to Halifax, 16 June 1938; also Mayer, *Egypt and the Palestine Question*, pp. 51ff.
118. AA, Büro des Staatssekretärs, Albrecht, Berlin, 30 September 1939; Tillmann, *Deutschlands Araberpolitik*, pp. 130–31; Francis Nicosia, "Arab Nationalism and National Socialist Germany, 1933–1939: Ideological and Strategic Incompatibility," *International Journal of Middle East Studies* 12 (1980): 351–72; *AMJY* 1940–41, pp. 441–42.
119. ʿAbd al-ʿAẓīm Ramaḍān, *Taṭawwur al-ḥaraka al-waṭanīya fī miṣr min sanat 1937 ilā sanat 1948*, vol. 2, passim; Mitchell, *The Society of the Muslim Brothers*, p. 22.
120. Tillmann, *Deutschlands Araberpolitik*; Yūnus al-Baḥrī, *Hunā Barlīn: Ḥayya al-ʿarab!* (Beirut, n.d.).
121. For lists of pro-German Egyptian personalities, see AA, Handakten Ritter, Ägypten, 6 August 1942; and FO 921/34, Lampson to Stone, 11 July 1942; see also Mitchell, *The Society of the Muslim Brothers*, pp. 23ff.
122. Tillmann, *Deutschlands Araberpolitik* (p. 56), quotes the following statement Hitler is said to have made on 22 August, 1939 in front of the Wehrmacht commanders: "We will continue to stir up unrest ... in Arabia. Let us think as masters and let us see in these people lacquered half apes at best who want to feel the whip [lit., knout]." The German original runs: "Wir werden weiterhin die Unruhe ... in Arabien schüren. Denken wir als Herren und sehen wir in diesen Völkern bestenfalls lackierte Halbaffen, die die Knute spüren wollen." See also Wild, *National Socialism in the Arab Near East*, pp. 139–47, 160–63.
123. AA, Inland II A/B, von Stohrer, Cairo, 24 June 1936; MAE, Afrique-Levant, Egypte 95, de Witasse, 22 June 1936; and François-Poncet, Berlin, 23 June 1936, both to Bonnet; *Egyptian Gazette*, 24 June 1936. On the problem of *Aufnordung* (Aryanization), see Tillmann, *Deutschlands Araberpolitik*, p. 67n262.
124. See, e.g., AA, Büro des Staatssekretärs, von Stohrer, Berlin, 18 November 1941.
125. Telegram as transmitted by AA, Büro des Staatssekretärs, Ettel, Tehran, 15 April 1941; and von Papen, Ankara, 10 November 1941; see also a secret report in CZA, Z4/14620, "Some Notes on Egypt's Attitude in the Present War," unsigned, n.d. (late 1942).
126. AA, Büro des Staatssekretärs, von Weizsäcker, Berlin, 26 June 1942.
127. AA, Büro des Staatssekretärs, Fellers Mackensen, Rome, 15 February 1942; Schwendemann, Paris, 27 April 1942; Abetz, Paris, 23 June

1942, and telegram from Sofia, 7 March 1942; see also Fayṣal ʿAbd al-Munʿim, *Ilā ʾl-amām yā Rūmīl!* (Cairo, 1976); Muḥammad Anīs, *Arbaʿ fabrāyir 1942 fī tārīkh miṣr al-siyāsī* (Beirut, 1972); and CZA, Z4/14620, Vilensky to Shertok, 9 March 1942.

128. AA, Handakten Ettel, Istanbul, 24 July 1942; and AA, Inland IIg 334, Schellenberg to Luther, 7 July 1942. Jewish fears are recorded in CZA, S5/490, unsigned, 5 March 1940; and CZA, S25/2027, "Aspects of the Situation in Egypt up to Wednesday July 1st, 1942 in the Evening," unsigned, Jerusalem, 5 July 1942. For exodus figures, see *Oriente Moderno* 1941, pp. 425, 525; *Oriente Moderno* 1942, p. 290; and Politi, *L'Egypte*, pp. 210–17. The atmosphere in Alexandria in 1942 was vividly portrayed by the Egyptian film-maker Yūsuf Shāhīn in his film "Iskandarīya leh?" (1978), see *l'Avant-scène cinéma*, no. 341 (June 1985), issue on Youssef Chahine, "Alexandrie pourquoi?"

129. CZA, S6/3840, July 1942, passim, especially 13 July 1942 and 25 October 1944 with lists of names; further OH(61)11, J. Lotan. Non-Jewish activists were also included, see Saʿd, *Ṣafaḥāt*, p. 45; and Gilles Perrault, *Un homme à part* (Paris, 1984), pp. 98–114.

130. CZA, S6/3840, Sonsino to Shertok, 20 July 1942; FO 921/34, Lampson to Eden, 12 July 1942.

131. MAE, Guerre 1939-45, Londres CNF 369, Afrique, Egypte, June 1940–December 1941, passim, especially 28 August 1940 for numbers; and MAE, Guerre 1939–45, Alger 1315, 17 May 1943; also Michel Laforge, *Au fil des jours en Orient: Grèce, Egypte, Pakistan, Jérusalem, 1922–1958* (Brussels, 1967), pp. 141–44.

132. David Prato, *Cinque anni di rabbinato*, 2 vols. (Alexandria, 1933), 2: 67–72; FO 371/19097, Fitzpatrick, "Intelligence Note," 5 September 1935. Fitzpatrick lists several Jews among the local leaders of the fascist party; see also FO 371/19097, 24 October 1935; and the reports by the head of the European (intelligence) Department, Keown-Boyd, in FO 371/20132, 23 January 1936, and FO 371/20133, 11 August 1936. For a pro-fascist view, see Sammarco, *Gli Italiani*, pp. 44ff.

133. FO 371/21981, Kelly, 7 September 1938, and Bateman to Halifax, 9 September 1938; FO 371/21880, Lampson to Oliphant, 13 September 1938; *al-Shams*, 21 September 1938 and 17 May 1940; on Italian anti-Semitic legislation, see Meir Michaelis, *Mussolini and the Jews: German-Italian Relations and the Jewish Question in Italy, 1922–1945* (London, 1978), pp. 169ff and 185–91.

134. DW/ʿAbidīn, Wizārat al-Dākhilīya, Taqārīr al-amn, Cairo City Police and Alexandria City Police, Special Branch, April 1940–January 1941, passim; for the lodges, see Cairo, 13 and 17 April, 14 May, and 9 August 1940, and Alexandria, 23 May 1940; FO 371/19097, Fitzpatrick, 5 September and 24 October 1935; also *Oriente Moderno*, 7 November 1937.

135. DW/'Abidīn, Taqārīr al-amn, Cairo, 20 November and 23 December 1940, 10 March and 20 May 1941.
136. For membership lists, see DW/'Abidīn, Taqārīr al-amn, Cairo, 14, 31 May, and 20 November 1940; for fascist lists, see Cairo, 10 August, 19, 26 September, 20 November, and 17 December 1940; for fascist sympathies, see Cairo, 15 January 1941, and Alexandria, 14 May 1940.
137. FO 371/63004, "Economic Report 1946," 7 August 1947; FO 371/73458, file 1011, Campbell, "Review of Political Events in Egypt for 1947," 20 April 1949; and Campbell, "General Political Review of Egypt for 1948," 7 June 1949; FO 921/310, Peers, 1 May 1944; Issawi, *Egypt at Mid-Century*, pp. 141ff and 208–9; and Berque, *L'Egypte*, pp. 634–38.
138. al-Sa'īd, *Tārīkh ... 1940–1950*, p. 59; CZA, Z4/14620, Vilensky to Shertok, "Report on the Situation in Egypt," Jerusalem, 9 March 1942.
139. Deeb, *Party Politics*, pp. 344–50; Yūnān Labīb Rizq, *al-Wafd wa-l-kitāb al-aswad* (Cairo, 1978); on Makram 'Ubayd, see Carter, *The Copts*, pp. 167–81.
140. Donald M. Reid, "Fu'ad Siraj ad-Din and the Egyptian Wafd," *Journal of Contemporary History* 15 (1980): 721–44; Ṭāriq al-Bishrī, *al-Ḥaraka al-siyāsīya fī miṣr, 1945–1952*, 2d ed. (Cairo, 1983), pp. 304–8, 340–41, 358; Mitchell, *The Society of the Muslim Brothers*, pp. 35ff; Jankowski, *Egypt's Young Rebels*, pp. 40ff, 72–74, and 118ff.
141. MAE, Guerre 1939-45, Alger 1036, Moeneclay to de Benoist, 2 December 1943; FO 921/199, 20 March 1943, and FO 371/52605, 17 January 1946, both Killearn to Eden; *AMJY* 1940–41, 17 June 1940, gives their number as 5,000.
142. FO 371/41331, Kellar to Scrivener, registered 31 August 1944.
143. FO 371/41331, Kellar to Scrivener, registered 31 August 1944; CZA, S25/5218, Alexander, "The Egyptian Jews on the Eve of the Great Decision," 24 October 1945; for articles, see e.g., *Jarīdat al-Ikhwān al-Muslimīn*, 13 October and 3 November 1945; for the Kutla party, see Carter, *The Copts*, pp. 188–94.
144. Michael J. Cohen, "The Moyne Assassination, November, 1944: A Political Analysis," *Middle Eastern Studies* 15 (October 1979): 358–73; on local Jewish reactions, see FO 371/45404, Jenkins to Tomlyn, 20 January 1945.
145. CZA, S25/1877, Gordon, Jerusalem, 17 February 1943; CZA, S25/5218, 1943–1945, passim.
146. Report included in FO 371/53333, Speaight to Egyptian Department, 30 October 1945; see also CZA, S25/5218, Alexander, "The Egyptian Jews on the Eve of the Great Decision," 24 October 1945.
147. CZA, S25/5218, "Incidents of 2 and 3 November 1945 in Cairo, Egypt," unsigned, Cairo, 21 November 1945 (based on a top-secret report written by an officer of the Egyptian secret police, dated 3 November 1945); CZA, Z4/14620, M to Mosche, 10 November 1945; FO 371/45394,

Bowker to Foreign Office, 2–6 November 1945; and FO 371/45394, Killearn to Bevin, 1 November 1945. See press reports in *Jewish Telegraphic Agency*, 2–5 November 1945; *al-Shams*, 9 November 1945; and *Jarīdat al-Ikhwān al-Muslimīn*, 3 November 1945.

148. FO 371/45394, Bowker to Foreign Office, 3 November 1945; and CZA, S25/5218, 21 November 1945. See also *Jarīdat al-Ikhwān al-Muslimīn*, 3 November 1945.
149. FO 371/45394, Bowker, 2 November 1945; FO 371/45395, Barnard, al-Manṣūra, 3 November 1945.
150. FO 371/45394, Bowker, 6 November 1945; *al-Shams*, 16 November 1945; CZA, S25/5218, S. A. to Dr. Joseph, 9 November 1945; and CZA, S25/5218, Appendix I.
151. CZA, S25/5218, Appendix II and III; *Progrès Egyptien*, 10 November 1945 quoting *al-Ahrām* of 9 November 1945; for the pressure thesis, see CZA, Z4/14620, M to Mosche, Cairo, 10 November 1945.
152. CZA, Z4/14620, M to Mosche, Cairo, 10 November 1945.
153. Mayer, *Egypt and the Palestine Question*, pp. 104–25, 164–283; 'Abd Allāh, *Taṭawwur fikrat al-qawmīya*, pp. 144ff and 174ff; for party programs, see Mutawallī, *Miṣr wa-l-ḥayāt al-ḥizbīya.*
154. Gershoni, "Arabization of Islam."
155. MAE, Guerre 1939–45, Alger 1036, Moeneclay to de Benoist, 2 December 1943.

CHAPTER FOUR

1. See Joseph Aslan Cattaoui in a letter to 'Alī 'Allūba Pāshā in *al-Shams*, 6 July 1938; also *al-Shams*, 8 June 1938, and 22 September 1944; and *L'Encyclopédie populaire juive 5706/1946*, edited by the Société des Editions Historiques Juives d'Egypte (Cairo, 1946), p. 14.
2. AIU, Egypt, XII.E.182.k, Somekh, Cairo, 1 November 1912.
3. CZA, Z4/2051, Berger, Jerusalem, December 1925; and CZA, KH4B/451, Kohn, Jerusalem, 10 December 1928.
4. Many of his poems appeared on the pages of *al-Shams* and *al-Kalīm*; see also Sasson Somekh, "Participation of Egyptian Jews in Modern Arabic Culture, and the Case of Murād Faraj," in *The Jews of Egypt*, edited by Shimon Shamir (Boulder, 1987), pp. 130–40.
5. See *al-Shams*, 14 September 1934; CZA, S25/5218, Sasson, Cairo, 14 April 1943; Naṣṣār, *al-Yahūd*, pp. 63–67; also Victor Nachmias, "'Al-Shams'–'Itton yehudi be-mitsrayim, 1934–1948," *Pe'amim* 16 (1983): 128–41.
6. For biographical notes, see Krämer, *Minderheit*, pp. 329–30.
7. *al-Shams*, 14 September 1934; statutes of the Association in *al-Shams*, 17 and 31 October 1935; see also *al-Shams*, 28 November and 5 December 1935; and Naṣṣār, *al-Yahūd*, pp. 103–12.

8. *al-Shams*, 23 May 1941; CZA, S5/490, Organization Department, Jerusalem, n.d. (summer 1938).
9. For Cattaoui, see CZA, Z4/3229I, Grünhut, Jerusalem, 29 November 1927; *Hamenora* (1924), nos. 4–5; *Kadima* 1 (September 1935). For Nahum see FO 371/13149, Murray memorandum, 6 June 1928, who quoted one of Nahum's political opponents, Jack Mosseri, as saying that Nahum, was "vain and ambitious and anxious to play a political role. He was encouraging the Orientalised Jews to stand in with the Egyptians, and had persuaded a number of them to give up their foreign nationality and become Egyptian nationals." See also CZA, Z4/2797/99, 22 October 1939.
10. *al-Shams*, 1 February, and 12, 19 December 1935; 13 February and 18 May 1942; 8 March 1946.
11. *al-Shams*, 21 September 1934, 29 March 1935, 8 June 1938, 28 November 1941, 13 July 1942, 22 September 1944, and 13 May 1948; also a series on the Jews and Arab culture in *al-Shams*, 1934–36, passim. For the Zionists, see, e.g., CZA Z3/115, Thon, Jaffa to Palaestina-Amt des Zionistischen Aktionskomitees, Berlin, 3 March 1913; or *La Revue Sioniste*, 4 January 1918.
12. *al-Shams*, 29 March 1935, and 7 November 1947.
13. *al-Shams*, 2 January 1936, 29 June 1938, 28 November 1941, 11 July 1947, and 23 April 1948.
14. *al-Shams*, 24 May 1935, 1 February 1943, 12 October 1944. CZA, KKL5/1143, James, Cairo, 10 July 1939, nonetheless described the members of the Cairo school committee as dedicated advocates of Egyptianization.
15. *al-Shams*, 7 February, 13 July and 3 August 1942; 21 May, 14 June 1943; 2 September, 1 November 1946.
16. FO 371/69250, registered 4 October 1948; and FO 371/69259, 14 June 1948, both Campbell to Bevin.
17. Gittelman, *Israël*, 25 March 1936.
18. See FO 141/779, file 9065, Alexandria City Police, "Note on Rosenthal," 20 March 1921; and FO 141/779, file 9065, Clayton to Macnaghten, 28 September 1921; FO 371/7745, Allenby to Curzon, 16 November 1922; MAE, Afrique-Asie, Egypte 14, Gaillard to Briand, 6 December 1921. See also Rif'at al-Sa'īd, *Tārīkh al-ḥaraka al-ishtirākīya fī miṣr, 1900-1925*, 2d ed. (Cairo, 1975), pp. 221ff; Selma Botman, "Oppositional Politics in Egypt: The Communist Movement, 1936–1954" (Ph.D. diss., Harvard University, 1984), pp. 114–19.
19. al-Sa'īd, *Tārīkh ... 1900-1925*, pp. 198, 249, and 285; 'Abbās, *al-Ḥaraka al-'ummālīya*, p. 240; FO 371/11024, Ingram to Anson, 4 November 1925; Perrault, *Un homme à part*, pp. 85ff.
20. al-Sa'īd, *Tārīkh ... 1900-1925*, p. 284.
21. FO 372/2564, Chancellor to Amery, 22 February 1929.

22. FO 372/2564, Lord Lloyd to Chamberlain, 3 May 1929.
23. AA, Abt. III, von Czibulinski, Alexandria, 30 July, 8 August, and 27 November 1935, 6 May 1936; al-Sa'īd, *Tārīkh ... 1940-1950*, pp. 119ff and 154ff; Sa'd, *Ṣafaḥāt*, pp. 35–37, 42; Botman, "Oppositional Politics," pp. 138–64. A considerable number of Jewish youth in the LISCA were close to Marxist thought and therefore clashed with the Zionist members of the Jewish antifascist movement (*Israël*, 14 August 1935).
24. FO 371/41003, Andsley memorandum, "Communism in Egypt," 28 August 1945; FO 371/53327, 1946, passim; Botman, "Oppositional Politics," pp. 156 and 300.
25. Ra'ūf 'Abbās, *Awrāq Hinrī Kūriyīl* (Cairo, 1988), passim; p. 163 for membership; al-Sa'īd, *Tārīkh ... 1940-1950*, pp. 328–57; Perrault, *Un homme à part*, pp. 47–50, 98ff, and 134–38.
26. For Taḥrīr al-Sha'b, see al-Sa'īd, *Tārīkh ... 1940–1950*, pp. 161–63 and 287–93; for al-Fajr al-Jadīd, see pp. 300–314; also Sa'd, *Ṣafaḥāt*, pp. 38ff and 53–60.
27. For Iskra, see al-Sa'īd, *Tārīkh ... 1940-1950*, pp. 264–67, 315–27, and 383–86; but also Perrault, *Un homme à part*, pp. 162–63, 186ff. For membership, see 'Abbās, *Awrāq Hinrī Kūriyīl*, p. 163.
28. al-Sa'īd, *Tārīkh ... 1940–1950*, pp. 371ff; 'Abbās, *Awrāq Hinrī Kūriyīl*, pp. 139–84 (numbers in June 1947, p. 163); Perrault, *Un homme à part*, pp. 197ff.
29. 'Abd al-Qādir Yāsīn, *al-Qaḍīya al-filasṭīnīya fī fikr al-yasār al-miṣrī* (Beirut, 1981), pp. 39ff, 56ff; Botman, "Oppositional Politics," pp. 269–73; Rif'at al-Sa'īd, *al-Yasār al-miṣrī wa-l-qaḍīya al-filasṭīnīya* (Beirut, 1974), pp. 32–37, 45, and 313ff; see also al-Bishrī, *al-Muslimūn wa-l-aqbāṭ*, pp. 641ff. For HADITU membership in June 1947, see 'Abbās, *Awrāq Hinrī Kūriyīl*,p. 163–64 (28% workers, 20% students, 14% intellectuals, 26% foreigners out of a total of 1,400 members. The Central Committee had a majority of Muslim Egyptians and only three Jewish members [Curiel, Schwartz, and Sidnī Salāmūn]).
30. Conversions in Sa'd, *Ṣafaḥāt*, pp. 45 and 50; for attacks on Curiel, see FO 371/69250, Campbell to Bevin, 1 May 1948; *Jarīdat al-Ikhwān al-Muslimīn*, 27 July and 3 August 1948; al-Sa'īd, *Tārīkh ... 1940–1950*, pp. 415–20; Botman, "Oppositional Politics," pp. 128–38.
31. al-Sa'īd, *Tārīkh ... 1940–1950*, pp. 190–96, and *Ṣawt al-Umma*, 20, 22, 26, and 27 April 1947. According to Yāsīn, the Anti-Zionist League was already founded in the summer of 1946 (*al-Qaḍīya al-filasṭīnīya*, pp. 33, and 73–98). For the Zionist point of view, see CZA, S25/5218, Peron, Cairo, 20 May 1947, listing the names of ninety-seven members of the Section Culturel; and unsigned report, CZA, S25/5218, 1 July 1947.
32. Included in CZA, S25/5218, report of 1 July 1947; see also al-Sa'īd, *al-Yasār*, pp. 304–5.

33. Manifestoes in al-Saʿīd, *al-Yasār*, pp. 184–92 (see also pp. 193–99); and FO 371/61759, Campbell to Bevin, 25 October 1947; for the ban on the Anti-Zionist League, see Yāsīn, *al-Qaḍīya al-filasṭīnīya*, pp. 92–93. For the Forum group, see FO 371/69210, Foreign Office Minute, Research Department, 30 December 1947 (with quotation); and FO 371/69250, Campbell to Bevin, 18 March 1948; for its impact, see al-Saʿīd, *al-Yasār*, p. 305, and CZA, S25/5218, report of 1 July 1947.
34. See, e.g., CZA, S6/1982, unsigned, 20 November 1943; and CZA, S5/793, Alexander, Cairo, 4 January 1944; OH(61)19, Y. Masri; OH(61)-43, A. Schlossberg; and OH(61)40, T. Weiss, 26 June 1970.
35. al-Saʿīd, *Tārīkh . . . 1940–1950*, pp. 420–35; Rifʿat al-Saʿīd, *Munaẓẓamāt al-yasār al-miṣrī 1950–1957* (Cairo, 1983), pp. 25-184. See also FO 371/69250, Campbell to Bevin, 20 February, 18 March, 1 May, and 4 October 1948; and FO 371/73476, file 10118, "Communism in Egypt 1949."
36. al-Saʿīd, *Tārīkh . . . 1940–1950*, pp. 411–57; al-Saʿīd, *Munaẓẓamāt . . . 1950-1957*, passim; al-Bishrī, *al-Ḥaraka al-siyāsīya*, pp. 416–55; Botman, "Oppositional Politics," pp. 321ff, 466ff. From Paris, a group of former Jewish activists led by Henri Curiel (Roma Group), which was affiliated with the French Communist Party, still tried to exercise some influence on the Egyptian communist movement; see ʿAbbās, *Awrāq Hinrī Kūriyīl*, pp. 187–246; and Perrault, *Un homme à part*, pp. 212ff.
37. See, e.g., *Le Journal d'Egypte*, 12 December 1953, and 4 January 1954, dealing with "La Grande Affaire Sioniste et Communiste."
38. For the early period of 1897–1917, see Landau, *Jews*, pp. 115–24; Ts'vi Yehuda, "ha-Irgunim ha-tsiyoniyim be-mitsrayim," in *Shevet we-ʿAm* (1978): 147–96; Haim Gittelman, "Le Sionisme en Egypte," *Israël*, 8 December 1933 to 15 July 1936; Alfred S. Yallouz, "Comment le mouvement sioniste a débuté en Egypte," *La Revue Sioniste, Supplément Illustré*, 24 to 31 May 1920, pp. 16–18. For Bar Kokhba, see Landau, *Jews*, pp. 115–17; and Gittelman, *Israël*, 20 and 27 June 1935, 14 August 1935; for a list of the groups active in 1916, see CZA, Z3/753, Jack Mosseri, Cairo, 5 June 1916.
39. AIU, Egypt, XII.E.182.k, Somekh, Cairo, 15 May 1913; CZA, F21/1, 24 May 1913; CZA, Z3/1449, Thon, 7 April 1913; CZA, Z2/373, 21 December 1910, and CZA, Z3/752, 24 December 1912, both Hasamsony, Cairo.
40. CZA, Z3/620, Copenhagen Bureau to Zentralkomitee Berlin, 30 July 1915; Taragan, *Les communautés israélites*, pp. 120–22.
41. Comité d'Assistance aux Réfugiés Israélites de Syrie et Palestine, *Rapport général*; AIU, Egypt, I.G.I, Sionisme 1915; Lichtheim, *Rückkehr*, pp. 250ff. For the period after 1917, see Bat Ye'or, *Zionism in Islamic Lands*; and Ghunaym and Abū Kaff, *al-Yahūd*.

42. *La Revue Sioniste*, 4 January 1918; FO 141/734, file 4843, 1917–18, passim; FO 141/802, 803, and 805, file 4759, 1917–19, passim. For the Alexandria Committee, see FO 141/802, file 4759, 5 September 1917, and FO 141/734, file 4843, 30 August 1917.
43. CZA, F21/2, 21 October 1917 for Weizmann demand and telegram; FO 141/802, file 4759, Mosseri to Weizmann, 30 October 1917 for Cairo; and CZA, F21/2, 15 December 1917 for the Alexandria meeting.
44. CZA, F21/2, 21 March 1918; *La Revue Sioniste*, 15 March and 5 April 1918; see also Muḥammad 'Abd al-Ra'ūf Salīm, *Tārīkh al-ḥaraka al-ṣahyūnīya al-ḥadītha, 1898–1918*, 2 vols. (Cairo, 1974), vol. 2: *Documents*.
45. For obituaries for Jack Mosseri, see *The Jewish Chronicle*, 11 May 1934; *Israël*, 4 May and 15 June 1934; for the federation, see CZA, F21/2, 8 June 1917.
46. *La Revue Sioniste*, 4 January 1918; and CZA, F21/2, 6 January 1918; for *La Revue Sioniste*, see OH IV, II, M. Mosseri; also *Israël*, 3, 24 March 1933.
47. Comité "Pro-Palestina" d'Alexandrie, *Rapport sur sa gestion du 13 aout 1918 au 30 novembre 1927* (Alexandria, 1928); Taragan, *Les communautés israélites*, pp. 126–29.
48. FO 141/802, file 4759, Allenby to Curzon, 10 May 1920; and *La Revue Sioniste*, 1 May 1920.
49. CZA, F21/3, 20 May 1920; Gittelman, *Israël*, 2 April 1936; *L'Aurore*, 30 January 1925.
50. FO 141/803, file 4759, Mosseri to Wingate, 24 August 1917; FO 141/803, file 4759, Foreign Office to Wingate, 3 November 1918; and Wingate to Foreign Office, 2 December 1917; see also FO 371/4995, Syme, "Press Reports," 29 April and 14 May 1920.
51. *Aperçu du travail sioniste*, passim; and CZA, Z4/3229I, Grünhut, 14 January 1927; for Alexandria, see CZA, KKL5/438, Union Sioniste d'Alexandrie, 27 January 1925. For Mosseri, see CZA, F21/2, 20, and 24 April 1918; *Israël*, 15 June 1934.
52. *Aperçu du travail sioniste*, pp. 8, 33–34, and 40–44; *L'Aurore*, 28 March 1924.
53. CZA, KKL5/1416, Keren Kayemeth to Saporta, 20 September 1943. On general activities, see *Aperçu du travail sioniste*.
54. CZA, KKL5/438, Organisation Sioniste du Cairo, 8 June 1925; *L'Aurore*, 15 February and 23 October 1925; *Israël*, 16 March 1934; for the federation, see CZA, Z4/2570, 1926, passim.
55. CZA, Z4/3229I, Grünhut, October 1927; quotation from CZA, KKL5/-324, Grünhut to Ussishkin, Alexandria, 1 November 1928.
56. CZA, KH4B/451, Kohn, 19 December 1929; CZA, KH4B/451, unsigned, Cairo, 17 February 1930; and Bension to Hermann, 18 December 1930; also CZA, KKL5/472, Weissman, Cairo, 29 January 1930.

57. For the ban, see CZA, KH4B/451, Bension, Alexandria, 21 February 1930; for the collections, see CZA, KH4B/451, unsigned, Cairo, 17 February 1930, and CZA, KKL5/617, unsigned, Alexandria, 12 July 1932.
58. CZA, KH4B/451, Bension to Hermann, 5 March 1930, and 17 January 1931; also CZA, KKL5/472 Grünhut to Haezrachi, 2 July 1930. The lists of donations to the Jewish funds in Alexandria nevertheless include the names of virtually all notables; CZA, KH4B/451, 17 February 1930.
59. CZA, KH4B/452, Helfmann, Jerusalem, 28 May 1933.
60. CZA, KKL5/949, Bassan, Cairo, 11 September 1936; for ha-'Ivri, see *Israël*, 20 December 1934 and 18 September 1935; for he-Ḥaluts, see *Israël*, 25 August 1933.
61. CZA, S5/2213, Blumberg, Alexandria, 2 May 1937; and CZA, S5/2213, Lauterbach, Jerusalem, 19 January 1937.
62. CZA, KH4B/451, Bassan, Cairo, 15 January 1932; CZA, KH4B/452, Erlich, 1935; and Ben Ascher, Alexandria, 11 February 1935; for membership, see OH(61)45, T. Shesh; and CZA, S5/490, n.d. (1938); for Staraselski, see Ghunaym and Abū Kaff, *al-Yahūd*, pp. 46 and 100ff.
63. CZA, S5/490, Lichtheim to Lauterbach, 8 December 1937; CZA, KKL5/-1143, Subotnik, 11 November 1938; and CZA, KKL5/1143, James, 10 July 1939, all Cairo.
64. CZA, KKL5/1143, James, Cairo, 10 July 1939; and CZA, KKL5/1143, Subotnik, Alexandria, 22 February 1939.
65. CZA, S5/490, Elmaleh, 3 January 1939; CZA, S5/490, Subotnik, April 1939; and Ben Ascher to Lauterbach, 10 November 1940; for a more positive assessment, see CZA, S5/2213, Blumberg to Lauterbach, 2 May 1937; and *Kadima* 19 (March 1937).
66. See, e.g., CZA, Z4/2051, Landsberg, 25 September 1924; *Israël*, 11 November 1935.
67. State of Israel, *Census of Population and Housing 1961*, table 8, p. 24. For the lack of demand, see, e.g., CZA, S6/3840, Shaool, Cairo, 20 July 1942; for numbers of certificates, see CZA, S6/2538, 1933 and 1934, passim; e.g., Weissman, Cairo, 1 November 1933.
68. CZA, S5/490, unsigned, n.d. (1938?); Fargeon, *Les juifs*, pp. 296 and 300.
69. *La Revue Sioniste*, 1 May 1920 quoting Léon Castro; CZA, KKL5/472, Grünhut to Haezrachi, 2 July 1930; and CZA, S5/940, Czernowitz, 9 January 1939. According to Vilensky (CZA, S25/5218, 8 November 1945), capital investment in Palestine of Egyptian Jews amounted to £E 1–1.5 million in 1945.
70. "Briefe aus Cairo," *Die Welt* 13 (1904): 3.
71. AIU, Egypt, I.G.24, Mme Benneys, Ṭanṭā, 25 March 1928; see also AIU, France, X.F.17, Nahon, Ṭanṭā, "Rapport 1915–16."
72. CZA, S5/490, Lichtheim to Lauterbach, 8 December 1937.

73. See, e.g., *Israël*, 21 August 1935; *al-Shams*, 2 January 1936, 3 and 24 November 1939, 2 May and 11 July 1947.
74. CZA, S5/793, 1 December 1943; also AIU, Egypt, I.E.10, Rabbi Arditi, Alexandria, 12 March 1899, and IX.E.182.a, Somekh, Alexandria, 13 January 1897.
75. Cohen, *The Jews*, p. 70–71.
76. See, e.g., AIU, Egypt, XIII.E.199, Benveniste, Ṭanṭā, 27 October 1905, who described the aims of education as follows: "If we want to make our boys into firm characters, manly hearts, men armed for life ... useful citizens, we want our girls later to become excellent mothers ... good housewives who are able to keep order and economy at home, to watch over the happiness of their husbands and the health of their children." See also AIU, France, X.F.17, 1901–5 and 1908–9, passim. There is little to indicate that educational goals changed significantly over the following decades; see, e.g., *al-Shams*, 7 September 1945.
77. See, e.g., AIU, Egypt, VIII.E.179, Tagger, Cairo, 30 April 1914; and AIU, Egypt, I.C.15, Danon, Alexandria, 8 May 1914 reporting 20 conversions among Jewish students at the Ecole des Frères Congreganistes in Cairo. In 1925, the Apostolic vicar in Egypt, Igino Nuti, listed 56 Jews among 313 recent converts to Catholicism (MAE, Afrique-Asie, Egypte 34, Gaillard to Briand, 29 November 1929); see also MAE, Afrique-Asie, Egypte 102, 12 June 1930.
78. MAE, Afrique-Asie, Egypte 103, Lescuyer to Ministry of Foreign Affairs, 26 September 1932; *Israël*, 30 September 1932.
79. See, e.g., CZA, KH4B/450, Berger, 9 April 1928; *Israël*, 23 February 1929 and 14 March 1930; for their failure, see *Israël*, 21 August 1935.
80. *Statuts de l'organisation sioniste d'Alexandrie (1937)* and *Programme d'action*, included in CZA, S6/1781.
81. See, e.g., CZA, KH4B/451, Bension to Hermann, 17 January 1931; CZA KH4B/452, Erlich, 1935.
82. See, e.g., CZA, S6/1982, Peron, Cairo, n.d. (late 1946); and CZA, KKL5/1697, Saporta, Cairo, 27 June 1947.
83. CZA, KH4B/451, Confédération Universelle des Juifs Sépharadim, Jerusalem to S. Abrabanel, Cairo, 31 January 1929; CZA, KH4B/450, Pazi, Alexandria, 14 February 1928; CZA, KH4B/452, Erlich, 1935; and CZA, S6/1982, Peron, Cairo, n.d. (late 1946).
84. See, e.g., CZA, Z4/3229I, Grünhut, Cairo, 16 November 1927; CZA, KH4B/451, Kohn, Jerusalem, 10 November 1928.
85. *Aperçu du travail sioniste*, p. 19; CZA, KKL5/438, Nemoi, Alexandria, 3 May 1925; CZA, Z4/3229I, Grünhut, 29 November 1927; and CZA, S5/490, Subotnik, April 1939; membership lists in CZA, S5/77, 12 October 1946; and CZA, S5/75, 25 October 1946.
86. CZA, S5/490, Lichtheim to Lauterbach, 8 December 1937; CZA, S5/793, Alexander, Cairo, 4 January 1944; for the Karaites, see *al-Ittiḥād al-*

Isrā'īlī, 4 May and 13 July 1924, 5 May and 3 November 1925; *al-Kalīm*, 1 July 1945; al-Gamil, *Toldot*, p. 168.

87. CZA, KKL5/1143, unsigned, Alexandria, 9 February 1938; and CZA, KH4B/451, Kohn, 10 December 1928, quoting Ralph Harari.
88. CZA, Z3/753, Mosseri, 5 June 1916, and Léon Castro quoted in CZA, F21/3, 26 February 1920.
89. *Kadima* 19 (March 1937) for Prato; *The Jewish Chronicle*, 31 December 1937 for Ventura; CZA, Z4/2051, Berger, December 1925; CZA, Z4/3229II, Grünhut, 18 January 1928; CZA, KH4B/450, Berger, 9 April 1928; CZA, KH4B/451, Kohn, 10 December 1928; and 19 December 1929; CZA, S5/490, Subotnik, April 1939; *al-Kalīm*, 1 June 1948.
90. *La Revue Sioniste*, 11 January 1918; *Hamenora*, 1923 and 1924, passim; CZA, KH4B/3229I, Grünhut, 29 November 1927; CZA, KH4B/450, Berger, 9 April 1928; CZA, KH4B/451, Kohn, 10 December 1928; CZA, S25/1887, Bension, 6 December 1930; and CZA, S5/490, Czernowitz, 9 January 1939.
91. CZA, Z4/3229I, Grünhut, 1 November 1927; CZA, KH4B/451, Kohn, 19 December 1929.
92. See, e.g., CZA, Z4/2051, Berger, Jerusalem, December 1925.
93. CZA, Z3/115, Thon, Jaffa to Palaestina-Amt des Zionistischen Aktionskomitees, Berlin, 9 March 1913. See also *La Revue Sioniste*, 4 January 1918; CZA, F21/2, 6 January 1918; CZA, KH4B/451, Bassan, Cairo, 15 January 1932; *al-Shams*, 29 March 1935; CZA, S5/490, Subotnik, April 1939; For a good illustration, see the quotation from *Hatikvah*, January 1936, above, p. 152.
94. See, e.g., *al-Shams*, 3 November 1944, and 11 October 1946.
95. See, e.g., CZA, S25/1887, Bension to Hermann, 10 February 1931; CZA, Z4/3229II, Prato to Weizmann, 7 May 1931.
96. Ben Ascher, Alexandria, in CZA, S5/490, 10 November 1940, 7 and 22 May 1941; CZA, S6/1982, Alexander, 14 November 1943, and 17 February 1944; CZA, S6/1982, unsigned, 20 November 1943; CZA, S5/793, Czernowitz, 1 August 1944.
97. For interviews with these emissaries, see OH(61)2, A. Eiger, 28 March 1969; OH(61)25, R. Ricanati; OH(61)16, G. Ben Avi; see also OH(61)6, A. Matalon, 18 February 1969. Emissaries from the independent leftist ha-Shomer ha-Tsa'ir seem to have arrived a few months earlier in 1942.
98. Léon Castro quoted in FO 371/45404, Jenkins to Smart, 2 February 1945; and author's interview with Shlomo Hillel, Jerusalem, 5 July 1980.
99. CZA, S6/1982, Alexander, 17 February 1944; CZA, S6/1982, unsigned, 20 November 1943; CZA, S5/793, unsigned, 6 March 1944; and the interviews in note 97 above. The group in the *ḥāra* was, however, regarded as unsuited for kibbuts life: "Their social standard, if compared to that

of the majority of Egyptian youth is very low.... Although Zionists at heart, they cannot be sent to a kibbutz or kvoutza, as, in our opinion such an utterly and integral communal life will be a difficult thing for them to understand" (CZA, S6/3841, unsigned, Cairo to Immigration Department, 14 May 1947).

100. CZA, S6/1982, unsigned, 20 November 1943; CZA, S6/1982, Alexander, 17 February 1944, and Lévy, 24 November 1947; for Port Said, see CZA, S5/793, Alexander, 21 June 1944; for ha-'Ivri, see CZA, KKL5/1697, Eiger, 26 October 1945; and CZA, KKL5/1697, ha-'Ivri ha-Tsa'ir, Cairo, 6 January 1947.
101. CZA, S5/490, Subotnik, April 1939; CZA, S5/490, Ben Ascher, 10 November 1940; CZA, S6/1982, he-Ḥaluts ha-Tsa'ir, 2 October 1942; CZA, S5/793, unsigned, 21 May 1945; CZA, S25/5218, Peron, Cairo, 20 May 1947; also *al-Shams*, 10 November 1938.
102. Author's interviews with Ovadia Danon and Shlomo Hillel, both Jerusalem, 3 July 1980.
103. CZA, S6/1982, Ben Avi, 8 February 1944; and CZA, S6/1982, Alexander, 17 February 1944; CZA, S5/76, memorandum of ha-'Ivri ha-Tsa'ir, Cairo, 12 November 1946.
104. CZA, S6/1982, Alexander, 17 February 1944; and interviews with former members Nadav Safran, Robert Dassa, and Yūsuf Marzūq, all Tel Aviv, 30 June 1980.
105. CZA, S5/793, Alexander, 21 June 1944; OH(61)5, B. Sedbon, 23 June 1969; and OH(61)14, Y. Do'ar, 31 March 1969; Ghunaym and Abū Kaff, *al-Yahūd*, pp. 100ff; for membership, see MAE, Guerre 1939–45, Alger 1313, 23 April 1944; and Alger 1037, 14 July 1944.
106. CZA, S6/1982, Peron, Cairo, n.d. (late 1946); and CZA, KKL5/1697, unsigned, 9 May 1946.
107. CZA, S5/793, Czernowitz, November 1943; and CZA, S6/1982, unsigned, 20 November 1943.
108. On Castro, see *AJEPO*; criticism in CZA, Z4/2570, Grünhut, 14 November 1926; and CZA, S5/490, Lichtheim to Lauterbach, 3 December 1937. On the Comité Provisoire, see CZA, S5/793, Shertok to Castro, 11 January 1944.
109. CZA, S5/76, Fédération Sioniste, Cairo, 7 November 1946; FO 371/-45404, Jenkins to Rifaat, 16 January 1945, and to Smart, 2 February 1945; also FO 371/45404, Killearn to Eden, 12 February 1945.
110. See, e.g., CZA, S25/5218, Alexander, "The Egyptian Jews on the Eve of the Great Decision," 24 October 1945; CZA, S6/1982, Peron, Cairo, n.d. (late 1946); and CZA, S6/1982, Alexander, 17 February 1944.
111. FO 371/45404, included in Killearn to Eden, 12 February 1945.
112. CZA, S5/75, Najar, 12 October 1946; and CZA, S5/75, Saul to Lauterbach, 25 October 1946; CZA, S5/77, 12 October 1946.

113. Castro on 7 January 1945 quoted in FO 371/45404, Jenkins to Smart, 2 February 1945. See also CZA, S6/1782, Klueger, 22 March 1943; and CZA, KKL5/1697, Do'ar, Alexandria, 26 March 1947.
114. See OH(61)44, D. Basri; OH(61)14, Y. Do'ar; and OH(61)2, A. Eiger.
115. CZA, S25/5218, "Incidents of 2 and 3 November 1945 in Cairo, Egypt," unsigned, Cairo, 21 November 1945, Appendix III.
116. Letter included in FO 371/45404, Killearn to Eden, 12 February 1945. Further protests against Zionist activities in Egypt are noted in CZA, S6/1982, unsigned, 20 November 1943; CZA, S5/793, unsigned, Cairo, 21 May 1945; and CZA, S25/5218, unsigned, 9 May 1947. See also Bartley C. Crum, *Behind the Silken Curtain: A Personal Account of Anglo-American Diplomacy in Palestine and the Middle East* (New York, 1947), pp. 155–58.
117. CZA, S5/793, Castro to Cattaoui, 17 October 1944; and CZA, S5/793, Fédération Sioniste to Cattaoui, 25 October 1944; Cattaoui's letter included in FO 371/45404, Killearn to Eden, 12 February 1945; see also CZA, S5/793, unsigned, 21 May 1945.
118. For Cattaoui, see CZA, S25/5218, Alexander, 24 October 1945; *al-Shams*, 2 September 1946; for Ventura, *al-Shams*, 16 January 1948, and *al-Kalīm*, 16 January and 1 June 1948.
119. CZA, S6/1982, unsigned, Cairo, 25 January 1948; OH(61)51, R. Dwek, 21 May 1972; OH(61)46, W. Sachs; and OH(61)43, A. Schlossberg.

CHAPTER FIVE

1. MAE, Guerre 1939-45, Alger 1310, "Note sur la situation politique et sociale de l'Egypte," unsigned, May 1944, addendum to a letter dated 24 May 1944.
2. FO 371/46018, Reid-Adam, 3 July 1945; FO 371/63004, "Economic Report 1946," 7 August 1947; FO 371/63065, Campbell to Bevin, 21 January, 17 and 20 February 1947. Lists contained in DW/'Abidīn, Maṣlaḥat al-sharikāt, 1947–61.
3. FO 371/62990, 21 March 1947.
4. *al-Shams*, 30 January 1948; *La Tribune Juive*, 28 January 1948.
5. FO 371/46018, 7 June 1945. See also FO 371/53297, Fitzgerald to Pollock, 4 June 1946; and FO 371/53293, memorandum "Christian Minorities in Egypt," July 1944, included in a dispatch dated 2 May 1946; also Carter, *The Copts*, pp. 209–23.
6. MAE, Guerre 1939–45, Alger 1310, "Note sur la situation politique et sociale de l'Egypte," May 1944. See also FO 371/20148, Lampson to Eden, 6 April 1936; and Shamir, "The Evolution of the Egyptian Nationality Laws," pp. 54–62.
7. *La Tribune Juive*, September 1947, and 8 October 1947; CZA, S6/1982, Alexander, 14 November 1943; and CZA, S6/1982, unsigned, 20 Novem-

ber 1943; *al-Shams*, 23 May, 4 July, and 28 November 1947, 30 January 1948; DW/ʿAbidīn, Maṣlaḥat al-sharikāt, 1947ff.

8. See, e.g., FO 371/53297, Fitzgerald to Pollock, 4 June 1946; FO 371/73458, file 1011, "Report of Political Events in Egypt for 1947," 20 April 1949; and FO 371/62930, Chancery to Foreign Office, 7 May 1947.
9. CZA, S6/1982, Peron, n.d. (late 1946); *La Tribune Juive*, 7 April 1948. Some anti-Jewish incidents are reported in *al-Shams*, 16 July 1946.
10. *al-Shams*, 2 March, 15 and 29 November 1946; *al-Ahrām*, 13 November 1946.
11. FO 371/52605, High Commissioner, Jerusalem to Colonial Office, 5 January 1946; and FO 371/52605, Killearn to Foreign Office, 17 January 1946; FO 371/53338, Egyptian embassy, London to Foreign Ministry, Cairo, 29 April 1946; FO 371/53339, British embassy, Athens to Chancery, Cairo, 29 April 1946. See also *al-Shams*, 15 November and 27 December 1946.
12. *al-Ahrām*, 19 and 25 November 1947; Muḥammad Ḥusayn Haykal, *Mudhakkirāt fī 'l-siyāsa al-miṣrīya*, 3 vols. (Cairo, 1977–78), 3: 27ff, 38; on 1947, see al-Bishrī, *al-Ḥaraka al-siyāsīya*, pp. 131–78.
13. See, e.g., Ṣāliḥ ʿAshmāwī in *Jarīdat al-Ikhwān al-Muslimīn*, 20 July 1946; on materialism and the desire to dominate the world, see 13 October 1945 and 29 May 1948; on arms smuggling to Palestine, 9 February 1946; on Jewish capitalism, see also *Ṣawt al-Umma*, 21 and 26 May, 6 June 1948.
14. CZA, S25/5218, Alexander, 24 October 1945; *La Tribune Juive*, 29 October 1947; for the general attitude, see FO 371/69259, cover note, 21 July 1947; for 1947, see FO 371/69259, Campbell to Foreign Office, 27 July 1947; *al-Ahrām*, 3 November 1947; and *La Tribune Juive*, 5 November 1947.
15. *La Tribune Juive*, 31 December 1947, 10 March 1948; *al-Shams*, 2 January 1948.
16. FO 371/62994, 2 to 6 December 1947; FO 371/62994, 21 and 24 December 1947, all Campbell to Foreign Office; *al-Ahrām*, 1 to 9 December 1947.
17. FO 371/62994, 6 and 8 December 1947; and FO 371/41331, "Defence Security Summary," 3 to 16 August 1944, included in Kellar to Scrivener, 31 August 1944; *La Tribune Juive*, 31 December 1947; FO 371/69212, Campbell to Foreign Office, 3 and 8 December 1948; Mitchell, *The Society of the Muslim Brothers*, pp. 56–78.
18. *La Tribune Juive*, 14 January and 10 March 1948.
19. *al-Ahrām*, 1 and 7 December 1947, 5 May 1948.
20. OH(61)38, R. Lumbroso; OH(61)2, A. Eiger, 10 October 1969; and OH(61)25, R. Ricanati; author's interview with Roger Oppenheim, one

of the former heads of the Zionist Organization of Alexandria, Haifa, 22 June 1980.

21. OH(49), Y. Benzakein, 10 December 1971; OH(61)6, A. Matalon, 18 February 1969; OH(61)43, A. Schlossberg; see also CZA, S5/793, Czernowitz, 1 August 1944.
22. CZA, S25/2027, Fédération Sioniste d'Egypte, Cairo to Immigration Department, Jerusalem, 8 and 10 February 1948; OH(61)51, R. Dwek, 21 May 1972; and OH(61)49, Y. Benzakein.
23. FO 371/69259, Chapman-Andrews to Foreign Office, 22 June 1948; and FO 371/69259, draft letter McNeil to Haughton, 19 June 1948.
24. al-Bishrī, *al-Ḥaraka al-siyāsīya*, pp. 231–74; Mitchell, *The Society of the Muslim Brothers*, pp. 35–79.
25. FO 371/69259, Campbell to Bevin, 14 June 1948; and FO 371/69211, 15 October 1948. King Fārūq, too, told Sir Ronald Campbell in August 1947 that one thing was clear—one was not going to let the Jews take power in Egypt, a remark that at the time appeared rather cryptic to his British interlocutor (FO 371/62992, 13 August 1947).
26. OH(61)11, J. Lotan; OH(61)5, B. Sedbon; OH(61)43, A. Schlossberg; author's interview with Ora Schweizer, former secretary in the Cairo office of the Jewish Agency, Tel Aviv, 16 June 1980.
27. Pace, ed., *Répertoire permanent*, vol. 3: *Conflit palestinien*, II.—*Proclamations 1948*; FO 371/69259, 1948, passim; their names were, however, included in a list of those interested in receiving Zionist information (see CZA, S5/793, Organisation Sioniste d'Alexandrie, 22 October 1943).
28. FO 371/69259, Campbell to Foreign Office, 26 June 1948.
29. FO 371/69259, Campbell to Foreign Office, 26 June and 23 July 1948; for complaints, see FO 371/69259, Speaight, 10 July 1948; and Cook, 1 September 1948, both to Foreign Office; Perrault, *Un homme à part*, pp. 200–11.
30. FO 371/69259, Campbell, "Aide-Mémoire," 8 June 1948; and FO 371/-69259, Campbell, 14 June 1948; Chapman-Andrews to Foreign Office, 22 June 1948; for French reports on protests, see FO 371/69260, Speaight to Foreign Office, 2 August 1948; FO 371/73648, Sir P. Nichols, The Hague, 21 October 1949.
31. Pace, ed., *Répertoire permanent*, vol. 3: *Conflit palestinien*, I.—*Législation spéciale 1948*, pp. 5ff; and II.—*Proclamations 1948* and *1949*; FO 371/69273, 22 November 1948.
32. For Fārūq, see *La Tribune Juive*, 12 May 1948; for Nahum, *al-Shams*, 15 August 1947; for Cattaoui and Goar, CZA, S6/1982, unsigned, Cairo, 25 January 1948.
33. *al-Ahrām*, 16 May 1948; FO 371/69190, weekly political summaries, 14 to 21 May 1948.

34. For Port Said, see FO 371/69190, weekly political summaries, 28 May to 4 June 1948; for Orebi, see *al-Balāgh*, 23 May 1948; and CZA, S25/2027, 14 October 1947. See further *al-Shams*, 29 March and 1 April 1946; *al-Kalīm*, 1 July 1945, and 1 June 1948.
35. *Ṣawt al-Umma*, 28 May 1948; blacklists, *Ṣawt al-Umma*, 23–26, 28 May; 2, 6, 8, 19, and 26 June 1948; also *al-Balāgh*, 22 and 27 May 1948.
36. FO 371/69259, McDermott to Mayhew, 2 June 1948; similar is FO 371/69259, draft letter McNeil to Haughton, 19 June 1948; and Campbell to Foreign Office, 26 June 1948; see also *La Tribune Juive*, 7 April 1948. For events of the weeks preceding the war, see *al-Shams*, 19 and 26 March, 23 April, and 7 May 1948.
37. FO 371/69259, McNeil quoted in Haughton to Mayhew, 12 June 1948.
38. FO 371/69259, 20 and 26 June, 20 and 24 July 1948; FO 371/69210, 21 and 23 June 1948; FO 371/69260, 29 and 30 July, 2 August and 11 October 1948; FO 371/69212, Campbell to McNeil, 3 December 1948; *Ṣawt al-Umma*, 21 June 1948; *al-Kalīm*, 1 July 1948.
39. FO 371/69260, Mayall to Foreign Office, 11 October 1948; for the bomb attacks, see FO 371/69260, Chapman-Andrews to Foreign Office, 22 September 1948; for evacuations, see Pace, ed., *Répertoire permanent*, vol. 3: *Conflit palestinien*, II.—*Proclamations 1948*, 26 July 1948: Proclamation no. 41; and FO 371/69373, 10 September 1948.
40. FO 371/69261, Embassy, Cairo to Foreign Office, 12 November 1948.
41. For visas, see FO 371/7346-48, Chancery, Cairo to Foreign Office, January–November 1949. For release, see Pace, ed., *Répertoire permanent*, vol. 3: *Conflit palestinien*, I.—*Législation spéciale 1950*; and OH(61)51, R. Dwek, 21 May 1972; Perrault, *Un homme à part*, pp. 208ff.
42. FO 371/69259, Campbell to Foreign Office, 20 and 24 July, 2 August 1948; FO 371/69182, 31 July 1948 (mentions an appeal to boycott the Jews and make life unbearable for them); FO 371/69260, 13 August 1948; FO 371/69212, 3 and 9 December 1948; Mitchell, *The Society of the Muslim Brothers*, pp. 63ff, 75–78, and 328.
43. FO 371/69259, Campbell to Foreign Office, 20 July 1948; also FO 371/69260, Speaight, 27 July 1948.
44. Pace, ed., *Répertoire permanent*, vol. 7: *Nationalité égyptienne 1950*, 13 September 1950: Law no. 160 on Egyptian nationality, art. 15, sec. 3; and *Nationalité égyptienne 1956*, 20 November 1956: Law no. 391 on Egyptian nationality, art. 1, sec. 1, excluding from Egyptian nationality (*a*) the Zionists and (*b*) "all those persons convicted of a crime injurious to their loyalty toward the country or involving an act of treason."
45. FO 371/69259, Campbell to Foreign Office, 14 and 27 June, 20 July 1948; author's interviews with Edmond Riso-Lévy, Cairo, 12 December 1980; and Ora Schweizer, Tel Aviv, 16 June 1980; see also Jean and Simonne Lacouture, *Egypt in Transition* (London, 1958), pp. 102–4.

46. See the earlier analysis written after the incidents of November 1945 by the journalist Vilensky to Dr. Joseph, CZA, S25/5218, 8 November 1945.
47. See OH(61)33, E. Barka, 29 June 1970; OH(61)38, R. Lumbroso; OH(61)44, D. Basri; author's interviews with Shlomo Hillel and Ovadia Danon, Jerusalem, 5 and 3 July 1980, respectively.
48. Estimates of emissaries from Ovadia Danon and OH(61)40, T. Weiss, 5 July 1970; Israeli data in State of Israel, *Census of Population and Housing 1961*, table 8, p. 24; and State of Israel, *Census of Population and Housing 1972*, series no. 10 (Jerusalem, 1976), table 25, p. 306.
49. See, e.g., CZA, S25/5218, Alexander, 24 October 1945.
50. Lacouture, *Egypt in Transition*, pp. 105–22; Muḥammad Anīs, *Ḥarīq al-Qāhira fī 26 yanāyir 1952 'alā ḍaw'i wathā'iq tunshar li-awwal marra* (Beirut, 1972); al-Bishrī, *al-Ḥaraka al-siyāsīya*, pp. 277–366.
51. Muhammad Khalil, *The Arab States and the Arab League: A Documentary Record*, 2 vols. (Beirut, 1962), 1: 592; Mizrahi, *L'Egypte et ses juifs*, pp. 53 and 65; *Oriente Moderno* 1953, pp. 33 and 39; *Oriente Moderno* 1954, p. 431.
52. *The Story of Zionist Espionage in Egypt* (Cairo, 1955); Avri El-Ad, *Decline of Honor* (Chicago, 1976); for the Israeli point of view, see Aviezer Golan, *Operation Susannah* (New York, 1978).
53. On legislation, see Pace, ed., *Répertoire permanent*, vol. 4 : *Etat de siège 1956*; and vol. 7: *Nationalité égyptienne 1956*; see also "The Situation of Jews in Egypt at the Beginning of 1957," unpublished letter to Dag Hammarskøld by CBJO, CCJO, and Agudas Israel, New York, 7 January 1957 included in CAHJP, ET. Inv. 592/1.
54. Lists of nationalized firms in Maḥmūd Murād, *Man kāna yaḥkum miṣr? Shahādāt wathā'iqīya* (Cairo, 1980).

CONCLUSION

1. OH(35)2, I. Lévy.
2. Landshut, *Jewish Communities*, p. 23; Nehemiah Robinson, *The Arab Countries of the Near East and Their Jewish Communities* (New York, 1951), p. 52.
3. Landau, *Jews*, pp. 18–79, and British report quoted by him on p. 228; further Landau, *Middle Eastern Themes*, pp. 143–56; and Adler, *Jews in Many Lands*, p. 25.
4. AIU, Egypt, X.E.182.f, Somekh, Cairo, 8 April 1904, who added: "To be fair, one has to remember that the Jews are ferociously intolerant within their quarter."
5. For a later reference, see Muḥammad Sayyid Ṭanṭāwī, *Banū Isrā'īl fī 'l-qur'ān wa-l-sunna* (Cairo, 1987; originally published as a Ph.D. diss. in 1966).

6. Nawal M. Nadim, "Family Relationships in a Harah in Cairo," in *Arab Society in Transition: A Reader*, edited by Saad Eddin Ibrahim and Nicholas S. Hopkins (Cairo, 1977), pp. 112; El-Messiri, *Ibn al-Balad*. Also author's interviews with, among others, Edmond Mosseri, Cairo, 7 February 1980; Edmond Riso-Lévi, Cairo, 27 December 1979; Jacques Hassoun, Paris, 6 September 1980. The references to be found in Rotraud Wielandt's comprehensive study of the image of the Europeans in twentieth-century Arab literature (pp. 8–9) do not add up to a full image of the Egyptian Jew; see her *Das Bild der Europäer in der modernen arabischen Erzähl- und Theaterliteratur* (Wiesbaden, 1980).
7. Hassoun, *Chroniques de la vie quotidienne*, pp. 191–92.
8. In 1936, Rosette de Menasce, the wife of Félix de Menasce, complained about the Syrians, who, according to her, believed themselves to be Aryans and who practiced "disguised, but certain anti-Semitism;" she did not think much better of the Greeks (see CZA, Z4/17220, Rosette de Menasce to Weizmann, 21 October 1936); further Lambelin, *L'Egypte*, p. 192; OH(35)4, E. Cohen; OH(35)6, J. Kahanoff.
9. *al-Shams*, 14 January 1944; OH(35)6, J. Kahanoff, 21 January 1965.
10. Abram Adda gave £E 25,000 for the construction of an Egyptian eye clinic in 1925; the Menasce family bequeathed their villa to the city of Alexandria to establish a library there in 1939; Joseph Aslan Cattaoui left considerable sums for charitable institutions of all confessions in 1942; and Denise Mosseri contributed generously to Muslim and Coptic as well as to Jewish works.
11. Hourani, *Minorities in the Arab World*, p. 25.
12. OH(35)4, E. Cohen; OH(35)1, Y. Shohet; author's interview with Edmond Mosseri, Cairo, 7 February 1980; Landau, *Jews*, p. 20; Landau, *Middle Eastern Themes*, p. 152.
13. FO 371/11586, Henderson to Murray, 23 October 1926.

Bibliography

PRIMARY SOURCES

Archives

Egypt

Dār al-Wathā'iq (DW), Cairo
'Abidīn Palace (DW/'Abidīn), files 1922–
Majlis al-Wuzarā' (DW/MW), files up to 1922

France

Archives de l'Alliance Israélite Universelle (AIU), Paris
AIU, Egypte
AIU, France

Ministère des Affaires Etrangères (MAE), Paris
Afrique-Asie 1918–40, Egypte et Levant
Guerre 1939–45, Alger CFLN-GPRF and Londres CNF

Federal Republic of Germany

Auswärtiges Amt (AA), Bonn
Büro des Staatssekretärs: Ägypten
Büro des Unterstaatssekretärs: Ägypten
Handakten E. Ettel, K. Ritter
Handelspolitische Abteilung: Handakten Clodius: Ägypten; Wiehl
Inland ID: Ägypten
Inland II A/B: Juden in Ägypten, 1938–44

Politische Abteilung II: Po25 Deutschtum im Ausland; Abteilung III: Vorderer Orient. Ägypten; Abteilung VII: Po36 Ägypten: Judenfragen; Orient: Judenfragen.

Referat Deutschland: Po5 N.E.: Boykottbewegung, etc.

Great Britain

Public Record Office (PRO), London
Foreign Office (FO), Series 141, 371, 372, 407, 847, 891, 921
Wiener Library, London

Israel

Central Archives for the History of the Jewish People (CAHJP), Jerusalem
Egypt files
Central Zionist Archives (CZA), Jerusalem
Protocols of the Fédération Sioniste d'Egypte, 1913–20 (F21)
Keren Hayesod, Jerusalem, 1926– (KH4B)
Keren Kayemet le-Yisra'el, Jerusalem, 1922–47 (KKL5)
Organization Department, Jerusalem, 1933–58 (S5)
Immigration Department, Jerusalem, 1919–48 (S6)
Political Department, Jerusalem, 1921–48 (S25)
Zionistisches Zentralbureau, Cologne, 1905–11 (Z2)
Zionistisches Zentralbureau, Berlin, 1911–20 (Z3)
Jewish Agency for Palestine, London, 1917–55 (Z4)

INTERVIEWS

Oral History Department (OH), Institute of Contemporary Jewry, Hebrew University, Jerusalem

(OH)35: Interviews in French with former members of the Jewish community in Egypt
4 Cohen, Edith (née Cattaoui), 11 April 1965
6 Kahanoff, Jacqueline (née Shohet), 21 January, 11 June, 18 July 1965
2 Lévy, Iris (née Romano), 18 January 1965
7 Shallon, Selim, 18 June 1965
1 Shohet, Yvonne, 20 November, 10, 16 December 1964

(OH)61: Interviews in Hebrew with former Zionist activists and emissaries
33 Barka, Eliahu, 29 June and 7 July 1970
44 Basri, David, 28 January 1971
15 Ben Ascher, Eleonor (?), n.d.
16 Ben Avi, Gershon, 30 April 1969
49 Benzakein, Ya'aḳov, 9, 10 December 1971
48 Ben Ze'ev (Wolfensohn), Israel, 15 July 1971
14 Do'ar, Ya'ir, 31 March and 21 April 1969
51 Dwek, Raphael, 19, 21 May 1972
2 Eiger, 'Aḳiva, 28 March and 10 October 1969

23 Farhi, Noury, 5 May 1969
20 Hourvitz, Avinoam and P'nina, 1 May 1969
39 Klueger (Aliav), Ruth, 27 June and 21 July 1970
35 Krause, Dr., 14 July 1970
11 Lotan, Dr. Joseph, 2 April 1969
38 Lumbroso, Renato, 21 August 1970
30 Masri, Moshe, 6 July 1970
19 Masri, Yoḥanan (Jean), 7 May 1969
6 Matalon, Avraham, 18, 25 February 1969
12 Rabin, Ya'aḳov, 6 April 1969
25 Ricanati, Raphael, 26 August 1969
46 Sachs, Willy, 25 March 1971
43 Schlossberg, Dr. Arieh, 30 January 1971
5 Sedbon, Benjamin, 23 June and 24 September 1969
45 Shesh, Ts'vi, 30 January 1971
– Tsur (Czernowitz), Yitsḥaḳ, 29 July 1970
40 Weiss, Tibor, 26 June and 5 July 1970
4 Zadikoff, Debora, n.d.

Further interviews in OH:

Littman, Gisèle, with R. Oppenheim, 10 November 1971
IV, II, Mosseri, Mazal Mathilda, with H. Cohen, 12 August 1964

Interviews with Author (former affiliation in parentheses)

Danon, Ovadia (head of the Cairo travel agency for *'aliya*, 1949–51), Jerusalem, 3 July 1980

Dassa, Robert (he-Ḥaluts), Tel Aviv, 30 June 1980

Dwek, Edmond (assistant to Léon Castro, secretary to Haim Nahum, secretary of the Jewish community in Cairo, 1980), Cairo, 17 February and 7 March 1980

Hārūn, Shiḥāta (communist movement), Cairo, 7, 10 March 1980, 13 April 1980

Hassoun, Jacques (communist movement), Paris, 6 September 1980

Hillel, Shlomo (Mossad, in charge of immigration from Oriental countries), Jerusalem, 5 July 1980

Iscaki, ? (1980 president of the Jewish community in Cairo), Cairo, 11 February 1980

Lévy, Joseph (he-Ḥaluts Alexandria), Tel Aviv, 5 June 1980

Lévy, Suzanne (née Kaufmann) (Zionist youth movement), Tel Aviv, 16 June 1980

Maleh, Jacques (*L'Aurore*), Paris, 27 June 1979

Marzūq, Yūsuf (Karaite, Maccabi, Bene 'Aḳiva), Tel Aviv, 30 June 1980

Mosseri, Edmond (businessman), Cairo, 4, 7, 16, 21 February 1980

Najar, Aviva (née Weissman) (WIZO), Jerusalem, 1 July 1980
Najar, Emile ('Amiel) (1944–47/48 secretary general of the Fédération Sioniste d'Egypte), Paris, 7 September 1980
Oppenheim, Roger Yitsḥaḳ (Zionist Organization of Alexandria), Haifa, 22 June 1980
Riso-Lévy, Edmond (physician), Cairo, 27 December 1979, 14 February, and 9 April 1980
al-Sa'īd, Rif'at (communist movement), Cairo, 1, 15 March and 11, 13 April 1980
Safran, Nadav (Bene 'Aḳiva), Tel Aviv, 16, 30 June 1980
Schweizer, Ora (née Zuckerman) (Cairo office of the Jewish Agency, 1944–48), Tel Aviv, 16 June 1980
Setton, Clément (1980 president of the Jewish community in Alexandria), Alexandria, 4 March 1980
Yūsuf, Ovadia (Karaite community), Cairo, 7 March 1980

Newspapers and Periodicals

Egyptian and European Press

al-Ahrām (Cairo)
al-Ahrām al-Iqtiṣādī (Cairo)
al-Balāgh (Cairo)
La Bourse Egyptienne (Cairo)
The Egyptian Gazette (Cairo)
Hamenora (B'nai B'rith, District d'Orient, Constantinople)
al-Jamāhīr (Cairo)
Jarīdat al-Ikhwān al-Muslimīn (Cairo)
The Jewish Chronicle (London)
Le Journal d'Egypte (Cairo)
Le Journal du Caire (Cairo)
Le Monde (Paris)
al-Muqaṭṭam (Cairo)
Oriente Moderno (Rome)
Le Progrès Egyptien (Cairo)
Rūz al-Yūsuf (Cairo)
Ṣawt al-Umma (Cairo)
Le Temps (Alexandria)
The Times (London)
La Tribune Juive (Paris)
Die Welt (Vienna)

Egyptian-Jewish Press

L'Aurore (independent; Cairo)

Hatikvah (pro-Zionist; Alexandria)
"Hérout" Liberté (he-Ḥaluts; Alexandria)
L'Illustration Juive (Alexandria)
Israël (independent; pro-Zionist; Cairo)
al-Ittiḥād al-Isrā'īlī (Karaite; Cairo)
Le Jeune Pionnier (he-Ḥaluts; Alexandria)
Kadima (monthly supplement of *al-Shams*; Cairo)
al-Kalīm (Karaite; Cairo)
La Renaissance Juive (Cairo)
Le Reveil (ha-'Ivri ha-Tsa'ir; Cairo)
La Revue Sioniste (Fédération des Sionistes d'Egypte; Cairo)
al-Shams (Association de la Jeunesse Juive Egyptienne; Cairo)
al-Tas'īra (business paper; pro-Wafd; Cairo)
La Tribune Juive (independent; Cairo/Alexandria)
La Voix Juive (Zionist revisionist; Cairo)

SECONDARY SOURCES

'Abbās, Ra'ūf. *al-Ḥaraka al-'ummālīya fī miṣr, 1899–1952*. Cairo, 1968.

———. *Awrāq Hinrī Kūriyīl wa-l-ḥaraka al-shuyū'īya al-miṣrīya*. Cairo, 1988.

'Abd Allāh, Nabīh Bayyūmī. *Taṭawwur fikrat al-qawmīya al-'arabīya fī miṣr*. Cairo, 1975.

'Abd al-Mun'im, Fayṣal. *Ilā 'l-amām ya Rūmīl!* Cairo, 1976.

'Abd al-Raḥmān, 'Awāṭif. *Ittijāhāt al-ṣiḥāfa al-miṣrīya izā' al-qaḍīya al-filasṭīnīya, 1922-1936*. Ph.D. diss., Cairo University, 1975.

———. *al-Ṣiḥāfa al-ṣahyūnīya fī miṣr, 1897-1954: Dirāsa taḥlīlīya*. Cairo, 1977.

Abdel-Fadil, Mahmoud. *Development, Income Distribution and Social Change in Rural Egypt (1952–1970): A Study in the Political Economy of Agrarian Transition*. Cambridge, 1975.

Abdou, Ali Ibrahim, and Khairieh Kasmieh. *Les juifs des pays arabes*. Beirut, 1971.

Abu-Lughod, Janet. *Cairo: 1001 Years of the City Victorious*. Princeton, 1971.

Adler, Elkan Nathan. *Jews in Many Lands*. London, 1905.

Agwani, Mohammed Shafi. *Communism in the Arab East*. London, 1969.

Ahmed, Jamal Mohammed. *The Intellectual Origins of Egyptian Nationalism*. London, 1960.

American Jewish Committee. *American Jewish Yearbook*. Philadelphia, 1938–42.

———. *The Plight of the Jews in Egypt*. New York, 1957.

American Jewish Congress. *The Black Record: Nasser's Persecution of Egyptian Jews*. New York, n.d.

American Jewish Yearbook. See American Jewish Committee.

Annuaire des juifs d'Egypte et du Proche Orient 1942, 5702–5703. Cairo: Société des Editions Historiques Juives d'Egypte, 1942.

Annuaire statistique 1907–1961. See Egypt, Ministry of Finance, Statistical Department.

Anīs, Muḥammad. *Arba' fabrāyir 1942 fī tārīkh miṣr al-siyāsī*. Beirut, 1972.

———. *Ḥarīq al-Qāhira fī 26 yanāyir 1952 'alā ḍaw'i wathā'iq tunshar li-awwal marra*. Beirut, 1972.

Aperçu du travail sioniste au Caire pendant les années 1920, 1921, 1922, 1923. Cairo, 1924.

al-'Aqqād, 'Abbās Maḥmūd. *Sa'd Zaghlūl: Sīra wa-taḥīya*. Beirut, n.d.

Baer, Gabriel. *A History of Landownership in Modern Egypt, 1800–1950*. London, 1962.

———. *Studies in the Social History of Modern Egypt*. Chicago, 1969.

Bahā al-Dīn, Aḥmad. *Ayyām lahā tārīkh*. 3rd ed. Cairo, 1967.

Baḥr, Samīra. *al-Aqbāṭ fī 'l-ḥayāt al-siyāsīya al-miṣrīya*. Cairo, 1979.

al-Baḥrī, Yūnus. *Hunā Barlīn: Ḥayya al-'arab!* Beirut, n.d.

al-Bannā, Ḥasan, *Majmū'at rasā'il al-imām al-shahīd Ḥasan al-Bannā*. n.p., n.d.

Barakāt, 'Alī. *Taṭawwur al-milkīya al-zirā'īya fī miṣr, 1813–1914, wa-atharuhā 'alā 'l-ḥaraka al-siyāsīya*. Cairo, 1978.

Bat Ye'or [pseud.]. "Zionism in Islamic Lands: The Case of Egypt." *Wiener Library Bulletin*. Vol. 30, n.s., nos. 43–44 (1977): 16–29.

———. *Le dhimmī: Profil de l'opprimé en Orient et en Afrique du Nord depuis la conquête arabe*. Paris, 1980.

Bayyūmī, Zakariyā Sulaymān. *al-Ikhwān al-muslimūn wa-l-jamā'āt al-islāmīya fī 'l-ḥayāt al-siyāsīya al-miṣrīya, 1928–1948*. Cairo, 1979.

Behrens-Abouseif, Doris. *Die Kopten in der ägyptischen Gesellschaft—von der Mitte des 19. Jahrhunderts bis 1923*. Freiburg, 1972.

———. "Locations of Non-Muslim Quarters in Medieval Cairo." *Annales Islamologiques* 32 (1986): 117–32.

Beinin, Joel. "Class Conflict and National Struggle: Labor and Politics in Egypt, 1936–1954." Ph.D. diss., University of Michigan, 1982.

Berger, Elmer. *Who Knows Better Must Say So*. New York, 1955.

Berque, Jacques. L'Egypte: Impérialisme et révolution. Paris, 1967.

al-Bishrī, Ṭāriq. *al-Muslimūn wa-l-aqbāṭ fī iṭār al-jamā'a al-waṭanīya*. Cairo, 1980.

———. *al-Ḥaraka al-siyāsīya fī miṣr, 1945–1952*. 2d ed. Cairo, 1983.

Black, Edwin. *The Transfer Agreement: The Untold Story of the Secret Agreement between the Third Reich and Jewish Palestine*. New York, 1984.

Botman, Selma. "Oppositional Politics in Egypt: The Communist Movement, 1936-1954." Ph.D. diss., Harvard University, 1984.

Braude, Benjamin, and Bernard Lewis, eds. *Christians and Jews in the Ottoman Empire: The Functioning of a Plural Society*. 2 vols. New York, 1982.

Brinton, J. Y. *The Mixed Courts of Egypt*. Rev. ed. New York, 1968.

Carter, Barbara L. *The Copts in Egyptian Politics, 1919–1952*. London, 1985.

Castro, Léon. *Le procès de l'antisémitisme. Mémoire déposé au Tribunal Mixte du Caire pour Umberto Jabès et contre le Club Allemand du Caire*. (Cairo?), 1934.

Cattaoui, Joseph. *Le khédive Ismail et la dette de l'Egypte*. Cairo, 1935.

Cattaoui, Joseph, ed. *L'Egypte: Aperçu historique et géographique, gouvernement et institutions, vie économique et sociale*. Cairo, 1926.

Cattaoui, René. *La règne de Mohamed Aly d'après les archives russes en Egypte*. 4 vols. Cairo, 1931–36.

Cattaoui, René, and Georges Cattaoui. *Muhammad Ali and Europe*. Cairo, 1952.

Cattaui Pasha, Joseph. *Coup d'oeil sur la chronologie de la nation égyptienne*. Cairo, 1931.

Chambre de Commerce d'Alexandrie. *La renaissance de l'Egypte*. Cairo, 1940.

Chouraqui, André. *Cent ans d'histoire: L'Alliance Israélite Universelle et la renaissance juive contemporaine (1860–1960)*. Paris, 1965.

———. *Between East and West: A History of the Jews of North Africa*. Philadelphia, 1968.

Cleland, Wendell. *The Population Problem in Egypt*. New York, 1936.

Cohen, Amnon, and Gabriel Baer, eds. *Egypt and Palestine: A Millennium of Association (868–1948)*. Jerusalem, 1984.

Cohen, Hayyim J. *The Jews of the Middle East, 1860–1972*. New York, 1973.

Cohen, Hayyim J., and Zvi Yehuda. *Asian and African Jews in the Middle East, 1860–1972: An Annotated Bibliography*. Jerusalem, 1976.

Cohen, Mark. *Jewish Self-Government in Medieval Egypt: The Origins of the Office of Head of the Jews, ca. 1065–1126*. Princeton, 1980.

Collins, Jeffrey G. *The Egyptian Elite under Cromer, 1882–1907*. Berlin, 1984.

Colloque international sur l'histoire du Caire. Cairo, 1969.

Colombe, Marcel. *L'Evolution de l'Egypte, 1924–1950*. Paris, 1951.

Comité d'Assistance aux Réfugiés Israélites de Syrie et Palestine. *Rapport général sur la période entière, 19 décembre 1914–15 juillet 1920*. Alexandria, 1921.

Comité "Pro-Palestina" d'Alexandrie. *Rapport sur sa gestion du 13 aout 1918 au 30 novembre 1927*. Alexandria, 1928.

Communauté Israélite d'Alexandrie. *Rapport général pour l'année 1933*. Alexandria, 1934.

Communauté Israélite du Caire. *Statuts de la Communauté Israélite du Caire*. Cairo, 1927.

Compte rendu du Comité d'Assistance aux Réfugiés Israélites de Syrie et Palestine. 19 décembre 1914–31 décembre 1915. Alexandria, 1916.

Coon, Carleton. *Caravan: The Story of the Middle East*. Rev. ed. New York, 1976.

Corneilhan, Georges. *Juifs et opportunistes: Le judaisme en Egypte et Syrie*. Paris, 1889.

Crider, Elizabeth Fortunado. "Italo-Egyptian Relations in the Interwar Period, 1922–1942." Ph.D. diss., Ohio State University, 1978.

Cromer, Earl of. *Modern Egypt*. 2 vols. New York, 1916.

Crum, Bartley C. *Behind the Silken Curtain: A Personal Account of Anglo-American Diplomacy in Palestine and the Middle East*. New York, 1947.

Davis, Eric. *Challenging Colonialism: Bank Misr and Egyptian Industrialization, 1920–1940*. Princeton, 1983.

al-Dasūqī, 'Aṣim. *Kibār mullāk al-arāḍī al-zirā'īya wa-dawruhum fī 'l-mujtama' al-miṣrī (1914–1952)*. Cairo, 1975.

Deeb, Marius. "Bank Misr and the Emergence of the Local Bourgeoisie in Egypt." *Middle Eastern Studies* 12 (October 1976): 69–86.

———. "The Socioeconomic Role of the Local Foreign Minorities in Modern Egypt, 1805–1961." *International Journal of Middle East Studies* 9 (1978): 11–22.

———. *Party Politics in Egypt: The Wafd and Its Rivals, 1919–1939*. London, 1979.

De Felice, Renzo. *Ebrei in un paese arabo: Gli ebrei nella Libia contemporanea tra colonialismo, nazionalismo arabo e sionismo (1835–1970)*. Bologna, 1978.

Delpujet, David. *Les juifs d'Alexandrie, de Jaffa et de Jérusalem en 1865*. Bordeaux, 1866.

Deshen, Shlomo, and Walter P. Zenner, eds. *Jewish Societies in the Middle East: Community, Culture, and Authority*. Washington, D.C., 1982.

Deutsch, André. *The Jewish Communities of the World: Demography, Political and Organizational Status, Religious Institutions*. London, 1971.

Diewerge, Wolfgang. *Als Sonderberichterstatter zum Kairoer Judenprozeß (1933): Gerichtlich erhärtetes Material zur Judenfrage*. Munich, 1935.

Directory of Social Agencies in Cairo. Prepared by Isis Istiphan. Social Research Center, American University in Cairo. Cairo, 1956.

Durrell, Lawrence. *The Alexandria Quartet*. London, 1962.

Egypt, Ministry of Finance, Statistical Department. *Annuaire statistique 1907–1961*. Cairo, 1909–.

———. *Population Census of Egypt, 1937*. Cairo, 1942.

Egypt, Republic of, Ministry of Finance and Economy, Statistical and Census Department. *Population Census of Egypt, 1947*. Cairo, 1954.

Encyclopaedia Judaica. 2d ed. 16 vols. Jerusalem, 1972.

L'Encyclopédie populaire juive 5706/1946. Edited by the Société des Editions Historiques Juives d'Egypte. Cairo, n.d. [1946].

Engle, Anita. *The Nili Spies*. London, 1959.

Ettinger, Shmuel, ed. *Toldot ha-yehudim be-artsot ha-islam*. Jerusalem, 1981.

Faraj, Murād. *al-Shu'arā' al-yahūd al-'arab*. Heliopolis, 1939.

Fargeon, Maurice. *Le tyran moderne: Hitler ou la vérité sur la vie du Fuehrer. (Un nouveau livre brun)*. Alexandria, 1934?

———. *Les juifs en Egypte depuis les origines jusqu'à ce jour*. Cairo, 1938.

———. *Médecins et avocats juifs au service de l'Egypte*. Vol. 1: *Les médecins juifs d'Egypte*. Cairo, 1939?

Fargeon, Raoul. *Silhouettes d'Egypte (Lettrés et mondains du Caire)*. Cairo, 1931.

Farhi, Noury. *La communauté juive d'Alexandrie de l'antiquité jusqu'à nos jours*. Conférence faite par M. Noury Farhi, 7 November 1945. Alexandria, 1946.

Fattal, Antoine. *Le statut légal des non-musulmans en pays d'islam*. Beirut, 1958.

Feilchenfeld, Werner, Dolf Michaelis, and Ludwig Pinner. *Haavara-Transfer nach Palästina und Einwanderung deutscher Juden nach Palästina 1933–1939*. Schriftenreihe wissenschaftlicher Abhandlungen des Leo Baeck Instituts, no. 26. Tübingen, 1972.

Fischel, Walter J. *Jews in the Economic and Political Life of Medieval Islam*. 2d ed. New York, 1969.

Galatoli, Anthony M. *Egypt in Midpassage*. Cairo, 1950.

al-Gamil, ha-Rav Yusuf. *Toldot ha-yahadut ha-ḳara'it*. Vol. 1. Ramla, 1979.

Gendzier, Irene L. *The Practical Visions of Ya'qūb Ṣanū'*. Cambridge, Mass., 1966.

Gershoni, Israel. "Arabization of Islam: The Egyptian Salafiyya and the Rise of Arabism in Pre-Revolutionary Egypt." *Asian and African Studies* (Haifa) 13 (1979): 22–57.

Gershoni, Israel, and James P. Jankowski. *Egypt, Islam, and the Arabs: The Search for Egyptian Nationhood, 1900–1930*. New York, 1986.

Ghunaym, Aḥmad Muḥammad, and Aḥmad Abū Kaff. *al-Yahūd wa-l-ḥaraka al-ṣahyūnīya fī miṣr, 1897–1947*. Cairo, 1969.

Gibb, Hamilton A. R., and Harold Bowen. *Islamic Society and the West: A Study of the Impact of Western Civilization in the Near East*. 2d ed. 2 vols. London, 1969.

Gilbert, Martin. *The Jews of Arab Lands: Their History in Maps*. Oxford, 1975.

Gittelman, Haim. "Le Sionisme en Egypte." *Israël* (Cairo), 8 December 1933 to 15 July 1936.

Giughese, Virginio. *Gli Italiani per la cognoscenza dell'Egitto sotto il regno di Mohammed Ali*. Diploma thesis, Istituto Superiore de Magistero de Piemonte, 1931–32.

Goitein, Shlomo Dov. *Jews and Arabs: Their Contacts through the Ages*. New York, 1964.

———. *A Mediterranean Society*. 4 vols. Berkeley and Los Angeles, 1967–83.

Golan, Aviezer. *Operation Susannah*. New York, 1978.

Grafftey-Smith, Laurence. *Bright Levant*. London, 1970.

Grant, Samuel Becker. "Modern Egypt and the New (Turco-Egyptian) Aristocracy." Ph.D. diss., University of Michigan, 1968.

Grunwald, Kurt. "'Windsor-Cassel': The Last Court Jew." *Leo Baeck Institute Yearbook* 14 (1969), pp. 119–61.

———. "On Cairo's Lombard Street." *Tradition* (Berlin) 1 (1972): 8–22.

De Guerville, A. B. *New Egypt*. London, 1905.

HaCohen, Devorah and Menachem. *One People: The Story of the Eastern Jews*. New York, 1969.

Haim, Sylvia G. "Arabic Anti-Semitic Literature." *Journal of Jewish Social Studies* 17 (1955): 307–12.

Harari, Edmond. "Quelques réflexions sur les origines, us et coutumes des habitants des quartiers israélites du Caire, par un témoin de son temps." Paris, May 1980. Unpublished manuscript.

Harkabi, Yehoshafat. *Arab Attitudes to Israel*. Jerusalem, 1972.

Harris, Murray. *Egypt under the Egyptians*. London, 1925.

Hassoun, Jacques. "Chroniques de la vie quotidienne." In *Juifs dul Nil*. Edited by Jacques Hassoun. Paris, 1981, pp. 106–92.

Hassoun, Jacques, ed. *Juifs du Nil*. Paris, 1981.

Haykal, Muḥammad Ḥusayn. *Mudhakkirāt fī 'l-siyāsa al-miṣrīya*. 3 vols. Cairo, 1977–78.

Heffening, Willy. "Die Entstehung der Kapitulationen in den islamischen Staaten." *Schmollers Jahrbuch* 51 (1927): 97–107.

Heyworth-Dunne, John. *An Introduction to the History of Education in Modern Egypt*. London, 1938.

———. *Religious and Political Trends in Modern Egypt*. Washington, D.C., 1950.

Hirschel, G. "Egypt, Zionism." In *Encyclopedia of Zionism and Israel.* Edited by Raphael Patai. New York, 1971. Vol. 1, pp. 178–281.

Hirszowics, Lukasz. *The Third Reich and the Arab East.* London, 1966.

Hourani, Albert. *Minorities in the Arab World.* London, 1947.

———. *Arabic Thought in the Liberal Age.* London, 1962.

———. "The Syrians in Egypt in the Eighteenth and Nineteenth Centuries." In *The Emergence of the Middle East.* London, 1981, pp. 103–23.

———. *The Emergence of the Modern Middle East.* London, 1981.

Hussein, Mahmoud. *L'Egypte: Lutte de classe et libération nationale.* 2 vols. Vol. 1: *1945–1967.* Paris, 1975.

Ibn Qayyim al-Jawzīya. *Aḥkām ahl al-dhimma.* Edited by Ṣubḥī Labīb. 2 vols. Damascus, 1961.

Institute of Jewish Affairs. *Jews in Arab Countries during the Middle East Crisis.* London, 1957.

———. *Jews in Arab Countries since the End of the Six-Day War.* London, 1967.

Israel, State of, Central Bureau of Statistics. *Census of Population and Housing 1961. Demographic Characteristics of the Population. Part IV.* Publication no. 22. Jerusalem, 1964.

———. *Census of Population and Housing 1961. Labour Force. Part IV. Occupations Abroad.* Publication no. 27. Jerusalem, 1965.

———. *Census of Population and Housing 1972. Demographic Characteristics of the Population. Part II.* Series no. 10. Jerusalem, 1976.

Israel Information Center. *Jews in Arab Lands.* Jerusalem, 1974.

Issa, Hossam. *Capitalisme et sociétés anonymes en Egypte.* Paris, 1970.

Issawi, Charles. *Egypt at Mid-Century: An Economic Survey.* London, 1954.

Jacobsen, Hans-Adolf. *Nationalsozialistische Außenpolitik, 1933–1938.* Frankfurt/Main, 1968.

Jankowski, James P. *Egypt's Young Rebels: "Young Egypt," 1933–1952.* Stanford, 1975.

———. "Egyptian Responses to the Palestine Problem in the Interwar Period." *International Journal of Middle East Studies* 12 (1980): 1–38.

———. "Nationalism in Twentieth Century Egypt." *Middle East Review* (Fall 1979): 37–48.

Les juifs d'Egypte par l'image. Paris, 1984.

Kahanoff, Jacqueline. *Mi-mizraḥ shemesh.* Tel Aviv, 1978.

Kāmil, Anas Muṣṭafā. "al-Ra'smālīya al-yahūdīya fī miṣr." *al-Ahrām al-Iqtiṣādī*, 23 March to 4 May 1981.

Kedourie, Elie. *The Chatham House Version, and Other Middle Eastern Studies.* London, 1969.

———. *Arabic Political Memoirs and Other Studies.* London, 1974.

Kerr, Malcolm. *The Political and Legal Theories of Muhammad 'Abduh and Rashid Rida*. Berkeley and Los Angeles, 1966.
Khalil, Muhammad. *The Arab States and the Arab League: A Documentary Record*. 2 vols. Beirut, 1962.
Khoury, Adel. *Toleranz im Islam*. Munich, 1980.
Khūrī, Ya'qūb. *al-Yahūd fī 'l-buldān al-'arabīya*. Beirut, 1970.
Killearn, Lord. *The Killearn Diaries: 1934–1946*. Edited by Trefor Evans. London, 1972.
Kisch, Frederick H. *Palestine Diary*. London, 1938.
Krämer, Gudrun. *Minderheit, Millet, Nation? Die Juden in Ägypten, 1914–1952*. Wiesbaden, 1982.
———. "Die Juden als Minderheit in Ägypten, 1914–1956. Islamische Toleranz im Zeichen des Antikolonialismus und des Antizionismus." *Saeculum* 34 (1983): 36–69.
———. "Zionism in Egypt, 1917–1948." In *Egypt and Palestine: A Millennium of Association (868–1948)*. Edited by Amnon Cohen and Gabriel Baer. Jerusalem, 1984, pp. 348–66.
Kramer, Thomas W. *Deutsch-ägyptische Beziehungen in Vergangenheit und Gegenwart*. Tübingen, 1974.
Kremer, Alfred von. *Aegypten*. 2 vols. Leipzig, 1863.
Lacouture, Jean and Simonne. *Egypt in Transition*. London, 1958.
Laforge, Michel. *Au fil des jours en Orient: Grèce, Egypte, Pakistan, Jérusalem, 1922–1958*. Brussels, 1967.
Lambelin, Roger. *L'Egypte et l'Angleterre vers l'indépendance, de Mohammed Ali au roi Fouad*. Paris, 1922.
Lane, Edward W. *An Account of the Manners and Customs of the Modern Egyptians*. 5th ed. Edited by Stanley Lane-Poole. London, 1860. Reprint. New York, 1973.
Landau, Jacob M. *Parliaments and Parties in Egypt*. Tel Aviv, 1953.
———. *Jews in Nineteenth-Century Egypt*. New York, 1969.
———. *Middle Eastern Themes: Papers in History and Politics*. London, 1973.
Landes, David S. *Bankers and Pashas: International Finance and Economic Imperialism in Egypt*. London, 1958.
Landshut, Siegfried. *Jewish Communities in the Muslim Countries of the Middle East*. London, 1950.
Laqueur, Walter Z. *Communism and Nationalism in the Middle East*. London, 1956.
Lāshīn, 'Abd al-Khāliq. *Sa'd Zaghlūl wa-dawruhu fī 'l-siyāsa al-miṣrīya*. Beirut, 1975.
Leprette, Fernand. *Egypte: Terre du Nil*. Paris, 1939.
Lévy, Clément, ed. *Stock Exchange Yearbook of Egypt*. Alexandria, 1937, 1939, 1942.

Lewis, Bernard. *The Jews of Islam*. Princeton, 1984.
Lichtheim, Richard. *Rückkehr: Lebenserinnerungen aus der Frühzeit des deutschen Zionismus*. Stuttgart, 1930.
Lilienthal, Alfred. *What Price Israel?* Chicago, 1953.
Livingston, John W. "Aly Bey al-Kabir and the Jews." *Middle Eastern Studies* 7 (1971): 221–28.
Lloyd, Lord George Ambrose. *Egypt since Cromer*. 2 vols. London, 1933.
Lorni, Henri. *L'Egypte d'aujourd'hui: Le pays et les hommes*. Cairo, 1926.
Maḥmūd, Ṣāliḥ Ramaḍān. "al-Jālīyāt al-ajnabīya fī miṣr fī 'l-qarn al-tāsi' 'ashar." Ph.D. diss., Cairo University, 1969.
Makarius, Raoul. *La jeunesse intellectuelle d'Egypte au lendemain de la deuxième guerre mondiale*. Paris, 1960.
Makāriyūs, Shāhīn. *Tārīkh al-isrā'īlīyīn*. Cairo, 1904.
Makkabi, Raḥel. *Mitsrayim sheli*. Merḥavia, 1968.
Mandel, Neville. *The Arabs and Zionism before World War I*. Berkeley and Los Angeles, 1976.
Mann, Jacob. *Jews in Egypt and Palestine under the Fatimid Caliphs*. 2 vols. Rev. ed. London, 1970.
Masri, Jean. *Le judaisme égyptien par l'image présenté par Jean Masri*. Vol. 1: *La communauté d'Alexandrie*. Alexandria, 1948.
Masriya, Yahudia [pseud.] *Les juifs en Egypte: Aperçu sur 3,000 ans d'histoire*. 2d rev. ed. Geneva, 1971.
Mayer, Thomas. *Egypt and the Palestine Question, 1936–1945*. Berlin, 1983.
Memmi, Albert. *Juifs et arabes*. Paris, 1975.
Memorandum on the Position of the Jewish Communities in the Oriental Countries, Submitted to the UN Special Committee on Palestine by the Jewish Agency for Palestine. Jerusalem, 1947.
El-Messiri, Sawsan. *Ibn al-Balad: A Concept of Egyptian Identity*. Leiden, 1978.
Michaelis, Meir. *Mussolini and the Jews: German-Italian Relations and the Jewish Question in Italy, 1922–1945*. London, 1978.
Mitchell, Richard P. *The Society of the Muslim Brothers*. London, 1969.
Mizrahi, Maurice. *L'Egypte et ses juifs: Le temps revolu (XIXè et XXè siècles)*. Geneva, 1977.
Le mondain égyptien et du Proche Orient: The Egyptian Who's Who. Edited by E. J. Blattner. Alexandria, 1937, 1945, 1954, 1957–58.
Moreh, Shmuel, ed. *Arabic Works by Jewish Writers, 1863–1973*. Jerusalem, 1973.
Motzki, Harald. *Ḏimma und Egalité: Die nichtmuslimischen Minderheiten Ägyptens in der zweiten Hälfte des 18. Jahrhunderts und die Expedition Bonapartes (1798–1801)*. Bonn, 1979.
Murād, Maḥmūd. *Man kāna yaḥkum miṣr? Shahādāt wathā'iqīya*. Cairo, 1980.

al-Mursī, Fu'ād. *al-'Alāqāt al-miṣrīya al-sūviyatīya, 1943–1956.* Cairo, n.d.

Mutawallī, Maḥmūd. *al-Uṣūl al-tārīkhīya lil-ra'smālīya al-miṣrīya wa-taṭawwuruhā.* Cairo, 1974.

———. *Miṣr wa-l-ḥayāt al-ḥizbīya wa-l-niyābīya qabla sanat 1952: Dirāsa tārīkhīya wathā'iqīya.* Cairo, 1980.

Najar, Albert. *Rapport sur l'Egypte.* Presented to the president of the Alliance Israélite Universelle. 1 July 1901.

Nassau, Rudolf. "Briefe aus Cairo." *Die Welt,* no. 13 (25 April 1904); no. 18 (29 April 1904); no. 20 (13 May 1904).

Naṣṣār, Sihām. *al-Yahūd al-miṣrīyūn bayna al-miṣrīya wa-l-ṣahyūnīya.* Beirut, 1980.

Nemoy, Leon. "A Modern Egyptian Manual of the Karaite Faith." *Jewish Quarterly Review* 62 (1971–72): 1–11.

Nicosia, Francis. "Arab Nationalism and National Socialist Germany, 1933–1939: Ideological and Strategic Incompatibility." *International Journal of Middle East Studies* 12 (1980): 351–72.

Nini, Yehuda. *Mi-mizraḥ u-mi-yam—yehude mitsrayim: Haye yom yom we-hishtaḳfutam be-sifrut ha-she'elot u-teshuvot, 5642–5674 (1882–1914).* Jerusalem, 1980.

Noth, Albrecht. "Möglichkeiten und Grenzen islamischer Toleranz." *Saeculum* 29 (1978): 190–204.

Owen, E. Roger J. *Cotton and the Egyptian Economy, 1820–1914: A Study in Trade and Development.* Oxford, 1969.

———. *The Middle East in the World Economy, 1800-1914.* London, 1981.

Pace, Umberto, ed. *Répertoire permanent de législation égyptienne.* Alexandria, 1934–.

Papasian, Edouard. *L'Egypte économique et financière.* Cairo, 1933.

Patai, Raphael, ed. *Encyclopedia of Zionism and Israel.* 2 vols. New York, 1971.

Patai, Raphael. *Israel between East and West: A Study in Human Relations.* 2d ed. Westport, Conn., 1970.

———. *The Vanished Worlds of Jewry.* London, 1981.

Peretz, Don. *Egyptian Jews Today.* New York, 1956.

Perrault, Gilles. *Un homme à part.* Paris, 1984.

Philipp, Thomas. *The Syrians in Egypt, 1725–1975.* Stuttgart, 1985.

Poliakov, Léon. *De l'antisionisme à l'antisémitisme.* Paris, 1969.

———. *The History of Anti-Semitism.* Vol. 2: *From Mohammed to the Marranos.* London, 1971.

Politi, Elie I. *L'Egypte de 1914 à "Suez" ... A travers une existence pas connue des autres.* Paris, 1965.

Politi, Elie I., ed. *Annuaire des sociétés égyptiennes par actions, études financières,* Alexandria, 1929–.

Politis, Athanase G. *L'Héllénisme et l'Egypte moderne*. 2 vols. Paris 1929–30.

Porath, Yehoshua. *The Palestinian Arab National Movement: From Riots to Rebellion*. Vol. 2: *1929–1939*. London, 1977.

Prato, David. *Cinque anni di rabbinato*. 2 vols. Alexandria, 1933.

Prittie, Terence, and Bernard Dineen. *The Double Exodus: A Study of Arab and Jewish Refugees in the Middle East*. London, n.d.

Qāsim, 'Abduh Qāsim. *al-Yahūd fī miṣr min al-fatḥ al-'arabī ḥattā 'l-ghazw al-'uthmānī*. Cairo, 1987.

al-Rāfi'ī, 'Abd al-Raḥmān. *Fī a'qāb al-thawra al-miṣrīya. Thawrat sanat 1919*. 2 vols. Cairo, 1966 and 1969.

Ramaḍān, 'Abd al-'Aẓīm. *al-Ikhwān al-muslimūn wa-l-tanẓīm al-sirrī*. Cairo, 1982.

———. *Taṭawwur al-ḥaraka al-waṭanīya fī miṣr min sanat 1937 ilā sanat 1948*. 2 vols. Beirut, n.d.

Reid, Donald M. "Syrian Christians, the Rags-to-Riches Story, and Free Enterprise." *International Journal of Middle East Studies* 1 (1970): 358–67.

Rizq, Yūnān Labīb. *Tārīkh al-wizārāt al-miṣrīya*. Cairo, 1975.

Robinson, Nehemiah. *The Arab Countries of the Near East and Their Jewish Communities*. New York, 1951.

Roshwald, Mordecai. "Marginal Jewish Sects in Israel, Part 1." *International Journal of Middle East Studies* 4 (1973): 219–37.

Roumani, Maurice M. *The Case of the Jews from Arab Countries: A Neglected Issue*. Tel Aviv, 1978.

Russell Pasha, Sir Thomas. *Egyptian Service, 1902–1946*. London, 1949.

Sa'd, Aḥmad Ṣādiq. *Ṣafaḥāt min al-yasār al-miṣrī fī a'qāb al-ḥarb al-'ālamīya al-thānīya, 1945–1946*. Cairo, n.d.

Safran, Nadav. *Egypt in Search of Political Community: An Analysis of the Intellectual and Political Evolution of Egypt, 1804–1952*. Cambridge, Mass., 1961.

al-Sa'īd, Rif'at. *al-Yasār al-miṣrī wa-l-qaḍīya al-filasṭīnīya*. Beirut, 1974.

———. *Tārīkh al-ḥaraka al-ishtirākīya fī miṣr, 1900–1925*. 2d ed. Cairo, 1975.

———. *Tārīkh al-munaẓẓamāt al-yasārīya al-miṣrīya, 1940–1950*. Cairo, 1976.

———. *Aḥmad Ḥusayn: Kalimāt wa-mawāqif*. Cairo, 1979.

———. *Munaẓẓamāt al-yasār al-miṣrī, 1950–1957*. Cairo, 1983.

Salīm, Muḥammad 'Abd al-Ra'ūf. *Tārīkh al-ḥaraka al-ṣahyūnīya al-ḥadītha, 1898–1918*. 2 vols. Cairo, 1974.

Sammarco, Angelo. *Gli Italiani in Egitto: Il contribuo italiano nella formazione dell'Egitto moderno*. Alexandria, 1937.

Samuel, Sydney Montague. *Jewish Life in the East*. London, 1881.

al-Sayyid-Marsot, Afaf Lutfi. *Egypt's Liberal Experiment: 1922-1936*. Berkeley and Los Angeles, 1977.

Schechtman, Joseph B. *On Wings of Eagles: The Plight, Exodus, and Homecoming of Oriental Jewry*. New York, 1961.

———. *The Mufti and the Fuehrer: The Rise and Fall of Haj Amin el-Husseini*. New York, 1965.

Schölch, Alexander. *Ägypten den Ägyptern! Die politische und gesellschaftliche Krise der Jahre 1878–1882 in Ägypten*. Zurich, 1972.

Schulze, Reinhard. *Die Rebellion der ägyptischen Fallahin 1919*. Berlin, 1981.

Schwarzbart, Isaac. *Tableau comparé des Séphardim dans la population juive mondiale, 1950–1954*. New York, 1954.

Le second Israël: La question sépharade. Special issue of *Les Temps Modernes*. 1979.

Sephiha, Haim Vidal. *L'Agonie des Judéo-Espagnols*. Paris, 1977.

Shamir, Shimon. "The Evolution of the Egyptian Nationality Laws and Their Application to the Jews in the Monarchy Period." In *The Jews of Egypt: A Mediterranean Society in Modern Times*. Edited by Shimon Shamir. Boulder, 1987, pp. 33–67.

Shamir, Shimon, ed. *The Jews of Egypt: A Mediterranean Society in Modern Times*. Boulder, 1987.

Shilsh, 'Alī. *al-Yahūd wa-l-māsūn fī miṣr. Dirāsa tārīkhīya*. Cairo, 1986.

Sid, Edgar. *Les derniers juifs d'Egypte*. Beirut, n.d.

Siṭon, David. *Ḳehilot yehude sefarad we-ha-mizraḥ ba-'olam be-yamenu*. Jerusalem, 1974.

La situation des juifs dans les pays du Proche Orient. Bulletin Intérieur d'Information, no. 11. Paris, 1948.

Le sort critique des juifs d'Iraq et d'Egypte. Bulletin Intérieur d'Information, no. 12. Paris, 1948.

Smith, Charles D. "The 'Crisis of Orientation': The Shift of Egyptian Intellectuals to Islamic Subjects in the 1930's." *International Journal of Middle East Studies* 4 (1973): 382–440.

———. *Islam and the Search for Social Order in Modern Egypt: A Biography of Muḥammad Ḥusayn Haykal*. Albany, N.Y., 1983.

Staffa, Susan J. *Conquest and Fusion: The Social Evolution of Cairo A.D. 642–1850*. Leiden, 1977.

Stillman, Norman A. *The Jews of Arab Lands: A History and Source Book*. Philadelphia, 1979.

The Story of Zionist Espionage in Egypt. Cairo, 1955.

Taragan, Bension. *Les communautés israélites d'Alexandrie: Aperçu historique, depuis les temps des Ptolémées jusqu'à nos jours*. Alexandria, 1932.

Terry, Janice J. *The Wafd, 1919–1952: Cornerstone of Egyptian Political Power*. London, 1982.

Tignor, Robert L. *Modernization and British Colonial Rule in Egypt, 1882–1914*. Princeton, 1966.

———. "The Egyptian Revolution of 1919: New Directions in the Egyptian Economy." *Middle Eastern Studies* 12 (October 1976): 41–46.

———. "The Economic Activities of Foreigners in Egypt, 1920–1950: From Millet to Haute Bourgeoisie." *Comparative Studies in Society and History* 22 (January 1980): 416–49.

———. *State, Private Enterprise, and Economic Change in Egypt, 1918–1952*. Princeton, 1984.

Tillmann, Heinz. *Deutschlands Araberpolitik im Zweiten Weltkrieg*. (East) Berlin, 1965.

Trevisan Semi, Emanuela. *Gli ebrei caraiti tra etnia e religione*. Testimonianze sull' ebraismo. Vol. 18. Rome, 1984.

Vatikiotis, Panayotis J. *The Modern History of Egypt*. London, 1969.

Wendell, Charles. *The Evolution of the Egyptian National Image from Its Origins to Ahmad Lutfi al-Sayyid*. Los Angeles, 1972.

Wielandt, Rotraud. *Das Bild der Europäer in der modernen arabischen Erzähl- und Theaterliteratur*. Wiesbaden, 1980.

Wild, Stefan. "National Socialism in the Arab Near East between 1933 and 1939." *Die Welt des Islams* 25 (1985): 126–73.

Woolfson, Marion. *Prophets in Babylon: Jews in the Arab World*. London, 1980.

World Jewish Congress. *The Treatment of Jews in Egypt and Iraq*. New York, 1948.

Wright, Arnold, ed. *Twentieth Century Impressions of Egypt: Its History, People, Commerce, Industries, and Resources*. London, 1909.

Yallouz, Alfred S. "Comment le mouvement sioniste a débuté en Egypte." *La Revue Sioniste, Supplément Illustré* (Cairo), 24 to 31 May 1920.

Yāsīn, 'Abd al-Qādir. *al-Qaḍīya al-filasṭīnīya fī fikr al-yasār al-miṣrī*. Beirut, 1981.

Yehuda, Ts'vi. "ha-Irgunim ha-tsiyoniyim be-mitsrayim." *Shevet we-'Am* (Jerusalem) (1978): 147–96.

Zakī, 'Abd al-Raḥmān. *Mawsū'at madīnat al-Qāhira fī alf 'ām*. Cairo, 1969.

Zimmels, H. J. *Ashkenazim and Sephardim: Their Relations, Differences, and Problems as Reflected in the Rabbinical Responsa*. London, 1958.

Index

Library of Congress Cataloging-in-Publication Data

Krämer, Gudrun.
The Jews in modern Egypt, 1914–1952 / Gudrun Krämer.
p. cm. – (Publications on the Near East, University of Washington ; no. 4)
Bibliography: p.
Includes index.
ISBN 0-295-96795-1
1. Jews—Egypt—History—20th century. 2. Egypt—Ethnic relations. I. Title. II. Series.
DS135.E4K68 1989 88-27805
962'.004924–dc19 CIP